Palgrave Studies in Religion, Politics, and Policy

Series Editors: Ted G. Jelen and Mark J. Rozell

A generation ago, many social scientists regarded religion as an anachronism, whose social, economic, and political importance would inevitably wane and disappear in the face of the inexorable forces of modernity. Of course, nothing of the sort has occurred; indeed, the public role of religion is resurgent in US domestic politics, in other nations, and in the international arena. Today, religion is widely acknowledged to be a key variable in candidate nominations, platforms, and elections; it is recognized as a major influence on domestic and foreign policies. National religious movements as diverse as the Christian Right in the United States and the Taliban in Afghanistan are important factors in the internal politics of particular nations. Moreover, such transnational religious actors as Al-Qaida, Falun Gong, and the Vatican have had important effects on the politics and policies of nations around the world.

Palgrave Studies in Religion, Politics, and Policy serves a growing niche in the discipline of political science. This subfield has proliferated rapidly during the past two decades, and has generated an enormous amount of scholarly studies and journalistic coverage. Five years ago, the journal *Politics and Religion* was created; in addition, works relating to religion and politics have been the subject of many articles in more general academic journals. The number of books and monographs on religion and politics has increased tremendously. In the past, many social scientists dismissed religion as a key variable in politics and government.

This series casts a broad net over the subfield, providing opportunities for scholars at all levels to publish their works with Palgrave. The series publishes monographs in all subfields of political science, including American Politics, Public Policy, Public Law, Comparative Politics, International Relations, and Political Theory.

The principal focus of the series is the public role of religion. "Religion" is construed broadly to include public opinion, religious institutions, and the legal frameworks under which religious politics are practiced. The "dependent variable" in which we are interested is *politics*, defined broadly to include analyses of the public sources and consequences of religious belief and behavior. These would include matters of public policy, as well as variations in the practice of political life. We welcome a diverse range of methodological perspectives, provided that the approaches taken are intellectually rigorous.

The series does not deal with works of theology, in that arguments about the validity or utility of religious beliefs are not a part of the series focus. Similarly, the authors of works about the private or personal consequences of religious belief and behavior, such as personal happiness, mental health, or family dysfunction, should seek other outlets for their writings. Although historical perspectives can often illuminate our understanding of modern political phenomena, our focus in the Religion, Politics, and Policy series is on the relationship between the sacred and the political in contemporary societies.

The Catholic Church in Polish History: Politics, Religion, and Cultural Resistance
By Sabrina P. Ramet

Global Religions and International Relations: A Diplomatic Perspective
By Pasquale Ferrara

Beyond Religious Right and Secular Left Rhetoric: The Road to Compromise
By Karin Fry

Christianity in Chinese Public Life: Religion, Society, and the Rule of Law
Edited by Joel A. Carpenter and Kevin R. den Dulk

Mitt Romney, Mormonism, and the 2012 Election
By Luke Perry

Clerical Sexual Abuse: How the Crisis Changed US Catholic Church–State Relations
By Jo Renee Formicola

Clerical Sexual Abuse

How the Crisis Changed US Catholic Church–State Relations

Jo Renee Formicola

palgrave
macmillan

First published in 2014 by
PALGRAVE MACMILLAN®
in the United States—a division of St. Martin's Press LLC,
175 Fifth Avenue, New York, NY 10010.

Where this book is distributed in the UK, Europe and the rest of the world,
this is by Palgrave Macmillan, a division of Macmillan Publishers Limited,
registered in England, company number 785998, of Houndmills,
Basingstoke, Hampshire RG21 6XS.

Palgrave Macmillan is the global academic imprint of the above companies
and has companies and representatives throughout the world.

Palgrave® and Macmillan® are registered trademarks in the United States,
the United Kingdom, Europe and other countries.

ISBN: 978–1–137–38402–7

Library of Congress Cataloging-in-Publication Data

Formicola, Jo Renee, 1941–
    Clerical sexual abuse : how the crisis changed U.S. Catholic church-state
relations / by Jo-Renee Formicola.
       pages cm
    Includes bibliographical references and index.
    ISBN 978–1–137–38402–7 (hardcover : alk. paper)
       1. Child sexual abuse by clergy—United States. 2. Catholic Church—
Clergy—Sexual behavior—United States. 3. Church and state—Catholic
Church. 4. Church and state—United States. I. Title.

BX1912.9.F67 2014
261.8′327208828273—dc23   2014012338

A catalogue record of the book is available from the British Library.

Design by Newgen Knowledge Works (P) Ltd., Chennai, India.

First edition: October 2014

To the Victims of Clerical Sexual Abuse
To their Parents, Spouses, and Supporters
For their Psychic healing, Physical health, and
Spiritual reconciliation

Contents

Introduction   1

1   Early Warnings and Denials:
Father Gauthe   9

2   Revelations and Scandals: Boston and
Beyond   45

3   Challenge and Complexity: Canon
Law and Civil Law   75

4   Too Little, Too Late: The Hierarchy
Responds   111

5   Pushback and Payback: The Laity and
the Lawyers   147

6   From Crisis to Power Shift and
the Future   193

Notes   217

Bibliography   243

Index   267

Introduction

The newspapers are full of it. Television commentators continue to report on it. The Internet is a growing repository of heinous stories related to it. So far, it has cost over three *billion* dollars to settle the lawsuits. But the cost in publicity and money is only a collateral consequence of Catholic clerical sexual abuse. The crisis is costing the Church its moral credibility and its long-standing, balanced relationship with civil authority in the United States.

Over the course of the last decade and a half, numerous cases have come before civil and criminal courts to redress priestly sexual crimes perpetrated against children. Stories have escalated about the rise of "pedophilia," or the adult attraction for, or a sex act with, a prepubescent child. Others tell of "ephebophilia," a different type of sexual deviance based on an adult attraction for, or sex with, a minor during his/her later teenage years.

When the first stories of clerical sexual abuse started to trickle out in the media, the general public was shocked. The tragedies of the victims, the heinous crimes of the priests, the arrogance and the naïveté of the hierarchy all stunned American society. Catholics, especially, could not believe that the most respected, educated, and spiritual members of their religious community were responsible for violating their innocent children. The laity's shock turned to anger. Their need for compassion changed into demands justice—but both were left unanswered.

The Church all but ignored and abandoned the victims of clerical sexual abuse. Its leadership hid behind a theology that stressed repentance and reconciliation. Church officials from the Pope on down blamed others for the predatory behavior of priests: the culture, American society, and homosexuality. The Church demanded ecclesiastical rights and relied on its own canon law to punish its clergy. It used secret financial settlements and confidentiality agreements to silence victims, a tactic that the hierarchy believed would heal the victims' psychic injuries and save the reputation of the Church. The bishops and other superiors acted as though money for therapy and suffering from past clerical molestations would wipe the slate clean. They behaved as though they could circumvent the need for the Church to be accountable for the lack of former criminal prosecutions and financial liability, *and* yet, somehow, protect other children from similar, reprehensible victimization in the future.

When Church officials refused to recognize not just the sin but the *crime* of sexual abuse, molested children and their aggrieved families had no place to go for justice other than civil authorities. It was the state—not the Church—that acted to protect their rights and address their grievances.

In the process, civil authorities have used civil law to challenge Church legal mandates known as the "canon law." State officials have used their various powers to overcome the perceived right of the Catholic religious leadership to invoke special ecclesiastical exemptions, privileges, superiority and secrecy in the handling of clerical sexual abusers. They have broadened the scope and use of the subpoena to access clerical personnel and medical records. They have investigated the hierarchical management of clergy. They have deposed high-ranking members of the Catholic leadership. They have become involved in Church financial matters related to bankruptcy. They have monitored Church employees working with minors. They have sent predator priests to jail for their crimes. In short, civil officials over the last 15 years have done what the hierarchy has been unable and unwilling to do: hold the clerical sexual abusers and their hierarchical enablers accountable for their crimes.

Chapter 1 of this book begins by looking at the traditional Catholic treatment of early clerical sexual abusers in the United States. By examining the case of Father Gilbert Gauthe in Louisiana, in 1984, it provides an early picture of the standard operating procedures of bishops with regard to sexual deviance. Their grand strategy was basically to deny any such occurrences, and their tactics could be characterized as ones that were totally secret and intimidating for the accusers. Sometimes bishops made referrals of priests for "treatment" to a variety of "facilities," which were then followed by unexplained reassignments of those clerics to other parishes. Their members were never told why a new priest had arrived.

Father Gauthe's story is important because it shows how three concerned men—a canon lawyer, a defense attorney, and a priest-psychiatrist—worked together to try to find a pragmatic and just solution to the problem of clerical sexual abuse. They understood that Gauthe's case was not an isolated one but that his sexual proclivities represented other potential problems for the Church in the future. They sought a consistent and accountable way to deal with such an eventuality. Father Thomas Doyle, F. Ray Mouton, and Father Michael Petersen tried to warn Church leaders that Gauthe's case was only the tip of the iceberg. They tried to send an alarm that the priest's crimes were going to cause irreparable damage to the Church in the future—but no one really listened to them until a decade later.

In chapter 2, the book moves to the year 2001 and looks at what happened in Boston with the revelations of the stunning sexual abuse cases of Reverend Paul Shanley and Father John Geoghan. This is when the working church-state relationship that had existed between the Catholics and the Commonwealth of Massachusetts began to change and erode, a portent of things to come beyond the Bay State and across the United States.

The cases of Shanley and Geoghan shed light on the public ramifications of the sexual abuse crisis. They show how the courts started to make legal demands on Church authorities for personnel and medical records of priests, deposed high-ranking Catholic leaders, and held the Catholic leadership responsible for the actions of its clergy. It charts the assertive, legal beginnings of state involvement in clerical sexual abuse cases.

The history of the Catholic Church and the role of canon or Church law in dealing with clerical behavior is articulated in chapter 3. It traces the earliest hierarchical punishments for such sins, and looks at how the mandates from the popes and other religious superiors on matters of Church management grew, became more complex, and were even absorbed into civil practices over time.

Indeed, it articulates how canon law evolved into a complex, convoluted, misunderstood, and inconsistently applied series of dictates in cases of clerical sexual abuse. Instead of simplifying and systematizing Church administration and the management of clergy, canon law eventually became an inefficient millstone around the necks of a hierarchy intent on dealing with such matters in its own way.

Chapter 4 looks at how the hierarchy has responded to the clerical sexual abuse crisis and how it has attempted to deal with it in the United States. It examines how bishops and other religious superiors tried to make *canonical* changes to Church law at their meeting in Dallas in 2002. They adopted a zero-tolerance policy toward predator priests and promised to accommodate to civil law. The chapter also shows why, without total Vatican recognition of some policies, their attempts were, in many ways, too little to late. Sadly it also discusses how some bishops today are still recalcitrant about making good on the promises they made to deal more effectively with clerical sexual abuse in the future.

The role of the laity and the aggressive actions of lawyers in clerical sexual abuse cases are explored in chapter 5. It shows how aggrieved, yet still committed, Church members have worked with the public and civil authorities to raise awareness about the legal implications of predatory priestly behavior. It shows how the laity, through various organizations such as Survivors Network of those Abused by Priests (SNAP) and Voice Of The Faithful (VOTF), along with other groups, have sought justice for victims. They have also been working for structural reform to make sure that institutional change will occur within the Catholic Church to protect children in the future.

The chapter also discusses several major cases that have been brought against the Vatican, the Holy See, and even the pope. It describes and analyzes legal actions designed to hold the church bureaucracy and its leader responsible for the sexual abuse of children and young people within the context of Church ministry. The cases illustrate the depth of American legal frustration to demand financial liability as well as morally culpability for the actions of predator priests at the very highest levels of the institutional Catholic Church.

Finally, this book will look at how the Vatican has dealt with clerical sexual abuse under Pope John Paul II and Pope Benedict XVI. Chapter 6 will make the argument that John Paul was conflicted by his theological beliefs—emphasizing that clerical sexual abuse was essentially a sin and a crime only secondarily—both of which were to be adjudicated by canon law. His faith in the ability of clerical sexual abusers to repent, to change, and to return to ministry colored his acceptance of the fact that punishment for predatory priestly behavior as a crime was just as critical to reconciliation with a perpetrator's victims and the larger society.

While John Paul was primarily concerned with penance, Benedict XVI was simply overwhelmed by the whole issue of clerical sexual abuse.

Both popes tried to use canon law to answer and "fix" the clerical sexual abuse scandal, but to no avail. They revised it. They set new procedures in place. But the canon law, in the end, simply imploded.

This last chapter ends by looking at the potential for the new pope, Francis I to make a difference in the Church. His election as pontiff holds out the hope of a compassionate, loving, just, and accountable Church. But will he be able to live up to the world's expectations and make meaningful institutional, and in turn, doctrinal change?

The research for this book has been formidable. It has required combing through innumerable grand jury reports, legal transcripts, depositions, newspaper accounts, Church documents, and personal stories. The investigations in Boston, Philadelphia, and Los Angeles give the earliest insight into how clerical sexual abuse was handled by religious officials in large archdioceses. But many smaller dioceses were investigated as well, and their reports provided similar concerns and patterns of abuse. The documents from all these hearings and cases are available from public sources and can also be accessed at http://www.bishop-accountability. org, a website that publishes an archive of information related to clerical sexual abuse. It has virtually catalogued every case, hearing, and report from civil and religious sources, the latter coming to light as courts have, and continue to, demand the information be made public in on-going investigations.

The Holy See also has a comprehensive website that provides all official information concerning clerical sexual abuse. It includes letters, documents, speeches, press releases, and statements by officials within the Vatican—including those of the pope and other leaders, and the agencies under him. All these sources are available at http://www.Vatican.va. in a variety of languages.

The United States Conference of Catholic Bishops also provides similar, critical Church policy information to the public. It can be accessed at http://www.usccb.org and contains all pertinent position papers and other documents as they relate to clerical sexual abuse in the United States.

Internationally, United Nations documents, along with those of Amnesty International, are sources that investigate clerical sexual abuse from a global perspective. They are available from both the organizations on line as well.

For newspaper reporting, the *Boston Globe* and the *New York Times* provided critical investigative reporting for those trying to understand the scope and meaning of Catholic clerical sexual abuse in the United States.

The *Boston Globe* broke the story of Father John Geoghan and fought before the civil courts for the right to open the proceedings against the accused priest. Its investigative staff has recounted its work on the crisis in a book entitled *Betrayal: The Crisis in the Catholic Church.*

The *New York Times* has also served as an objective source on clerical sexual abuse, reporting consistently about the actions and reactions of the American bishops, the Catholic hierarchy, and the Holy See. It has covered the stories of victims and those seeking justice as well, giving critical details and analyses of the claims and challenges of both groups involved the continuing tragedy.

The media across the United States has played a critical role in reporting information and investigating clerical sexual abuse cases across the country as well. Its commitment to finding the truth has been inspiring, to say the least.

Certain books have also been invaluable to this research. They have provided the historical context and personal information that is often lost when trying to understand a complex problem.

Among these works are *Lead Us Not Into Temptation: Catholic Priests and the Sexual Abuse of Children* by Jason Berry. He was the reporter who covered the Gauthe case in 1984, providing detailed interviews and insight into the early handling of clerical sexual abuse in the United States. Berry is also the author of *Vows of Silence: The Abuse of Power in the Papacy of John Paul II* with Gerald Renner. Together, they chronicled the internal workings of the Vatican infrastructure and how it deals with clerical sexual abuse. Their book is also the definitive work on the case of Father Marciel Maciel, the founder of the Mexican religious order, the Legion of Christ, and his double life as a predator priest and a husband/father.

Michael D'Antonio's book, *Mortal Sins: Sex, Crime, and the Era of Catholic Scandal*, relates important interviews and analysis about the clerical sexual abuse scandal. His book helps to round out the complex picture of those in the laity who were trying to find a way to reverse the handling of the tragedy by Church officials.

Finally, the autobiography of Archbishop Rembert Weakland, entitled *A Pilgrim in a Pilgrim Church: Memoirs of a Catholic Archbishop*, gives insight into the decision-making process of a major Church leader about how to deal with predator priests. He sets out to explain why he attempted to deal with clerical sexual abuse as he did in the Archdiocese of Milwaukee. In many ways, his story is the sad rationale of many of others in the hierarchy.

Other critical contributions to the literature on clerical sexual abuse have been made by Father Thomas Doyle. A canon lawyer and an outspoken critic of the institutional Church's handling of the tragedy, Doyle has written extensively in journals, magazines, and on the Internet on the internal workings of the Church and its decision-making processes. Doyle has served as an expert witness in a significant number of cases and an attorney for those seeking redress from the Church.

This work has been difficult to research—not because it has required long hours to do it but because it has been so hard to deal with the details of the crimes perpetrated by priests on young children and teenagers. The grand jury hearings and lawsuits left nothing to the imagination. There was clearly no deviant act that the priests had not committed, and committed over and over again. It has been hard to be objective, to be a political scientist, and to look at the whole issue of clerical sexual abuse from the detached, objective view of its implications on church-state relations in the United States.

The personal stories of the victims of these crimes, however, have given even greater justification for the actions of the state to limit and monitor the Catholic Church's handling of predator priests in the clerical sexual abuse crisis. For clearly, the central research question of this book throughout its pages is what role, if any, the state should play in the clerical sexual abuse crisis. And there is no denying the argument that will inevitably be made here: that the state must take the lead to implement what is without doubt, one of the most compelling state interests of all—the need to protect children.

Any work of this depth and magnitude requires help. So I must first thank my husband, Dr. Allan Formicola, who not only encouraged me throughout this project, but also acted as critic, editor, and colleague. I am solely responsible for any unintended errors that might exist in this book.

Sarina Roth, one of my ablest students, worked on this manuscript, helping me to get it ready for publication. She made sure that endnotes and bibliographic entries were as close to perfect as possible and that the logistics and the work timeline were met.

The members of the political science department, my chairperson, the dean of my college, and the provost all supported and provided me with the release time and much of the funding to make this book a reality. Their belief in my ability to make a meaningful contribution to the church-state debate has made the work possible. Indeed, as I have said in the past—a book is like a baby: easy to conceive, but hard to deliver. Finally, it is also important to thank Oxford University Press for allowing me to use parts of three articles that I published in the *Journal of Church and State* during the last decade.

It is important at this point to make a sad statement here as well. Children, teenagers, and their families were not the only people who were victimized by clerical sexual abusers. So were many holy, committed priests. I work and interact with many of them and have watched some people treat them as though they have *all* done something wrong. Their vocations have been questioned; their careers scrutinized. I hope the reader will consider how many good religious men there still are, how much they can give, and how selflessly they continue to serve our young people by their examples, spirituality, and academic knowledge.

Jo Renee Formicola, Ph. D.

28 February 2014

1

Early Warnings and Denials: Father Gauthe

Introduction

When did it all start, this dirty little secret of clerical sexual abuse in the American Catholic Church? And why didn't anybody in the Church leadership do anything to stop it?

Even now, more than a decade after the shocking, public revelations and responses to the Catholic clerical abuse scandals in so many places, it is apparent that there were plenty of rumors, whispers, and serious, unheeded warnings about predator priests. There were scandalous allegations floating around in small towns and hierarchical circles for more years than anyone cared to remember—like the accusations against Father Gilbert Gauthe in Henry, Louisiana in 1984.

What is so incredible is that the most religious, supposedly well-educated, politically astute, and elite leaders among Catholic Church officials understood little to nothing about the behavior of sexually perverted priests. And they did even less to try to understand the pathology of the disease, paying virtually no attention to the criminal ramifications of what their fellow clergymen were perpetrating on young, innocent children for a long, long time.

Experts[1] now seem to think that denial, ignorance, arrogance, and deference were what the victims, the perpetrators, and the enablers of sexual abusers used as their means to cope with their own personal and emotional stress. Compounded by institutional pressures to deal quietly and swiftly with misunderstood, priestly perversions, Church leaders also often reacted by simply refusing to accept, or even consider, the charges against child abusers. Instead, in many cases, they simply ignored them.

The victims had to build up their own emotional defenses in order to survive. They existed alone within their own world of fear—isolated, embarrassed, and angry. It was through these psychological responses that the abused were able to survive within their Catholic religion and culture.

As a result, many minors and their families simply succumbed to the bishops' ecclesiastical control, prestige, and wealth. They reluctantly accepted the Church leaders' ability to use the weight and legitimacy of their power and canon law, a means to confuse and defeat accusers.

In time, victims faced the fact that bishops also existed within their own separate institutional realm as well—a place where they were totally committed to the protection of their priest-brethren and the reputation of the Church. It was a world of hierarchical silence and loyalty to the clerical culture and Church law that would never give children an equal chance to pursue justice for sexual molestation. In reality, that recognition was the only way for victims to deal with Catholic religious chauvinism and ecclesiastical privilege in matters of clerical sexual abuse.

On the other hand, the priest-perpetrators often could not, and usually would not, face their own spiritual failings, psychological debilitation, and heinous crimes. It was as though they existed in another kind of world, a sexually duplicitous one in which they were unable to escape the perverted double lives that they led.

Their almost schizophrenic sexual existences were further *enabled* by many Church leaders, too. The members of the hierarchy who sent abusive priests for psychological "treatment" or moved them from parish to parish were actually or unconsciously complicit in the sexual abuse. They believed that by following such a plan of therapy and reassignment, they would somehow help abusive clerics to rest and repent, to become reconciled with their personal spirituality, and to make psychic recoveries. In the process, however, the cardinals, archbishops and bishops who approved various treatments and new ministries for clerical sexual abusers essentially covered up the sins as well as the crimes of the priests.

They believed they were protecting the Church's religious interests by protecting its clergy and reputation. But instead, they ultimately hindered the Church's ability and responsibility to face the truth and to deal with it. The ecclesiastical leadership neglected its duty to pursue justice for those who lost their innocence and to reform the system of dysfunctional hierarchical management that allowed it to happen and of which they were a part.

Such behaviors by those involved in the sexual abuse crisis reflected the power relationship between the Church hierarchy, the clergy, and the laity. It was one that had traditionally been based on a privileged and monopolistic connection, a lay dependence created by the Church leadership due to its perceived religious affinity to the supernatural, advanced education, and political involvement throughout Christian history. Eventually, the hierarchy controlled more and more matters among itself and the clergy, its adherents and its opposition, as well as its relations with civil structures. It did this through the development of its own legal system, known as canon law.

Over the centuries, the Church's legal system empowered it to dominate or form "concordats," politically advantageous alliances with emerging civil states. These privileged legal and political positions allowed Church leaders to carry out both the Church's religious and social missions effectively, and to assume controlling spiritual and temporal roles that waxed and waned in a number of countries throughout the last two millenniums.

This historical church-state relationship, however, was complicated and interrupted in the United States by a unique, new, and complex situation. It developed a different rapport between the Catholic Church and the US government through the First Amendment and the notion of the separation of Church and State.

The continuing evolution of the right to religious freedom and the civil strictures on the establishment of a state religion in the First Amendment formed a dynamic tension in church-state relations. Both the freedom and the limits were balanced and counter balanced during American history by the belief in the principle of the separation of Church and State. This notion clashed with traditional papal and hierarchical teachings regarding the Church's right to preferential religious treatment and, often, political power as well.

It was Pope Leo XIII, in the late nineteenth century, who clearly responded in a negative way to American constitutional principles. He believed that modernism, liberalism, and secularism were the doctrinal enemies of the Church. He maintained that the Church's appropriate relations with civil states, including those with the United States government, had to guarantee the Church a superior position in a civil-religious relationship.

He based this view on four religious perspectives. First, Pope Leo contended that the state had the obligation to protect and assure the freedom of the Church to carry out its salvific mission, that is, to teach, preach and sanctify its adherents. Second, he believed that civil governments should accept Catholicism as the one, true religion; that it should be given a preferred status or at least an accommodation within civil infrastructures. Third, he asserted that the spiritual order and its sphere of interest should take precedence over the temporal and civil concerns. And fourth, he believed that there should be harmonious cooperation between Church and State for the common good.

Pope Leo's numerous encyclicals reflected the traditional reluctance of Church leaders to give up any perceived Church authority in its own sphere of competence, even within the context of the US democratic experiment.[2] In fact, he clearly opposed the model of the American principle of the separation of Church and State, saying that the "dissevered and divorced" relationship in the United States is not "the type of the most desirable status of the Church."[3] Instead, he insisted, "It is to the Church that God has assigned the charge of seeing to, and legislating all that concerns religion...in accordance with her own judgment in all matters that fall within its competence."[4]

In other words, Pope Leo, like his predecessors, wished to have no interference from civil authorities about managing any of the internal affairs of the Church. Instead, he expected Catholic adherents "to be ruled and directed by the authority and leadership of bishops, and above all, of the Apostolic See."[5]

Thus, lay Catholics, even those belonging to the Church during the twentieth century, obeyed Church teachings without question. The members existed within a hierarchical structure where power was controlled from the top down. It was an autocratic religious system characterized by spiritual sovereignty and religious superiority inculcated over centuries by popes and implemented by bishops.

Church members were, therefore, even in the United States, often torn between papal edicts carried out on the local level by the hierarchy and clergy, and demands that were often contrary to accepted social and political norms.[6] As a result, American Catholics were considered politically suspect by other religious denominations who challenged their political loyalty to the pope rather than the United States government during much of its history.

It wasn't until the 1940s and '50s, however, that progressive Catholic theologians, such as John Courtney Murray, S. J., began to question the hierarchy's traditional reticence to accept the notion of the separation of Church and State.[7] Murray, an influential Jesuit, argued that theology was evolutionary, and thus able to change in the light of time, place, and circumstance. As a result, he put forward an innovative way of thinking about Catholic church-state relations. He stressed the need for a new reliance on religious pragmatism. In order to accomplish this, Murray emphasized the importance of the development of an educated citizenry, one that would be able to bring about church-state cooperation and concord in America.

These ideas, which Murray believed would lead to civil peace, were published in influential Catholic journals. They caused him, however, to be "silenced" by Vatican officials, and to be denied the right to publish on church-state theory.

Then, in 1962, the pope of the Catholic Church at the time, John XXIII, called a General Council, or meeting of all the hierarchy, to come to Rome to discuss church renewal. Murray was invited to attend by Francis Cardinal Spellman of New York, even though the priest was essentially censured. He was credentialed at the conference, known as Vatican II, as a theological expert, a status that allowed Murray the ability to influence the course of future Church thinking about church-state relations. He, along with other like-minded theologians advanced the notion of freedom of conscience and, in turn, religious freedom. It was significant because it had the potential to catapult official Catholic thinking into a new, modern phase of church-state relations—a move that would reflect American constitutional principles.

A number of socially progressive documents, then, were promulgated at the Church's General Council at Vatican II.[8] These included, first and most importantly, *Lumen Gentium*. It stressed, with the approval of all the hierarchy, that the Church had to recognize its role vis-à-vis governments based on changing situations. In essence, it recognized the rights of states in temporal matters and repudiated the ideas of earlier popes such as Leo XIII. The document clearly stated that "Christ, to be sure, gave his Church no proper mission in the political, economic or social order. The purpose he set before her is a religious one."⁹ In fact, *Lumen Gentium* went so far as to say that the Church "does not lodge her hope in privileges conferred by civil authority. Indeed she stands ready to renounce the exercise of certain legitimately acquired rights if it becomes clear that their use raises doubt about the sincerity of her witness or that new conditions of life demand some other arrangement."¹⁰

Church officials also passed another critical document at Vatican II, entitled *Dignitatas Humane*. It recognized freedom of religion as an inherent and civil, constitutional right. It said:

> This Vatican Synod declares that the human person has a right to religious freedom. This freedom means that all men are to be immune from coercion on the part of individuals or of social groups of any human power, in such wise that in matters religious no one is to be forced to act in a manner contrary to his own beliefs. Nor is anyone to be restrained from acting in accordance with his own beliefs, whether privately or publicly, whether alone or in association with others, within due limits... This right of the human person to religious freedom is to be recognized in the constitutional law whereby society is governed. This is to become a civil right.¹¹

In making such a statement, the hierarchy essentially changed the traditional, Leonine principles that demanded civil states recognize the superiority of Catholicism, and to accept, instead, the principles of the First Amendment and the notion of the separation of church and state. These potential changes between the Church officials in Rome created a more equal relationship with the United States government and had the potential to end the traditional antagonism that had existed throughout most of American history.

In addition to recognition of their loyalty to the United States in World War I and World War II, their enhanced education and financial status meant Catholics began to become part of the American social and economic structures. Along with the election of one of their own, John Fitzgerald Kennedy, to the presidency in 1960, ordinary lay Catholics started participating in the American political mainstream by the end of the decade.

But old ideas die slowly. While some progressive clergyman, like John Courtney Murray, adhered to a more liberal ideology characterized by notions of social justice and the view that religion was a constitutional right, other theologians held more doctrinally conservative views.¹² They still adhered to vestiges of Leonine thinking. This often placed the laity in a quandary about how to relate to the teachings and management of the leaders of Catholics in a particular "diocese" or geographical area.

Those Catholics in a parish led by the more conservative clergymen were more likely to follow the Church leadership and doctrine in an unquestioning manner. They relied on the authority of the Pope and bishops, and the historical notion that the Church should be allowed "to administer freely and without hindrance in accordance with her own judgment all matters that fall within its competence."[13]

This was meant to include all spiritual and internal matters that the Church had held to be within its own purview, particularly perceived—then, as now—as the management of the clergy, the administration of Church property, and the disposition of all matters tangential to Church affairs. Taken broadly, these were considered to be part of the pastoral responsibilities and prerogatives of the bishop. Most personnel and financial issues were dealt with privately and in accordance with a particular Church leader's interpretation and implementation of the canon, or Church law.

On a more personal level, the Church was an integral part of many people's lives. It was natural for its parishioners to volunteer for projects, and it was normal for them to send their sons to become altar boys. They got to know their priests personally, and often invited them to their homes for dinner. Church involvement was incorporated into their everyday hustle and bustle, and reflected the ordinary religious and social practices of the people. Most importantly, their close relationship with the clergy was a way of life, a fact that constantly reinforced the laity's spiritual values and ties to their priests as well as to the Church.

This grew out of the Catholic immigrant experience, historically one in which its European adherents were both a religious minority and part of an economic underclass. It wasn't until the Irish potato feminine in the 1840s that a mass migration of Catholics to the United States began to occur. Mostly, they were treated with disdain by the majority and wealthy classes because of their religious beliefs and papal demands for political loyalty. As a result, Irish immigrants and other Catholics who came to the United States essentially moved into ethnic ghettos for social protection, to a place whose center was their neighborhood church. Within those community confines, they inter-married, sent their children to parish schools, took up blue-collar jobs, and made their lives within familiar, insular surroundings.

Central to this self-chosen, isolated way of life was hierarchical religious "guidance," or command and control. It was a traditional form of Church leadership based on an autocratic model of Catholic leadership. This meant that Church adherents were given religious and even political directives from above: dictates that were interpreted and implemented by spiritual superiors, and expected to be practiced in an obedient and unquestioning manner.

Within this organizational system were the bishops of their dioceses, the pastors of their parishes, and the priests who ministered to the religious, social, and economic needs of the laity. Each played a crucial role in the interlocking autocratic power structure.

As the diocesan leader, the bishop represented Church religious and economic interests to the state. He controlled all the Church's property and operated schools, houses of worship, cemeteries, hospitals and orphanages. He was the personal connection between his institution and the civil authorities, particularly on economic matters. The bishop had the right to make appointments of pastors and priests, to remove or reassign them as he saw fit, to adjudicate personnel issues in canonical matters, to administer church-owned organizations, and to deal with civil authorities and state challenges to Church interests should such matters arise.

As a powerful individual, the bishop resided in a special, formidable residence and had a staff to assist him in his various responsibilities. Usually, someone who was called a "vicar general" or a "vicar for administration" carried out the oversight of clerical personnel and ecclesiastical record keeping.

The pastor of a particular church was appointed by the bishop. In his capacity as a sort of local administrator, the pastor managed the running of the parish church and its school. He was also the person who worked most closely with his staff: nuns and fellow priests. He lived in a common residence (rectory) with the clerics and ministered with them by providing the sacraments, visiting the sick, offering solace to the depressed, and making the church the center of parishioners' lives.

The priests were under the bishop and the pastor. They were the men who served on the front line of the Church and the community. Besides being clerics, they became surrogate brothers and fathers to those who needed or sought such relationships. They were confidants, friends, and role models. They trained altar boys, coached teams, developed young men and women spiritually, and even helped them get jobs. Families with sons who became priests were given special respect among their peers. They were considered privileged to have a son in the service of God and received a type of social status by having someone in the priesthood.

The public story of clerical sexual abuse involving the priest, Father Gilbert Gauthe, then, begins within this type of Catholic culture in Louisiana. Much of its religious and social atmosphere was traditional, accepted as part of the cultural practice of the times. The laity was removed from church-state matters and generally unaware of the dynamics of the power plays between its hierarchy and public officials.

It was this more conventional relationship that still pervaded the atmosphere in 1983 when the first real inkling of the coming sexual abuse crisis started to come to light. It happened in Henry, Louisiana. A small town estimated to be about 65 percent Catholic at the time, the Cajun community was located in a county that boasted 13 Catholic churches and a greater percentage of Catholics per capita than even the bastion of Catholicism, the Boston Archdiocese!

The religious culture of Henry was a microcosm of Catholic society in rural Louisiana during the 1980s: a conservative, still accepted type of religious inbreeding. It reflected the dynamic, traditional, assertive interplay of Catholic church-state relations, and a background of expectations of ecclesiastical privileges, hierarchical and priestly respect, as well as the very earliest beginnings of a lay questioning of deference to both.

A significant part of the Gauthe story has been told by Jason Berry in his excellent book, *Lead us Not into Temptation*.[14] His narrative is extremely well-documented, complex, and telling. Now in hindsight, it is possible to see how the Gauthe case sowed the seeds that brought about the beginnings of a shift in the church-state power equation, if only in Louisiana. In a small way, it started to erode the relationship between the leaders of the Catholic Church, its adherents and civil authorities. The case began to question hierarchical decisions about the treatment of clergy in sexual abuse matters and ecclesiastical privileges that had formerly been protected by the state. In the end, they would be negated, secrecy denied, and victims of clerical sexual abuse would finally be recognized.

Other parts of the Gauthe story have be gleaned from media interviews with family members and victims, as well as newspaper accounts, and many, many legal documents. In trying to pull it all together and make some sense out of why and how the story of clerical sexual abuse unfolded and what it meant in the church-state context, it is necessary to understand the events, along with the role, the power, the indifference, and the eventual impotence of the Church leadership to bring an end to the most serious religious malignancy in its history.

The Beginning

The time is the early 1980s. The place is a rural Catholic town. The actors are a trusted priest, a number of innocent young boys, their shocked and furious parents, committed lawyers, a dysfunctional bishop, and an ineffective vicar.

Wayne Sagrera was just a typical Catholic resident of a small Louisiana town, a man who had a wife and four sons. He was an alligator farmer, and like many of the other people in his hometown, Sagrera and his family attended the local parish church, St. John's. They got to know their priest, Father Gilbert Gauthe, through church attendance, service, and family dinners. They felt so comfortable in their relationship with him, in fact, that they allowed their boys to go to sleepovers at the rectory.

The bottom fell out of the close relationship between the Sagrera family and Father Gauthe when Craig, the youngest boy in the family, told his father that he and two of his older brothers had all been molested by the parish priest when they were altar boys. Incensed, their father immediately reported the crimes to the vicar for administration, Monsignor Henri Alexandre Larroque. He was Bishop Gerard Frey's aide, and it was his job to handle all personnel matters, especially such allegations.

But Sagrera, in an interview on *Sixty Minutes* some time later, said that the vicar was not surprised by his allegations; he actually seemed to have been aware that the sexual abuse had been going on for quite a while.[15] Sagrera said that the Monsignor told him that when Father Gauthe was transferred to this new parish, St. John's, the vicar made sure that the reassigned priest slept in an upstairs bedroom. This was to make it more difficult for the priest to have boys over and to have them leave the rectory secretly by "climb[ing] in and out of the window."[16]

In the course of talking to Sagrera about the allegations of sexual abuse, Larroque also played the religious guilt card in order to keep the matter confidential. The monsignor told the father that Sagrera would be responsible for whatever happened if and when the allegations became public: If "someone hurts themselves or there's a divorce or a suicide, all of this guilt is on your shoulders…"[17] And then, in a final ecclesiastical insult, the monsignor told Sagrera that Father Gauthe would, nonetheless, have to stay at the parish because there was no replacement for him.

Stunned, Sagrera let other parents know. Some joined with him to confront the bishop, who was the ultimate authority on the matter. The bishop had the right to suspend Gauthe from his ministry. But at that point, the bishop and other officials in the Church would not even warn families about the danger of Gauthe in an official way—from the pulpit.

Then, on another night in Henry, Louisiana, a distraught nine-year-old boy, Pete Robichaux, sobbed as he told his mother that he had done bad things with the priest at their Church. Reportedly she was "nauseated"[18] when she told her husband, Roy. He tried to soothe the boy while crying himself.

A recovering alcoholic, the father pulled himself together, and questioned his older sons about the priest's behavior. When they said the same things, he went to a lawyer, Paul Herbert, who contacted the office of the head of their diocese, Bishop Frey, and his aide, Monsignor Larroque, who was responsible for the oversight of the priests in the diocese.

The bishop was out of town, but Robichaux reached his second in command, the vicar, Larroque. It was obvious to the father that the bishop's aide recognized the criticality of the call. The Vicar said he would be willing to meet with the furious parent and his lawyer at once.

The father became even more incensed when Larroque, also a recovering alcoholic, tried to befriend him. Robichaux did not want a buddy; he wanted someone who could end the sexual abuse of his sons. Reportedly, the vicar, again, was not surprised at the allegations about the priest. Accounts say that he told the boy's father, "We've known that Father Gauthe had a problem for some time, but we thought it had been resolved.[19]

The vicar promised to call Bishop Frey and take care of the matter. He reached the bishop, who has been described as "shy," "aloof," and often "detached," a man who spent long vacations at his family's resort camp.[20] Larroque got permission from him to suspend the priest immediately based on a specific part of canon law (Canon 2359, 2). He also got a signed confession from Father Gauthe in which the accused priest admitted to having engaged in sexual acts with minors.

The vicar told the priest to get out of town in 24 hours and gave him some cash so that he could check into a motel. Some ten days later, Gauthe went back to his rectory, called one of his earlier victims, a 15-year-old, molested the boy, packed up his belongings, and appeared to get out of town for good. But the matter had to be resolved in a better way, lest the victims' parents made further trouble.

Father Gilbert Gauthe's parishioners at St. John's Church were simply told by Monsignor Larroque that the priest had been relieved of his position for "grievous misconduct," but Larroque gave no clearer reason for his dismissal as he announced the removal. While rumors of a nervous breakdown and medical reasons were rife, the head of the diocese, Bishop Frey, decided that the best way to handle the mess was to ship Gauthe off to a treatment facility in Massachusetts known as the House of Affirmation. He also quietly agreed to pay for therapy for the molested boys.

This was standard operating procedure at the time. The bishop had the authority under canon law to handle such situations. There were no civil laws in place in Louisiana or anywhere else to force him to report such clerical actions to civil authorities. So the drill was pretty much the same from diocese to diocese. Keep everything quiet. Make sure the police are not involved. Send the priest away. Pay for the victims' treatments.

But this was neither the solution nor the justice that the Sagreras, Robichauxs, and others expected when they eventually came forward with allegations from nine of their sons. Dissatisfied with the bishop's response, they wanted more: they wanted to bring *criminal* charges against Gauthe.

The parents and their attorney, Paul Herbert, contacted the district prosecutor, Nathan Stansbury, who was anxious to prosecute the case in criminal court. But when the parents realized that their boys would have to testify in public, they began to reconsider their actions.

Stansbury, however, who was totally committed to the case, pushed forward, thinking that he might be able to get a pre-indictment deal and save the boys from having to tell their stories. So he started to prepare a criminal indictment.

In the meantime, Paul Herbert and his co-counsel, Raul Bencomo, moved forward as well, helping the families they represented in the Gauthe case to mount a major *civil* lawsuit, instead of a criminal case. At least this way, they could sue the Church for financial damages.

But this kind of civil action was also new legal territory for the plaintiffs. They, of course, had been brought up to be obedient and deferential to the clergy. But Herbert and Bencomo believed that the plaintiffs' retribution should go beyond receiving a quiet check for therapy for their sons. They knew that the diocese had corporate status, and therefore could be sued publically. They also knew that the Church had plenty of its own money as well as insurance funds to cover all kinds of catastrophes, including personal injuries. Thus, Herbert and Bencomo wanted to sue the Church so that its insurers and the institution itself would have to pay dearly for the sexual abuse perpetrated by Gauthe, a sexual abuser *known* to Church officials.

Ultimately, the families opposed pursuing a criminal case and an open civil suit.[21] Instead, they agreed to a financial settlement that would keep their sons from having to testify openly in court. The potential publicity and stigma to both the boys and the Church ended in silence. Gauthe's sexual abuse remained a secret in return for $4.2 million,[22] a payout to cover the cost of therapy and minimal damages that would be settled by the diocese and its insurers. The money would be divided among the families of the predator priest's victims. The ordeal would be over for everyone.

Immediately after the families and Church representatives signed the agreement, the judge placed a protective order on the settlement filing, even though state law required that such agreements were to be filed with the court and available to the public for scrutiny. The contents of the proceedings were sealed, and Paul Herbert, just to be sure to protect the victims, redacted their names and the amounts of the individual settlements as well.

What would become usual practice occurred: a financial agreement tied to confidentiality. In the case of the first set of Gauthe's accusers, a secret settlement between the parents and the diocese protected the identities of the young boys, the stories of their victimization, the name of their perpetrator, and the fact that Gauthe would be required to undergo psychiatric treatment. The reputation of the Church was intact. Again, this was just part of the standard operating procedure at the time. The court facilitated the adjudication of the matter in as quiet a way as possible.

In the meantime, Gauthe was sent off to the House of Affirmation by his superior, Bishop Frey. A treatment facility for clergy, the place seemed to be one of the best around at the time and quite unique. Founded in 1973 by Sister Anna Polcino, MD, and the Reverend Dr. Thomas Kane, a priest with a PhD in psychology, the facility was a place for priests with psychological and psychosexual problems. The approach to abusive behavior and the type of treatment administered at the facility garnered the confidence of Pope Paul VI when it opened. The Pontiff referred to the work of its staff as a "special gift to the Church."[23]

The House of Affirmation ran several facilities. These were located in Whitinsville, Hopedale, Boston, and Natick, Massachusetts; Middletown, Connecticut; Montara, California; Webster Groves, Missouri; and Clearwater, Florida.

In its brochure and in other published articles, the founders of the House of Affirmation said that its mission was to provide clergy members with an opportunity for self discovery, emotional growth, and a "cure"—a cure for those who had "non-affirmed identities."[24] It had both a credible board of directors and even an international advisory board. And it stayed open until 1990, when the main House of Affirmation in Worcester closed due to allegations against the director, Father Thomas Kane, of financial improprieties and sexual abuse.

There were a number of other "facilities" as well that existed to help priests with their problems. Some were run by the Church, itself, while some private centers dealt with various clerical addictions. Most handled cases of alcoholism and drug abuse, but some facilities also tried to handle "sexual perversions," too. There are now estimates that the Church spent as much as $50 million dollars for "treatments" for priests in a number of centers over a 25-year period *prior* to 2002 when the Boston scandal publically erupted.[25]

What is known today is that early medical/psychiatric interventions in some of these religious and private treatment centers were often new and untested, with the therapists believing they had accomplished some sort of positive change. Some simply wanted to send the priests back to the service of the Church, anxious to prove that a predator priest was "fixable."[26]

There are no credible statistics, even today, about the recidivism rates among individuals, much less priests, who have been treated for sexual abuse. This is due to the fact that the definition of what constitutes a sexual crime differs from state to state. These can include anything from public urination to prostitution, to pornography, sexting, and molestation (adult sexual contact with a child) to sexual assault, rape, incest and bestiality. But what does come into focus is the fact that the lack of meaningful therapeutic follow-up, professional explanations, or warnings about sexual abuse, coupled with the lack of hierarchical understanding and communications, meant that many religious superiors often did not comprehend the depth of the psychic damage of the priests.

More frightening is the fact that they also had no real knowledge of the predator priest's danger to the community and to the parishes to which they were often returned or reassigned. Religious leaders also had no legal obligation and no sense of ethical responsibility to report such crimes to civil authorities. They never disclosed such information to the laity at large since no canonical laws enjoined them to do it.

But this was the only way the hierarchy knew how to respond to clerical sexual abuse in 1983—to send a sexually abusive priest like Father Gilbert Gauthe to an out-of-town facility for "treatment." Other official responses were often defensive: using confidentiality agreements to hush up the problems; turning to lawyers who could use delaying tactics to limit or stave off financial and criminal claims against a priest, allowing ecclesiastical personnel to obfuscate the facts surrounding specific cases of clerical sexual abuse and, in a final desperate act, simply following through with an institutional cover-up.

It came as a shock, then, to the parishioners of St. John's when the gossip about Father Gauthe started to leak out and become the topic of incredulous discussion. Little by little, people began to put together his salacious past and understand the jeopardy to which their children had been exposed.

The seemingly pious priest in his late 30s who could ride a horse, fish and hunt, shoot a gun, be "a man's man," and charm older ladies,[27] had been assigned to six different parishes and sent to a number of "centers" for therapy to deal with his sexual perversions over the years.

It was even more astounding to learn that Gauthe had been living a double life for a long time. He had formerly been suspended from his ministerial duties and sent for treatment and therapy even before Sagrera, Robichaux and other boys had secretly accused him of molestation.

He had been "treated" a number of times at various "facilities" and had been moved from parish to parish during the course of his priesthood— and his actions were never reported to civil authorities. In fact, at one point, he was even appointed chaplain of the diocesan Boy Scouts by his superior, Gerard Frey, Bishop of the Diocese of Lafayette, Louisiana. He had been aware of Gauthe's behavior since becoming his superior there in 1975.

Gauthe had also been promoted to the position of pastor at St. John's, although in confidential Church circles he had been a known pedophile for more than a decade. In fact, evidence showed that there were at least seven other priests in the diocese who had also been accused of molesting children prior to the allegations against Gauthe. So the Church leadership, from the bishop on down, was aware of the Gauthe problem and even of the larger cancer within its ranks for a long time.[28]

The predator priest's way of luring children was devious *and* simple. He would first win the trust of his victims' parents, create situations where the kids would be alone with him, and then find places to molest them—even in the rectory and inside the Church.

Some of the parents who were so trusting and vulnerable were single, or working mothers, or busy fathers who were tending to farms. The point was that they were all unable to spend the bulk of their time with their children. Gauthe would call altar boy practices in the mornings, buy ice cream for the youngsters afterwards, and tell their parents not to worry about picking them up because he would be happy to keep the boys overnight at his house. Sometimes, the kids were even invited to Gauthe's cabin in the woods to learn about nature and to appreciate the wilderness. Under the trees and next to the lake, he reportedly would ply them with all sorts of gifts and games, and during the sleepovers, he would sexually abuse them

It was during 1984 then, that the rumors about Gauthe started to leak out to the public. He had been suspended for deviant acts and had had nine credible law suits filed against him. But the hardest part was that no one could verify anything because the case had been quietly settled and *sealed* by the court.

The parents of the molested boys, especially, were still upset because Gauthe's superiors didn't understand either the psychological or *criminal* ramifications of their former pastor's problem. However, they couldn't say anything because they had signed a confidential agreement with Church authorities.

The first wave of victims, then, received financial compensation and therapy. Gauthe was getting treatment—again. The crisis seemed to have been averted and settled as far as Church leaders were concerned. But the matter did not end there.

State criminal proceedings were still quietly being prepared by the county prosecutor, Nathan Stansbury, who wanted life imprisonment for Gauthe, especially when other allegations against him appeared soon after the settlement of the first large group case. These demands came from four other victims led by the family of an 11-year-old sexual abuse victim named Scott Gastal.

The boy's parents were determined to disclose their son's allegations of molestation against Gauthe. No confidentiality agreements for them. No puny settlements. No rehab for the predator priest. No simple apologies from the higher-ups. No compromises. They wanted the Church to pay, and they wanted Gauthe to go to jail as well.

In order to assure justice, the Gastal family was willing to allow their young son to appear in court and blow the whistle on the predator priest. Stansbury took notice. Church officials took notice, too.

The first group settlement between the Church, the Sagreras, the Robichauxs, and the other clerical abuse victims had been taken care of, but it was clear that the Gastal family, in particular, wanted no part of a similar type of agreement in the new case that was gaining traction. They were dissatisfied with the outcome of the earlier case and remained upset about their son's victimization.

The Gastals did not care about the particulars of the Church pay-outs or the fact that the priest was in "treatment." They wanted transparency and accountability for their son, more than the satisfaction or the settlements that the other victims had received. So in order to get justice, they looked around for an aggressive, unorthodox lawyer who would represent their concerns. They found him in J. Minos Simon of Lafayette, Louisiana.

The 63-year-old Simon was considered crusty and tough in legal circles. He reportedly had a commanding presence because of his demeanor, which was physically reinforced by his graying mustache and silver hair. He was a tough litigator, and not afraid of anyone, according to those who knew him.

From the start, he was willing to take on the Gastals case, and to push the legal envelope in a new direction. One way he was going to do this was to take on the Church itself—to challenge its silence and superiority. He was going to build his case on the principle of *respondent superior*— that is, he intended to pursue a legal strategy that would seek to hold not just the predatory priest Gilbert Gauthe responsible for his actions, but his religious superiors as well.

This had never before been used as a legal strategy in Louisiana. Simon was going to argue that religious officials, up and down the line, were complicit in Gauthe's actions due to their *systematic* neglect of their administrative duties to deal with sick, perverted members of the clergy. He was going to challenge the hierarchy's sacrosanct internal, eccesiastical power to manage and protect the clergy! This approach was predicated on the fact that Bishop Frey, the leader of the diocese, Monsignor Larroque, his aide, and the ranking bishop of the state, Bishop Philip Hannan of New Orleans, had "failed to enforce canonical codes that demanded celibacy."[29]

Simon contended that they had not performed the appropriate oversight of Gauthe. In other words, the Church leaders were negligent because they reassigned a predator priest to various parishes after his continuous record of recidivism.

Simon, in fact, was essentially challenging the legality of the revered, respected, and unquestioned canon law—its prerogatives and the underlying notion that Church law was supposed to supersede civil law in matters that dealt with the treatment of the clergy. He planned to challenge the canon law's validity in matters of sexual abuse and the right of bishops to act outside civil law in such criminal acts. In fact, some reports indicated that Simon also intended to indict the Pope, himself.

Simon started by filing a motion to break the court's protective seal on the discovery or the evidentiary findings of the impending Gastal case. The seal preserved the identity and victimization of the boy, but it also kept the actions of the priest and his superiors a secret as well. If Simon won and got the court to refuse to seal the information, it would set a precedent that would allow open testimony in court about the Gastal molestation. The information would not be suppressed. The media would know everything. The public would be told. The Church would lose its protected status. Civil authorities would be under pressure to change their usual protective approach to such cases. Indeed, if Simon were successful, he could then deal with the more senior religious officials later!

Stansbury, the prosecutor waiting in the wings, now saw the opening for a criminal indictment as well. With a boy on the stand, he would be able to bring charges of sexual abuse against the priest.

Suddenly, the Catholic hierarchy in Louisiana sat up and got very nervous as news of the coming criminal and civil lawsuits began to circulate within legal and religious circles. The gravity of the situation caused the higher-ups to become deeply concerned about an immediate, serious diocesan dilemma: how to assure damage control if the Gauthe accusations were aired publically.

There were, however, even bigger problems on the horizon—major church-state implications from the new Gauthe case that could impact their religious autonomy and protection from civil intrusions. How would they deal with the potentially devastating legal consequences that such a case could have on the Church's financial interests? Would it lessen their ability to carry out social services and parochial education? What would be the outcome of a potential civil challenge to canon law? Would it affect the Church's traditional ecclesiastical privilege to manage and even punish its own personnel? Could the state suddenly demand clerical personnel files, which had traditionally been held in secret? Could the content of these files become public knowledge? Would their moral reputation be compromised? Would it affect the Church's ability to influence public policy?

A well-connected person in the diocese suggested that Monsignor Larroque, the bishop's aide, set up a meeting with F. Ray Mouton, a personal injury lawyer and a Catholic with a "social pedigree."[30] They approached Mouton to see if he was up to the legal task that they were dreading.

Mouton could be the Church's answer. His family had founded the city of Lafayette, Louisiana, and Mouton, himself, was a fifth generation Catholic. In fact, his grandfather donated the land on which the cathedral in Lafayette stood. During the lunch, it was becoming clear to the higher-ups that Mouton was their best hope: a lawyer who had the credentials to defend Gauthe, and in turn, possibly a credible Catholic who would be able to minimize the harm that could come to the bishop and the institutional Church if the case made it to court.

A few days after the meeting, Mouton got a call from the bishop's office asking him to defend Gauthe. He accepted. In doing so, he faced the most serious challenge of his legal career *and* his life. Why, in God's name, did he agree to defend the accused child molester?

The reasons went to his core commitment to the American judicial system. From the beginning, Mouton was dedicated to two basic legal principles: that everyone was innocent until proven guilty and that each person deserved the best legal defense possible. He believed that a jury would do the right thing and that he had to be the one to show the way. His goals were clear: to make sure Gauthe would go to jail for about 20 years, that the alleged sexual predator would be completely removed from the priesthood, and that he would receive the psychological help that he needed.[31]

So despite public threats and acrimony, Mouton decided that he would serve as the defense attorney for the accused, Gilbert Gauthe. His strategy was simple: use an insanity plea. By doing so, Gauthe would receive the justice and treatment he deserved.

Stansbury, however, was still moving forward on the criminal case, and did not want Gauthe in a prison hospital; he wanted him to spend his life in a very secure prison instead. The prosecutor, however, allowed Gauthe to remain in treatment while the case was being prepared. This was a condition in the settlement of the earlier group civil case brought by Sagrera, Robicaux, et al. Stansbury did this with the understanding that Gauthe would have to return to Louisiana when an arraignment date could be set for a possible criminal trial. The only way the prosecutor would agree to Gauthe continuing to have treatment was if he would be denied freedom of movement.

The preparation for the trial was grueling and complex, but as Mouton was slowly gathering information, Monsignor Larroque suggested that the lawyer get in touch with Father Michael Peterson, a highly respected priest-psychiatrist who ran a treatment facility for priests in Suitland, Maryland called the St. Luke Institute. The vicar had heard good things about the man as well as the center, and thought Peterson might be just the right type of psychiatrist to treat Gauthe. Mouton called Peterson, and they agreed to meet a few months later, in early 1985.

In the meantime, Mouton continued to prepare for Gauthe's criminal case. He flew to Boston where his client was being treated, at the House of Affirmation. The place has been described as a "psycho-theological community,"[32] but its staff referred to it as a "counseling center." According to its own literature, the organization described the general mission of the House of Affirmation as one focused on helping its patients deal with their severe emotional distress. As clinicians, then, the staff at the House of Affirmation concentrated on treating mental illnesses, rather than trying to eliminate clerical criminal behaviors and their consequences. Their approach to a mental "cure" was based on their three-pronged program of service, education and research, or therapy.

In the facility's brochure, one of its founders, Father Kane, said that their purpose was to help an individual become "a fully human, consistently free person within the context of the ecclesial calling and in relationship to society."[33] In fact, he said that their treatment was designed to help restore priests to the service of their community and also to help the patients attain a "level of happiness commensurate with their potential."[34]

It was this total emphasis on a psychological approach to a cure and the lack of attention to the criminal aspect of Gauthe's behavior that most concerned Mouton when he visited Gauthe. He was stunned, in fact, when he learned that the staff at the facility recommended that

Gauthe, an accused pedophile priest, should be released. They wanted to send him to Gulfport, Mississippi to work as an EMT on an ambulance squad after some in-house training on how to care for the sick.

Mouton didn't believe, as the staff obviously did, that Gauthe could be repaired, repurposed, and sent back into society to still do meaningful work. Mouton was worried that there were still sexual abuse allegations pending against Gauthe in the state of Louisiana, criminal charges that would have to be resolved in court.

The former priest was abnormally anxious when Mouton met with him at the House of Affirmation; he was reportedly afraid and confused about his future. Gauthe told Mouton he knew about the violence that happened in jails when child molesters were serving time. "I'll kill myself," he cried. "I am not going to prison."[35] But Mouton, committed to helping the suspended priest, tried to reassure Gauthe and promised that he would help him and be with him every step of the way though the trial.

Totally dissatisfied with the House of Affirmation's limited form of treatment for Gauthe, Mouton demanded that Bishop Frey, the superior in charge of the priest, send him somewhere else, namely to a different facility for clerics. The one that Mouton had heard about was the Institute of Living in Hartford, Connecticut.

Founded as a private psychiatric hospital in 1822, it was the first facility of its kind in the state, and the only one committed to comprehensive patient care, research, and education. By the 1980s, the Institute had developed a relationship with the Church, treating many sexually abusive priests during its long history. Thus, Mouton felt that Gauthe would be better served in the Institute of Living than at the House of Affirmation. Later, he learned that moving Gauthe would cost $9000 a month and that the Diocese of Lafayette would have to pick up that part of the tab for Gauthe that was not covered by insurance. But considering the alternative of public disgrace for the Church, Bishop Frey quickly agreed. The priest was kept away from the rest of the psychiatric population—cloistered—just as Stansbury had demanded.

It wasn't long after Mouton completed his investigation with Gauthe and got him transferred to the Institute of Living, that the former priest's case became more complicated. Gastal's lawyer, J. Minos Simon, had won his motion to open the files on the impending Gastal case. The judge removed the previous gag order on what could have been the confidential proceedings against the predator priest. Now the public would be allowed to hear the testimony of Scott Gastal. The discovery rights of the Gastal family could now be made known; they could give media interviews about Gauthe. No holds barred.

Instantly, the dynamic about the case totally changed: everything would be made public; the media would investigate; the case could be tried in the press and in the court of public opinion. The Church would no longer be able to hide behind confidential proceedings. Stansbury could prosecute the priest and plead for justice in a criminal court.

Other legal decisions were also tipping the scales in favor of the plaintiff. In 1985, the Supreme Court of Louisiana ruled that Bishop Frey and Monsignor Larroque, the bishop's second in command, could be and would be compelled to give depositions and answer questions put to them by the Gastal's lawyer, Simon.[36] This was a first in state demands on religious leaders. Gauthe was openly deposed as well, and the plaintiff's attorney quickly offered audio tapes of the accused priest's statements to the media.

Simon continued on his quest for information previously considered privileged. He obtained a number of subpoenas to get information on other accused Catholic clergy from Church personnel files. This was a major breakthrough in church-state relations, as well. While the lawyers for the Church argued that this was a violation of the First Amendment and an intrusion into its internal canonical affairs, the judge ruled the motion to be without merit. He claimed that the Church had no special prerogative in the case: the matter was ended at that point.

None of the parties realized that this ruling would become so significant in the future. For now, however, information about other accused priests could come forward in Louisiana, and Simon could use it to show a pattern of managerial and pastoral neglect by the bishop and the vicar.

It was clear that there was not going to be an out of court settlement, under any circumstances, as the Catholic higher-ups had hoped. The Gastal family was anxious to settle and collect a rumored $12.5 million dollar claim against the Church: realistic damages according to them, and money that Simon believed could be awarded if they threatened to go public.

Although the parents of the victim wanted the money badly, Church officials underestimated their greater desire for justice. The Gastals wanted, more than anything else, to reveal Gauthe's sexual deviancy and to force the Church to take responsibility for the actions of the predator priest who molested their son. Criminal proceedings would soon begin to bring the predator priest and his superiors down.

Bishop Frey and Monsignor Larroque would also have some serious explaining to do. Why the quick dismissal of Gauthe in the Sagrera case? Why had he been sent off to the House of Affirmation then? What justified their decision to bypass canon law on the subject? Why didn't they set up a canonical court to suspend the accused priest? The bishop and the vicar, who in past could carry out unquestionable ecclesiastical actions, were suddenly subject to both public and Church scrutiny as well.

Mouton would have to change his legal strategy, too, in light of the fact that the criminal trial was going to be open. Originally attempting to show that Gauthe was a victim of a terrible mental illness,[37] Mouton realized that pleading Gauthe to insanity and requesting a 20-year sentence might no longer work. It would all depend on the testimony of a victimized, and possibly credible, Scott Gastal.

It was time to rethink everything, and time for Mouton to meet what he hoped would be his ace in the hole, Father Michael Peterson. The priest-psychiatrist who had been recommended by Bishop Frey and Monsignor Larroque was in charge of St. Luke Institute just outside of Washington, DC. Peterson was critical to the case. But Mouton thought the twin objectives of trying to get both justice and treatment for Gauthe weren't going to be as easy as it first seemed.

Matters of such delicacy as clerical sexual abuse that involved a priest, the hierarchy, diocesan finances, canon law, and possibly even a suit against the Pope, had to be handled in a special, discrete way through proper channels—especially in the 1980s when a new phase of Catholic church-state relations began.

In 1984, the Reagan Administration established official diplomatic ties with the Vatican. It was expected, on both sides, that there would be a significant, positive political change in the relationship between the Catholic Church and the United States government.[38] Based on similar concerns about communist control of Eastern Europe, the president and Pope John Paul II had begun to pursue a clandestine, unified approach to diplomatically support democracy in that atheistic, totalitarian part of the world.[39]

There was an official Vatican embassy in Washington, DC, headed by a papal nuncio (ambassador), Archbishop Pio Laghi, and a continuous dialogue between the two governments to carry out their similar political/religious agendas. Could the new potential relationship for global social justice, human rights, and political cooperation to bring about democracy in communist states be in jeopardy due to the scandal of clerical sexual abuse in Louisiana?

In order to assure diplomatic protocol and convergence, Mouton would have to work through a canon lawyer at the highest international level. Father Thomas Doyle, a Dominican priest, was the Church lawyer who would now be the linchpin between the Gauthe defense team and the Vatican. Doyle handled the legal affairs at the embassy. He was assigned, among other things, the responsibility of monitoring correspondence on the Gauthe case and reporting on it to the Holy See, that is, the governmental instrumentalities at the Vatican.

Doyle had clout and was well-connected in ecclesiastical circles. He had reportedly earned several Master's degrees and two legal degrees by the time he was 34 years old. A gifted intellect and a pilot as well, the young, dynamic clerical power broker was serving at the Vatican Embassy in 1984 when the Gauthe case broke. In fact, it has been reported that he had so much influence while he was assigned at the Embassy that he was able to recommend two men, namely Bernard Law and John O'Connor, to Pio Laghi, the papal nuncio, for promotions to the position of archbishop in both Boston and New York. Both his recommendations were accepted by the nuncio and the pope.

Doyle seemed to know the right people in a lot of critical positions: bishops, cardinals and important up-and-coming priests in ecclesiastical management circles. One of them was Father Peterson of the St. Luke Institute. He introduced Peterson to Gauthe's lawyer, Mouton, and brought the priest-psychiatrist and the Louisiana attorney together to work on the Gauthe case.

The Triad

Peterson was real.[40] That's what Mouton thought of him when Doyle made it possible for them to collaborate on the Gauthe case. The therapist's credentials were impeccable. A physician, Peterson trained at the University of California San Francisco where he became what might be called a pragmatic psychiatrist.

He was born a Mormon, converted to Catholicism, and soon after, became a priest. He had worked at the National Institutes of Health and founded St. Luke Institute near the nation's capital. He did all this while collaborating with the staff at the Marsalin Institute in Holliston, Massachusetts, a treatment center for alcoholic priests. He became director of both the Maryland and the Massachusetts facilities when the priest in charge at Marsalin died in 1977.

By the early 1980s, Marsalin closed, the Gauthe case had broken open, and Peterson had become increasingly convinced that St. Luke's needed to enlarge its mission. He felt there was a need to address the number of escalating clerical sexual abuse deviants that were being referred to him by their religious superiors.

Taking a holistic approach, St. Luke's provided mental evaluation and therapy for six months at its residential center. It also ran a halfway house and a step-down program for addicts, and helped with spiritual redevelopment, education, and continuing care for clergy and nuns.

When Peterson met Mouton, it was obvious that they were on the same page about how to help Gauthe: provide him with both long-term psychiatric treatment and safe incarceration. Later, they also realized something even more important—that they had a mutual commitment to do something about clerical sexual abuse in a larger, national context as well.

Within a few months, a personal and professional nexus developed between Mouton and Peterson, with Doyle being the point man at the Vatican Embassy. So while Mouton was involved in preparing to defend Gauthe in Louisiana, he stayed in touch with the two priests in the Washington area, even sending his client's depositions to Peterson and Doyle.

As the canon lawyer in the triad, Doyle described his early part in trying to deal with the problems of clerical sexual abuse within the Church infrastructure. He said, on the record, that information from both Mouton and Peterson attested to the fact that there were other priests besides Gauthe in Louisiana and across the United States who were involved in sexual abuse, and that he had informed the papal nuncio of the "gravity of the situation."[41]

In turn, the Vatican official called Archbishop Philip Hannan of New Orleans, Bishop Frey, Father Peterson, Monsignor Larroque, and the bishop's lawyers to Washington to assess the situation. Subsequently, and after conversations with Mouton and Peterson, Doyle suggested to the nuncio that Bishop A.J. Quinn of Cleveland, who had a legal background, should go to Louisiana to assist in managing the crisis.

After a series of "alarming reports" from Doyle to the Vatican, the appropriate authorities concurred. Indeed, it appeared as though a consensus was beginning to emerge among the higher-ups: that since the Gauthe case was becoming public, it could no longer be contained, and that other cases were going to be coming forward routinely in the future. This was 1985, well before the scandal of clerical sexual abuse came to light in Boston.

Doyle recognized almost immediately the seriousness of the potential clerical sexual crisis and wanted to set up some sort of an educational manual—simple, with a question and answer format to provide information about sexual abuse for the bishops who would have to deal with such issues in the future. He felt that it was important to establish a research committee along with guidelines for all the American bishops: a clear and systematic framework for case management that they or Church agencies could follow. Mouton and Peterson also wanted to establish a crisis intervention team.

Stressing that immediate action was critical, Doyle briefed the papal nuncio daily. Later, Doyle recounted that he, Mouton, and Peterson wrote a document known as *The Manual* as an "entirely private venture,"[42] in order to deal with the molestation problems that were inevitably going to come to light within the Church

The original document was hammered out in secrecy in Chicago in 1985. The authors of *The Manual* were also joined by a few American bishops to make sure that their work would be acceptable to the US canonical organization, the National Conference of Catholic Bishops (NCCB).[43]

Made up of all of the bishops in the United States, the NCCB was charged with the pastoral and social responsibilities to teach religious doctrine, to inform the consciences of the Catholic laity, and to work to develop moral public policies in the United States. It was also the organization that brought together all the bishops annually, both formally and informally, to discuss serious problems facing the Church leadership.

One of the invitees to the secret Chicago meeting was Archbishop Philip Hannan of New Orleans because he was one of Father Gauthe's superiors. He was also one of the people involved in a civil suit as well, since he was being sued by the Gastal family.

According to Mouton, another bishop who was at the Chicago meeting was William Levada, a member of the NCCB Committee on Research and Pastoral Practices, a group that was headed up by the new, powerful archbishop of Boston at the time, Bernard Law. Mouton claimed that Levada, from California, supposedly "vetted every word of the document and seemed to be in full support"[44] of bringing *The Manual* to the NCCB.

The Doyle-Peterson-Mouton triad pointed out in their document at the Chicago meeting that hundreds of millions of dollars in claims had already been made against just *one* diocese in 1985—Lafayette, Louisiana—the place where Gauthe had ministered. They argued that ten *billion* dollars had already been threatened in a number of other potential lawsuits. Expected investigations by a growing number of civil authorities, the American Bar Association, legal consultants, interested authors, and the press were closing in on the scandal that could do irreparable damage to the Church.

Doyle, Peterson, and Mouton wanted to stave off such a public disgrace. They urged the NCCB to move immediately to discuss the civil, criminal, insurance, canonical, medical, and pastoral implications of clerical sexual abuse and to prepare a systematic plan to deal with them.

They suggested five basic guidelines for the bishops to adopt: 1) to respond promptly to allegations by relieving the alleged offender from his ministerial duties; 2) to refer him for medical evaluation and intervention; 3) to comply with civil law by reporting and cooperating with legal investigations; 4) to reach out to the victims and their families while respecting the privacy of all individuals involved; and 5) to deal openly with members of the community.

The Manual and its recommendations, however, had difficulty getting attention and acceptance in hierarchical circles, even though the triad worked to create a realistic picture of the coming crisis. Suggestions that the NCCB fund the project, establish a crisis control team, and set up a policy planning response group never went anywhere.

That was the middle of 1985. Shortly after the Chicago meeting, Bishop Levada reportedly contacted Doyle and basically told him to scrap the plan, that the bishops had a plan of their own and were planning to form a committee to deal with the issue. So after a press conference by Bishop Quinn, who had been sent by the papal nuncio to advise on establishing an NCCB group to study the problem, nothing really happened to advance *The Manual*.

Two cardinals, Krol of Philadelphia and Law of Boston, had agreed to place the Doyle-Peterson-Mouton's recommendations on the NCCB's upcoming agenda for its annual meeting. But in the end, the general counsel of the bishop's organization, Mark Chopko, who spoke for the bishops, opposed setting up a committee that included the members of the triad and accepting any of their prescribed actions. Chopko claimed that the bishops were aware of the information that Doyle, Peterson, and Mouton wanted to discuss, and claimed that the bishops had "already taken appropriate action"[45] to deal with clerical sexual abuse.

With official NCCB consideration of a systematic framework to deal with clerical sexual abuse closed to them, Doyle, Mouton and Peterson sent copies of their manual to each of the American diocesan bishops as a mailing from the St. Luke Institute. Although some bishops personally admitted that it was useful, Doyle claimed that "The [US] NCCB...never acknowledged its existence nor have they ever contacted Mouton or I [sic] in relation to any of the meetings which they had had concerning the issue since that time."[46]

In short, the triad was frozen out of any meaningful early participation with Church officials on how to deal with the problem of clerical sexual abuse in the United States. Thus, the status quo remained a secret, potentially scandalous situation. In fact, in 1988, Bishop A. J. Quinn of Cleveland, who had approved the authors' *Manual* to start with, wrote to the Vatican nuncio complaining about Doyle's negative comments to the secular press about clerical sexual abuse.

Monsignor Daniel Hoye, General Secretary of the NCCB in 1989, also accused Doyle, Peterson, and Mouton of giving "short shrift" to "diocesan and NCCB/USCC efforts" in dealing with sexual abuse, while also implying that "one of the authors intended to be...retained at considerable expense by the NCCB/USCC."[47] These comments and the attitudes of a number of high ranking Church leaders fueled the internal turf war over how and who would control the response to the sexual abuse crisis for almost another decade.

In the midst of all the Church confusion and institutional infighting, Mouton still had to maintain his composure and relationship with Louisiana Church officials as he continued to work on the Gauthe case. He had to let the internal politics between the triad and the bishops' organization play out as all the parties sought to protect their own turf on national and institutional levels.

Mouton's immediate priority was clear: he wanted to keep Gauthe alive. Peterson did, too. The priest-psychiatrist thought the accused predator priest would try to kill himself if he had to stand trial. Doyle continued to sound alarms, write letters, and make calls to try to get the attention of the US hierarchy about the impending crisis.

The prosecutor in the criminal proceedings, Nathan Stansbury, wanted to be sure that Gauthe would be incarcerated for life. Church officials from the Vatican on down knew only one thing: that they wanted no part of a public trial; it could only damage the credibility and moral posture of the Church, regardless of the verdict.

As the legal situation grew more grave for Gauthe, with motions and judicial decisions beginning to favor the plaintiffs, he and Mouton agreed that the best course of action for the accused sexual abuser was to simply plead guilty to 33 charges of sexual abuse in the criminal case. With no consideration of an insanity defense, the judge sentenced Gauthe to 20 years in the Wade Correctional Facility in Homer, a medium-security prison in northern Louisiana. There was no salacious testimony. Gauthe was sent to a place where his family could visit him, and where he would presumably be safe. Unfortunately, however, Gauthe would not receive the extended psychiatric care that he needed, as Mouton and Peterson had hoped.

Then in 1986, a year after Gauthe was convicted and jailed, and with careful consideration, the family of 11-year-old Scott Gastal decided to file charges against the pedophile priest and to sue for damages.[48] His parents were deadly serious about their willingness to allow their son to testify in open court to tell how and when he had been sexually abused by the predator priest.

What they wanted was the church to admit liability in the case. It was not enough to punish Gauthe, and it was not enough to pay them secret hush money. Therefore, the civil courtroom action would essentially provide this; it would determine the amount of the damages that they would receive, but more importantly, it would tell in a very public, graphic way what Gauthe had done and how the hierarchy had enabled him. The story would be out, and the court of public opinion could reconvict the priest and damn his superiors.

The Gastal case went forward in a shocked atmosphere. Simon, the boy's lawyer, who had also subpoenaed the dioceses for the personnel files of 27 other priests,[49] pulled no punches. He "bore down on anatomical details," and as one account says, "the clerics seemed frozen in their seats."[50] Scott Gastal was a more than effective witness. It only took the jury a little less than two hours to provide the Gastals with a significant financial settlement.

The Aftermath

The case took a devastating personal toll on all involved. Gauthe spent the next ten years, half of his original sentence, in jail. He was released early for good behavior, but in less than 12 months, he was again arrested in Texas for molesting a three-year-old boy. Because the child's mother did not want her son to play any public part in Gauthe's case, the prosecutor dropped the charge of molestation to one of injury to a child. This allowed Gauthe to be given seven years' probation rather than a prison sentence.

In 2008, the convicted pedophile priest again ran afoul of the law and was sentenced to two years in the Galveston Country Jail for failing to register as a sex offender. It has been reported that he is in poor health and suffering from high blood pressure. No one knows where he is now.

It's now known that the Robichauxs, the Sagreras, and the first group of parents of the victims of Gauthe's sexual abuse settled quietly with the Church for approximately $1.2 million each. Craig Sagrera went to a psychiatric hospital at age 11 to get treatment for deep depression. His parents have admitted that as they try to move forward, the memories of their situation keep resurfacing with each new case that appears.

Scott Gastal's family turned down a $3 million structured settlement and instead allowed their son to be deposed in the county courthouse. His testimony was so compelling that he and his family got slightly more than $1 million in a lump sum settlement. In a television interview he gave as an adult, though, Gastal told reporters that no one in the church apologized to him and that he was treated "like a liar."[51] The money was released to his parents after the judgment, but after legal fees, they reportedly managed to lose most of it in poor investments.

Their attorney, J. Minos Simon, played a critical part in making Church-State changes in the relationship between the civil authorities and the Catholic Church in Louisiana. He demanded openness and redress for Gauthe's actions. Many of his legal strategies were cutting edge at the time, and laid the ground-work for other cases, especially those that would break open in Boston a number of years later. Simon demanded and got subpoenas from the diocese for letters and records that pertained to Gauthe—files that had always been held in strict confidence by the diocese. This was an entirely new church-state legal tactic. He was able to bring all the pain and the cover-up out into the open by filing and winning motions to prevent the sealing of settlements between victims and the Church officials. He was able to subpoena information about other priests who were accused of sexual abuse as well, thus breaking new ground that the Church would consider as a civil incursion in the future. Because of his legal actions, demands by civil authorities became more prevalent in later cases. Simon opened the way for more aggressive criminal and civil strategies that were to come.

F. Ray Mouton, the Catholic lawyer with the social pedigree, however, lost his faith. "I have no belief in the Catholic Church. None," he said. "It's all gone. I went too many places I saw too many things. Today I'm fine. But I'm not in the Church."[52]

The only good thing that came out of the Gastal-Gauthe case, according to Mouton, was that for the first time the Church admitted liability for the former priest's actions. But Mouton has consistently faulted the Church hierarchy, saying that leaders were aware that he wanted to reach out to victims, but that they never supported him. Sadly, he admitted that "I never was in a meeting with Church personnel where children were discussed." Instead, he said, all they talked about was "the Church, defense motions, money [and the] press." As far as Mouton was concerned, Church leaders never had any intention of giving an apology, providing counseling, or approving of therapy.[53]

Mouton seemed to have intuited this because, during the course of the Gauthe trial and later, he admitted that the frightening realization came to him: that the priests and the bishops covered up such crimes. He claimed that they were "afflicted with a deeper, darker pathology that pose[d] a great threat, or even a great threat to society, for it was the bishops and the Vatican that empowered and enabled these criminals...to avoid scandal to the church."[54]

When the case was over, Mouton spent two years traveling the country talking with various bishops about clerical sexual abuse—without any real impact. The report that he wrote with Doyle and Peterson went nowhere, although in 1993, almost a decade later, the NCCB developed a series of responses to the crisis.

Afterwards, it was reported that Mouton "became an alcoholic, was diagnosed with bipolar disorder, got a divorce, and stopped practicing law."[55] He essentially refused to give interviews about the Gauthe case, and today the blogosphere reports that he is retired and writing a novel about a scandal and a cover-up in the Catholic Church.

Doyle also paid a price for his intervention into the Gauthe case and the alarms he raised about clerical sexual abuse. In 1986, after the completion of the predator priest's case, Doyle was relieved of his duties as a canon lawyer at the Vatican Embassy in Washington, DC. He was reassigned and commissioned as a reserve officer in the US Air Force as a chaplin. He has said in interviews that he was "too much of a maverick for them" in the embassy, but rumors also circulated that he opposed the idea of "cloaking damaging records with diplomatic immunity"[56] at that office. Since then, he has been stationed at Dover AFB, Andrews AFB, Lackland AFB, Maxwell AFB, Grissom AFB, and at posts in the Azores and Germany.

From these outposts, he has continued his critique of the Catholic hierarchy and its handling of the sexual abuse crisis in America, even though it was logical to assume that he would lose his platform and effectively be silenced by the duties in his new jobs. But that was not the case.

He was honored in 1992 for his "Moral Courage in Government and Business" by the Survivors Network for Those Abused by Priests (SNAP) as well as by military and humanitarian organizations too numerous to mention. In 2001, he was vindicated and called in as the expert witness when the US bishops hammered out their document to protect children after the Boston sexual abuse scandal.

It was in Germany, at Ramstein AFB, however, that Doyle was finally done in. He was removed from his job as an Air Force chaplain in 2004 due to a pastoral disagreement with his superior. He currently resides in Vienna, Virginia and is still active in working as a canon lawyer. Doyle has reportedly testified as an expert witness in clerical abuse cases over 1000 times in the past decade.

Doyle continues to fight for transparency and accountability within the Church. He has also recently been appointed a member of the panel that is investigating the voluntary audit of the Capuchins, a Catholic religious order, and allegations of clerical sexual abuse. They have opened their files back to the nineteenth century in order to clear the order's reputation, to show that it has been concerned about clerical sexual abuse, and to explain how it has been dealing with the issue going as far back as 1932. Doyle has given credibility to the panel overseeing the audit, and says that he hopes the "process will lead other entities in the Church...to have the courage and the Christian decency to do the same thing."[57] The former rising star in the ecclesiastical ranks is a recovering alcoholic and is now being characterized as a hero, a whistle-blower, and a troublemaker—depending on who is discussing him.

In 1987, two years after the Gauthe case and the publication of the Doyle-Mouton-Peterson report, Father Michael Peterson, the priest-psychiatrist and founder of St. Luke's Institute, died in Washington, DC. Only 44 years old, he had contracted AIDs and decided to go public with the news. When he sent a letter about his deteriorating condition to each of the US Catholic bishops in the country a few months before his death, his admission was met with mixed feelings. Only seven members of the hierarchy—but hundreds of priests—attended his burial Mass in the nation's capital.

The two Church officials in the center of the Gauthe case, Bishop Gerard Frey and Monsignor Alexandre Larroque were also affected by the case. Frey did not resign, nor was he removed from office, but instead, he was assigned a "coadjutor," co-leader of the diocese, who was designated to be his successor as bishop. Frey retired soon after and has since died. Larroque also shared his office for a number of years with other priests, and is currently in ill health.

Until recently, Bishop William Levada, the NCCB's observer/vetter of *The Manual* in Chicago, served as head of the Congregation of the Doctrine of the Faith (CDF) at the Vatican. After the Gauthe debacle, Levada rose to the highest ranks of the Church power structure in Rome. First, as a worker at the Congregation for the Doctrine of the Faith from 1976 to 1982, he was later appointed Archbishop of Portland in 1986, Archbishop of San Francisco in 1995, and Cardinal in 2005. Finally, he served as the prefect (head) of the Congregation of the Doctrine of the Faith, thus dealing with all matters of religious orthodoxy and clerical sexual abuse. The same cleric who vetted *The Manual* in 1985 and who brought the cease and desist news from the American bishops to Mouton, Peterson, and Doyle ended up being at the center of the religious universe in Rome until his eventual retirement in 2012.

Significant institutional changes occurred within the Catholic Church in the United States as a result of the Gauthe case as well, and had an early effect on United States' church-state relations. The NCCB, the bishops' canonical organization, recognized the gravity of the impending clerical sexual crisis. In 1993 it set up a Joint Study Commission with Vatican officials and started to work on getting some policies in place, but it was not until 2003 that their recommendations finally became institutionalized.[58] In short, there were no systematic ways of handling clerical sexual abuse matters that enjoined the bishops or their vicars up to that time within a church-state context.

The hierarchical organization, however, finally issued a three-part document[59] in 1994 that set up guidelines for dealing with clerical sexual abuse. Known as *Restoring Trust,* the bishops finally reviewed Church policies in place and appropriate ways to deal with allegations of clerical molestations. Interestingly, they followed part of the guidelines set down by Mouton, Doyle, and Peterson in *The Manual.*

The bishops were told to respond promptly to allegations of abuse where there was a reasonable belief that abuse had occurred, to relieve an alleged offender from his ministerial duties, and to refer him for medical evaluation and intervention, even if there was insufficient evidence. Bishops were told to comply with civil law, to report and cooperate with legal investigations, and to reach out to victims and their families. The bishops were expected to make a sincere commitment to the victims' spiritual and emotional well being, to respect the privacy of the individuals involved, and to be open about the issues with the members of the community. The bishops' compliance with such guidelines was mixed and uneven, at best, as later developments will show.

The *Restoring Trust* documents also provided public descriptions of viable treatment centers that the bishops could use for inpatient referrals. There were ten centers that an ad hoc bishops' Committee solicited for criteria to assess potential facilities that the hierarchy might use for sexually abusive priests. Some were church-related while others were located in private institutions. Among those run by the Church were the Institute of Living in Hartford; the New Life Center in Middleburg, Virginia; St. Luke Institute in Suitland, Maryland; St. Michael's Community run by the Servants of the Paraclete in Missouri; The Albuquerque Villa of the Servants of the Paraclete in New Mexico; Southdown, a treatment facility supported by the Canadian Conference of Catholic Bishops in Aurora, Canada; Villa St. John Vianney Hospital in Downingtown, Pennsylvania; and Our Lady of Peace Hospital in Louisville, Kentucky. Priests were also routinely referred to the Department of Psychiatry and Behavior Sciences at Johns Hopkins and the Department of Family Practice and Community Health of the University of Minnesota Medical School.

All of the facilities dealt with various addictions, emotional stress, and psychosexual disorders. They provided residential treatment as well as some form of outpatient and aftercare. They provided a variety of approaches to treatment: some were like the Institute of Living— committed to the "least restrictive" care; others such as the New Life

Center, Servants of the Paraclete, and Southdown emphasized "holistic" treatment, while St. Luke Institute provided intensive therapy, and St. John Vianney sought to help patients to be personally accountable, functional within boundaries, and become part of a support system.

Each of the centers maintained that all patient information was confidential and required patient approval if they were to share it with the patient's bishop. The Institute of Living, however, was willing to provide information that could have a bearing on a priest's ministry. What was part of every protocol in the treatment of disordered priests was the fact that the bishop, or his designee such as a vicar for administration, was expected to be in contact, either in person, by phone, or by fax, with the staff at each of the facilities to discuss outcomes and evaluations of priest-patients. The University of Minnesota even had a go-between who made sure that contact between the staff and the bishops or his designee were informed of the progress of patients. *Restoring Trust* explained ways to care for victims/survivors, and reported about ongoing official canonical efforts to deal with the matter.

At the same time, *Restoring Trust* raised many questions after the Gauthe case. How involved were the bishops or their designees supposed to be in the ongoing treatment of the priest-patients? What part, if any, should they play in aftercare? How knowledgeable or honest were they in the referrals of the priests in the first place?

In 2002, the Institute for Living in Hartford, which had treated Gauthe almost two decades before, had a falling out with Cardinal Edward Eagan of New York and other church officials. At that time, Dr. Harold Schwartz, the chief of psychiatry for the institute, accused the Church of having "misconstrued" its evaluations "in order to return priests to ministry."[60] This extraordinary allegation essentially accused Church officials of using the institute as a "clinical cover" to justify hierarchical reassignments of priests. Further, the institute maintained that in the future "the Church would have to attest, in writing, that it…disclosed any past allegations against priests referred for treatment."[61]

Just as importantly, one must also ask, What role did the various types of treatments play in the bishops' differing decisions to reassign priests with sexual abuse problems? Should the bishops have relied on many untested therapies in their decisions about how to deal with sexual abusers? Why wasn't there any kind of database or information pool on such priests? Were there any canonical courts in the United States dealing with such matters at the time?

In 1994, there still was no clear official canonical policy in place, as the three-part document *Restoring Trust* shows. A variety of responses for reassignment included counseling, a return to non-parochial ministry, resignation, retraining, restricted ministry, laicization, a formal ecclesiastical trial, and expulsion from active priestly ministry if a priest were convicted of pedophilia. Such decisions, however, were often made in light of differing legal proceedings; the advice of professionals, the well-being of the laity, and the best interests of the Church.[62] Bishops were often conflicted by their obligations to the clergy, the laity, and the Church, unsure about how to use the information and advice that they received, and ignorant about sexual deviance, generally.

While the hierarchy struggled to find ways to deal with the effects of clerical sexual abuse, the National Conference of Catholic Bishops (NCCB) and Vatican officials tried to deal with the problem, too. Essentially they held meetings, assisted individual diocese in their attempts to develop uniform advice and policies about clerical sexual abuse, enforced canon law, and carried out other ecclesiastical procedures that had the force of Church sanctions behind them.

There were no definitive policies, though, from the pope or officers in the Vatican about how the hierarchy in the United States should interact with civil authorities. In a top-down hierarchical structure, such a void was catastrophic. There were no real guidelines about how the Church leaders should manage and/or punish clerics for the *crime* of clerical sexual abuse. The canon law still prevailed on matters of *sin*. Church management of clerical personnel was still considered to be within the purview of ecclesiastical rights and privilege.

As a result, it would eventually have to be the power of the civil authority—its legal system and the investigations of the press and media—in the United States that would finally break open the tragedy that had been festering for such a long time. They would demand retribution for the victims of clerical sexual abuse and punishment for the priests/perpetrators. They would insist on transparency and accountability. They would take the lead, challenge the Church and its canon law, and enforce the compelling state interest to protect children. They would force the institutional Church to revisit its legal system and reconsider its eroding ecclesiastical privileges in the United States. The church-state power shift would soon begin to happen.

2
Revelations and Scandals: Boston and Beyond

Introduction

The EMTs brought the corpse to the hospital about an hour after an alert had been sounded at the maximum security prison. Dr. Richard Freniere, the attending physician on duty in the emergency room, declared the man dead at 1:17 p.m. Several days later, the chief medical examiner in Boston, Dr. Richard Evans, listed the official cause of death as ligature strangulation, blunt chest trauma, broken ribs, and a punctured lung: in short, a homicide.

The deceased was known as a "skinner" in jailhouse slang, the name inmates use to identify a child molester. Confined in cell no. 2 at the Souza-Baranowki Correction Center in Shirley, Massachusetts, the predator existed in a stifling space. It had a bunk, two shelves for his possessions, a toilet, a small sink, a footlocker, and a piece of metal that served as a mirror.

The skinner was in protective custody, living within 20 feet of the guard's duty station. That way, he could be watched closely by the officers 24/7. This particular inmate, however, who needed so much attention, was frequently harassed by other felons and sometimes by his jailers, too. They taunted him and often told him that he would burn in hell for his crimes. Within the prison walls, skinners were the worst of the worst, and this one was no exception because he was a *serial* pedophile.

The skinner's murderer, Joseph Druce, was already serving a 30-year life sentence without the possibility of parole. He had beaten a guy to death for making a pass at him while he was hitchhiking, an assault he would never forget. That could have motivated Druce as he began to think about killing the skinner in the cell next to him.

The murderer had originally been assigned to cell no. 3, but had been sent to solitary confinement for awhile for a fight. When he returned, Druce was transferred to another cell, no. 21, further away from the child molester. Nevertheless, he continued to become increasingly interested in teaching the skinner a lesson.

Druce was going to take care of the little old man that some said looked like a kindly uncle or a friendly neighborhood shopkeeper. The future killer, however, saw somebody else: a dangerous, convicted, unremorseful felon—living close enough to him to be made to pay with his life for his disgusting past acts.

Druce planned to kill the molester for more than a month, and stalked him with his eyes, according to an inmate.[1] He decided that his type of justice would take place on a Saturday because the normal lunch procedure was different then. On that day, groups of inmates were allowed to leave their cells, get their own food off a cart in the middle of the cellblock, and eat it in their unlocked cubicles.

The Saturday of the murder, however, the guards deviated from their usual lunch practice. Instead of mechanically opening a group of cell doors a few at a time, the guards automatically opened all of the 24 cells in the maximum security wing at once. This made it possible for all of the inmates to leave their cubicles and mix with each other in the center of the cellblock. No one was sure why the guards changed from the normal procedure, but Druce instinctively realized that this shift in the meal routine would be his opportunity to kill the skinner.

He watched as the molester looked over the food cart and took some pizza. And, he continued to eye the skinner as he carried his lunch back to his cell and ate alone. When the molester went to return his tray to the open space, Druce quickly followed him and sneaked into his prey's small living area. Then, just before the guards were to close the doors automatically, Druce jammed the upper track of the cell door mechanism with a paperback book, and the lower track with the prisoner's nail clipper and a toothbrush. That way he could be sure that the door couldn't be opened electronically by the guards if the skinner cried out. It was also the way he could prevent his detection until he took care of business.

Two inmates saw Druce enter the cell and reported what was going on to the guards, but reports say that by the time the guards reacted, the murderer had already been in the skinner's cell for about five minutes. Interestingly, there were 366 cameras[2] surveying the cellblock at the time, but no one in authority saw anything happening. By the time the officers issued an alert, and before the other guards could respond, Druce had all but finished his chore.

He brought a t-shirt to tie his victim's hands together. Somehow, Druce had persuaded the skinner to be quiet, telling him that everything was a joke. Just to be sure, though, he also brought a pair socks to stuff in the pedophile's mouth if he decided to cry out—and a razor. But he only had a short amount of time, so Druce hurriedly tied the inmate's shoes together and tightened a pillowcase around the skinner's neck to strangle him. Druce killed him quickly and, seemingly, without notice.

Then, just to be sure that the child molester was dead, Druce jumped from the victim's cot onto the skinner's chest a number of times. He was about to castrate him with the razor he brought, but stopped when at least six guards arrived and tried to open the cell door.

It took a few minutes before they could force it off its track and gain access to the scene. Losing time while they waited for a large crowbar to be sent down to them, the guards could do nothing until they were finally able to get inside after some frantic, crucial minutes.[3]

That was when they saw what they had suspected. The skinner was laying face down and unresponsive. Druce was on the floor, too, looking up at the guards. They immediately placed Druce in wrist restraints and called the medics.

The guards began nonstop CPR on the inmate, but by 12:58, only 11 minutes after the alert, it was all over. The skinner was dead. They rushed him to the local hospital anyway, but it was too late.[4]

The murderer has been characterized as satisfied and proud. The prosecutor told the jury at his subsequent trial that Druce got his "prize."[5]

Druce, himself, had been beaten and molested as a youngster, and maybe that was part of the reason why he carried out his own jail-house justice on the skinner. But in a letter to the Catholic Free Press of Worcester, Druce explained his motivation. He said he carried this childhood hatred with him and that he often heard conversations in prison—talk among pedophiles who expressed "no remorse, only gloating and reminissing [*sic*] over past victims."[6]

Punishing their actions, and taking revenge for his own sexual abuse, were both powerful reasons for the murder. But at Druce's trial three years later, the jury refused to accept any mitigating circumstances or psychological excuses for his actions. The jury turned down an insanity defense and found Druce guilty.

The pedophile's murderer was ultimately sentenced to life in prison without the possibility of parole—for a second time—but no one really cared. In fact, a lot of people thought the killer performed a public service, that he had saved the state millions of dollars. That was because Druce had murdered the notorious Catholic predator priest: the former Reverend, John J. Geoghan.

The dead man was a defrocked cleric who was 68 years old when he was strangled. He had been accused of sexually abusing somewhere between 130 and 150 children during the course of his religious ministry. Even worse, high-level Church leaders knew about his sexual deviance but still continued to reassign him from one parish to another. Geoghan had been moved to six different parishes by his superiors over two decades.

The sickening situation began in 1962, when the newly ordained Father John Geoghan was sent to his first parish, Blessed Sacrament in Saugus, Massachusetts. After four years there, he was moved to St. Bernard's in Concord, then a year later to St. Paul's in Hingham. After another seven years, he was sent to St. Andrew's in Jamaica Plain, six years later to St. Brendan's in Dorchester, and then, finally, three years later to St. Julia's in Weston.

During his active ministry, Geoghan had repeatedly been reported and accused of molesting young boys, the first time being at his initial ministry at Blessed Sacrament. Although he later admitted to molesting four boys for two and a half years, he wasn't reprimanded or sent away for his first "treatment" until 1968, when a number of accusations were leveled against him at his new parish assignment at St. Paul's in Hingham.

Five years into his ministry, he was sent for help for the first time. He stayed for a while at the Seton Institute in Baltimore, but was allowed to leave, apparently without a change in his behavior. There were other accusations during the 1970s too, but it wasn't until a decade later that Geoghan was finally placed on sick leave for his predatory actions.

In 1980, he was ordered for a second time by his superiors to get counseling and psychoanalysis with a private therapist and a physician. Soon after entering treatment, Geoghan sent a handwritten report to his superior, the vicar for administration. The man in that position who served as the bishop's aide was Bishop Thomas Daily. He received a note from Geoghan saying that he had been through a psychological evaluation, and his personal physician, John Brennan, thought he was "making good progress."[7] Geoghan reported that his physician put him on medication and suggested that he continue with therapy. That is what the priest referred to as "my little routine."[8]

The therapy consisted of weekly meetings with a psychiatrist, Dr. Robert Mullins, for psychotherapy, and return visits to Dr. Brennan for medication every two weeks. After an extended leave of absence and outpatient treatment, Dr. Mullins sent the following letter to his superior at the Boston Archdiocese about his patient's progress:

> Rev. John Geoghan, a long-time friend and patient of mine, has recently terminated his ministry at St. Brendan's parish, due to a rather unfortunate traumatic experience. Following a brief, but beneficial, respite from his duties, Father Geoghan has adjusted remarkably well.
>
> In my opinion, he is now able to resume full pastoral activities without any need for specific restrictions.[9]

Dr. Brennan, Geoghan's physician, however, was more cautious. He waited a few months longer before concurring with the psychiatrist's opinion. At that time, however, he wrote to another superior at the archdiocese that Father Geoghan, who had been under his care for *seven years*, [italics added] was emotionally "stable and very satisfactory," presumably so satisfactory that he could also say, "There are no psychiatric contraindications or restrictions to his work as a parish priest."[10]

Even with a clean bill of health, though, many sexual abuse accusations against Geoghan proliferated. In response, his superiors referred him to St. Luke Institute in Maryland, then to the Institute of Living in Hartford, and then back to St. Luke's again. In a final attempt to help him, the vicar packed him off to another treatment facility, Southdown, in Ontario in 1996.[11]

During all that time, for more than three decades, there were mixed messages about the mental state of Father Geoghan. He was declared fully able to carry out his pastoral activities by some private psychotherapists while receiving mixed diagnoses from others. Experts at the Institute of Living, where Geoghan received treatment for three months, were typical with equivocations. They said that "the probability that he (Geoghan) would sexually act out again is quite low. However, we cannot guarantee that it could not re-occur. It is both reasonable and therapeutic for him to be reassigned back to his parish."[12]

Geoghan was released from the institute with a diagnosis of "atypical pedophilia in remission"[13] in 1989. But Geoghan's superiors, who relied heavily on a variety of mental evaluations, were only sure of one thing: that the priest's behavior kept reoccurring despite repeated therapy, sick leaves, and hospitalization. At no point did they know, with total certainty, how to handle the pedophile priest who had been in their midst for many years.

Finally, after continued claims of sexual abuse, Geoghan's superiors dismissed him from active ministry in 1989. They sent him to work with retired priests at the Regina Cleri residence in 1993. But Geoghan was still not rehabilitated. They placed him on administrative leave in 1994, put him on sick leave in 1996, and finally requested him to retire at that time. After four mandated psychiatric and therapeutic confinements, extensive outpatient treatments, and various prognoses, Geoghan had been assigned and reassigned before he was finally defrocked in 1998 for pedophilic behavior. He was gone for good—a pyrrhic victory.

Geoghan's religious and psychic care was the direct responsibility of three cardinals. The first was Richard Cardinal Cushing, who headed up the Boston Archdiocese when Geoghan was ordained in 1962. Cushing retired in 1970. Then, the Geoghan problem fell to Humberto Cardinal Maderios, who served from 1970 until his death in 1983. It was finally left to Bernard Cardinal Law who ran the archdiocese from 1984 until December 2002 to clean up the Geoghan mess.

In spite of the predator priest's continual psychosexual problems, all three cardinals and their assistants, or vicars, claimed to have relied on psychiatric recommendations over the years to justify reassigning him to new parishes. This was true with Geoghan's last appointment to St. Julia's, in Weston, when his transfer occurred without informing the parishioners about their new priest's past.

The investigative staff of the *Boston Globe* broke the story about the pedophile priest in early 2002. Its "Spotlight Team," which looked into all kinds of corruption and scandals for over three decades, had seen it all. But according to its editor, Walter V. Robinson, the paper had "nary a file folder on a priest, much less a bishop or a cardinal."[14] In fact, the only other such story that was close to matching the impending Geoghan scandal occurred about a decade before, and it involved crimes that had been committed almost 40 years earlier by a *former* priest, James Porter.

Porter's was the case of a priest who had been ordained in 1964 and shuffled off to a number of different parishes for molesting children between then and 1970. Although there were many allegations against him, none resulted in any Church discipline—only his movement from parish to parish. In 1973, Porter reportedly acknowledged to his superiors that he had become sexually involved with some young men in his Fall River parish and requested to be released from his vows. He was quickly defrocked by the Vatican that same year.

Porter subsequently married and had children, but was finally prosecuted for his alleged sexual abuse crimes in 1993, when more than 100 of his victims came forward to testify against him. The former priest was eventually convicted of 43 counts of sexual abuse and sentenced to 18–20 years in prison. The Diocese of Fall River was left to pay a $7 million dollar settlement in a civil suit brought by other accusers as well. Porter died quietly of cancer in 2005.

So when members of the *Globe*'s staff[15] were looking into a routine arrest in early 1999, they weren't expecting to come across a case involving a priest—of any kind—former or defrocked. Nor did they expect to find an "extraordinary admission"[16] in the court filings related to the arrest and subsequent indictment of Father John Geoghan for committing indecent assault and battery on a boy at the Waltham Boys and Girls Club. What they did find, surprisingly, was a statement by Bernard Cardinal Law, the head of the Boston Archdiocese about his knowledge of Geoghan, the defrocked priest.

The filing in the case revealed that Bernard Cardinal Law admitted to having appointed Geoghan as the leader of a suburban parish several years earlier. He did this, the records showed, even though he knew before he made that assignment that the priest had molested seven boys. Now, the media flood gates were about to open.

The investigative team at the *Globe* followed up on the cardinal's admission after Geoghan's arrest and found another startling fact: Church lawyers had asked for a protective order—or a seal of confidentiality on Geoghan's personnel records from his first assignment in ministry until he was indicted. Indeed, there had been an imposed legal silence on the defrocked priest's past by a judge, James Hughes. But the *Globe* refused to be deterred or "intimidated"[17] and tried to find out more about Geoghan's alleged predatory behavior.

The newspaper brought several suits[18] to open the files sealed by the protective order and used its unique public position as well to get around it. Besides petitioning the court for transparency regarding Church records connected to Geoghan, the *Globe* also asked for other clerical sexual abuse victims who might be among their readers to come forward and provide information. Hundreds of victims responded, changing the salacious story to a quickly escalating public scandal, one that resulted in the newspaper ultimately publishing more than 900 news stories about various sexually abusive priests.[19]

But many leads and other claims dried up because earlier clerical records were often either sealed or impounded by judges. As a result, they were rendered virtually nonexistent as far as the public was concerned. Judges in the Massachusetts District Courts had the right to place a protective seal in a "widely publicized or sensation criminal or civil case" if either the litigants or the judge decided to do so because the parties or witnesses were likely "to interfere with the rights of the accused or the litigants to a fair trial."[20] Many did so.

Records could also be impounded, or kept sealed for a specific period of time, as well, for a variety of reasons such as the need for confidentiality, the need to protect the public health and safety, and a "compelling" reason to seal court documents.[21] Thus, the Boston Archdiocese's canon lawyers used one of their usual strategies to protect minor victims and the reputation of the Church: they filed a motion to seal the records of the case being brought against John Geoghan.

Undeterred, the *Globe* challenged the request in the Geoghan case. Lawyers for the paper filed a motion for transparency based on the public's right to know about the sexual abuse accusations against Geoghan—but they also went one step further. They demanded files on other accused predator priests as well.

Countering, the Church's lawyers argued for a protective seal based on the principle of separation of church and state, and the bishop's responsibility to protect the due process rights of the accused priest. In essence, however, the Church was asserting its traditional ecclesiastical right to privacy, a privilege that actually protected the personnel files and medical records of clergy. This was simply code for the Church's assertion of its power: its insistence on the supremacy of canon law over civil law to deal with the management and possible punishment of a member of the clergy.

During the legal maneuvering, what the public record did not yet show was that Cardinal Law did nothing definitive to remove Geoghan from his ministerial position after many years of allegations of sexual abuse. The *Globe* staff was able to show that despite such claims by the Church, it was not until the 1990s that Cardinal Law finally accepted a different diagnosis by some new psychiatrists who maintained that Goeghan suffered from a "deep rooted sexual perversion" and "homo-sexual pedophilia."[22]

Up to that time, Geoghan's superiors reportedly relied on indefinite diagnostic claims: that sexual deviance could be cured or curbed by therapy. As a result, the Boston Church officials accepted as fact that Geoghan could be transformed spiritually and psychically after counseling—indeed, that he would be able carry out his ministerial duties. So Church higher-ups simply transferred Geoghan around to different parishes in the greater Boston area, a routine action by pastors, bishops, and even cardinals, who were misguided, in denial, ignorant, unconcerned, or simply protecting the "old boy network" and the reputation of the Church. In fact, at one point they were so sure that Geoghan was cured, they even put him in charge of the altar boys at one parish where he served.

The media also reported the tragic fact that Cardinal Law allowed Geoghan to stay at St. Julia's, his last parish, for eight years. This was dur-ing extended leaves, periods of treatment, and other allegations, before the religious superior finally relieved him of his priestly post in 1993. After subsequent failed treatments during the decade, Geoghan was sent to work at a retired priests' home known as Regina Cleri. But multiple civil suits and criminal charges followed him there, too.

Finally, when Geoghan's superiors defrocked him in 1998, they took away his right to perform any spiritual functions. They worked out a way, however, to allow him to remain at Regina Cleri. In fact, the newspapers reported that as his address when he was finally arrested in Waltham and discovered by the *Globe*.

The newspaper's staff dug further into the case and exposed other shocking information. With leads from informants, the newspaper team was able to reveal many other instances of clerical sexual abuse.

And it unmasked another, frightening clandestine action of the lead-ers of the Catholic Church: numerous financial settlements in a number of lawsuits in pedophilia cases within and around the Archdiocese of Boston. In fact, in 2003, it was reported that at least $21.2 million in settle-ments went to 149 people from 1994–2001—pay-outs made for instances of clerical sexual abuse *before* the Geoghan case even broke open.[23]

So the public's shock over the news of the Geoghan case and the defrocked priest's heinous crimes reached the level of outrage when it became public knowledge that Geoghan's acts were not unique. Even more astounding was the fact that a cover-up by the Catholic higher ups within the Boston area was standard operating procedure in other dioceses as well.

In fact, the *Globe* disclosed that the behavior of the Church leaders in Geoghan's case was merely routine and part of a secret, systematic policy of Church hush money that was paid to cover up crimes against innocent children. How could that happen? Didn't anyone remember Louisiana or the Gauthe case? Didn't anyone pay attention to the guidelines put out by the NCCB?

The way the clandestine arrangements were carried out in Boston and other places, as it turns out, was quite simple. The results of a number of grand jury hearings in a variety of cities show a definite pattern of how the cover-up business was carried out in most dioceses.

Financial settlements between the Church and alleged victims of clerical sexual abuse were supposed to be based on covert payments for therapy, pain, and suffering. Children and their families received money in the name of an impersonal, corporate body known as a "diocese," a term which technically referred to a number of parishes under the control of a bishop.

In this way, the bishop acted in his capacity as the powerful leader of an ecclesiastical *entity* (the diocese), rather than simply as an *individual*. This enabled and legitimized the bishop's secret actions, explained to the victims and their families as the best way to protect minors. The strategy of concealment inferred that it was only through confidentiality and the bishop's generosity that the "diocese" would grant funds to the victim. At the same time, however, secrecy also protected the accused members of the clergy and, in turn, served to deflect personal responsibility from the bishop. In a final stroke of control, the "diocese" would solemnly promise to impose the penalties of the canon or Church law in clerical sexual abuse cases. In return for often lucrative financial settlements, then, the "diocese" would demand total written parental and child confidentiality. Later, this policy was justified by Church officials as a way to protect the identity of the minors who were abused, the reputations of the alleged priests, and the moral credibility of the Church.

The routine policy of using confidentiality agreements came to light during the Geoghan case as well. This occurred when the records of an accused second molester in the Boston area, Reverend Paul Shanley, were unsealed as part of the Geoghan case.

Judge Constance Sweeny of the Massachusetts Superior Court, a Catholic-educated woman, herself, was the person who heard the *Globe's* motion to release documents related to Geoghan. The newspaper claimed that the public had a right to know about the clerical sexual abuse that had occurred and that was still happening in the Boston Archdiocese. The Church, on the other hand, wanted to continue its strategy of delay and demands for confidentiality to protect the reputation of the Church.

In November of 2002, Judge Sweeny agreed with the *Globe's* motion and ordered the public release of 10,000 Church documents that dealt not only with the criminal case against Geoghan, but with 84 other lawsuits as well. She brought about what an earlier confidential Church report had foretold: "Our dependence in the past on Roman Catholic judges and attorneys protecting the Diocese and clerics is GONE."[24]

One of the accused clerics revealed in the documents was the Reverend Paul Shanley. His case shed light on how the Church used the strategy of filing motions to place a protective seal on court findings and rulings regarding clerical sexual abuse cases. Shanley's case was being conducted almost at the same time as Geoghan's.

Early in his career, Shanley was regarded as a "hippie priest," a 1970s man of the cloth who ministered to alcoholics, addicts, and homeless people who needed his care. Somewhere along the line, though, Shanley's demons took over. He became a founding member of the North American Man Boy Love Association (NAMBLA),[25] advocating the abolition of age of consent laws for sex, and calling for the decriminalizing of adult sex with consenting minors.

The newly unsealed documents that were permitted in the Geoghan case gave civil authorities and lawyers access to the accused's personnel records and those of other priests who had also been reported as sexual abusers to Church administrators. The documents had been formerly considered privileged, but now these diocesan records proved that high-level church officials knew about early sexual abuse accusations against priests like Shanley—and that they had settled civil lawsuits brought against him. Further, they brought to light the pattern of hierarchical protection and silence in clerical sexual abuse cases. Such evidence was now made available thanks to the ruling by Judge Sweeny

The records showed that in 1990, Shanley's superiors in Boston sent him to California, but did not inform the predator priest's new bishop about previous sexual abuse charges leveled against him. When the West Coast hierarchy finally became aware of Shanley's history, he was dismissed from Church duties there.

The Boston Church records also revealed that Shanley was sent for mental evaluation and had personally admitted to being attracted to adolescents three years later in 1993. Even more shocking, they showed that his superior, Cardinal Law, settled a number of lawsuits based on that confession through confidentiality agreements, providing more proof of the Church leader's knowledge of Shanley's sexual deviance over a long period of time. Ultimately, the predator priest was defrocked by Pope John Paul II in 2004 at the age of 73, and then convicted in court of two counts of rape and indecent assault in 2005.

Judge Sweeney, then, is critically important in breaking open the whole clerical sexual abuse scandal in Massachusetts. In fact, she did more than just set the precedent to unseal clerical personnel records. She also castigated Church lawyers publically. She maintained that they were filing motions that appeared to have been "designed to escape the full force of the court's multiple orders to produce documents...open to public inspection...[and that] they still resist public disclosure of those documents."[26] She denied the hierarchical legal inference that the records were ecclesiastically privileged and should remain sealed. Instead, she allowed clerical personnel and medical records to be subpoenaed in the state, taking a tough stance and warning that the "court simply will not be toyed with."[27]

Sweeney's decision in the Geoghan case set a legal precedent in Massachusetts, ensuring that previously protected personnel records, including medical and psychiatric reports of Catholic priests, could and would now be opened. The public's right to know would be given priority over Church control of secret information in alleged clerical criminal matters. This meant that the totality of the damage and the facts in the case against Geoghan would be presented for all to see when he came to trial. The same would be true in the Shanley case.

Transparency and civil investigations of Church management were now a totally new part of the civil and canonical legal equation. The criminal prosecution of predatory priests and civil lawsuits against them would result in a new way that Church leaders would be treated. The canon law would be challenged in matters of clerical sexual abuse, and legal cooperation, instead of accommodation, would be expected to prevail. The church-state equation in Massachusetts had changed forever.

The legal rulings and judicial expectations in Boston did not stop there. They were later repeated in subsequent state investigations as well. For example, in Westchester County, New York, a grand jury found that settlements between victims of clerical sexual abuse and the archdiocese were nothing more than a "sham."[28] The jurors came to this conclusion because payments for free counseling services for the victims of molestations were tied to total silence.

The panel concluded that confidentiality agreements with victims enabled the hierarchy to "maintain a shroud of secrecy"[29] over the behavior of pedophile priests. In fact, the grand jury maintained that by outlawing such practices, civil authorities could finally help to alleviate the victims' isolation and continued victimization.

In Cincinnati, another grand jury made a similar recommendation and went even further. In a settlement mediated between Hamilton County and the archdiocese, the Church was required to provide the names and addresses of accusers, the dates of their charges, and their current addresses, along with the assignments and other information about the accused priests. But more importantly, the Cincinnati settlement also required the archdiocese to release victims from previously agreed upon confidentiality obligations![30]

The secret way of doing Church legal business was quickly ending. As soon as the decision came down, the archbishop of Cincinnati, Daniel E. Pilarczyk, set up a $3 million fund to assist the victims.[31]

With the disclosure of the previously privileged medical and psychiatric information about Shanley, Geoghan, and other pedophile priests in the Boston area, the depth of the national crisis began to emerge. Geoghan went through a sensational criminal trial in court and in the press. The decision of the jury in the criminal case against him resulted in a conviction with a 9–10-year sentence in a maximum security prison.

Geoghan and church authorities were also sued in a group civil suit brought by victims of the priest's sexual abuse as well. There were attempts to win a financial settlement of $30 million dollars that was to be split among 86 victims of the predator priest. But under canon law, any expenditure beyond $1 million had to be approved by the finance council of the Boston Archdiocese. When the council learned that there could be as many as 600 potential claims, the advisors refused to approve the settlement that had previously been agreed to by Cardinal Law. They argued that $50 million dollars[32] would be the final amount that the Church could afford to pay out *in toto*—no matter how many victims came forward in the future. They claimed that to give $30 million dollars to Geoghan's accusers could have placed the mission of the Church "at risk."[33]

This led to a new church-state predicament. The finance council recommended the establishment of a non-litigious, global assistance fund for all victims, paid from a source of money that would not compromise the ability of the church to teach, preach, and sanctify its adherents. If civil lawyers would not accept such a deal, then the Church attorneys would delay the settlement and invoke Massachusetts' "charitable immunity" law. It limited the Church's liability, as was the case with every other charitable institution, to an earlier, statutory payment of $20,000 per victim.

Lawyers for the victims, however, refused to accept the Church's arguments. They would not accept money from the capped fund, saying that they would take on the diocese and its five highest ranking officers as well. They were willing to go to trial no matter what the Church's legal team decided.

After several more months of legal wrangling between canon and civil lawyers, however, the Geoghan victims decided to take the course of least resistance. They agreed to accept a $10 million dollar settlement— with no formal apology or spiritual outreach from the Church, and no opportunity for the victims to make statements in court.[34]

In short, the Church dodged a bullet. It got a confidentiality agreement in the Geoghan civil case, and had to pay out a smaller financial settlement than was originally demanded by the victims. It received greater secrecy than the hierarchy could have expected.

The archdiocese was punished in other ways, though. Financially, it was required to pay $18 million in settlements for other past acts of clerical sexual abuse—but that was only the tip of the iceberg. Other cases continued to come forward, and greater monetary problems were the result. Emotionally, the scandal, fueled by the revelations in the Shanley case along with Geoghan's conviction and his subsequent murder, resulted in anger, outrage, and a public mistrust of other clerics and members of the Church leadership. Throughout the Boston Archdiocese, there were rumors about hierarchical complicity and sexual abuse cover-ups: whispers of a long history of such predatory priestly behavior. It was time for the civil authorities to get to the real story.

Civil Challenges to the Catholic Church

A flood of sexual abuse allegations began to emerge during the clerical abuse cases of Shanley, Geoghan, and other priests in the Boston Archdiocese and its environs. In response, the state investigated the numerous victims' claims that had been ignored prior to 2002, a fact that was about to change the church-state relationship in the Bay State.

The attorney general for the Commonwealth of Massachusetts, Thomas F. Reilly, decided to go to the top and depose high-ranking Church leaders in the Boston Archdiocese. He wanted to know what they knew and what they did in instances of clerical sexual abuse before the Geoghan and Shanley cases. These were to be open depositions with no promise of confidentiality attached to them. Among the superiors to be questioned were Bernard Cardinal Law and a number of his most important assistants.

The deposition of a cardinal was a very significant civil action. It was rarely, if ever, done, and certainly not publically in a Catholic bastion like Boston, Massachusetts. In essence, a deposition is a civil discovery tool, testimony that is required under oath to gain evidence before going to a trial. Usually it is part of a civil action that would involve suits for financial damages.

In a deposition, questions can be broad, and even based on hearsay. The person being deposed can also refuse to answer based on "privilege," that is, the confidentiality between an attorney and his client, a physician and his patient, or a priest and his penitent. Would the cardinal expect to be treated in a special way, with an ecclesiastical exemption if the state started to probe into the personnel matters of the Boston Archdiocese? Could the relationship between an archbishop and a clergyman under his pastoral protection be breached by a subpoena for information by civil authorities? Church-state issues were definitely going to be tested by Reilly and his prosecutorial team.

This was new legal ground. It foretold the beginning of the end for some of the Catholic hierarchy's rationale for, and insistence on, the ecclesiastical privilege of secrecy and silence attached to its power. All bishops believed they had certain canonical rights that were attached to their positions: rights to deal with the clergy, to protect priests' due process rights, and to preserve the autonomy and reputation of the Church. This was especially true as the hierarchy applied such thinking to Law, the ruling cardinal of the Boston Archdiocese, a "Prince of the Church."

The deferential title was first used in medieval times because cardinals held the highest rank in the ecclesiastical feudal order. That position afforded them the same privileges and protocols as secular princes, those men who were part of the nobility in civil society. The title was also given to elite churchmen because cardinals were equated with "prince-electors," like those members of the royalty who had the right to choose a new emperor upon the death of the king in the feudal Holy Roman Empire.

Traditionally, then, the respect for the position of a cardinal revolved around his papal appointment to the College of Cardinals, a position that allowed him to vote for a new pope on the death of the pontiff. This is a position held today by only a small number of individuals; in fact, there are currently only a few more than 200 cardinals in the world who have been "enthroned." The number may vary if a reigning pope decides to lessen or enlarge the College of Cardinals, as popes have always done during their pontificates. Modern cardinals may also be called to a "consistory" or a meeting with the pope in order to advise the Church's supreme leader on a specific ecclesiastical matter.

Cardinal Law was one of five active, governing "princes" of the Church in the United States during his tenure. The Boston Archdiocese, which he headed from 1984–2002, was the third largest archdiocese at the time, and a major enclave of Catholics in the country. He was part of the upper ecclesiastical elite of the Catholic hierarchy in the United States and, in turn, part of the Vatican inner circle and power structure as well.

Law rose through the ecclesiastical ranks quickly. He was an only child whose father was a World War II flier and whose mother was a Catholic convert. Because of his father's work, the family moved around, and he lived in a variety of places.

The future cardinal attended Harvard and graduated with a degree in medieval history. When he completed his religious training, he became a civil rights activist while serving at St. Paul's parish in Vicksburg, Mississippi.

Law worked on ecumenical issues during and after Vatican II, the major Church council held in Rome in the 1960s. With his reputation for religious outreach and conciliation, he secured a papal appointment as Bishop of the Diocese of Springfield-Cape Girardeau in southern Missouri in 1973.

Eleven years later, he was elevated to the leadership of one of the most prestigious Catholic archdioceses in the United States by Pope John Paul II, an appointment that reportedly caused Law to say "After Boston, there's only heaven." A year later, he was enthroned as a cardinal as well.

Law was at the top of his game, and he never forgot how he made it there. He had been praised earlier by Charles Evers, the brother of the slain civil rights activist, Medgar Evers, for his commitment to racial justice when he served in the South. And Law continued to work for equality and social justice in the Archdiocese of Boston, as well, by trying to get affordable housing for immigrants and minorities. He reached out to Jewish leaders in the community; he spoke Spanish and mingled easily with newcomers to America. He was a determined and staunch opponent of abortion.

The new cardinal even gave up the traditional, automatic membership in the Atheneum Club for the crème de la crème of Boston society because he didn't think he would use it: he preferred to project the image of a man of the people. Although he was not a part of Boston's Irish clerical gentry, it was reported that Law was affable and could still move easily in the Kennedy, O'Neill, and Kerry political circles.

Within his own religious realm, however, the cardinal was different. He expected his staff to call him "Your Eminence" at the chancery office and to follow his orders precisely. In his own formidable way, Law was able to run the archdiocese's $50 million dollar a year operation without any internal opposition and direct its hundreds of millions of dollars worth of real estate. He was also reputedly a workaholic. He lived in a palatial three-story, 28-acre Italianate residence on Boston's most prestigious street in a home that at one time was valued at $85 million dollars.

Cardinal Law's administration was based on the traditional pyramid model of management like the rest of the Catholic institutional church. A medieval vestige of organization still existing in the modern era, it was typical of the Vatican paradigm: one in which most decisions were made at the top by the pope and a relatively few senior members below. The assistants were men who were loyal and responsible for line and staff matters, as they say in the military. In terms of Church management, they were faithful aides who dealt with either administrative issues of diocesan business, or pastoral religious matters that dealt with clergy and religious issues.

Following the pattern of his predecessor, Humberto Cardinal Maderios, the new cardinal, Bernard Law reappointed an auxiliary, or a bishop-assistant, to serve as his second in command. Bishop Thomas Daily, known as the vicar for administration, the right-hand man to the former cardinal, was a holdover in the new leadership team of Cardinal Law and carried out the day-to-day running of the archdiocese. Daily was helped by Bishop John McCormack, a sort of equal who worked as the secretary for ministerial affairs, handling all personnel matters, pastoral and religious. Both men reported to the cardinal. Remember these names—Daily and McCormack—because the civil authorities intended to depose them, too.

A year after the Geoghan case broke in 2002 and clerical sexual abuse claims were mounting, the attorney general of the Commonwealth of Massachusetts started a civil investigation into the functioning of the Boston Archdiocese that lasted for more than a year. He wanted to find out three things: if clerical sexual claims were recent or ongoing, if any actions or inactions of the archdiocese and its leaders were subject to criminal prosecution, and if children in the archdiocese would be safe in the future.

In order to do this, Reilly started looking at the ecclesiastical policies in place to deal with clerical sexual abuse. This, again, was new legal ground as far as church-state relations were concerned. Previous Catholic leaders had never had to explain the reasons for what they considered to be their internal management of the clergy or the administration of Church affairs. But Reilly now investigated the role and responsibilities of the archbishop and other superiors in the process, as well as the treatment of priests after the disposition of their cases.

Cardinal Law had actually put a "Misconduct Policy" in place in 1993, since there were no written policies about how to handle complaints of clergy sexual abuse before that time. Specific positions were set up and individuals appointed to deal with all types of personnel matters. Nonetheless, he still claimed ignorance about the clerical sexual abuse cases when the civil authorities confronted him. Even with an extensive investigation involving prosecutors, state police, civilian investigators and a grand jury, and after a year of intense scrutiny, the attorney general was only able to show that there was no recent or ongoing sexual abuse of children in the Archdiocese of Boston.

However, Reilly qualified the finding with an admonition. He claimed that it was too soon to say that there were procedures in place that had stopped—and would continue to stop— such actions in the future. This, Reilly said, was due in part to the archdiocese's lack of a true sense of "urgency" about predator priests.[35]

Then Reilly went on to question new diocesan processes put in place in early 2003 after Law retired. Reilly claimed that in these processes, entitled *Policies and Procedures for the Protection of Children,* many of the modes of investigation and discipline were inconsistent and allowed too much discretion (read "power") for the diocesan leader. Further, he maintained that the plan lacked a true independent review board and an objective organization to provide services to victims, provided inadequate supervision of abusive priests, and had no accountability for those superiors in charge of disciplining clerics. Finally, Reilly criticized the procedures for their inability to deal with anonymous complaints and the absence of an appointed person within the Church infrastructure who would implement and run an Office for Child Advocacy.

Indeed, this was a church-state first. Civil authorities were now telling religious leaders how to set up systems, both independent and in-house, to deal with children, clergy and the laity.

The grand jury also found that the culture of secrecy within the offices of the Boston Archdiocese protected the institution of the Church at the expense of children. It reported that individuals were discouraged from attempting to speak to the cardinal or other members of the diocesan leadership, that the diocese provided information at a "slow pace" and refused to produce records voluntarily. It also claimed that this was the case with regard to disclosing correspondence with the Vatican and papal nuncio on clerical sexual abuse matters. Indeed, communications of such a nature had always been held in the utmost confidentiality and considered privileged by the Church leadership. These were further challenges to the freedom of the Catholic Church to carry out its affairs without civil interference.

Unfortunately, the attorney general's report did not find sufficient evidence to charge the cardinal or other superiors with any crimes under Massachusetts state law. This was because there were no mandatory reporting requirements for Church officials in clerical sexual allegations. Nevertheless, Reilly was able to show that there was "an institutional acceptance of abuse and a massive and pervasive failure of leadership[36] when it came to clerical sexual abuse. He claimed that senior Church officials were aware of multiple accusations as far back as the 1940s, and that Law had "first-hand knowledge" of substantial cases of clerical sexual abuse "for many years."[37]

In fact, the report showed that Law had received a letter in 1986, five years before the Geoghan tragedy came to light—correspondence from Dr. Kane, the psychiatrist who dealt with an earlier pedophile, Gilbert Gauthe, and who, himself, was later ousted as director of the House of Affirmation. Kane wrote to Law regarding the treatment and cure of predator priests, saying that "In general practice, the clinical literature seems to support that there has been a great deal of recidivism among treated pedophiles. Often these people are referred to the House of Affirmation after repeated offenses."[38] The message was clear: these patients are rarely cured.

In the end, the attorney general claimed that the archdiocese's lack of response and the secrecy of its reports placed children in the Archdiocese of Boston at risk. Reilly said such actions "reflected tragically misguided priorities,"[39] and that top Church officials put the needs of sexually abusive priests ahead of those of their victims. The attorney general's report did not mince words. With regard to Cardinal Law, it stated quite plainly:

> He had direct knowledge of the scope, duration and severity of the crisis experienced by children in the archdiocese; he participated directly in crucial decisions concerning the assignment of abusive priests, decisions that typically increased the risk to children; and he knew or should have known that the policies, practices and procedure of the archdiocese for addressing sexual misconduct were woefully inadequate given the magnitude of the problem.[40]

Soon, mounting public outrage, pressures from the press, and legal criticisms put Law in a position where he had to do something. So he turned over the names of suspected pedophile priests to the police. But a spokesperson for the archdiocese admitted that none of those named were in active service in the Boston area any longer.

Next, the cardinal sent an open letter to the laity promising that the Church would work for the detection and deterrence of sexual abuse, provide education and pastoral care for victims, and report such matters to civil authorities. But the local newspapers summed up the public's feeling about the cardinal: he lost his moral authority to make any such promises and most people just didn't believe him.

As the months wore on, Law became more and more culpable in the cover-up of priest predators, especially as the formerly privileged personal records of priests began to come to light. Law's subsequent depositions demanded by Reilly, the attorney general, and ordered by Judge Sweeny, as well as the damning information that was uncovered increasingly by the press, further fueled the downfall of the once powerful cardinal archbishop of Boston.

Did his denial of knowledge or understanding of treatments allow him to seriously deny responsibility for what was happening on his watch? That's what civil authorities wanted to know. In April of 2002, Law was also deposed as a defendant in the other scandalous sexual abuse lawsuit underway in Boston. He was called to answer questions regarding accusations of rape and indecent assault and battery involving Reverend Paul Shanley.

The revelations and gravity of the Shanley and Geoghan cases destroyed the reputation and credibility of the cardinal of Boston and several of his assistants as well. In an act of desperation, Law finally apologized from the pulpit and accepted responsibility for decisions that he realized had led to intense suffering. But it was too little, too late.

By the fall of 2002, about nine months after the conclusion of the Geoghan criminal case, and several months into the extensive grand jury investigation of the Boston Archdiocese, Reilly complained publically that the government's work had been slowed because of the pace and refusal of the archdiocese to provide information, especially medical and psychiatric records of priests.

Judge Sweeney had the same criticism. She accused lawyers for the archdiocese of "sandbagging"[41] and delaying the investigation.

Finally, by the end of the year, the attorney general's office had issued 53 subpoenas, went over 500 formerly secret files, reviewed 30,000 pages of documents, and heard 100 hours of testimony from Law and 30 other individuals within the archdiocesan infrastructure. This evidence allowed Reilly to conclude that there was "an institutional acceptance of abuse and a massive and pervasive failure of leadership" for "at least six decades" through "three successive archbishops, their bishops and others in positions of authority" in the Boston Archdiocese.[42]

Although the grand jury concluded that 250 priests and other diocesan workers were involved in the sexual abuse of minors, there were no personal indictments of members of the hierarchy who had covered up the sexual abuse of children. During the time that Shanley, Geoghan, and others had molested children, the Church had no legal responsibility to report incidents of sexual abuse to police for possible prosecution. Its clergy was exempt from such a legally mandated obligation. There were no laws in place in Massachusetts to hold the hierarchy criminally liable for its past inaction.

Charitable institutions such as the Catholic Church also had financial immunity under the law. They had financial exemptions as well. Statutes of limitations in the Bay State also had run out on most cases of clerical sexual abuse, or the priests had died. Thus, there was no way to get justice for most of the past crimes of clerical sexual abuse.

As a result of the attorney general's investigation, however, new laws were enacted in Massachusetts that created important tools to prevent the systematic abuse of children in the future.[43] These included mandatory reporting of sexual molestations of children by priests or other Church personnel working or dealing with young people; longer time limits for victims to report crimes of sexual abuse; and an extension of the statute of limitations for civil suits in abuse matters.

Finally, the attorney general called on Church officials to show that they understood that clerical sexual abuse was a criminal act. In his official report, Reilly made critical demands: that the archdiocese end the culture of secrecy about clerical sexual abuse, that it work to prevent such heinous behavior in the future, that it respond to all allegations of priestly molestations, and that it ensure the protection of children in the future.

The Shanley and Geoghan cases brought the Boston clerical sexual abuse scandal to prominence and revealed patterns of church-state behavior that would change for all time. Sealed and impounded court records would now be subject to much closer scrutiny and would be based on the compelling state interest to protect children rather than to preserve the identity of a victim, the due process rights of a priest, or the reputation of the Church. Transparency would become the norm in all such cases. Delaying tactics by the Church would not be tolerated. Statutes of limitations were extended in cases of clerical sexual abuse. Clerical medical and psychiatric records would be subject to subpoenas. High-ranking Church personnel would be deposed, and done so publically. Ecclesiastical privilege would become a thing of the past.

Even so, all of this was only the shocking prelude to numerous other revelations about similar hierarchical cover-ups. In the pursuit of truth and justice for the victims, the Catholic Church, as an institution, began to suffer a loss of moral credibility, financial stability, and Church superiority with regard to canon law. Just as important, the decision of the court of public opinion condemning the Church hierarchy, its policies and practices, was clear, as clear as those echoed by Reilly.

The Aftermath of Boston

The attorney general's investigation in Boston and his subsequent report brought strong and unintended public consequences. Financial donations to the Church all but dried up after the revelations of Shanley's, Geoghan's, and other clerical sexual abuse cases.

Catholic Charities, the biggest private provider of social services in Massachusetts, called off its annual garden party fundraiser after the Geoghan trial. Donors refused to attend an event that involved Cardinal Law, or as Jay Leno referred to him, "Cardinal Above the Law."

On a national level, the American Catholic Bishops, meeting in Washington in 2002 at their annual meeting, were asked by prominent philanthropists to allow a nationwide audit of Church financial documents— but the collective body of bishops denied access to its records. It was a fateful decision, even as parishes in the Boston Archdiocese withheld money from the cardinal's office, creating an almost million dollar deficit that continued into 2005.[44]

Bankruptcy was considered by a finance panel of the Archdiocese of Boston but eventually rejected. Instead, it was decided that the archdiocese would sell its headquarters, plus 43 acres adjacent to the complex, as well as the archbishop's residence. It was purchased for about $172 million dollars by Boston College, a Jesuit Catholic institution near the Brighton property.

The section of the city, which consisted of the college, St. John's Seminary, and St. Elizabeth's Hospital, was considered like a mini-Vatican. To Catholics who were educated there, and to those who served with such a deep commitment and dedication to the Church in the area, it was affectionately known as "little Rome."[45]

But everything, excluding the seminary, moved in 2008 to an office park in Braintree, a suburb of Boston. The new building, off Route 128, is known today as the Pastoral Center of the Archdiocese of Boston.

Cardinal Law's successor, Sean Cardinal O'Malley, is nothing like his predecessor. A Capuchin Franciscan, he wears the traditional brown robe and sandals of his order. He lives humbly in the rectory of the Cathedral of the Holy Cross in the south end of Boston, and takes his vow of poverty seriously. It is this man who has had to lead the negotiations on the settlements of many of the molestation cases in the archdiocese, trying to straddle the demands of justice and economic realities.

The general view of O'Malley is that he is honest, down-to-earth, and feels the pain of the victims of clerical sexual abuse. In an attempt at Church transparency, O'Malley has published a partial list of clerics who have been accused of sexual abuse.[46] It is available on the archdiocese's web site and includes the names of current priests who are on administrative leave while their sexual abuse cases are being investigated. He was elevated from archbishop to cardinal in 2006 and was mentioned as a possible successor to the pope in the last election. But Pope Francis I was chosen instead. Nevertheless, O'Malley has the new Pope's attention. In 2013, he was appointed by Francis to two criticial Vatican positions. The first was to be part of an eight-member hierarchical papal committee to reform the central administration of the Church, and the second was to head up a mixed papal commission to find ways to prevent clerical sexual abuse and to help molested victims. He remains a powerful presence in Boston and Rome *and* a serious contender for the role of ultimate Church leader in the future.

The financial situation continues to be a problem for the Archdiocese of Boston, however. Money from the sale of the Church property where the official offices were located was originally to be used to pay off loans of about $90 million dollars that the archdiocese had borrowed to settle sexual abuse claims. But since then, the number of claims against the archdiocese has continued to climb, causing much of the money that was made on the sale of the Church enclave to simply erode.

The "Prince of the Church," Bernard Cardinal Law, became a pariah and the butt of jokes, and was considered to be complicit in sexual abuse crimes in the eyes of much of the public. His fall from grace was swift. After withering questioning by the attorney general over a number of long sessions before a grand jury, the cardinal spent some time in seclusion at a retreat house. Several months later, he tendered his resignation to the pope, and retired as the cardinal-archbishop of Boston.

His parting words were that his decision "was motivated by a desire to do what is best for the archdiocese,"[47] as well as to bring about healing, reconciliation, and unity among its members. He apologized and asked for forgiveness. As always, though, it was primarily about the Church: its reputation, its interests, and its needs, rather than about the people who were its victims.

But not to worry about Law—he was able to retain his title and status as cardinal. He was also appointed by Pope John Paul II to the position of "archpriest" at St. Mary Major Basilica in Rome, a plush reassignment for the disgraced cardinal.

The Basilica is one of the four most important Catholic churches in the city—so significant, in fact, that its administrator, or archpriest, reportedly is paid a $12,000 a month stipend. That was Law's position and residence until he retired in 2012.

The apple didn't fall far from the tree with his subordinates either. When the Geoghan scandal broke in Boston, the attorney general had a lot to say about Bishop Daily, the vicar for administration, too. He had worked for Law's predecessor from 1976 until 1983, and then for Law for a short time in 1984.

The grand jury concluded that Daily "had a clear preference for keeping priests who sexually abused children in pastoral ministry and generally followed a practice of transferring those priests without supervision or notification to new parishes rather than removing them from pastoral ministry."[48] He did this all the while he served as a top aide to two cardinals. Further, the bishop was accused of investigating allegations only superficially, of moving accused predator priests around quietly, and of shielding the clerical violators from the police. Daily's response? He was only following procedures generally accepted at the time.

Daily, who had presided so poorly over the sexual abuse allegations in the Boston Archdiocese under Cardinals Maderios and Law, was rewarded for his service to the Church with two consecutive posh assignments. First, Daily was appointed head of the Diocese of Palm Beach, Florida. Then, six years later, was made leader of the Brooklyn, New York diocese, the second largest in the Empire State.

As the Church leader in Brooklyn, he retired parish debts, was a successful fund raiser and began a major study of parish elementary schools. However, his past reputation about how he dealt with sexual abuse allegations followed him from Boston to Florida to New York. Even as he was preparing to retire, after more than a decade of service to the Brooklyn diocese, a pending lawsuit followed him out the door. The diocese and Daily were named as defendants by 42 people in a sexual abuse case.[49] That legacy followed him, even as Daily tried to retire quietly in 2003.

Bishop McCormack, who also served Law as his secretary for ministerial personnel, and who spent part of his tenure with Daily, was responsible for dealing with certain aspects of cases of sexual abuse, too. While he served at the Archdiocese in Boston, McCormack was a defendant in multiple lawsuits brought by victims who claimed they were sexually abused by clerical serial pedophiles, such as Shanley and Geoghan, as well as George Rosenkranz, Paul Mahan, Robert Gale, and others.

The attorney general of the Commonwealth of Massachusetts found McCormack's greatest failing to be his inability to establish a means to deal with deviant priests. These included offenders who pursued some type of sexual relations or contact with minors. He also accused McCormack of failing to turn to public authorities for advice or assistance, and faulted his policy of treating each case of clerical sexual abuse as an internal matter.

The vicar denied the allegations, but the attorney general was able to prove that it was at McCormack's insistence that all information received from victims was to "remain in confidence and not be shared with the relevant parishes."[50] McCormack followed the policy of diocesan secrecy and keeping parishioners in the dark about the crimes of the priests who were reassigned to their churches.

Even so, in 1998, before the news reached the public, McCormack had already been appointed as the bishop of the Diocese of Manchester, New Hampshire. But in his new position, he was still challenged by sexual abuse allegations against his fellow clergymen.

In Manchester, McCormack was sued by a priest who claimed that as bishop in New Hampshire, McCormack had covered up, a "tawdry sexual liaison,"[51] according to *The New York Times*. It was between a dead priest and his lover. The accuser said that the bishop did this by sending a group of men to clean up the priest's apartment after his death in order to remove and destroy anything that might embarrass the Church. Reportedly, the workers found "artificial genitalia, leather thongs, sex-enhancing drugs and scores of pornographic videos."[52] McCormack kept the situation quiet and supposedly did nothing.

The bishop was also accused of another cover-up about a priest in his diocese soon after. This time he was blamed for reassigning a priest, Reverend Roland Cote, to a new parish after finding out that he had had a six-year affair with a teenager.

Although the boy's age was disputed—some said he was 16, others 18—the parishioners were incensed when they found out that McCormack had transferred him to their church without telling them of Cote's background. Completely insensitive to the situation, McCormack wrote a letter to church members assuring them that Cote was not a risk to children or young people. Nevertheless, Cote resigned.

Later, when McCormack attempted to apologize for his deception in person, he was shouted down by the parishioners at the new parish as he stood in the pulpit. In the midst of the furor, he appeared on television and begged the congregation's forgiveness.

McCormack soon found himself in hot water with the civil authorities as well. The attorney general of Manchester, New Hampshire began an investigation of "the diocese" for endangering the welfare of children, particularly by its handling of allegations of clerical sexual abuse. It was similar to what had occurred in Boston.

In March 2003, after extensive scrutiny, the attorney general charged the Diocese of Manchester with multiple counts of child endangerment. Resulting in a consent agreement, "the diocese" (rather than the bishop, personally) admitted "that the State had evidence likely to sustain a conviction against the Diocese for child endangerment."[53] The admission was catastrophic for the Church, the diocese, and the bishop.

Subsequently, officials at the diocese were forced to provide complete disclosure about how the Church handled sexual abuse allegations to state authorities. And, Church leaders were required to comply with other legal requirements as well. These included state mandates that obliged the diocese to report allegations of sexual abuse to civil authorities, to train clerical and lay personnel about such matters, to establish policies and protocols to handle cases, and to maintain records on all related situations. Further, the diocese had to submit to an annual audit by the attorney general's office for five years. This would allow state officials "to review, and comment on policies, protocols and training materials"[54] regarding the sexual abuse of children.

After its admission of child endangerment, the Diocese of Manchester then sued the state of New Hampshire over its demands for the civil oversight provision of the consent agreement. It did so for three reasons. First, the diocese challenged the Church's obligation to pay for the cost of the mandated performance audit. Second, it opposed the right of the state to establish the scope of the future oversight. And third, it argued against the right of the state to assess the effectiveness of the Church's program for child safety.

In short, the Diocese of Manchester maintained that the state exceeded its authority by making demands on the Church's right to carry out its own management and administration of internal personnel functions. It contended that the civil authorities had established an intrusive relationship between the government and the Catholic Church.

These were actions that the Church considered to be in direct violation of church-state principles that had been set down in an earlier Supreme Court case, *Lemon v Kurtzman*.[55] That case denied the constitutionality of any government action that had, as one of its consequences, an "entangling alliance" between Church and State. That effect, according to the Church's lawyers, would occur as a result of the state's intrusion into the oversight and monitoring of the Church's means to protect children.

But in 2005, after the Church's appeal, the New Hampshire Superior Court ruled for the attorney general and the right of the state to oversee the policies and implementation of actions to report and prevent clerical sexual abuse. The court said that the state's actions did not compromise the First Amendment guarantee of religious protection from intrusion or involvement by the government in the compelling state matter to protect children. In essence, then, the Superior Court ruled that the Church had to obey civil law rather than try to hide behind its own interpretation of the constitution. A new day was dawning in the relationship between the Catholic Church and Massachusetts, and now the State of New Hampshire, too.

In the midst of all this, and in a stroke of total arrogance or ignorance, the United States Conference of Catholic Bishops (USCCB), formerly known as the National Conference of Catholic Bishops (NCCB), appointed McCormack to chair its national ad hoc committee on sexual abuse. The shamed bishop of Manchester, who had publically begged for forgiveness from his flock, was now in charge of leading all of his fellow bishops to respond to allegations of clerical sexual abuse cover-ups, and to rebuild trust in the American hierarchy. As head of the Committee, McCormack would serve with two other bishops who were were also under investigation for possible cover-ups in their own diocese as well.

The attorney for many clerical abuse victims in Dallas, Jeffrey Anderson, talked to the press and brought the information to light. He said it best: the bishops on the committee were on the most wanted list—the list of concealers. With such mounting pressure, McCormack realized he had to step down from his visible national position. It left much of the incredulous public to ask, How do these kinds of men get such sensitive, critical jobs? McCormack finally retired as Bishop Emeritus in 2011.

The Boston tragedy never ends. The Internet has been abuzz in recent years about Joseph Druce, the murderer of John Geoghan, because he now has a fiancé. Her name is Shirl Borden, a Christian minister and an Air Force veteran, who reportedly fell in love with him after a long correspondence.

Internet sources have reported that she said her relationship with Druce was based on the fact that he was an advocate against people being abused. Borden, who has helped Druce in several jailhouse lawsuits, tried to get permission to marry him while he serves out his two life-time sentences. The petition has been denied.[56]

The defrocked Shanley is still claiming that he is innocent of sexually abusing minors. His lawyer appealed the pedophile priest's conviction to the Massachusetts appellate court, claiming that Shanley's accuser had used a suspicious, sudden repressed memory testimony to charge him with sexual abuse. The former cleric's lawyer argued that the charges of his accuser were unreliable and should be thrown out.[57] Shanley's final appeal has been denied, and he is still in jail.

And Geoghan's legacy lives on, too. In 2008, Patrick McSorley, a young accuser of the pedophile priest who remained troubled in his drug-addicted adult life, committed suicide years after he had been molested. Only 12 years old[58] at the time, McSorley had claimed that Geoghan took him out for ice cream—after McSorley's father had just committed suicide—and then sexually abused him. Although the young man shared a $10 million dollar legal settlement in September 2002 with 85 other victims, he sadly admitted to the press that the money didn't bring closure to this pain.

3

Challenge and Complexity: Canon Law and Civil Law

Introduction

Why has the Vatican and the American Catholic hierarchy responded to clerical sexual abuse so slowly, so secretly, and, basically, so haphazardly? Why has the Church's hierarchical structure and legal system protected predator priests? Indeed, why have Church leaders obfuscated, excused, denied, and even blamed others for the tragedy?

One way to gain some insight into the types of official Church responses to clerical sexual abuse is to examine the Church's internal legal system. Known as canon law, it is separate from evolving national civil legal systems or mores. Instead, it is purported to be based on the natural universal law that applies to all people, as well as on Catholic religious teachings and Christian moral values.

Canon law evolved in an *ad hoc* way, since the founding of what is now known as the Roman Catholic Church. That legal system established and legitimized the Church's religious authority and autonomy throughout the last two millenniums. This occurred first for the sake of expediency of its administration and management. Then later on it took on a different purpose—to gain power and to control most aspects of religious freedom within civil society—teachings, rites, clerical appointments, civil obligations, and the treatment of clergy.

A second way to try to understand the hierarchical mind-set and its responses to clerical sexual abuse is to examine the ways that the popes and the bishops have used canon law in the past. By doing so, it becomes possible to see how and why they use it in the present. Basically, it serves as a model for the current institutional thinking and decision-making of Church leaders; it is their rationale to respond as they do to the tragedy. Indeed, from an organizational perspective, the implementation of canon law also sheds light on how the Church administration works to preserve and maintain itself in order to carry out both its religious and social missions.

Canon law, then, has been able to create a type of religious-legal symbiosis throughout history and within much of civil society. It has enabled the Church to maneuver for institutional benefits and prerogatives, since it has existed long before the development of most secular, governmental and social systems. And it has been the catalyst to centralize, implement, and enforce the Church's religious power even to the point of claiming Church superiority over civil power at certain times.

As popes and their minions played the roles of civil advisors and co-rulers with sovereigns in the political realm, they developed a culture of spiritual superiority and sought exclusive ecclesiastical prerogatives within many civil infrastructures. No surprise, then, that the Church/ State dynamic between Catholicism and civil governments has always been fraught with tension and competition for power.

Both institutions have historically attempted to gain dual control over religious and secular power, giving impetus to the Catholic institution's willingness to pursue, embrace, and even confront power for the sake of its religious mission—to teach, preach, and sanctify (spiritually save) it adherents. And in the process, each time the Church gained greater religious freedom, it also fought to acquire more social and political influence to advance its religious interests, as well.

Coupled with its uncanny expertise at accommodating to changing mores and still remaining orthodox in its theology and social *magisterium* (teachings), the Church has been able to learn the hard lessons of social progress and political failures in the past. It has mentored and critiqued governmental processes and practices from its own moral vantage point and canon law, followed the secular lead when necessary, and taken charge of the civil order when expedient.

But the question that everyone is asking now is whether or not the Church can continue to act as it has: imposing canon law on civil society and carrying out its religious and social missions in light of the clerical sexual abuse scandal? Can the hierarchy survive in its traditional leadership role? And will canon law of today be sufficient or effective or relevant enough to deal with the tragedy of predator priests? Indeed, will canon law have to bow to civil law when it comes to the investigation and punishment of its accused clergy in matters of sexual abuse? And, how if at all, will the Church respond to such a potential seismic change?

The Canon Law: Long Story, Short

Sexual deviance has always been part of the dark side of the Catholic clergy, but historically, molestations have always been viewed primarily as a "sin." As a result, priestly sexual abuse has been dealt with in *uneven* ways by the Church's superiors, men who were intent on bringing about the spiritual remorse and reconciliation of their brothers. They did this by the way they enforced canon law.

This institutional Catholic legal code was put in place by a variety of religious leaders over the last 2,000 years. Through the establishment of Church rules, the ecclesiastical superiors were able to govern the clergy and administer the Church institution, itself, by a number of different hierarchical guidelines.

These norms were originally based on the Scriptures and the Gospels, as well as apostolic and missionary teachings, religious instructions and the Biblical interpretations of the fathers and doctors of the Church. Papal decrees, bishop's rulings, and statements issued at council meetings of Church officials were added later, until these disparate ordinances evolved into the earliest mandates, laws, or "canons" of the Church.

Together, they set up an ethical framework of moral behavior that was expected of Church clergy. The canons also established substantive legal processes and procedures to punish transgressions of Chuch law. Many "sins" were also recognized as "*religious* crimes," and historically they had differing "prescriptions" or statutes of limitations attached to them. The way various Church leaders interpreted and carried out the canons depended on the context, time, and grievous nature of an offense.

Some of the first guidelines regarding the behavior of churchmen were found in the letters of St. Paul, the earliest Christian missionary. The son of a wealthy tent maker, Saul, as he was named in Hebrew, or Paul as he was called in Greek, was well-educated in both those languages as well as Latin. He held the equivalent of a Ph.D. in theology today and was part of the religious elite of laymen known as the Pharisees.

Saul was a purist, committed to the most orthodox form of Jewish law. So when Jesus began to preach and gain large numbers of followers, Saul, like other members of the conservative religious establishment in Judea, believed that the Nazarean was a renegade and a rebel—a troublemaker. In fact, after Jesus' death, and the claims of his followers that He arose from the dead, Saul joined with his fellow religious compatriots and took part in the persecution of Christians. He was the one who gave the permission for the stoning of Stephen, the first martyr, and did "great harm to the church" going "from house to house arresting both men and women and sending them to prison."[1]

Saul threatened to slaughter Christians and sent letters to the high priests for the authority to arrest them in Jerusalem. But while waiting for a response on his way to Damascus, the Bible says that he was surrounded by light, struck from his horse, and visited by a Voice saying, "Why are you persecuting me?"

The voice identified Himself as Jesus, and Saul—struck speechless—got up and was led to Damascus to the house of a Christian disciple. It was there that the Lord told Saul that he would be God's "chosen instrument" and bring "His name before gentiles and kings and before the people of Israel."[2] Thereafter, he was referred to as Paul.

From that point on, the convert began to teach, baptize and spread Christianity, even beyond the borders of Judea. Having been divinely transformed, Paul changed from a persecutor to a proselytizer of Christianity.

Paul visited many small clutches of converts on Asia Minor, especially in cities like Antioch, Thessolonica, Athens, Corinth, and Ephesus. He wrote letters, or epistles, to their various leaders, such as Timothy and Titus, to reiterate Christian teachings and to encourage their burgeoning faith in his absence.

The letters that Paul wrote to Timothy and Titus were unique because they were personal: sent to two men who had later become his friends and missionary companions. They received special instructions from Paul about church leadership. He told them that elders, or presbyters, should be appointed to preside over the various Christian communities, and that they should have one wife and be temperate, discreet, courteous, hospitable, and good teachers. Yes, that's right. The earliest churchmen were allowed to marry, most likely because they were already married before they became Christian converts and religious leaders.

They were expected to carefully manage their own households and to have children who obeyed them and who were well-behaved. The only other religious expectations and requirements were that they "work hard at preaching and teaching."[3]

In his letter to Titus, Paul restates his views. He says that elders are to be impartial, sensible, upright, devout, self-controlled, and lovers of goodness. In short, they were to be representatives of God—men of "irreproachable character."[4] Deacons, or helpers to the priests, as he wrote earlier, were expected to be "respectable…moderate…" and generous, as well.[5]

Paul did not legislate hard and fast rules. He understood that early priests often married, but he also wrote that those who were unmarried should "stay as they are, like me," without a wife, but that "if they could not exercise self-control, let them marry."[6] Instead, Paul, pointed out that "the unmarried man gives his mind to the Lord's affairs and to how he can please the Lord."[7] Thus, the early members of the clergy appear to have lived different lifestyles and had diverse understandings about both their vocations and sex.

By about AD 100, these early instructions of Paul and others are believed to have been gathered together by an unknown source into what has come to be known as the *The Didache: The Teachings of the Twelve Apostles*. Basically, it was a four-part compendium of the rules that applied to the teachers, preachers, doctors and prophets of the church. *The Didache* discussed the Christian way of life, the religious rituals attached to certain sacraments, principles regarding ministry, and the coming of the apocalypse.

It laid down the broad rule that Christians do not murder, do not commit adultery, do not practice pederasty, and do not fornicate. They were not to steal, practice magic or witchcraft, or murder a child by abortion or kill one that is already born. More specifically, clergy were supposed to be known by their morals, worthy of the Lord, and ordained to carry out their religious tasks.[8] *The Didache* also tried to bring some uniformity to the rites for the practice of the liturgy, that is, the public rituals for the performance of the sacraments.

By the third century, the roles and rules for the clergy were beginning to become more connected and clarified. But as the Church tried to establish a more consistent organizational infrastructure and to develop a code of conduct for its evolving clerical cadre, many of its rules still lacked uniformity and clerical acceptance. Church leaders increasingly attempted to set up expedient rules for the religious administration of Church affairs and to systematize its religious rituals, but many personal norms, such as those requiring sexual purity, only received lip service.

During all this time, the number of Christians was growing quickly within the Roman Empire, so much so that they were referred to as "katoliki." It was the Greek word for "universal," and was first used by St. Ignatius of Antioch around AD 110. It seemed as though these "katoliki" were everywhere and beginning to gain critical mass by the time Constantine, the most significant fourth-century Roman emperor, came to power.

When he won an unexpected critical military victory at the Milvian Bridge, where his army was greatly outnumbered, Constantine's life and the trajectory of Christianity in the known world changed. Constantine attributed his victory to the intervention of the Christian God, whom he claimed told him in a dream to draw a cross on the shields of his men and to fight in His name. Their defeat of the larger numbers of enemy fighters was a sign to him that the increasing population of Christians in the empire was favored by a more powerful god than those of the Romans.

In thanksgiving, Constantine allowed the free practice of Christianity in the empire in AD 313. Under him, Christians were allowed to build churches, receive bequests and donations, and serve in the government. Finally, he decreed Christianity to be the official state religion of the Roman Empire in AD 379.

Further, Constantine showed his political support of Christianity by issuing secular decrees that were designed to increase the number of Christian converts. These people, in turn, would bring about greater loyalty to the emperor.

But as an unintended consequence, the growth of "katoliki" led to the need for more members of the clergy and a highly defined hierarchy of religious leaders. Senior clergy, or "bishops," increased; so did the promulgation of a larger number of Church organizational rules. Soon, the rules, or canons, were subject to diverse interpretations, all of which eventually led to internal religious problems and the fear of civil unrest.

In response, Constantine, who exercised civil control rather than religious power, attempted to unify the ever-growing Roman Catholic Church in order to assure internal peace. He did this by trying to bring some order to Christian theological beliefs, liturgical practices, internal administration, and clerical behavior.

Many canons, or Church laws, were increasingly becoming inconsistent since they developed haphazardly and were implemented in a variety of ways by diverse churchmen. This was especially true with regard to the issue of clerical marriage. While there were those who wanted clarifications, no definitive decisions were made on the issue or accepted by Church leaders before Constantine's assent to political power. Instead, theological beliefs were often confused and challenging, too: some were even branded as heresy. Clerics and laymen alike took sides in theological battles, causing Christianity to begin to splinter from within and to disrupt the civil order.

To rectify this situation, Constantine called a Church Council at Nicea in AD 325. Its purpose was to bring about greater religious unity and clarity, thus assuring *political* loyalty from the Christians. Acting as what some might call a "bishop-at-large," Constantine insisted that Church theologians codify religious doctrines and define heresies. He demanded that they promulgate an official creed to serve as both a clarification of religious orthodoxy and a political litmus test for those who wanted to serve in the army or be part of the government within the empire. The Nicene Creed, as it was called, emerged as a listing of the beliefs that all Christians were supposed to espouse, and was intended to separate the true believers from pagans and heretics. Indeed, it was a test for those who sought favor within the empire: economic, political, social and religious prerogatives.

Constantine's strong secular and religious roles were further carried out in the eastern part of the Roman Empire as well. During his reign, Constantine moved to Byzantium, where he ruled with total control. He renamed the city after himself (Constantinople), playing a critical role in the development of the Eastern Orthodox Church, and appointing its church leaders, too.

In this part of the empire, clerical marriage was accepted, and Constantine, rather than the pope in Rome, assumed the power to appoint the early patriarchs of Antioch, Jerusalem, and Constantinople. For his religious protection and other accomplishments, Constantine was declared a saint and is held as "isapostolas" among Eastern Christians, that is, in the same esteem as the Apostles.

The differences between the Roman Catholic Church and the Byzantine (Eastern Catholic) Church were significant. And the attempts of a number of secular rulers to control the beliefs and practices of both were further complicated and compromised by "decretals," or spiritual rulings, from the popes in Rome.

The exercise of this type of personal, papal authority from the Eternal City began in AD 385, when Pope Siricius produced an edict that forbade priests and deacons to have relations with their wives. He also attempted to supersede secular control of the Church by asserting the exclusive papal right to deal with ecclesiastical discipline, hierarchical appeals, and the adjudication of internal problems within the Church. The Eastern Church, developing in its own way, would have none of it, and continued to function on its own. The "decretals," however, became part of canon law.

In AD 410, however, a major political catastrophe occurred: the city of Rome was sacked by Alaric and his barbarian cohorts; the political supremacy of the Eternal City was in shambles. Having had to fend off attacks from the Germanic tribes, the Saxons, and others, as well as having absorbed the expense of maintaining armies in North Africa and the Middle East, the Western Roman Empire was all but destroyed. Most vestiges of Roman secular authority had become corrupted, weakened, or eliminated.

The institutional Roman Catholic Church was essentially the only truly functioning organization still standing after the barbarian hoards burned and looted the Eternal City. As a religious—and now an unwitting social/political—organization, the Roman Catholic Church stepped into the political breach and social void. This was a consequence of the loss of an ineffective secular ruling class, one that had been decimated by the exit of many leaders, their families, and their fortunes to Constantinople with the emperor years earlier.

Social services, education, and even political matters fell to the Church. It became involved, whether consciously or by default, in secular matters as well as religious ones. And as a result, it became a significant political power within the western part of the empire, controlling most major institutions that were needed to keep it functioning.

In AD 529, Justinian, the Roman ruler in Constantinople at the time, codified the secular or civil law, reinforcing the legitimacy of Christianity within both the eastern and western empires. It gave Roman Catholic and Eastern Orthodox Christianity a protected position within the entire imperial state. The new legal system outlawed heresies against Christian teachings, and forbade the practices of paganism. Further, the

Justinian Code disallowed the consecration of any priest to the position of a bishop if he had children or even nephews, due to concerns that his affinity to them might compromise his religious or political decisions.

As a consequence, civil authorities, trying to regain religious power, also attempted to regulate many other internal practices of the Christian religious organization during the rest of the millennium. Particularly, secular rulers attempted to appoint Church leaders in both the eastern and western parts of the Empire. This process, known as "lay investiture," caused escalating church-state struggles over secular selections of high Church officials, a fact of political controversy that existed throughout much of the Middle Ages.

By AD 800, however, the Roman Catholic popes, who had consolidated significant religious and secular power in western Europe, became the equals of most of their political challengers. In fact, in many places, they had essentially supplanted the power of kings, emperors, and all kinds of sovereigns by their ability to unify huge territories and emerging states under the religious aegis of Christianity and the elements of canon law. Similar religious beliefs started to bring political unity to evolving civil states that had not yet developed a sense of nationalism.

The popes and the hierarchy claimed the moral high ground and gained the political clout to back it up. For example, Leo III insisted that developing states were part of the "Holy" Roman Empire, and when he crowned Charlemagne as the "Holy Roman Emperor," the pope elevated the office of the papacy above that of the emperor. Thus, the pope seized political superiority, playing the role of the dispenser of secular power and the religious legitimizer of civil power. In effect, he created a system of dual political leadership in which both pope *and* emperor ruled, a symbiotic model that lasted for over six centuries.

It took until the first millennium for the Church to develop its internal organization and to systematize its belief system. But as it entered into the second millennium, it still needed to provide a more unified management system and religious infrastructure, due to the complexity of its growing number of clergy and adherents within a changing civil power structure.

For example, the issue of clerical marriage was still unresolved. By AD 1123, at the First Latern Council, Church leaders enacted a canon that disallowed marriage for ecclesiastics and those studying for the priesthood, a policy that was reiterated and clarified in canon law at the Council of the Lateran in 1215, and again at the Council of Trent in 1545.

At that point, then, just about 1500 years into Christian history, celibacy became an uncontested requirement of the life of the Roman Catholic clergy.

Thus, an evolution in the type of leadership and expected clerical behavior was occurring within the Church. In an almost parallel way, its hierarchy had also gained *political* power after the fall of the western part of the Roman Empire, and used its position to solidify the Church's legal prerogatives within the evolving civil organizations that it guided and, in some cases, ruled.

No surprise then, that by the twelfth century, the Roman Catholic Church established a definitive codified legal system. This was due to the efforts of Gratian, a Camaldolese monk. He brought together the more than 4000 Church canons, or laws, that had been promulgated out of expediency and the desire for hierarchical control over religious practice within civil society during the first millennium. This legal system has come to be known as the *Decretum Gratiani* or the *Corpus Juris Canonici*, the first Code of Canon Law.

As the canons became clarified and unified, a system of Church law developed into a discipline of its own. As an area of systematic study, first at the University of Bologna, canon law became part of the curriculum at many other schools of higher learning in the Middle Ages. Priests became the earliest students and practitioners of canon law. Therefore, they were basically the only people who understood it and who could interpret it. As a result, they used their educations and expertise to elevate Chuch law to a position of spiritual and legal prominence within Christian society.

The *Decretum* of Gratian was supplemented later by the *Brevarium* of St. Bernard, adding more canons to Chuch law. Then, as more decretal collections began to appear, popes periodically published their own canons, in what came to be known as the *Bullaria*. As a result, the Roman Catholic Church, which had originally functioned as part of a pagan state, and then as a leader in Christian society, developed a separate, internal, and legal system of its own. It was considered by the Church as both spiritually inspired and superior to civil law.

Canon law set out procedural laws, as well as regulations that controlled church taxation, tithing and indulgences. It also dealt with Church governance structures, rules regarding the treatment of clerics and hierarchy, and penal laws that applied to them for both religious and *secular* infractions of the law.

To be sure, the individual concerns of popes and bishops about clerical sexual sins existed throughout the growth of the Church. But their worries had been addressed in a spiritual, sporadic way, and as was considered necessary. During early and medieval times, clerical sexual sins were dealt with in a religious way: through the implementation of *ad hoc*, ecclesiastical canons and decretals that reflected religious understandings of impurity.

For example, homosexuality was understood in biblical terms as "sodomy," and pedophilia (adult-child sex) or ephebophilic behavior (adult on young adolescents) as "pederastic" acts. As early as AD 177, Bishop Athenagoras referred to individuals involved in such practices as anti-Christian, and called for their excommunication from the Church. Later, at the Council of Ancyra (AD 314), the Church demanded strict penances and excommunication for homosexuality.[9]

Spiritual books also described sexual sins. For example, the *Paenitentiale Bede,* or the *Penitential Book* of St. Bede, written in England in the eighth century, called for severe penances for sodomites. In it, St. Bede demanded that the higher the clerical position, the harder the punishment. For sexual involvement with minors, adultery, rape, bestiality, sodomy, traffic in vice, and incest, punishments could include anything from confession and repentance to public flogging and the shaving of a cleric's or monk's hair.

Some punishments, in essence, were considered as expiatory penalties: that is, actions designed to restore order and repair harm to an individual's or the Church's reputation. These punishments often resulted in removing the offender from his ministry. Other penalties were treated as medicinal condemnations—ways to reform the offender by either suspension or excommunication.[10]

In 1051, St. Peter Damien wrote *The Book of Gommorah* to deal with abuses within the Church. A Benedictine reformer, he called for changes within the infrastructure arising from simony—the buying and selling of Church offices—and the moral behavior of the clergy. He maintained that a sexual abuser could be "foully besmeared with spit and . . . bound in iron chains."[11]

For his *crime,* the abuser was supposed to be held in confinement for an unspecified period of time and forced to fast three days during each week, being allowed to eat only barley bread for his evening meal. For his *sin,* the offender would be required to spend six months under the custodial care of a spiritual elder and be required to remain in a segregated cell doing manual work and prayer. He would only be allowed to go for supervised walks and could never again associate with youths, either in private conversation or a counseling situation. In severe cases, he could also be deprived of his office within the Church: his ministry and all benefits that other priests could expect as being part of the clergy.

In AD 1179, the Third Latern Council called for clerics who committed sins against nature, as sexual deviance was defined, to be dismissed from their ministries. Alternately, they could be confined for life in a monastery and be required to perform penance.

As the expanding power and wealth of the papacy stimulated the Crusades, advanced commerce and art, and led to the development of towns, social services, and charitable institutions in western Europe, all manner of abuses became rife within the Church. Leading to the challenges for reformation, then, Church leaders responded by considering the need for further moral, religious, and administrative reforms.

At the Council of Trent (1545–1563), the hierarchy clarified and defined religious dogma, ended notions of group authority, and declared the supremacy of the pope as the "Vicar of Christ on Earth." Celibacy for the clergy was definitive. Among other issues, the hierarchy dealt with the eroding morality of the lives led by priests, and called for disciplinary action by local bishops.

In many cases, however, law and custom were used unevenly to punish those who committed sexual sins. Prayer, fasting, exclusion from Communion, torture, being turned over to civil authorities, and even civil executions have been reported, but none were applied to all clerics in the same way everywhere.

Papal religious power began to erode, however, as the ideas of the Renaissance and Reformation challenged Catholic theology, pontifical prestige, and church resources from the twelfth to the sixteenth centuries. The emergence of nation-states and capitalism, and the movement toward liberal democracy, eventually led to the unification of Italy in 1870.

It also brought about the subsequent loss of the Papal States that had existed as a Church benefit since the days of the Roman Empire. Attempting to reassert his political and religious control at the time, Pope Pius IX called a Church council in Rome. His supporters subsequently declared him infallible on matters of faith and morals, but they could do nothing to restore the Papal States to the Church and their former rulers, the popes.

So by the turn of the twentieth century, although papal religious power was stronger, Catholic political power was severely compromised by growing Italian nationalism and the rise of secular states in Europe and elsewhere. There were also fears within the religious leadership about the authority, disposition, and continued implementation of approximately 10,000 canons that had been promulgated from the inception of the Church's legal system to modern times. Each canon also had multiple attachments that spelled out specific canonical legal procedures, practices, exemptions, and clarifications.

So many canons were considered redundant; some were simply inconsistent and unclear, while others required reexamination, and even reconciliation with new, opposing secular legal systems that had developed over the centuries—like the Napoleonic Code. Would these disparate canons still be considered valid and relevant in Italy after its unification? Would the pope have to submit to civil authority? How would the pope be able to continue to rule a universal institution, its clergy, and its adherents without uniform procedures applicable to all? Would Church privileges be compromised by new principles like the separation of Church and State? How could the Church maintain its sovereignty—the internal, and in some cases, even external power over its own affairs?

The answer had to be found in the legitimacy and implementation of canon law. It would have to be the glue to hold the Church together, as it were. It could bind the institution's priests and insure their loyalty. It could be used as a means to protect the spiritual interests of the Church within civil states. Canon law could secure the civil autonomy needed to carry out its religious and social missions—to teach, preach, and sanctify its adherents. And it could be used to protect the many ecclesiastical privileges, hard fought for and won over the millennia, to guard the privacy of Church processes and procedures that were used to administer its finances and control its personnel. But somehow, the leaders of the Church would have to figure out how to control and systematize its legal system.

Among the thousands of canons that existed at the turn of the century were a variety of punishments for violations of the sixth commandment and the sins associated with "impurity" that had emerged during the almost 2,000-year history of the Roman Catholic Church. Therefore, it is easy to see that the codification of so many different canons and practices that dealt with everything from clerical behavior to liturgical practices to religious tradition, needed to be revisited and reorganized. Their reconsideration was key to maintaining religious order and control of the Church infrastructure for modern times within emerging secular states.

Over the years, then, canon law became critical to the functioning of the Roman Catholic Church. It gradually became the vehicle that separated spiritual control from civil power; indeed, it even became the rationale for Church leaders to assert the legitimacy of canon law, even maintaining it as being *above* civil authority at times.

Because the Church's legal system dealt with the regulation of a *spiritual* institution and was used to implement moral values based on the natural law—or law known by one's conscience—the Church leadership contended that the canon law's lengthy existence also allowed it to supersede many transient, newly drafted, and potentially changeable national, man-made laws. The popes believed, in short, that emerging states could not impose their civil laws over the spiritual law, nor limit the political autonomy of the universal Roman Catholic Church to carry out its religious mission. Indeed, some have contended that as a result "the Church...institutionalized...[a] power imbalance in its theology, law, and pastoral practice."[12]

The Canon Law in the Twentieth Century and Beyond

As the Church moved into the twentieth century, canon law became more important for the maintenance of religious power, prestige, and preferential treatment in an increasingly secular world. Pope Pius X, in order to assert the legitimacy and superiority of canon law within a newly united Italian state, ordered the development of the first modern Code of Canon Law in 1918 to regulate the Church's legal system.

This new, modern compendium of Church laws established a *systematic, religious, legal* code that clarified the rights and responsibilities of the Church within a civil state. It was designed to codify the *universal* rules that were to govern the ecclesiastical infrastructure and to define the behavior and treatment of clergy within the institution. It also set down punishments for transgressions of canon law—including sexual perversions.

In 1922, and again in 1962, these offenses were further defined by an appended section to the code that dealt with homosexual and pederasty acts. Then in 1983, a second major revision of the Code of Canon Law, designed to deal with so many political, social, economic and political changes in civil infrastructures, appeared during the pontificate of John Paul II. Containing a number of sanctions that he added later in 2001, this is essentially the Church's legal code that is in effect today.

Each of the modern codes, promulgated in 1918 and 1983, was significant in its own way. In the 1918 version, several major issues were clarified. First, pedophilia was recognized as a sin everywhere, indeed, a violation to be prosecuted and punished by specific, comprehensive Church laws. In fact, Canon 2359 said that priests who are involved sexually

> with a minor below the age of sixteen, or engage in adultery debauchery, bestiality, sodomy, pandering, incest with blood-relatives...are suspended, declared infamous, and are deprived of any office, benefice, dignity, responsibility, if they have such whatsoever and in more serious cases they are to be deposed.[13]

Second, in the 1918 Code of Canon Law, a bishop was given significant discretion to impose a treatment or punishment on a priest accused of certain "delicts," or grave offenses. This occurred when such acts were public, or part of the "occult." Over the years, bishops interpreted this power to include their right and responsibility to deal with matters of sexual abuse as well, particularly if there were witnesses to the delict, if it involved children who might be traumatized, or if harm might occur to the Church. In these instances, the bishop served as judge and jury and ruled on the final disposition of such matters.

Third, according to the 1918 Code, the bishop could justify his power to punish clerics for delicts under the principle of *ex informatia conscienti*, which was used to legitimize a bishop's judgments based on the validity of his informed conscience (i.e., directed by religious teachings and education). This allowed a particular bishop to pass on the guilt or innocence of a cleric without a canonical investigation or trial. Witnesses did not have to be heard, nor did the accused necessarily have the right to defend himself.[14]

Fourth, the offending priest could be "defrocked," that is, deprived of his religious functions and ministerial duties by the bishop. The bishop could also recommend that the cleric be "laicized" by the Congregation for the Doctrine of the Faith (CDF) in Rome. This meant that, on the bishop's request, the cleric could be removed from the priestly state for leading a depraved life by a usually lengthy canonical trial in Rome.

In 1922, and later in 1962, the Code of Canon Law was enlarged by refined and secret instructions from one of the highest offices in the Vatican.[15] These policies were explained in a document entitled *Crimen sollicitationis,* as an addendum to the 1918 code. They dealt with the severe punishment of a priest for soliciting sex or homosexual acts with boys in the confessional. Recognized as a sin, rather than a crime, the means by which priests were penalized for such acts was through the Church's legal court in Rome.[16]

In 1983, the new version of the Code of Canon Law emerged under Pope John Paul II. It appeared essentially one year before the Gauthe case broke open in Louisiana. The 1983 Code redefined the legal canonical procedures and mandates that currently enjoin all clerics. Significantly, it also serves as the basis for church-state cooperation as well as conflict today, especially in the United States.

The Code of Canon Law as promulgated in 1983 emphasized that all churchmen must be celibate and must abstain from sexual activity. Canon 1395, for example, specifically defines pedophilia as a delict, or a willful crime, against the sixth commandment. And the code, at the time, made a change stating that a six-year statute of limitations would apply if an alleged victim wanted to bring charges against a cleric for sexual abuse. Further, it said, "If the delict was committed by force or threats or publicly or with a minor below the age of sixteen years, it is to be punished with just penalties, not excluding dismissal from the clerical state if the case so warrants."[17]

So what can be understood about canon law that dealt with clerical sexual abuse when increasing rumors about priestly molestations began to appear in the United States in the 1980s? What impact did individuals like Doyle, Mouton, and Peterson have, if any, as they sounded the alarms about the tragedy that was about to befall the Church during the Gauthe case?

First, there was a transitional time between the 1918 code, its 1922 and 1962 addendums, and the new, more evolved 1983 code. During most of the twentieth century, bishops held the tightest power over the clergy they managed. They could decide whether or not to send cases of grave transgressions on to Rome for adjudication; however, that was about to change.

During the decade of the 1980s, some legal confusion existed within the Church about how to handle clerical sexual abuse allegations that were coming to light. There were now recommendations for types of punishments coming from local pastors, vicars, and lawyers about how to handle such delicts. The bishops were no longer able to make all decisions, in secret, about the treatment of clerical sexual abusers without clerical, lay, and legal advice.

Second, in 1983, the Church still did not fully understand clerical sexual abuse. It was only able to grasp it in terms of *sin*. It was discerned within the spiritual belief that the individual could to rise above his own human frailty and receive grace or some sort of spiritual aid that would enable him to repent for his past transgressions, and with God's love, be forgiven. Clerical sexual abuse was not understood in any real way—a way that would lead to knowledge of its causes, psychological damage, treatment, or criminal ramifications.

In the clerical culture, then, sexual abuse was only considered in terms of a priest's ability to successfully carry out his ministry. The criminal aspects of clerical sexual abuse were not part of the decision-making process in the treatment of a priest. Instead, canon law confirmed the historical and ecclesiastical right to punish transgressors, even sexual abusers, within the Church's own legal system.

Third, victims were, therefore, were always considered skeptically and secretly rather than as the main focus of a canonical investigation. They were kept in isolation by Church officials, who demanded confidentiality agreements. They were treated in different ways by various Church leaders at particular times and in different places. Canon law did not apply to them: it applied to the clergy. Only the generosity or the compassion of the bishop played a role in the dispensation of religious justice and financial settlements.

Fourth, civil law was challenged at almost every turn by Church officials, even after the promulgation of the 1983 Code of Canon Law. In fact, the legal ramifications of the crimes of predator priests were basically ignored, and resolved, essentially, by the traditional Church measures: confidentiality agreements between religious officials and victims along with hospitalizations and therapy for predator priests. These responses to allegations of clerical sexual abuse not only provided secrecy, thus protecting the Church's reputation, but they were also often used as the means to circumvent criminal proceedings against accused priests.

So while major cases, like those involving Gauthe, Geoghan, Shanley, and so many others, were being adjudicated under canon law, they were not necessarily carried out under the *revised* 1983 instructions. There was still essentially only a religious understanding for their delicts rather than a concern for their criminal behavior.

In reality, there was no real knowledge or concern for their criminal offenses, and no standard way to canonically treat predator priests within the context of civil law that was followed by bishops. In fact, in most states, there were no requirements for religious superiors to turn such perpetrators over to civil authorities, so they did not. The question as to why that was the case remains unclear even today.

Thus, despite the enactment of newer and revised canonical codes that dealt with clerical sexual abuse in the 1983 Code of Canon Law, continued misunderstandings about the issue itself, and the failure of the Church leadership to follow the new rules set down by the Vatican, all added to confusion and blurred lines of authority between many bishops and the Holy See.

The 1983 Code of Canon Law set up specific and different procedures from the 1918 code, especially with regard to dealing with specific delicts—particularly accusations of clerical sexual abuse. While the revised code still defined such offenses in terms of sin and the sixth commandment, it now also considered whether force, threats, or public actions occurred, and if the abuse involved a minor below the age of 16.[18] Age now entered into the picture, a sign of the new awareness of pedophilia: molestations of children by priests.

For the first time, as well, the 1983 Code required that an investigation of allegations against a priest had to take place at the diocesan level. A bishop was newly required to appoint a number of investigators to gather evidence and to present their findings to him. The bishop, then, would decide if there were enough evidence to proceed with further action. These proceedings were similar to a civil grand jury hearing and an indictment.

A bishop could move for either a full judicial process or canonical hearing. The 1983 code was supposed to be similar to a trial in civil judicial procedure. It allowed the accused priest to have a lawyer, to have witnesses, to confront his accusers, and to have his case heard before a panel of three to five judges, appointed by the bishop

In the case of a priest being found guilty, the highest punishment the jury could impose was a restriction on his clerical state. This would mean that the priest could not function as a cleric or carry out his ministry any longer. He would not be able to administer the sacraments or say Mass publicly. Defrocked, he would, however, still remain a priest in name only, but without the ability to perform the rites associated with his former religious duties.

A priest found guilty of a delict would, nevertheless, have the right of appeal. Such an appeal would be heard by the Congregation of the Doctrine of the Faith (CDF) in Rome. If he were also found guilty there, he could be laicized (returned to the laity) and excommunicated, that is, turned out of the Church.

A bishop, however, was still allowed two other alternatives when allegations of sexual abuse were brought against a priest in his diocese. These consisted of bypassing the whole process of a judicial canonical hearing in Rome for purposes of expediency,[19] or the bishop dealing with the issue himself, due to mitigating circumstances. Both options were more familiar to the members of the hierarchy and canon lawyers than the new canons. This was because they were, in fact, the practices used, for the most part, in the past.

Specifically, these new procedures would apply to offenses that were beyond a simple correction, reproof, or pastoral care. In essence, if a priest's scandalous actions left a victim without justice and no possibility of reform for the offender,[20] the bishop could pursue a varied number of punishments. These could include the suspension of the priest, his retirement, the requirement to attend a facility for treatment, or seclusion in a monastery or some sort of a religious residence to do penance for the rest of his life or for a specified period of time.

If there were some kind of mitigating circumstances—diminished mental capacity or lack of pre-meditation in the commission of an offense forbidden by certain canons (1387 and 1395)—the bishop would not be expected to impose the most extreme penalties after considering the mental state of the cleric.[21] Instead, he could call for an administrative process, by himself, or a pastoral admonition.

In the 1983 Code of Canon Law, then, the power of the bishop of each diocese was supposed to be limited. It was intended that he would no longer take swift or secret action because of the new requirement to investigate allegations with other individuals within his diocese. He was also expected to take into consideration the use of the full canonical juridical process when dealing with clerical sexual abuse.

The former significant leeway to deal with the pastoral needs and/or problems of the priests within his care as the bishops saw fit (i.e, based on his own informed conscience), now became more complicated. This was due, in part, to the involvement of individuals other than the bishop in the investigation of clergy and an increase in procedures that were to be followed in a particular case of clerical sexual abuse. It was also predicated on the fact that the Church, one the hand, wanted to protect the canonical rights of its clergy, perceived traditionally as protected privileges by their victims, and to stave off the challenges of intense media coverage and legal challenges to canon law itself by public attorneys.

The 1983 Code of Canon Law also set down a six-year statute of limitations that could have hampered the full judicial canonical process in Rome. Many canon lawyers now thought that the time factor to adjudicate acute clerical sexual abuse allegations was too short: it could allow many priests to escape investigation and impede action to deal with religious crimes that had been committed years earlier.

Thus, the use of the full judicial canonical process was often considered a hindrance rather than a viable and pragmatic way to deal with clerical abuse allegations. This, then, led many bishops to revert to their former personal penal decision-making in such matters.

Another difficulty in applying the 1983 Code of Canon law arose from the frequent inability of the bishops to determine the state of mind of the accused priest. This meant that in many cases, the hierarchy was unsure about how to proceed to appropriately deal with clerical sexual abusers.[22]

An account of this quandary appears in the memoirs of Archbishop Rembert G. Weakland, the former Archbishop of Milwaukee. A Church leader with impeccable scholarly credentials, and a leader within both his own Benedictine order and the ecclesiastical infrastructure in Rome, Weakland was disgraced toward the end of his career when news of an adult homosexual affair came to light. He submitted his resignation to the pope, retired, and now lives a contemplative life.

Regarding his decision-making about clerical sexual abuse matters, the former archbishop admits that he has spent many of his last years "reflecting on my knowledge of this phenomenon, my presuppositions about it, and my reactions to it."[23]

His dealings with Father Bill Effinger, an accused sexual abuser and an alcoholic within his own archdiocese, reveal not only Weakland's own basic ignorance of the whole issue of pedophilia, but likely the problems of many other Church leaders charged with adjudicating such matters. He says in his autobiography that

> At the time no one spoke to criminal charges:...I ask myself why I did not even consider the possibility of reporting the matter to the police. It was simply not done...The legal aspects of these cases, if any, I now suppose must have been

handled behind closed doors...bishops had the power to restrict the ministry of a priest, but not to dismiss him from the priesthood. Only Rome could do that, and even then, I knew of no case in which this penalty was inflicted. Furthermore, psychologists and therapists were not always helpful.[24]

The Bishop's statements reflect an unexplained ignorance and naïveté about clerical sexual abuse in his early years as the Archbishop of Milwaukee, as well as his lack of involvement in the criminal aspects of it. These were actions that Weakland believed, as a newly installed member of the hierarchy, were somehow going to be fixed by his staff. He seemed to feel a sense of impotence to impose what he considered to be significant penalties. And he also appeared to misunderstand what he was told by professionals, whom he believed, in hindsight, contributed to his own "insensitivity"[25] toward the vulnerability of the young victims of clerical sexual abuse.

There were many other mixed hierarchical responses, and even denials about the clerical sexual abuse crisis in the United States. Practices over the years show that the bishops' approaches could be characterized as individual, pragmatic ways of coping with a difficult internal problem within a complex, restrictive canonical process. The situations in Boston and other dioceses reflected this as they come to light. They were further complicated by external pressures to punish priests by the imposition of the civil legal procedures as well.

So to expedite matters, canonical procedures were often simplified or fast-tracked by a bishop who dealt with clerical sexual abuse in his own way, in his own diocese, even with the promulgation of the new 1983 Code of Canon Law. Therefore, very often such matters were process-driven for efficiency, secrecy, restitution, and resolution. What the bishops overlooked in their preferred ecclesiastical concerns for the rights of the perpetrators and the institutional Church was the lack of personal focus on the physical and psychic abuse of the priests' victims. Allegations against clergy were treated as issues that had to be resolved swiftly and silently by high-ranking authorities who were often ignorant, arrogant, confused, defensive, and conflicted as they tried to mete out Church justice, and forgiveness as well, to clerics.

It has also been said that the 1983 Code of Canon Law and its tighter controls from Rome resulted in the fact that the American bishops "seldom" conducted trials of clerics accused of sexual abuse because it placed too much emphasis on the individual rights of priests while deemphasizing the penalty part of the process.[26] By the latter part of the

1980s, the National Conference of Catholic Bishops tried to bring about changes that would restore more power to the bishops as they discussed clerical sexual abuse with Vatican officials.

Most of their proposed changes regarding the penal process, which sought to limit the full, judicial, canonical procedures, were not accepted by the powers in Rome. The bishop was still required to use the judicial rules in place in the 1983 Code. The appeals process for priests still remained in practice.

By early 1992, the NCCB, still trying to make changes to the Code of Canon Law, issued a public statement through its president, Bishop Daniel Pilarczyk of Cincinnati. It said that the bishops in the United States would now review and refine the original process and the five guidelines proposed by Mouton, Doyle, and Peterson almost a decade earlier to deal with clerical sexual abuse! The bishops had come full circle and were now willing to reconsider the quick removal of an offender from ministerial duty, sending him for medical evaluation and intervention, complying with civil law, reporting and cooperating with legal investigations, reaching out to victims, and dealing openly with members of affected communities.

Within the year, the bishops brought together a number of experts for a special meeting in St. Louis, refined the various aspects of the guidelines, and continued to work with Vatican officials to work out changes to canon law. As a result, the NCCB was able to form a Joint Study Commission with officials in Rome to finally deal with the sexual abuse problem. In 1993, the NCCB appointed an *ad hoc* committee on sexual abuse and officially recommended that the bishops accept the five broad recommendations suggested by Mouton, Doyle, and Peterson almost a decade earlier.

In 1994, the Vatican was only willing to accept two specific changes among the many recommended by the American bishops. The first was that the sexual abuse of anyone under the age of 18 (rather than 16) should be considered as an elemental component in decision-making about a delict for the next ten years. This was eventually incorporated into the Code of Canon Law in 2001. A second recommendation was also accepted: that the statute of limitations be extended. It would allow an individual to bring charges against a priest until the accuser's 28th birthday. This became part of the Code of Canon Law as well.[27]

The lack of more positive Vatican responses to the bishops' concerns resulted in bishops establishing different sexual misconduct policies for personnel in their own diocese. Although the NCCB sent out advisory guidelines about how to deal with clerical sexual abuse, they were too late to serve as official policy responses.

Basically, then, individual bishops and the bishops acting together as a canonical body through the NCCB had little impact on revising Vatican policies and procedures concerning clerical sexual abuse in the 1983 Code of Canon Law. There was a lack of uniformity and collegiality among the bishops. Past practices died hard, and the American hierarchy continued in its own, old way when it came to the treatment of predator priests.

Official Papal Responses to the Clerical Sexual Abuse Crisis

This highly contrived, misunderstood, and often misdirected religious legal system, the canon law, is part of the workings of two other curious Church institutions: the papacy and the Vatican State. It is important to understand that everything in Catholicism revolves around the fact that all Church power and policy flows from the sitting pope, directly, to the rest of the Church leadership. He is at the top of a hierarchical structure: one that is autocratic rather than democratic, secretive rather than transparent, and one that requires no accountability to its constituency—the laity. The pope only answers to the Church's founder, Jesus Christ. In Catholic thinking, the Church provides salvation; the laity supplies obedience and loyalty.

The Vatican, that is, the territory from which the pontiff operates, is as unique as the papacy itself. As both a sovereign state and a religious entity, the Vatican consists of a labyrinth of diplomatic agencies, inter-locking directorates, and spiritual offices. These are referred to as "the curia" or the "Holy See." This infrastructure, too, is an anomaly: a geo-political, yet religious state, within a nationalistic and secular world.

The current pope, Francis I, rules over a one-mile square, neutral civil state created by the Italian government and the papacy in 1929. By the Treaty of the Lateran, the pope controls St. Peter's Basilica, all buildings and palaces, and everything within its proximate environs. The pope serves as the chief executive of the Vatican's infrastructure, which consists of its own bank, police force, post office, radio and TV station, website, newspaper, and hospital.

The pope rules the Vatican totally, and as its administrative and political leader, is charged with carrying out both domestic and foreign affairs without external controls. He is, in effect, the geopolitical voice of the Vatican. He appoints the Vatican religious bureaucracy (the Curia) and key diplomats who carry out international relations with over 190 other sovereign states. The pope does not have to stand for reelection, answer to a cabinet or a constituency, or watch the polls.

The papacy's origin and legitimacy are traced to Jesus Christ, according to Roman Catholics. They hold that Christ passed his mission to teach, preach, and sanctify His followers to St. Peter with the Biblical statement that "thou art Peter and upon this rock I will build my Church and the gates of hell shall not prevail against it."[28]

Traditionally popes have interpreted and extrapolated their spiritual responsibilities. From a church-state perspective, these include the obligation to maintain, protect, and advance the freedom of the Church within the confines of state infrastructures and legal systems, so they can carry out their religious and social missions.

In modern times, these missions have been renewed and modernized. Pope John XXIII called a General Council of Church leaders, known as Vatican II, in 1960, which stressed the Church's need to support human rights, social justice and ecumenism, to reach out to developing states, and to bring about the transformation of society based on the principles of Jesus Christ.

From an internal, governing perspective, however, another important reform occurred at Vatican II. Bishops gained more collegial authority within the Church infrastructure. They were given the right to create regional and/or national organizations to discuss matters of religious import, particularly as they intersected with the political, economic, and social concerns of their respective states and regions.

Subsequently, the National Conference of Catholic Bishops and its administrative arm, the United States Conference of Catholic Bishops, were founded in 1966. Even with this new, concerted power, though, the bishops could not make binding social, political, or religious policy without the approval of the pope. His was still the final word. This is a critical point to remember when examining how the Vatican and hierarchical responses to clerical abuse scandal unfolded in 2001 with the Geoghan and Shanley cases in Boston.

At the time, Pope John Paul II was sitting on the Chair of St. Peter. He was a popular Pope: charismatic, young, and dynamic—a skier, an actor, a mountain climber! Elected in 1979, he was the first Polish Pope to head up the Roman Catholic Church in its almost 2,000-year history.

Born Karol Wojtyla in Wadowice, Poland, the future pope was the son of a retired military officer and a mother who died when her son was only nine. His older brother attended medical school, but died during an epidemic, leaving the future pope and his father alone.

Wojtyla attended the Jagiellonian University in Krakow, where both he and his father lived together in a basement apartment. He studied philosophy and linguistics, participated in theatre groups, and wrote poetry.

When the Germans invaded Poland on September 1, 1939, and Wojtyla was about to start his second year at the university, the Nazis virtually closed down the school by deporting all its Jewish professors. Forced to take a menial job, then, the future pope became a stonecutter to support himself and his father. Then one day, after completing his shift, he found his beloved father dead.

The loss led Wojtyla to the decision to become a priest. He studied in a secret seminary in Krakow and, by the time the Russians liberated the city from the Nazis in 1945, the future pope only needed one more year to complete his religious studies. He was ordained very soon thereafter, and then sent to Rome for advanced study at the Angelicum University.

He received a doctorate there in sacred theology in 1948, returned to Poland, and within the year became the assistant pastor at a church in Krakow. Because of its proximity to the Jagiellonian University, he served as the chaplin for the student community, occasionally taught a course in Catholic social ethics there, and managed to earned a second doctorate in philosophy in 1953.

As an assistant pastor and a part-time academic, Wojtyla became intimately aware of the politics of the Communist party in Krakow as they related to the Catholic Church and higher education in Poland. Within a short time, he simultaneously attained a position as a full-time professor at the Catholic University of Lublin and was also appointed an auxiliary bishop (aide) to the Archbishop of Krakow. Now on the fast track as both a scholar and ecclesiastical leader, Wojtyla began to have both an academic and *political* impact within his home country.

This began when Wojytla ran a series of "mediation days" or retreats for lawyers, physicians, teachers, and students. They became a way to counter the Communist propaganda machine and its efforts to influence the educated and professional class of Poles. Soon, though, Wojytla was beginning to get too much political attention.

In 1962, he was invited to attend the General Council in Rome, and while there, he developed relationships with some of the most influential people in the Church hierarchy at the time. He emerged as the spokesperson for the Polish episcopate on theological issues and was recognized as distinguished intellect by the time he left.

Wojtlya received a variety of papal appointments after his time in the Eternal City. After the death of the Archbishop of Krakow, he was appointed to that open position. He built a new cathedral in Nova Huta, and by 1967, was named to the College of Cardinals. He became part of Pope Paul VI's inner theological circle after supporting the pontiff's pro-life and birth control policies. As a reward, Wojtyla was subsequently appointed to the Congregation for the Clergy, the Congregation for the Sacraments and Worship, and the Congregation for Education, major offices of the Holy See at the Vatican. These appointments allowed him to be a frequent visitor to Rome and a repeated dinner companion to the pope.

He was part of the conclave that chose John Paul I as pope, but when the newly elected pontiff died after only one month in office, Wojtyla, who was both known and influential, became a leading contender for the position of pope. Well respected among the highest levels of the Vatican leadership, he was elected as Pope John Paul II in 1979. He was, after all, committed to pro-life principles and social justice, just as his successor had been.

The Polish political leadership assumed that the pontiff would take a religious approach to Church-state problems—a notion that the ruling party came to rue after its confrontation with labor opposition and the new *Polish* Pope.[29] In 1981, only two years after being elected the leader of the Catholic Church, John Paul lent his moral support to Lech Walensa, the leader of the trade union, Solidarity. In a public statement, he asked that the union be allowed to exist without Soviet interference.[30] Using his geopolitical platform, the pope was able to provide guidance and moral protection to Walesa and the union, to garner the support of the media, and even to give limited financial support to the growing union.

He visited Poland several times, and after the Reagan Administration recognized the Vatican state in 1984, even secured what some have called a "secret alliance" with the White House to unseat the atheistic, Communist government. In the end, his efforts paid off: Solidarity won political power; Poland was forced to transition to a democratic state in 1989, and United States-Vatican relations were stronger than ever before.

If John Paul could be a global political activist, stand up to the Communists in Poland, carry out an eight-year moral war against those who had compromised religious and civil rights in his homeland, and speak out for worker's rights, why couldn't or didn't he work as tirelessly to protect the safety of children and punish priestly predators?

The answer, as they say, is complicated. John Paul II exercised his authority to handle the clerical abuse crisis through two distinct prisms, one spiritual and one political.[31] Spiritually, he approached the crisis from the perspective of a theological conservative, being committed to the Biblical belief that the individual is made in the image of likeness of God—that is, with a human and a spiritual dimension. To him, man's duality made each person worthy of dignity and respect. That religious notion impelled the pope's political action to advance human rights for all, especially the unborn and the vulnerable, to stand up to dictators, to work for social justice, and to support economic development. It also was the basis for his thinking about how to deal with clerical sexual abuse.

As a priest himself, John Paul II tried to understand the tragedy of clerical sexual abuse, theologically and philosophically in the context of *sin.* Thus, as the spiritual leader of the world's one billion Catholics, the pope believed, first and foremost, that priests who were guilty of the *sin* of sexual abuse could admit guilt, seek forgiveness, pursue treatment, repent, and change. It was his seminal belief that individuals could transform themselves psychically because they have a soul, the spiritual capacity that leads them to do so. John Paul's own forgiveness of Mohamet Ali Aga, the man who attempted to kill him, serves to illustrate his personal commitment to this principle.

What was missing in these papal theological and philosophical beliefs, however, was the lack of material concern for the victims of clerical sexual abuse. They were not sinners like their priestly sexual abusers, so they had nothing to repent. Yet, the victims had so much to overcome, in a non-spiritual sense, in order to recover their own human dignity and respect. The pursuit of justice by their church leader for the *crimes* that were perpetrated against them never became the prime focus of John Paul's spiritual attention.

As the ruler of the Vatican state, the pope also acted in a sovereign capacity. He was a civil executive; he initiated the Church's foreign and domestic policy, managed its personnel, and administered the universal canon law. He could punish those within his state for sins and for *crimes*, and had the power to define both, as well.

Thus, the pope maintained the historical position that the Church had the right to prosecute and punish its own—the clergy—for proven instances of sexual abuse. This was based on the pope's sovereign position, the Vatican's autonomy, its definition of crimes within a civil context, and the validity of canon law.

As a result, John Paul attempted to frame the resolution of the sexual abuse scandal within the context of both his religious and political *power* during his pontificate. In fact, on his watch, John Paul did eventually define clerical sexual abuse as both a grave *sin* and a *crime*.

Why then, did John Paul handle the US clerical sex abuse crisis in the way that he did? Did he see the solution to the emergency in terms of religion, philosophy, sovereignty, or canon law? Or was everything related? Did he see it as a risk to his religious control over the hierarchy, or the laity in the United States? Or did he see it as a legal challenge to church-state relations in America and the Vatican's geopolitical presence in the rest of the world?

The answers are not easy because, in hindsight, John Paul had been troubled with the problem of clerical sexual abuse in America during much of his papacy. He had been made aware of the tragedy by the National Conference of Catholic Bishops (NCCB) during the mid-to-late 1980s after the secret Chicago meeting with Mouton, Peterson and Doyle, all of whom rang the alarm for the crisis that was about to happen. He knew that the NCCB began to study the problem confidentially and initiated discussions with high-ranking members of the Vatican on matters of treatment, culpability, the Code of Canon Law, and penal provisions for offender priests.

Becoming aware of the situation behind closed doors, John Paul began to respond to the festering problem. In particular, he showed his concern for the dilemma in America by sending a defensive letter to the US bishops in 1993. Writing that the conduct of predatory priests was the result of an "irresponsibly permissive" society, he blamed the clerics' predilections on the fact that American culture was "hyper-inflated with sexuality."[32] Calling that the "real culprit,"[33] the pope chose to place blame on secular externals rather than on the individuals and the institution that were responsible for such actions. Could this have been due to the fact that he also admitted publicly that lawsuits against US clergy had already reached the level of $400 million?[34]

Later that year, in a very candid statement, while in Denver for World Youth Day in August of 1993, the pope seemed to change his thinking. While there he castigated the clergy, saying, "at a time when all institutions are suspect, the Church herself has not escaped reproach."[35]

The US bishops responded to John Paul's accusations with a flurry of activities: reviews of diocesan policies, public descriptions of treatment centers, ways to care for victims/survivors, and reports of efforts to deal with the matter. But while they tried to find ways to handle the *effects* of clerical sexual abuse, neither the US bishops nor the Vatican, itself, took any action at that time to figure out how to understand, manage, or cope with its root *causes*.

In 1995, however, the scandals began to spread to Ireland and Germany, and later to Canada, Australia, Britain, France, Mexico, and Poland. The notion that a permissive American society was somehow responsible for clerical sexual abuse in the United States suddenly seemed to lose its credibility within Vatican circles, as the matter gained global notoriety. Trying to grasp the cause, the pope instructed Archbishop Jorge Mejia, a troubleshooter for the Vatican, to prepare a report on the problem.

By December 1998, on a trip to Australia and New Zealand, John Paul referred to the information that had been gathered on the growing crisis of clerical sexual abuse and offered a formal apology to the victims in Oceania. He said,

> Sexual abuse by some clergy and religious has caused great suffering and spiritual harm to victims…Sexual abuse within the Church is a profound contradiction of the teaching and witness of Jesus Christ. The Synod Fathers wished to apologize unreservedly to the victims for the pain and disillusionment caused to them. The Church in Oceania is seeking open and just procedures to respond to complaints…and is unequivocally committed to compassionate and effective care for the victims, their families, the whole community and the offenders themselves.[36]

In John Paul's understanding of reconciliation, both apology and true repentance are critical steps for forgiveness, reconciliation, and reintegration into the spiritual community. Now in the matter of clerical sexual abuse, the pope began to slowly acknowledge the outrageous behavior of offender priests officially, and to seek forgiveness for the institutional Church insofar as it was culpable for sexual victimization.

In 2001, Pope John Paul showed his growing concern about clerical sexual abuse by issuing a major document on the problem. As mentioned earlier, his responses to the NCCB's petitions for certain changes were incorporated into canon law.

His Apostolic Letter, or papal announcement, entitled *The Norms of the Moto Proprio "Sacramentorum Sancititatis Tutela,"*[37] reiterated more strongly that clerical sexual abuse was a *delicta graviora,* or grave sin. It also gave more power to the Congregation for the Defense of the Faith (CDF) in Rome to deal with the matter, requiring that it be informed about diocesan investigations into clerical sexual abuse, as well as empowering it, alone, to handle full judicial proceedings and appeals in the matter.

As the institution in charge of protecting religious orthodoxy, the CDF was the successor to the office that instigated the Inquisition in Spain and excommunicated Galileo for teaching the "heresy" that the earth revolved around the sun. There was no more conservative office in the Church infrastructure or anyone who was more committed to his cause than its head.

Pope John Paul had appointed Joseph Cardinal Ratzinger as the leader of the Congregation for the Defense of the Faith. (CDF) A theological clone of the pope, he was often referred to as the pope's "Rotweiller," doing the tough, religiously correct, orthodox interpretations of the Church's teachings.

Together with Ratzinger, John Paul eradicated liberation theology in Latin America. He warned politically active clerics that they were priests, rather than politicians, and that they were not supposed to be in the business of trying to destroy the political structures in Latin America that marginalized people.

As a team, John Paul and Ratzinger worked to bring more conservative theological principles to the fore in the beliefs and policies of the Church. No surprise then, that Pope John Paul charged Ratzinger, as head of the (CDF), with the authority to issue specific guidelines on how to deal with the problem of clerical sexual abuse.

Just to make sure the hierarchy recognized the lines of authority, Ratzinger sent a letter to all the members of the hierarchy, ordering them that if "even a hint" of clerical sexual abuse existed, the bishop in charge "must open an investigation and inform"[38] Rome of the matter. At the same time, however, he requested silence from the members of the hierarchy about such issues. Again, no mention was made in the document of the responsibility of the bishop to report clerical sexual abuse to legal authorities.

But these papal directives were too little too late, when early in 2002, reports began to appear in the American press that secret trials were being carried out at the Vatican to handle a burgeoning number of cases of pedophilia from around the world. The *New York Times* and the *Boston Globe* confirmed rumors that the Boston Archdiocese had settled numerous lawsuits against Father Joseph Geoghan and a number of other priests from 1962 to the present. The secret of clerical sexual abuse was now out in the open, and Vatican attempts to deal with it in-house were futile in the face of the media and public outrage.

Now seeking to deal with reality rather than rumors about clerical sexual abuse, the pope's official spokesman, Joaquin Navarro-Valls, attempted to shift the blame for clerical sexual abuse from American society in general to homosexual clerics, in particular. He reportedly said "People with these inclinations just cannot be ordained,"[39] leaving the Vatican and the pope open to criticism for oversimplifying a much more complex problem.

As the issue proceeded into a full-blown crisis in the spring of 2002, the pope expressed "great compassion" and "fraternal solidarity" with the US bishops.[40] He charged the members of the hierarchy, themselves, to resolve the dilemma of clerical sexual abuse, but this was out of character for the pope. In fact, he had often been accused of micromanaging church administration.

For example, in 1998, he had issued an Apostolic Letter entitled *Ad Tenendam Fidem,*[41] making it impossible for regional hierarchical organizations to issue binding statements on matters of doctrine or of public policy. In the document, specific canons were revisited to remind the hierarchy and clergy of their duties to obey all aspects of Church teachings on faith and morals. They were "bound to avoid any contrary doctrines" including the word of God as written or handed down by tradition, professions of faith, and teachings (*magisterium*).[42]

Thus, the pope's new, hands-off treatment of the clerical sexual abuse issue in the United States surprised everyone. This was especially the case of the US Catholic bishops who had been required to submit to the will of the pontiff in all matters of priestly deviance prior to this.

By 2002, then, the general public had seen the pope change his attitude toward clerical sexual abuse several times. First, he viewed it strictly as a grave sin, then as an American problem based on a permissive society, then as a behavioral issue nurtured in homosexuality, and finally as a dilemma that the American bishops should handle on their own.

In reality, however, recent published reports by the National Review Board of the newly renamed NCCB (now known as the United States Catholic Conference) reveal some startling information. They say that "the Vatican did not recognize the scope of gravity of the problem...despite numerous waning signs; and it rebuffed earlier attempts to reform procedures for removing predator priests."[43]

In trying to interpret the various papal responses, some in the media called it a "cultural chasm."[44] Others saw it as a division between American openness and Vatican secrecy. Some thought it reflected a split between American freedom and democracy and Vatican centralization. There were even some who framed it as a clash of American accountability with Vatican deference and a belief in forgiveness.[45]

Whatever the case, everyone in the Church hierarchy appeared to be at a loss—flummoxed. This was particularly case of the American bishops and their leader, Bishop Wilton Gregory, President of the USCCB at the time. He was called to Rome to confer with Vatican officials about the handling of the clerical sexual abuse crisis in the United States in 2002.

As the bishop of Bellville, Illinois and head of the American hierarchical organization, the USCCB, Gregory went to Rome defensively and apologetically, accepting responsibility for the mishandling of the clerical sexual abuse problem. Taking one for the team, he admitted openly after meeting with the pope that the hierarchy had "misplaced" its faith in therapy and the judgments of therapists.[46]

But these admissions were insufficient for the pope, who was still dissatisfied, and apparently still concerned with the American hierarchical disposition of the clerical abuse matter. Finally understanding the severity of the crisis, John Paul decided to summon all of the American cardinals to Rome. He recalled Gregory, and insisted on a full accounting of the scandal in April 2002.

The pope's demand for attendance by the highest members of the US leadership reflected a need to restore control, trust, and credibility to the pope and the Church's mission. It was also interpreted by the press as an attempt at damage control and a way to coordinate a collective response to the scandal. According to Vatican officials, though, the meeting was simply characterized as a way to inform those in power at the Holy See about the matter of clerical sexual abuse, to evaluate the situation, and to develop ways to move forward in addressing the issues.[47]

In reality, the discussions between the American Catholic leadership and John Paul were a way for the pope to exercise religious control over the clerical abuse scandal: a way to exert papal authority over how the situation would be handled in the United States. Catching most of the American church leaders off guard, the meeting included not only the highest-ranking members of the US hierarchy, but Cardinal Ratzinger, the man who would be the future Pope Benedict XVI, and the most senior leaders of the Roman Curia, or Vatican infrastructure.

While awaiting the arrival of the US cardinals, the pope met with Bernard Cardinal Law of Boston privately about the crisis of pedophilia in his archdiocese. What was said has been kept private, but one can only assume that the meeting was uncomfortable, at least, for both parties. The pope also publically ordered a group of Nigerian bishops to investigate clerical sexual abuse accusations diligently in their home country. Thus, John Paul began to set the tone for the arrival of the American cardinals a few days later, openly discussing the issue, remarking on the value of celibacy and the life of chastity, poverty, and obedience.

As the pope began to grapple with the problem of clerical sexual abuse, his faith and training turned toward his theological concerns, particularly the internal question of priestly formation and the development of the religious education of seminarians. As he emphasized the need for better spiritual training and the ideal of clerical service, another shift in papal thinking occurred, but not a change in John Paul's desire to control the outcome of the problem.

At the meeting with the American Church leadership, John Paul expressed grief over the sexual scandals that had occurred in the United States. Characterizing them as "wrong by every standard," and "rightly considered a crime by society," the pope called pedophilia "an appalling sin in the eyes of God," and offered a profound sense of solidarity and concern to the victims and their families.[48]

He thanked the clergy who had dedicated their lives to priestly service, and admitted to the Church's lack of knowledge in this area. But then, he instinctively returned to his theological and philosophical positions. Stressing the power of conversion, the pope emphasized that true transformation "reaches to the depth of a person's soul and can work extraordinary change," but that "there is no place in the priesthood and religious life for those who would harm the young."[49]

Then, in a joint statement, the cardinals and John Paul affirmed six basic principles with regard to clerical sexual abuse. First, they maintained that it is a crime and an appalling sin, particularly when perpetrated by priests and religious on the young. Second, they asserted that the Church must provide a sense of solidarity and assistance to the victims and their families. Third, all the Church leadership recognized the gravity of the problem, regardless of the number of cases. Fourth, the cardinals and Pope maintained that there is no link between celibacy and pedophilia. Fifth, Church leaders agreed to promote the correct moral teaching about sexual abuse, to visit seminaries in order to screen those who chose to become candidates to the priesthood, and to observe a national day of prayer and penance. And finally, all recognized "the power of Christian conversion, that radical decision to turn away from sin and back to God."[50]

John Paul controlled the final statement from the cardinals. In it, they acknowledged, along with him, the gravity of clerical sexual abuse, defended the traditional unmarried state of the clergy, and reasserted the theological notion of personal transformation. All of this was done *without any erosion of papal power, or acquiescence to civil authorities to deal with the punishment of ecclesiastical personnel.*

Leaving the Vatican, Bishop Gregory, who was obviously chastened, spoke for the American bishops. He expressed his outward satisfaction with the papal meeting, telling the press about the pope, "He gets it."[51] Trying to put the issue and the discussions into some kind of context, he reverted to Vatican speak: "The church doesn't do crime," he said. It "does sin."[52]

What that meant was left unsaid at the time, but Gregory left Rome optimistically. Believing that those in power in the Vatican were not civil obstructionists, he led the public and the Catholic laity to believe that the members of the hierarchy were simply men in need of education and that they would respond appropriately to clerical sexual abuse with the proper information and understanding. Subsequently, however, his impressions proved to be wrong.

Gregory's confusion was indicative of American misunderstanding in general, for the matter was unsettled and left a cloud over the credibility of the Church in America. A month later, in May 2002, President George W. Bush met with the pope on a trip to Rome and told the pontiff that he was "concerned about the Catholic Church in America…its standing. And I say that because the Catholic Church is an incredibly important institution in our country."[53]

Did this give the Vatican pause? Did the Vatican suddenly see the potential interference of the US government in the prosecution of clerical sexual abusers after the visit of the president? Did Church leaders fear that they were losing their moral credibility in America? Or worse, did they see an erosion of their political influence on American public policy? It's hard to say, but within a month, the US bishops took up the matter of clerical sexual abuse at their bi-annual meeting in Dallas.

There would have to be a new approach to the problem of clerical sexual abuse. The canons of the past had proved ineffective to deal with the realities of the present because there were so many individual interpretations of canon law and such confusion over its convoluted processes. Bishops understood their power to investigate and punish alleged clerical sexual abusers differently. In most cases, they acted as judges and juries. Yet as decision-makers they were naïve, subjective, and often conflicted about their pastoral roles and punitive responsibilities. They enforced questionable treatments and secretive ministry reassignments. They bypassed canon law whenever possible.

In short, the hierarchy was still functioning in an *ad hoc* way, as it did in the earliest part of Church history. All the efforts at systemizing and codifying canon law seemed like an exercise in futility. From their elite positions of authority, shored up by centuries of claims to moral legitimacy, the bishops unwittingly contributed to the sexual abuse scandal by their own actions and inactions and by their attempts to cover up the allegations that have been leveled in thousands of molestation cases in the United States. Perhaps they would regain some credibility at their upcoming meeting in Dallas. Only time would tell.

4
Too Little, Too Late: The Hierarchy Responds

Introduction

The biannual US bishops' meeting in Dallas two months after the papal summons to Rome was a media circus. More than 700 members of the press, TV, and various Internet sites were in place and credentialed, supposedly about the same number of reporters who would usually cover a papal visit, and about 10 times more than would be expected to report on a gathering of the American hierarchy.

Before the Church leaders even showed up, photographs of 112 US bishops appeared in the *Dallas Morning News.* They were part of a five-page spread showing pictures of the diocesan elite across the United States who had been accused of transferring pedophile priests from one parish to another. The paper made sure that even if the bishops thought they could run from the allegations, there was no place for them to hide in Dallas.

The polltakers were also on the job. They were able to empirically verify the overwhelming lay dissatisfaction with the bishops' handling of the clerical sexual abuse problem. The numbers characterized a fiasco. On the eve of the Dallas meeting, the Quinnapiac Poll reported that 87 percent of the faithful believed that the Catholic Church should have a zero tolerance policy towards priests who sexually abused young people, even if it only occurred once. Sixty-nine percent also thought that Church leaders who transferred predator priests should resign. And 89 percent wanted every US diocese to report all accusations of sexual abuse to civil authorities. When it came to what role the laity should have in fixing the problem, 70 percent wanted to make sure that they had an equal voice with the hierarchy in deciding how to deal with predator priests. Indeed, only 23 percent had confidence in the bishops, with an overwhelming majority responding that the USCCB would not produce meaningful improvements on its own.[1]

With gavel-to-gavel coverage of the Dallas meeting of the US bishops on the Catholic television network (EWTN), the cameras highlighted the difficult discussions of over 250 bishops during a two-day period. Nevertheless, Bishop Wilton Gregory, the head of the USCCB at the time, remained optimistic. Speaking before the meeting, he pointed out that the hierarchy would be dealing with an "unprecedented" topic about which "not enough ha[d] been done" in the past, and one where there hadn't been a "consistent implementation of the recommendations... arrived at even 10 years ago."[2]

With these admissions, Gregory promised that things would change, and that the US hierarchy would take the lead in rectifying clerical sexual abuse. He tried to assure the public that a systematic protocol to deal with the problem would, indeed, come out of the meeting. He even hinted at the fact that an obligatory policy of action could occur and would most likely be monitored by the establishment of a new national review board.[3]

Later, in his keynote address to the assembled bishops in Dallas, Gregory, speaking as the head of the USCCB, sought forgiveness for the tragic priestly behavior in the name of his fellow Church leaders. He asked silent victims to come forward and report their abuse to Church and civil authorities, and appealed to abusers to do the same. He struck a compassionate and conciliatory tone, while holding out the hope that clerical sexual abuse would be addressed the same way in each diocese across the United States and finally ended.

The media was not as optimistic or as easily convinced that any of Gregory's agenda or pleas would actually be translated into positive results. The press had a different impression of what was going to happen at the meeting—basically, very little—and reported instead on the serious disagreements among the bishops who were attempting to develop a collective, canonical response to the clerical sexual crisis.

The press, especially, contrasted the views of Church leaders. There were those, according to reports, who were willing to exempt priests from dismissal from the clerical state if they had committed only one sexual offense. There were other hardliners, however, who refused to give clerical abusers another chance and wanted to remove them from ministry altogether. The press also emphasized the concerns of those bishops who took into account what the laity expected of them as well. This could be seen in articles about the stance of Archbishop Daniel Pilarczyk of Cincinnati, particularly, who opposed creating a soft document or one that appeared to provide "wiggle room"[4] in dealing with predatory priestly behavior.

With so much pressure on the bishops, from both the laity and the press, a draft of a document on clerical sexual abuse appeared quickly. It was characterized by overwhelming support for a zero tolerance policy regarding clerical sexual abuse. The hierarchy immediately rallied behind this principle, and the exemption clause for one-time offenders never even reached the floor at the Dallas meeting.

The press also reported on discussions among the bishops who wanted to hear from the victims of clerical sexual abuse versus those who did not. One story recounted a conversation with a cardinal who said he had never heard from a victim, while another reported that other members of the hierarchy said that they had met with many abused individuals. In the end, it didn't matter because only four people—four survivors—out of thousands of victims, actually got a chance to address the convened bishops. They were joined by a scholar, a magazine editor, and a clinician.

Each of the seven individuals provided "withering"[5] indictments of the bishops at the televised sessions. The crux of their criticisms revolved around accusations of systemic corruption in the hierarchy, ecclesiastical secrecy, denial, and self protection as well as a deferential attitude toward the Vatican.[6] According to the people allowed to speak, such actions continuously cultivated a clandestine clerical culture devoid of accountability to the laity.

These accusations were countered by some members of the hierarchy who were canon lawyers themselves, and who had come to the meeting with strong defensive arguments of their own. Some were already disturbed by larger internal issues, specifically, the growing overreach of civil demands for ecclesiastical records. They saw this as a larger threat to the autonomy of the Church and its ability to carry out its religious and social mission. For example, Bishop Thomas Doran of Rockford, Illinois opposed actions by certain state authorities and was reported as saying that bishops shouldn't "rat out our priests."[7] Others, such as Archbishop John J. Myers of Newark, New Jersey tried to find a middle of the road approach. He saw the value of conducting an internal annual audit of each dioceses' compliance with the new regulations that were about to be put in place and made such a recommendation to the body. Even though these concerns were aired, the central focus of the meeting—how to deal with clerical sexual abuse—seemed to only be a by-product of the hierarchy's larger interests. These issues specifically involved the US church-state ramifications of the scandal. How could the institutional Catholic Church maintain its power and autonomy in the administration and management of its clergy? How could it preserve the legitimacy of canon law? And how could it assure its role as a moral arbiter in the development of social, economic, and public policy in the United States?

What is a surprise to observers, however, is Bishop Gregory's recollection about what happened at the Dallas meeting. When he discussed the event two years later with the media, what Gregory remembered, most emphatically, and what he believed should have been the real news, was the behavior of the bishops—rather than the stress on the victims of clerical sexual abuse. Instead, he praised how the bishops worked together even though there were "matters of an intense debate at that time."[8]

In his recollection, Gregory also emphasized that, in the end, the bishops did pass two important policy documents that set the tone for their future hierarchical actions regarding the treatment of accused clerical sexual abusers. Left unsaid by Gregory, however, was how many years it took for the bishops finally to act, to systematize, and to approve those two policies at the Dallas meeting in 2002. It had been nearly three decades since the prosecution of Father Gilbert Gauthe in Louisiana in 1984, and about the same amount of time since Doyle, Peterson, and Mouton had tried to warn the hierarchy to set up guidelines to deal with predator priests.

One Church leader who took an assertive position among the differing members of the hierarchy and who tried to answer the papal request for a national strategy to deal with clerical sexual abuse was Theodore Cardinal McCarrick. At the time, he was head of the archdiocese of Washington, DC, having risen within the ecclesiastical ranks due to his leadership abilities, his interpersonal skills, and his political connections.

McCarrick was ordained a priest in 1958 after attending Fordham University and St. Joseph's Seminary in Yonkers, New York. He held both a Master's degree in the social sciences and a Ph.D. in sociology. He had served as the president of the Catholic University of Puerto Rico in the latter 1960s and was recognized as a comer in the ecclesiastical ranks as well.

McCarrick was soon tapped for higher office, becoming the private secretary to the cardinal of New York, Terence Cooke, a position he held for six years, from 1971 to 1977. From there, he was appointed to the position of an auxiliary or assistant bishop to Cardinal Cooke for East Manhattan and Harlem. McCarrick continued on the fast track by becoming the founding bishop of the Diocese of Metuchen, New Jersey in 1982, and then archbishop of Newark in 1986. From that vantage point, McCarrick is said to have traveled to Rome often, sometimes monthly, to visit with his longtime friend, Pope John Paul II.

McCarrick was also involved in a variety of significant political activities during his ecclesiastical career. He was an official observer to the commission that issued the Helsinki Accords on human rights; he attended an interfaith meeting in 1988 with Fidel Castro; he visited a number of countries in Eastern and Central Europe due to his international committee chairmanships within the USCCB. He visited China as part of a delegation representing President Bill Clinton. He even hosted Mother Teresa and Pope John Paul on their visits to the United States. No surprise then that he would have been appointed archbishop of Washington DC in November 2000, and just a few weeks later, also named a cardinal by the new pope, Benedict XVI.

Here's how astute McCarrick was: Only five days after President George Bush's inauguration in 2001, the *Washington Post* reported that his eminence was having a dinner party for the new chief executive and his wife, Laura. Billed as a "friendly, get-to-know-you-dinner" by the spokeswoman for the Washington Archdiocese, the guest list included influential Church leaders along with government officials such as Alberto Gonzalez, the general counsel at the White House and National Security Adviser Condoleeza Rice. An evening of cocktails, sea bass and politics! What a start to a year that would begin with an attempt by the cardinal to develop a close relationship with the President and members of his staff, and end with the horrific revelations from the *Boston Globe* and the *New York Times* about Catholic clerical sexual abuse.

When the US bishops met in Dallas, then, in 2002, McCarrick was a potential linchpin: an outspoken leader among his peers, the most politically connected member of the US hierarchy with the American government, and a major player at the Vatican as well. It was anticipated that his connections and influence would bring the bishops together and encourage them to create policies that would protect children, respect the due process rights of priests, and accomplish both those tasks within Vatican expectations and canonical parameters. And this is what he was able to do. In fact, at the Dallas meeting, he set the tone for reconciliation by meeting with a group of sexual abuse survivors for the first time.

The bishops worked on two documents in Dallas. The first was "The Charter for the Protection of Children and Young People." Broadly, its purpose was to help the victims of clerical sexual abuse. The second document was "The Essential Norms for Diocesan/Eparchial Policies Dealing with Allegations of Sexual Abuses of Minors by Priests or Deacons." Its goal was to deal with the rights of priests and to establish national standards in the United States to deal with sexual abuse charges that respected both canon and civil law. In the end, both the Charter and the Norms were tied together.

The Charter's emphasis was intended to focus on victims: to prevent clerical sexual abuse in the future and to bring about the reconciliation of all parties. It was based on precedents established from a variety of past legal, psychological, and canonical attempts to deal with clerical sexual abuse. These included the original guidelines set down earlier by Mouton, Peterson, and Doyle, principles adopted by the legal department of the NCCB in 1988, clarifications of the problem set down by the American bishops at their biannual meeting in June 1992, as well as the canonical and religious standards hammered out in 2002 by the cardinals, the American bishops and Pope John Paul at the Vatican, prior to the Dallas meeting.

The new document, however, would ultimately be different. It reflected a distinctly American, hierarchical approach to dealing with clerical sexual abuse, one that called for more independence in hierarchical governance, and one that reflected the need for more immediate and transparent action on behalf of the Church. The American bishops wanted to expand their power and to take control of dealing with predator priests within their own diocese—without any interference from Rome. This was especially true when it came to removing priests from their ministries and reporting them to civil authorities.

Those at the highest levels of the Church infrastructure in Rome, however, were most concerned with the bigger picture: the application and implementation of canon law in the United States and *other* national states. The Holy See feared the loss of its ability to judge, punish, and/ or acquit the members of its own clergy, an historical prerogative forged over two millennia before nation-states and other legal codes even existed. Indeed questions of "lay investiture" or government appointment of Church personnel and control of its seminaries and Churches, as in China today, could also be at risk if civil authorities could make demands on ecclesiastical records and exemptions in the United State. The loss of power vis-à-vis its own institutional control, within hierarchical thinking, could mean a rupture within the ancient, hierarchical structure of the very Church founded by Jesus Christ 2,000 years ago.

The Documents and the Aftermath

The Charter, as it emerged from Dallas essentially dealt with five main issues. First, it called for the Church to promote healing and reconciliation with victims/survivors of the sexual abuse of minors. It stressed outreach and the establishment of mechanisms to respond promptly to allegations, and also ended the use of confidentiality agreements unless victims requested such action.

Second, the bishops guaranteed effective responses to allegations of the sexual abuse of minors. These actions included reports to public authorities, and applied even when the person was no longer a minor. Victims would now be advised of their right to make reports to public authorities. The bishops took the initiative and gave themselves, rather than Vatican officials, the power to relieve an alleged offender of his ministerial duty. This would come into effect after the preliminary investigation of a complaint and the referral of the alleged offender for appropriate medical and psychological evaluation. Most importantly, this would occur, as Article 5 of the Charter stated, "for even a single act of sexual abuse of a minor – past, present, or future." In short, it established a zero tolerance policy for priestly predators and set a higher bar for the Vatican and other national episcopates to follow.

Third, the bishops promised to ensure the accountability of their procedures. They agreed to establish an office for child and youth protection at their national headquarters and to put into place a national review board. It would be made up of mostly lay Catholics that would be responsible to monitor the implementation of the Charter.

At the conference, Bishop Gregory announced that the former Catholic governor of Oklahoma, Frank Keating, would serve as the chairman of the board. He and his team were empowered to audit how the Charter would be implemented by Church leaders in each of the US dioceses, a fact that was later fraught with dissension and resulted in his resignation.

Fourth, the bishops called for the protection of children in the future. To this end, they established safe environment programs, set up an Office for Youth and Child Protection at the USCCB, better screening for candidates for the priesthood, and more transparent communications in cases of reassignments. All of this was designed to protect young people from clerical sexual abuse and expected to translate into radical changes in Church administration.

Fifth, the hierarchy was still careful to protect the clergy. Again, as in the past, the Charter called for the right of Church officials to withhold files and personnel records of priests accused of clerical sexual abuse from civil authorities. These were still considered to be "canonically privileged," within the sphere of canon law, and not subject to civil intrusion. This exclusionary principle of clerical files was based on traditional, clandestine record-keeping and the Church's reticence to reveal anything in such records to civil authorities. As incorporated into "The Charter" and set down in "The Essential Norms" as well, this claim for confidentiality still remains a critical stumbling block in the Church solution of the clerical abuse scandal.

The other document to emerge from Dallas, "The Essential Norms," dealt with the treatment and rights of priests, and was important because it covered those parts of canon law that were at odds with American civil law. As might be expected, they represented a potential clash between church-state relations in the United States.

The main stumbling blocks all revolved around what the Church considered a civil intrusion and overreach into its right to manage its clergy. This especially involved the Church's perceived right to retain the personnel and medical records of priests. Such files had always been held in complete confidentiality by the vicar for administration in each diocese, and the thought that they could or would be subpoenaed by civil authorities and made public in clerical sexual abuse cases caused serious concern within the canonical legal system. It quickly led to major Church litigation against a variety of states within the civil judicial process.

Civil authorities believed that the state had the right to demand clerical records, treating the Church just as it would any other organization or corporation. Prosecutors across the United States believed they were able to subpoena any and all Church records to obtain information about employees, even within religious institutions, for the compelling state interest to protect children.

Even in light of this clash, "The Charter" and "The Essential Norms" passed without any significant opposition: 239 to 13 among those attendees who could vote at the Dallas meeting. The small number of bishops with serious reservations included some Church leaders who thought that past abuse should not be treated publicly, or those who challenged the right of the state to intrude into Church affairs, and those who opposed the definition of sexual abuse as a crime.

But the Geoghan case in Boston had already seen civil authorities set a precedent in Massachusetts by allowing the records of clerics and former clerics to be subpoenaed and used in cases against accused pedophile priests. So, in spite of the overwhelming number of affirmative votes, there were some bishops who still opposed the broad nature and scope of subpoenas and the demands of civil authorities for information the bishops continued to consider as privileged.

There was still going to be opposition and legal problems in the future. The conservative bishops remained concerned about continued and potentially increasing investigations into records that the Church had controlled since its inception, and had little inclination to turn over any ecclesiastical records to district attorneys.

In spite of this, the times were beginning to change, and bishops across the United States were increasingly being called before grand juries. Vicars (i.e., administrators/record keepers) were more frequently being required to turn over documents. While the Church tried to protect its ecclesiastical secrecy based on the legitimacy and supremacy of canon law, it was becoming more difficult to maintain such a position of prerogative within the American judicial process.

After the *Boston Globe* broke the story about clerical sexual abuse in Boston in 2001, subpoenas increasingly became the method of choice to access the personnel files of priests. By the time the bishops met for their meeting in Dallas the next year to discuss how to deal with the crisis, the hierarchy was already on the run, trying to figure out how to retain their "secret archives" and how to direct their Vicars to carry out mandated, canonical responsibilities.[9] For sure, the aura of religious privilege was beginning to evaporate within the US hierarchy. Major civil investigations into clerical sexual abuse were already in progress in Boston when the Dallas meeting was underway in 2002, and inquiries in other large dioceses were expected to start soon after.

The hierarchy did not expect and did not know how to respond to the grand jury hearings that began to proliferate across the United States. Some lasted for as little as three months, as in Westchester County, New York, while others that had begun around that time ultimately lasted for as long as three years, as in Philadelphia.

The investigations occurred because civil authorities issued subpoenas for confidential files, exhibits, records, memos, and notes, and required the testimony of victims, psychological counselors, and legal experts. In the Diocese of Davenport, Iowa, for example, imagine how surprised the bishop was when the district attorney sought records going as far back as 50 years!

Some of the grand jury findings and their reports varied in length from 17 to over 400 pages. In Boston, during the course of a year and a half, the attorney general's investigative team reported that it reviewed the personnel files of at least 102 priests, indexed and read over 30,000 pages of documents, and interviewed present and former diocesan priests, senior managers, experts, academics, and victims of clerical sexual abuse.[10]

But it is critically important to point out that even with all the grand jury investigations, relatively few indictments were handed down for the criminal prosecution of predator priests in the earliest civil quests for information. Most grand juries, instead, recommended the enactment of legislation for the protection of victims, while others, as in Cincinnati, Ohio, simply ended in mediated financial diocesan settlements.

In June and July of 2002, however, the situation grew more intense. Going on at the same time as the finalizing of "The Charter" and "The Norms," two grand juries were seated to investigate clerical sexual abuse in California: one in Ventura County and one in Los Angeles County. What happened there illustrates the increasing scope and use of the subpoena power by civil authorities and the early responses of Church leaders—even though the bishops had just passed two significant documents to deal with clerical sexual abuse.

In the Los Angeles Archdiocese, which encompasses both Ventura and Los Angeles Counties, the district attorneys served subpoenas to the custodian of the Church records, the vicar for administration. He was required to provide personnel records and documents relating to alleged molestations by priests.

At just about the same time, the California legislature had also enacted a law to extend the statute of limitations for child molestation. It was intended to have an impact on the length of time that victims would have to bring allegations against priests or other sexual abusers.

The archdiocese complied with the subpoenas in Ventura County and delivered the required documents to the court—except those it still considered "privileged." The county accepted the Church's response, and as a result, only three priests, who had been previously removed from their ministries, were criminally charged.

While the Los Angeles Archdiocese was developing its response to the other civil authorities in Los Angeles County, the US Supreme Court handed down a decision in a molestation case[11] that the Church could use as a defense in allegations against predator priests. In a new ruling on statutes of limitations, the court said that the state could not extend the time limits for victims to accuse sexual abusers beyond current law. Thus, the new decision meant that many of the charges against priests for past molestations could subsequently be dismissed. However, the California state legislators revisited the statute again and allowed another year, at least, for victims to bring civil suits against the Church.

When the Los Angeles Archdiocese attempted to comply with the district attorney's subpoena for personnel records in Los Angeles County, then, several priests filed motions to quash them based on the new Supreme Court decision. Resulting in a series of legal challenges, the archdiocese eventually brought suit against the State of California, shifting tactics as it appealed the case. It did not argue the merits of the differences in the statute of limitations, but appealed the fact that it had to produce records that revealed confidential information about the spiritual, pastoral, and psychological counseling of the clerics to civil authorities. Now, the case was framed as an internal/intrusive matter—one that went to the heart of, and challenged, the First Amendment right of the freedom of religion. It would also involve church-state relations as well.

Lawyers for the archdiocese argued that the demand for clerical records a) breached the canonical responsibility of a bishops to care for his clergy, b) compromised the right of a priest to have private communication with his Bishop, and c) violated the First Amendment of the Constitution by issuing subpoenas for privileged employee communications with psychotherapists. But the County Superior Court ruled against the Church,[12] refusing to accept such reasoning. This led the Archdiocese of Los Angeles to take its case to the court of Appeal of the State of California.

After two years of legal maneuvering, the court finally resolved the issue between the archdiocese and the grand jury of Los Angeles in September 2004. Of the 285 documents that had been subpoenaed, 53 were barred on the attorney-client privilege and the rest were required to be entered into evidence. While the narrow decision might have sufficed in the case, the court went further and dismissed all of the church-state arguments that the archdiocese had contended.

It maintained, first, that the free exercise of religion as guaranteed in the First Amendment was not violated in this case. The court reasoned that the state's demand for clerical files did not breach the priest-penitent right of confidentiality since the information in the records had already been turned over to a third party, in this case the vicar for administration.[13]

Second, the court held that the archdiocese had a legal obligation to produce the records that had been subpoenaed. In so doing, it rejected every aspect of Church "privilege" and "exemption." It maintained that the subpoenaed documents were not part of an internal Church dispute, and thus not privileged. Turning over such personnel files, the court said, was about more than just looking at the records of an employee, as the Church argued.

Third, it held that there was no undue burden placed on religion by the grand jury. The Court held that the requirement to turn over personnel records did not create an excessive state entanglement with the Church. Instead, it asserted its authority to decide the "relevance, burdensomeness and the applicability" of that requirement.

And finally, the court also held definitively that the compelling interest of the state of California to prevent the molestation of children survived "strict scrutiny." That was a legal test that showed that the state's purpose was critical, narrowly tailored, and the least restrictive means to attain its ends. In short, the court ruled that the state's obligation to protect children overrode all of the other legal claims of the Catholic Church against the state.

As a result, the Archdiocese of Los Angeles reported that it was required to turn over 10,000 pages of documents, including information of a spiritual, pastoral, and psychological nature with regard to 647 claims against 211 accused priests, of which 64 were deceased.[14] By 2007, however, after further investigations, the local papers revealed news of even more lawsuits, with the final disposition being that 508 lawsuits were finally settled for $660 million dollars with the Archdiocese of Los Angeles.

This settlement, however, was just the tip of the iceberg. While Catholic dioceses had historically protected their ecclesiastical structure, which was formidable and clandestine at best, and intimidating at worst, not only to lawyers, but to anyone attempting to bring an allegation against a priest, the Los Angeles investigation was merely an example of the new changes about how clerical sexual abuse would be handled by civil authorities in the future.

For example, in Westchester County, New York, a grand jury met 15 times during April-June of 2002 to investigate the archdiocese. It also reviewed thousands of pages of documents, according to its final report, and made three major legal recommendations. The first category of proposals consisted of eliminating the statute of limitations when the victim of the abuse is a minor, and requiring clergy, employees, and officials of a religious institution to immediately report allegations of sexual abuse to law enforcement authorities, and making it a felony to fail to report such allegations. The second proposal recommended that the New York State legislature enact a law to provide criminal penalties to individuals as well as all *organizations* that allowed known child sexual abusers to have access to minors. This would place sanctions on the institutional Church and its diocesan activities for decisions to relocate or reassign pedophile priests. Finally, the third proposal called for a prohibition of confidentiality agreements as part of the settlement of any claims of sexual abuse and misconduct involving minors.

This last recommendation was a significant call for change. The concept of the confidentiality agreements was a major area of concern to the members of the Westchester grand jury. In all cases, previous settlements with the archdiocese were tied to free counseling services, but as a consequence, the archdiocese was able to "maintain a shroud of secrecy over the clergy member's sexual misconduct."[15] Those clandestine agreements barred the victim from ever being able to report his abuse, thus leaving him isolated and other children vulnerable to victimization again.

At about the same time, a special grand jury was convened in Suffolk County (Long Island) to investigate charges that approximately 20 priests had sexually abused children and teenagers in the Diocese of Rockville

Center. Meeting for nine months during 2002, the grand jury heard testimony from 97 witnesses and considered 257 exhibits consisting of a variety of documents.[16] But because New York did not have a law on the books requiring religious authorities to report such acts to civil officials, the investigation did not lead to the indictments of any priests.

Nevertheless, the grand jury referred to the response of the diocesan hierarchy to sexual abuse as a "sham." It articulated a pattern of behavior that was quite telling and that could be found in many other dioceses. The grand jury uncovered information that revealed that priests accused of sexual abuse were transferred from parish to parish, protected under the guise of confidentiality, and denied professional treatment when it was often recommended. The bishops minimized the conduct of the priests and maintained strict administrative oversight. They monitored legal responses, supervised priests themselves, and maintained personal contacts with the accuser.[17] In so doing, they implemented conscious diocesan policies to expend as little capital as possible and to be prepared for the eventuality of potential financial and legal liability in the future. In short, the Diocese of Rockville used aggressive legal strategies and deceived victims—all with the intention of protecting the reputation and finances of the Church.

Thus, while the number of criminal indictments in the United States had been relatively few up to that point, grand juries were beginning to successfully expose a Church pattern of clerical secrecy. They drew a picture of hierarchical behavior characterized by cover-ups of confidentiality agreements, of a mind-set that minimized the severity of clerical sexual abuse, and the motivations that allowed sexual abuse to continue within priestly communities.

No wonder the bishops were so concerned about the treatment of the victims of clerical sexual abuse at their meeting in Dallas—the writing was on the wall. No wonder they wanted to create documents that would not only protect children but accused predator priests as well. They knew that if the grand jury investigations continued, the Church would be in for devastating moral and legal blows, financial liability problems, and challenges to both its religious and social missions. No wonder the bishops decided on a course of action that they thought could save the Catholic Church in America—to create a zero-tolerance policy that could mitigate all of the religious, economic, spiritual, and social fall-out that was about to emerge. What they did not count on, however, was the way their new approach would be met by strident officials at the Vatican.

The Bishops, the Vatican, and their Clash

"The Charter" as passed by the Catholic hierarchy in 2002 took no prisoners and allowed bishops to exercise their zero tolerance policy without any outside interference. An alleged predator priest or deacon could be dealt with spiritually by being relieved of his ministerial duties after a preliminary investigation of a complaint of sexual abuse. His punishment would be imposed *by a bishop*. An accused clergyman was also supposed to be referred for appropriate medical and psychological evaluation by his superior, or bishop. When and if sexual abuse was admitted or proven, the cleric would be removed from his ministry and offered professional assistance for his own healing and well-being. This would be done after one proven allegation.

Although the Canon Law of 1983 had to be considered, the bishop would be empowered to dismiss a cleric and provide him with canonical counsel. The offender could also be confined to a life or prayer and penance *by the bishop*, be denied the right to celebrate Mass publicly, to wear clerical garb, and to present himself publicly as a priest. The bishops' powers were now much more substantial, and in some ways separate from the judicial authority of the Congregation for the Doctrine of the Faith (CDF) at the Vatican when dealing with priestly molestations.

With regard to "The Charter" and the bishops' responsibilities to deal with the *crime* of clerical sexual abuse, the bishops adopted a zero-tolerance policy—something that had not even been hinted at in Vatican circles. It essentially set up mandatory punishments and abrogated legal control over clerical personnel accused of sexual abuse. It required bishops to cooperate with the police and others even when the person alleged to have been abused was no longer a minor. It placed the onus on the bishops, rather than the accuser, to bring the matter to the civil authorities. And it called for publically revealing the names of those priests who had been sanctioned for pedophilia in the past.

On the other hand, "The Essential Norms" elevated the powers of the bishops within the ecclesiastical order to deal with predator priests and deacons. The document redefined terms such as "sexual abuse," the conditions under which alleged offenders could be removed from ministerial duties, and reorganized the appeals process within canon law. In short, the bishops had challenged earlier Vatican directives, and in some cases, even the means to carry out canon law.

The tough stance of the American bishops was not so easy to implement, however. The drafting of "The Charter" and "The Essential
Norms" required Vatican approval or "recognitio." The hierarchy was
not empowered to make Church policy or to amend, modify, or in any
way change canon law. Thus, when the bishops sought Vatican approval
for "The Charter" and "The Essential Norms," two documents that
contained "derogations," or changes to canon law, the pope asserted his
religious authority and attempted to limit the hierarchy's pastoral and
legal control of priests and deacons.

In order to qualify for the "recognitio," or papal approval, the pope at
the time, John Paul, insisted on the establishment of a mixed commission of four Vatican officials from the offices of the Congregation for the
Doctrine of the Faith (CDF) headed by Cardinal Ratizinger (the future
Pope Benedict XVI), the Congregation for Bishops, the Congregation
for Clergy, and the Pontifical Council for Legislative Texts. On the
American side, it was to include four members of the USCCB.

Reports at the time indicated that the purpose of the mixed commission was to reconcile what the pope perceived as a conflict between
canon and civil law and a way to maintain a hierarchical balance of
power with civil authorities in the United States. In reality, however,
John Paul's demands were also a way to bring the American bishops
into line with papal authority, as well as a way to reassert the papal
prerogative to forgive sin and to punish "crime" as it applied to those in
religious life.

It should have come as no surprise to the American bishops. Total
acceptance of "The Charter" and "The Essential Norms" by the Vatican
would have indicated papal approval of its three main principles: a "zero
tolerance" policy for present and future clerical offenders, justice for
victims in the past, and support for the current criminal prosecution of
priests within US courts.

Papal endorsement would have allowed the Church to take the pastoral lead in the repentance and forgiveness of its priests, and to assure
the legal representation of priests by canon and civil lawyers. But it
would have also limited the Church's right to decide whether or not,
and under what conditions, its hierarchy would be required to report
clerical sexual abuse. Canon law might have been subject to 50 different
interpretations of state laws in the United States alone, thus opening the
doors to more challenges in other countries. Evidently, the pope was not
of a mind to concede this power by allowing bishops to make unilateral,

national changes to canon law by the passage of "The Charter" and "The Essential Norms."

More broadly, there was a possibility that total acceptance of the charter might encourage antagonistic governments toward the Vatican, such as those in China, Cuba, and Russia, to challenge fragile ecclesiastical positions. These could include church-state relations regarding the papal right to make clerical/hierarchical appointments, as well as the ability of the Church to carry out educational or social services, and to select and train its own clergy.

John Paul also had the possibility of totally rejecting the American hierarchy's solution to the crisis as spelled out in "The Charter" and "The Essential Norms," but this would have negated those religious parts of "The Charter" regarding spiritual repentance and forgiveness. It would have, therefore, resulted in a veto of the spiritual treatment of past, present, and future clerical sexual abusers, as well as all the mechanisms, both clerical and lay, established by the American bishops to ensure pastoral compassion and communal solidarity with the survivors/victims of sexual abuse.

At the same time, total rejection of "The Essential Norms" would have judicially challenged hierarchical obligations to report pedophilia and other crimes to state officials. This could have brought about a major disruption of church-state relations in the United States and with the Vatican.

Officially, then, as the Vatican opposition to the Dallas policies unfolded, four main Church interests emerged. A variety of reports pointed to the need to protect the due process and appellate rights of priests, particularly those granted to them under church law. Another was the concern for the lack of uniformity about statutes of limitations on sexual abuse. Questions about the civil definition of "sexual abuse" were also unclear. And the problem of how all of the proposed changes would apply to countries outside of the United States needed to be clarified.

A compromise, of sorts, emerged between the American hierarchy and the Vatican. First, the mixed commission of Vatican and American religious officials resolved the matter of due process rights by establishing mandatory church tribunals in each diocese. Composed of clergy and laity, they would deal with accusations of sexual abuse and have the right to decide on the removal of accused priests from their ministerial positions. Before they could do this however, the tribunals would have to send their suspension recommendations to Cardinal Ratzinger's office (i.e., the CDF) in Rome. That body would have the right to review the case and return it for diocesan action while still retaining the right to serve as the court of final appeal. Another possibility was that the CDF could hear the case itself and treat it as part of its original jurisdiction. Thus, Rome, rather than the American bishops or members of church tribunals, remained as the final arbiter in all cases regarding the removal of priests from their religious positions. There was no civil involvement allowed in the process.

Second, the question of the statute of limitations was more difficult to resolve. The pope's total theological and philosophical commitment to the belief in the human being's ability to confess guilt, feel remorse, transform him/herself, and attain spiritual reconciliation with God clashed with the bishop's call to turn over even one-time, past offenders to civil authorities for punishment. The matter ended with the bishops and the pope maintaining that equal penalties would be imposed regardless of when the reported molestation occurred.[18] However, the CDF would still have to be contacted by the church tribunals for each case of priestly removal, and an *exemption* would have to be granted in each case that went beyond the limitations set by canon law. If the CDF refused, the bishops would theoretically still have the right to ban a priest permanently from his ministry.

A major problem remained, however, complicated by the fact that those in Catholic "religious orders," such as Jesuits, Benedictines, Franciscans and Dominicans, were not under the authority of bishops. Approximately one-third, or about 15,000, American Catholic priests are members of orders,[19] and are answerable to their superiors, provincials, or abbots rather than to bishops. They were technically, then, exempt from the policies set down in the bishops' charter.

The leaders of those in religious orders are responsible to the Institutes of Consecrated Life (ICL) at the Vatican office. In turn, the ICL answers directly to the pope. Dismissal for individuals in religious orders found guilty of sexual abuse would also have to come from Rome. Again, civil authorities were excluded from involvement with these priests who often live in a community/group home or a monastery, have a familial relationship with their peers, and receive virtually no pay. Instead, they receive housing, medical care, and retirement benefits from their orders until their deaths. Recently, the Conference of Major Superiors of Men, an umbrella organization of the leaders of most orders, announced that it is in favor of closely supervising abusive priests, but of not expelling sexual predators from their ranks.[20] Again, civil authority is not recognized in these cases.

Third, the Vatican wanted to change the meaning of the term "sexual abuse," as it was used in "The Charter." Contending that it could be a source of "confusion and ambiguity, it argued that "some aspects are difficult to reconcile with the universal law of the Church."[21] Originally the term, "sexual abuse" was described in "The Charter" as "contacts or interactions between a child and an adult when the child is being used as an object of sexual gratification for the adult."[22] Not necessarily equated with intercourse or molestations, or even with other legal definitions in civil law, the American bishops had broadened the meaning of the term. They declared that "A child is abused whether or not this activity involves explicit force, whether or not it involves genital or physical contact, whether or not it is initiated by the child, and whether or not there is discernible harmful outcome."[23] The bishops further stated that if there were doubts about the definition, the writings of theologians should be consulted, but that Church policies "must be in accord with the civil law."[24]

The definition finally agreed upon by the mixed commission and contained in the revised edition of "The Charter" was based not on civil law but rather on "obligations arising from divine commands regarding human sexual interaction as conveyed…by the sixth commandment."[25] In the final Vatican approved version, the standard for sexual abuse would be a religious, rather than a civil one. It would be based on whether or not the "conduct or interaction with a minor qualifies as an external, objectively grave violation of the sixth commandment … [and that it] need not be a complete act of intercourse. Nor, to be objectively grave, does an act need to involve force, physical contact, or a discernible harmful outcome."[26] The religious leadership held that moral responsibility for a canonical offense was presumed upon external violation, but that in case of doubt, the writing of theologians should be consulted. However, it maintained that "ultimately, it is the responsibility of the diocesan bishop/eparch, with the advice of a qualified review board, to determine the gravity of the alleged act."[27]

Thus, the decision was to be made by the bishop and the laity without civil law parameters. What did that mean? Could the group empowered to make such a decision be able to advise a bishop about removing a priest based on its own definition of sexual abuse, leaving a priest to deal with any personal injury after the fact? The situation was murky at best. Could a bishop appoint his own supporters and control the tribunals?

In summary then, the revisions to "The Charter" and "The Essential Norms" mirrored the dominance of the pope's spiritual authority, his ability to frame the clerical abuse issue within a religious, and therefore, a canonical context, and the required subservience of the American hierarchy to him. Just as importantly, however, the bishops were also able to send a strong message to the Vatican and other organizations of national hierarchies that regardless of such pressures, "zero tolerance" would still be the norm in the United States and sufficient to remove sexual offenders from ministry. And to assure such a policy, the bishops promised that they would turn alleged pedophiles over to civil authorities.

Unexpected Political Consequences

Unexpected consequences within both a constitutional and a political context, however, began to emerge during and immediately after the Dallas meeting. Primarily, the clerical sexual abuse problem began to lead to seriously strained relations in Catholic church-state relations in America.

By 2003, one year after the acceptance of "The Charter" and "The Essential Norms," civil investigations of dioceses for clerical sexual abuse started to proliferate. As mentioned earlier, the Attorney General's Office (AGO) in Manchester, New Hampshire investigated "the diocese," and the way supervisory officials handled allegations of clerical sexual abuse. It charged the diocese, rather than the bishops, with multiple counts of endangering minors, imposed legal conditions to protect children, and monitored Church actions to comply with its civil demands.

Such civil confrontations continued in other states even though the bishops had put specific, tighter, systematized policies in place to deal with clerical sexual abuse in "The Charter" and "The Essential Norms." Most notably, this was due to the fact that attorneys general were not willing to overlook prosecutions for such past crimes in light of new hierarchical approaches to handle predatory priests. Justice, to the civil authorities, required the pursuit of all sexual abusers within the statutes of limitations in all states.

For example, in November of 2003, the Diocese of Cincinnati entered into a settlement agreement with the Hamilton County district attorney after an eighteen-month battle with prosecutors who sought access to archdiocesan documents. The settlement with the county required all those who worked with children to be mandatory reporters of alleged clerical sexual abuse. It also released victims from previously agreed upon confidentiality obligations,[28] and required the archdiocese to set up a $3 million dollar victims' compensation fund.[29] Civil authorities also forced the archdiocese to provide names, last known addresses of accusers, dates of charges, and current addresses, assignments, and information on the accused.[30] The pursuit of clerical sexual offenders would not end with the present, but would go back to the past to assure prosecution of possible predator priests.

In Phoenix, Arizona, a year-long grand jury investigation begun in 2003 and led by district attorney Richard M. Romley, reportedly examined more than 200,000 documents and the personnel records of 70 priests, former priests, and church employees accused of sexual misconduct during the 30 years prior.[31] It ended with an agreement between Maricopa County and the archdiocese in which Bishop Thomas O'Brien avoided indictment on a felony charge of obstructing justice by agreeing to "acknowledge that he allowed Roman Catholic priests under his supervision to have contact with minors after becoming aware of allegations of criminal sexual misconduct."[32]

In exchange for immunity from prosecution, the bishop also agreed 1) to appoint a chief of staff to deal with issues relating to sexual misconduct policy, 2) to appoint an independent youth protection advocate 3) to accept a special counsel to the youth protection advocate with input from the county 4) to review the diocesan policy on sexual misconduct 5) to implement a training program for diocesan personnel on sexual misconduct issues, and 6) to apologize and express contrition. These were, according to Bishop O'Brien, already part of a comprehensive plan that had been initiated by the Phoenix Diocese earlier.[33] In effect, though, the agreement allowed state intervention into Church management, a perceived intrusion that later raised questions about the boundaries of civil and ecclesiastical authority, and became a matter of disputed interpretation between the district attorney and the bishop.

The diocese also had to contribute $300,000 to the county's victims' compensation fund, create a victim assistance panel, provide up to $50,000 per victim for counseling fees, meet to exchange information on sexual abuse with country officials, and pay $100,000 for the investigative costs to the county.[34]

The onslaught of civil investigations into past cases of clerical sexual abuse continued. While they are too numerous to mention here, several grand jury hearings stand out and reveal major flagrant disregard for the safety of children. For example, in 2005, the district attorney of Philadelphia, Pennsylvania published the findings of the grand jury that had been convened for three years. Its purpose was to investigate the alleged cover up of clerical sexual abuse within the archdiocese by reviewing "thousands of documents from archdiocese files," and hearing statements and testimonies from over 100 witnesses.

The grand jury concluded that 63 priests had sexually abused hundreds of minors over several decades, but due to the statute of limitations only one priest could be prosecuted. Further, two previous archbishops, John Cardinal Krol and Anthony Cardinal Bevilacqua, were found to have covered up the abuse—and their aides were found to have been complicit, as well.

The cover-up seemed to follow a similar pattern in many dioceses. The Philadelphia grand jury said it consisted of 1) persuading parents not to report crimes to the police, 2) transferring a predator priest, and 3) concealing a crime from parishioners, police, and the general public.

This was carried out in a variety of ways. It included discouraging priests from reporting on their fellow priests, misinforming or not informing the members of parishes about why priests were removed, sending priests to distant parishes, denying access to the "secret archives," and accepting only oral rather than written complaints, most likely to prevent having such information in retrievable records.

The vicars and bishops who dealt with such issues were also found to be at fault. They questioned diagnoses of pedophilia, manipulated treatments, placed individuals in "limited" ministries, intimidated victims, blamed victims for seducing priests, and delegated responsibilities for handling such matters to their underlings.

The grand jury in Philadelphia concluded that Cardinals Krol and Bevilacqua "excused and enabled the abuse," and "put the legal and financial interest and moral reputation of the archdiocese ahead of protecting the children."[35] But again, because there were inadequate laws to prevent such actions, no criminal indictments could be brought against members of the hierarchy who had played a part in the crimes that the grand jury said ranged from rape to the endangerment of a minor.

What did emerge at the time from the 400+ page Philadelphia grand jury report, however, were some critical recommendations. These called for the abolition of the statute of limitations for sexual offenses against children, and the expansion of legislation regarding the offense of endangering the welfare of children. The grand jury called for an increase of the penalty for indecent assault where there is a pattern of abuse, a tightening of Pennsylvania Child Protection Service Law, a requirement that those who learn of sexual abuse (even indirectly) report it to authorities, and a required background check for school employees as well as any employees of any organization that supervises children.

Further, the grand jury called for legislation that would hold *associations* to the same standards as *corporations* for crimes concerning the sexual assault of children. This meant that the Catholic dioceses, some of which were incorporated legally for purposes of business and real estate, as well as other dioceses which were not incorporated, could be held to the same civil and criminal statutes that enjoined all economic, financial, and other non-profit agencies. It also recommended an enlargement or elimination of statutes of limitations on *civil suits,* as well as those criminal ones involving child sexual assault.[36] This would again change church-state relations, especially if those in power within the Catholic hierarchical infrastructure were to be treated like any other CEOs of major institutions. They would be subject to civil law and its investigative authority as would any other organization. Thus, the continued erosion of Church exemption continued even after the Dallas bishops' meeting, when they tried to stave off civil attempts to limit Church management and control of what it perceived to be its own internal affairs.

The unintended consequences of these hearings and recommendations came full circle when Seth Williams, the district attorney for Philadelphia, called for a second round of grand jury hearings in 2011. After more allegations of sexual abuse continued to come to light and the principles of "The Charter" did not appear to be implemented, he decided to investigate allegations of continued molestation of children in the "City of Brotherly Love."

His inquiry was held almost six years after the first Philadelphia grand jury hearings that found that more than 50 priests had been involved in sexual abuse; In 2011, Williams accused 37 more priests of similar crimes.

The sitting archbishop, Anthony Cardinal Bevilaqua, who had been found guilty of a cover-up of sexual abusive priests earlier, had retired just before the 2011 investigation. That left his successor, Archbishop Charles Chaput, and the secretary of the clergy, Monsignor William

Lynn, to deal with the matter of continued sexual abuse. Chaput was not a target of the investigation, since he was new—but Lynn was going to be held responsible since he had been on the job from 1992–2004.

As secretary of the clergy, Lynn was essentially the personnel director for the priests in the Philadelphia Archdiocese. He had two main jobs. One was to investigate allegations of sexual abuse, which meant that he was supposed to review such reports, recommend action, and to monitor the abuser's future conduct. His second duty was to assign and/or make recommendations for assignments or reassignments of priests to particular parishes.

Lynn repeatedly moved a number of predator priests around during his tenure, and the grand jury focused on the large number of reassignments that he had made. The movements of three particular clerics emerged as the worst: those of Father James Brennan, Father Charles Englehardt, and Father Edward Avery.

Father Brennan, a teacher and a live-in chaplin at a residential facility for young women with developmental disabilities, was accused by nuns for giving alcohol to underage kids and living with a boy at the home. Brennan subsequently requested a leave of absence to deal with his own psychological problems, but Lynn assured him that, even though there were rumors about this behavior, "the archdiocese would take no action against him—that he was safe."[37] Then in 1996, Brennan raped a young boy. He was investigated by an archdiocesan review board which registered its concerns to the Church leadership, but nothing was done. Instead, Brennan was reassigned to a new parish, and then voluntarily entered a monastery. In 2006, he was removed from active ministry, but his current status as a priest is still pending before a canonical jury. Lynn was the person in charge of the Brennan case.

Father Charles Englehardt, a second priest managed by Lynn, was accused of sodomizing a 10-year-old boy and sharing him with his fellow priest-associate, Father Edward Avery, at the parish where they served together. Then the boy was passed by Avery to a lay teacher, Bernard Shero, who worked in the school attached to the parish. Shero ultimately raped the boy. Avery knew what was going on, but he did not report the incidents to police. Rather than do so, Lynn assigned Avery to a new parish where he would essentially continue to have access to children.

Father Avery had been a major problem for the diocese for some time. He had a drinking problem. He had sexual problem. He moonlighted as a disc jockey, picked up boys, plied them with alcohol, and abused them at the events he emceed. He "adopted" children, and acted as their "father." After reports of abuse, he was finally sent for evaluation at St. John Vianney Hospital in 1992, a facility that had a center for sexual deviants. There the staff recommended that Avery be kept for inpatient treatment. After a year, Avery finally resigned from his parish duties—officially for health reasons, which some referred to as bipolarity and alcoholism. According to the grand jury, the cardinal at the time, Bevilacqua, was "insistent" that "parishioners not be informed of the truth."[38]

Lynn took orders from the cardinal and attempted to quash rumors about Avery. In 1993, the staff at the St. John Vianney facility recommended that Avery should not be allowed to work with adolescents, should enter a 12-step Alcoholics Anonymous group, and stay away from children. Nevertheless, Lynn assigned Avery as an associate pastor at Our Lady of Ransom, a parish in Philadelphia with an elementary school.

Avery continued to work with the teenagers, increased his disc jockey gigs to 25 out of 31 Saturdays in 1995, and found his double life a perfect way to meet young people. He continued with this lifestyle until 1997 when Lynn met with him, not to discuss his lifestyle or behavior, but to tell him that Bevilacqua would not recommend him for a doctoral program that he wanted to get into! Instead, Lynn provided the recommendation himself, citing Avery as an honest individual.

By 2002, a victim reported that Avery was still hanging around minors and drinking. The victim wanted him to admit what he had done in the past and wanted the archdiocese to protect other children.[39] The demands were finally accepted when, in 2003, the situation was finally resolved by a new cardinal, Justin Rigali, who ordered the removal of Avery from all assignments and prohibited him from performing public ministry.

But this wasn't the end of the story. The grand jury that was convened in 2011 revealed that Lynn carried out a cover-up of many other priests engaged in sexual abuse. Worse, it found that he "purposefully... placed sexual predators in positions where they would have easy access to trusting minors, just as long as the archdiocese was spared public exposure or costly lawsuits... [and that] he consistently endangered them."[40] The grand jury found that the procedures carried out within the offices of the Archdiocese of Philadelphia helped the abusers, and the archdiocese' practices allowed many pedophile priests to remain in ministry.

Lynn was indicted. Although he was acquitted of conspiracy to cover up crimes of clerical sexual abuse with his former boss, Cardinal

Bevilacqua, Lynn was convicted of one count of felony child endangerment in 2012.

He was serving a 3–6 year sentence in a Pennsylvania prison when he
was released on a legal technicality. After spending only 18 months in
jail, Lynn's lawyers were able to gain his freedom because at the time of
his conviction, the law did not cover people like Lynn who didn't directly
supervise children. Lynn is out of jail now but required to wear an ankle
monitor. He is considered a priest in good standing with the Church.

Brennan, an accused pedophile, remains in canonical limbo within
a monastery. He is waiting retrial in criminal court after a jury could
not reach a decision in his original case. Englehart and the lay teacher,
Bernard Shero, have both been convicted of rape. Englehart has recanted
his former confession and is seeking a retrial.[41] Cardinal Bevilacqua is
dead.

These stories are not unique; they appear repeatedly in the news. They
refuse to go away, and, in their own ways, give continuing courage to
other victims/survivors. Unfortunately, "The Charter" and "The Essential
Norms" have not effectively changed the way that the US bishops are
carrying out the promises and policies that they made in Dallas in 2002.
The statements they made to carry out their responsibilities to keep
youngsters safe from clerical sexual abuse and to maintain a "zero tolerance" for priestly perversions are only as good as their actions. These
documents are worthless without the hierarchical will and courage to
come forward and do what their canonical and civil responsibilities
require.

The abuse cases of so many other priests and their cover-ups cannot
even begin to be told here. There was a $17.65 million settlement to final-
ize 26 lawsuits of past sexual abuse in Vermont[42] in 2010. Bishop Robert
W. Finn of the Diocese of Kansas City-St Joseph was convicted and is
out on parole for refusing to report the pornography practices of Father
Shawn Ratigan to either civil or canonical authorities[43] in 2012. There
was a settlement of 11 more priest sexual abuses cases in Vermont in
2013.[44] Roger Cardinal Mahoney, the retired cardinal-bishop of the Los
Angeles Archdiocese was found guilty of "shielding accused priests and
protecting the church"[45] in 2013. The accusations, the findings, and the
prosecutions go on.

Civil authorities, to their credit, have been diligent in continuing their
fight to protect children though the courts, by the use of subpoenas, and
the investigations of grand juries. As a result, the dynamic between the

US government and the Catholic Church has gone through a power shift, an evolving change from a delicate balance between secular and sacred attempts to uphold institutional Church interests and privileges to a prioritized compelling state responsibility to protect the individual rights of children. This fact has brought an escalating and often aggressive clash between those who control internal Church governance and those who would impose external civil powers for the larger concern of child safety.

Unexpected Financial Consequences

Another unexpected consequence of the clerical sexual abuse crisis in the United States has been the financial disaster that followed it. No one ever dreamed that it would cost the Catholic Church upwards of $3 billion.[46] Mouton, Peterson, and Doyle thought that a one billion dollar estimate would set off alarm bells for the hierarchy and get the bishops' attention in the 1980s, but as the increase in allegations occurred, and the bishops seemed unable or unwilling to respond, so did a growth in civil liability suits and court mandated payouts.

In 2004, a study commissioned by the National Review Board of the Catholic Laity reported that over $573 million had been paid to settle sexual abuse claims up to 2002.[47] That number skyrocketed, hitting the $1 billion mark in 2005,[48] $1.5 billion in 2006,[49] and $2.5 billion in 2013.[50]

Although the bishops continue to maintain that sexual abuse claims are diminishing, lawsuits are still being filed in many dioceses across the United States. This has created critical, broad economic dilemmas for the Church. From a church-state perspective, how would Church leaders deal with a change in the power shift that was occurring? Could it lead to a loss of government assistance for its charitable, educational, and health agencies in the United States? And could the civil implications of potential diocesen bankruptcies result in civil intrusions into questions of Church finances, parish ownership, and the disposition of its properties?

These were distinct possibilities and fears surrounding the escalating clerical sexual abuse settlements. As the largest single charitable organization in the United States, the Catholic Church through Catholic Charities distributes about $1 billion annually to the poor in America—which represents about 60 percent of the Church's total charitable donations globally.[51] It is also a major recipient of local and federal monies from Medicare, Medicaid, and student loans used at its hospitals and colleges. The loss of its financial viability could have disastrous social and financial effects not only nationally, but internationally.

At the same time, the Catholic Church is also a major real estate owner in many parts of the United States. It is rumored that it is Manhattan's largest landowner. Church-state clashes, then, over property ownership as well as over the use and/or need to sell off diocesan assets to pay victims abused by priests had the potential to destroy its internal financial viability as well as its ability to control the monetary assets on the part of the wealthiest institution in the world.

This has become a fact of the Church's monetary life since nine Catholic dioceses, up to this point, have been forced into bankruptcy, and others may have to do the same in the not too distant future. They have used bankruptcy as a financial strategy in civil courts to settle, and try to limit, huge claims in clerical sexual abuse cases. Dioceses in Portland, Oregon, Tucson, Arizona, and Spokane, Washington were the first to declare bankruptcy in 2004. They were followed by Davenport, Iowa in 2006, San Diego, California in 2007, Fairbanks, Alaska in 2008, Wilmington, Delaware in 2009, Milwaukee, Wisconsin in 2011, and Helena, Montana in 2014. The Dioceses of Stockton, California and Gallup, New Mexico are currently in the process of declaring bankruptcy as well.

In general, the Church has argued that, in many cases, a bankruptcy strategy is the only way it can deal with the clerical sexual abuse claims against it. Declaring insolvency, according to Church officials, is a result of insufficient insurance and a lack of financial resources. It is the most effective way to prevent the possibility of having to sell school buildings, churches, cemeteries, hospitals, or other real estate holdings in order to pay claims by litigants in sexual abuse cases.

The church-state concerns and questions of Church officials are related to four major legal challenges: Who owns the Church's assets? Who can dictate how they can be used? Who would ultimately mediate such civil financial claims? And what role would state or federal bankruptcy courts play in the financial reorganization of dioceses? More broadly, there were also hierarchical concerns about the continued ability of the Church to carry out its spiritual mission. This role could be compromised by the state if the Church's holdings were mandated to be sold to pay sexual abuse claims rather than used to serve its own religious and charitable missions.

The complexity, power, and inconsistency of the state to deal with the civil liability consequences of clerical sexual abuse became pronounced when the Archdiocese of Portland, the first Catholic "corporation," filed for bankruptcy in 2004. It was reported that the diocese had spent more than $6.5 million in attorneys' fees to settle $53 million in claims for 100 lawsuits up to that point.[52] Rumors said that it also faced more than $100 million in claims by other alleged victims as well.

The Archdiocese of Portland is an ecclesiastical, as well as a corporate, entity. Within the Catholic hierarchical structure, an "archdiocese" or a "diocese" is a geographical area made up of an aggregate of local parishes. As an ecclesiastical entity, an archdiocese or diocese is headed by an archbishop or a bishop, who is appointed by the pope. His purpose is to serve as a spiritual leader of the faithful and a superior of all the priests in each of the parishes.[53]

The Archdiocese of Portland is also a civil entity because it applied for, and received, a charter from the state to be able to act as a "corporation." As such, the archdiocese voluntarily entered into a relationship with the state, in the past, which allowed it to hold and manage property, to sue others, and to participate in binding contracts. The archbishop in such cases acts as the "corporation sole," the person who embodies the corporation, or who is the face of the corporation.

He has limited personal liability in most property suits, and in most states, depending on the incorporation regulations, the archbishop can hold diocesan, as well as parish property in trust.[54] This type of corporation usually lacks members or officers or a board of directors, but provides a legal framework that assures the perpetual existence of the corporate body even if the natural person (archbishop) should die. The Archdiocese of Portland, then, is both an ecclesiastical body as well as a voluntary, legal creation, a corporation led by a corporation sole.

This whole notion of the corporation sole, however, along with church-planning and organization, according to the legal counsel for the USCCB at the time, Mark Chopko, was considered to be "under a microscope" by civil authorities across the United States, a situation he opposed.[55] While Chopko believed that liability follows responsibility, he maintained that the church's autonomy should be the basis for it to create its own structures of responsibility.[56] In short, he did not want the civil courts to set up mechanisms to reorganize canonical, diocesan financial systems.

The validity of state law in matters of Church bankruptcy first came into dispute in Portland. Litigants sued the archdiocese for financial damages arising from clerical sexual abuse settlements when the Church maintained that it could not afford to pay them. Filing for Chapter 11, the archdiocese attempted 1) to settle with as many victims as possible within its financial capacity, 2) to enable the "corporation" to pay out potential claims against its creditors in the future, and 3) to assure its ability to carry out its religious mission.

Canon lawyers argued that the real and personal property of the Church's individual parishes, schools and cemeteries were not part of the estate of the Church as a "corporation," or a portion of the holdings of the archbishop as its "corporation sole." Instead, they claimed that the assets were "ecclesiastical," that is owned by the pope and administered through officials at the Vatican and elsewhere, appointed by him. As such, they argued that such properties could not be used (or sold) to pay the claims of the victims of sexual abuse.

In 2005, the United States Bankruptcy Court for Portland[57] asserted that it had jurisdiction in the case involving the archdiocese, since bankruptcy was a corporate, rather than an ecclesiastical, matter. It held that the parish and Church buildings were legal assets, that they were under the control of the archdiocese, and that they were held in the name of the archbishop as the "corporation sole." It rejected the "ecclesiastical" arguments of Church canon lawyers. Nevertheless, the court held that even if the archdiocese chose to organize its property assets by forming a corporation, "civil courts did not have to rely on canon law to determine rights in property held by the corporation sole."[58] Thus, ecclesiastical rules and canon law did not necessarily apply to the legal corporate activities of the archbishop acting as the "corporation sole."[59] This struck a major church-state blow to the Church's assertion of ecclesiastical property rights.

The court also maintained that the jurisdiction of a federal court in a bankruptcy matter does not violate the First Amendment rights of the Church. Forcing it to obey state law rather than church law on the matter of property ownership was ruled permissible. It claimed that using neutral civil (Oregon) law to determine the Church's property interests was considered to be consistent with the "tenets of the church.[60]

Most significantly, the court ruled that obedience to state law in this case did not impose a substantial burden on its members. This would apply even if parishioners had to help pay claims against the archdiocese,[61] or even if the congregants had to worship at different buildings because church closings might be necessary to pay such claims.[62]

The court, however, left the door open for an appeal. It held that if the Church could show that a substantial burden had been placed on religion, and that the government did not have a compelling state interest to demand the sales of significant properties to pay lawsuits, the Church could bring the case before the court again to determine what would be an appropriate remedy for such a burden.[63]

The appeal did not go forward. Instead, a $75 million settlement plan was worked out between the Archdiocese of Portland and the sexual abuse claimants in 2006. Although it did not require the sale of Church assets such as schools, churches, or hospitals,[64] it called for the archdiocese to take loans and use other financial assets, such as insurance, to pay for sexual abuse claims. The final disposition of the settlement required approval by the bankruptcy court, and other questions of transparency, accountability, and the use of donated funds to the Church for other causes were considered.

The Diocese of Spokane also filed a bankruptcy suit in Washington State in 2004 – but with a different result. The Associated Press reported that the diocese had assets of $11.1 million and liabilities of $81.8 million, the majority coming from sexual abuse claims.[65]

In the Spokane case, the US Bankruptcy Court originally ruled that the state could apply federal bankruptcy law to a religious organization.[66] It held that the bishop as the "corporation sole" could dispose of churches, schools, and other real property to satisfy claims for clerical sexual abuse because they were held in trust and part of the property of the estate of the archdiocese.

Very soon thereafter, the bankruptcy case was appealed, reversed, and returned to the lower bankruptcy court for mediation.[67] The US District Court ruled that the parishes, rather than the diocese (as a corporation) or the bishop (as the corporation sole), owned their churches and schools. Because parishioners purchased, built, operated and maintained their churches by donations and tithes, the court held that a "resulting trust" was created, one that allowed each parish to be treated as a separate legal entity with rights, and to maintain its individual assets.

Regardless of their legal financial independence, though, parishes were called on by the archdiocese to help pay $10 million in attorney's fees, with several parishes also being used as collateral in the mediated sexual abuse claims. The consensual agreement hammered out in 2006 called for $48 million to be paid to victims by diocesan insurance and the sale of diocesan properties, other organizations such as Catholic Cemeteries and Catholic Charities, as well as the bishop as "corporation sole."[68]

The Tuscon bankruptcy in 2004 was, again, a different matter. In a simple case that lasted only one year, the diocese settled claims for sexual abuse for $22.2 million, for 31 victims.[69] It declared bankruptcy and went through a quiet reorganization that allowed it to move forward with its religious and social mission.

But that was not the case for many other financially strapped dioceses. In 2006 and 2007 two other Chapter 11 filings occurred: one in the Diocese of Davenport, Iowa, and the other by the Diocese of San Diego, California. Filing at the eleventh hour—before major cases involving civil suits dealing with clerical sexual abuse were about to begin—the bishops of both the dioceses claimed that bankruptcy was the best way for the Church to compensate victims equally and to continue its spiritual mission.

In Davenport, bankruptcy was recognized as the way that the diocese could deal with the claims of 25 victims of clerical sexual abuse. The bishop, William Franklin, said that it was "the best opportunity for healing and for the just and fair compensation of those who have suffered sexual abuse by clergy in our diocese."[70] Noting that all parishes and schools were incorporated, *separately*, canon lawyers for the diocese said that only the land on which the diocesan headquarters was located, which included its buildings and the bishop's residence, would be subject to financial claims and reorganization. Incorporating parishes separately has now become a new means to protect Church real property and assets in civil liability claims for clerical sexual abuse settlements.

In San Diego, the diocese, in an electronic filing, claimed that it had assets of more than $100 million,[71] but public information revealed that the diocese settled a major lawsuit for $200 million, which depleted most of its resources. Opponents maintained that bankruptcy had simply been a way to hide from embarrassing allegations, to eliminate certain assets from reorganization, and to limit demands for personnel records as well as documents about the handling of abusive priests.

As the suits piled up, questions of the rights of civil authorities began to wane; it seemed as though canon lawyers were at the end of their legal ropes, and that it was time to admit defeat, pay up, and make the best deals possible. But in 2008, when the diocese of Fairbanks declared bankruptcy, another legal twist occurred.

Twenty-eight Eskimo victims accused Joseph Lundowski, a volunteer Catholic missionary who was not an ordained priest, of having molested them. Lundowski had helped Father George Endal, a Jesuit cleric, from 1959 to 1975, serving as a *de facto* deacon. He conducted religious services, taught native children, and provided sacraments to the laity. According to the Associated Press, the number of claims from this case and others rose from 110 to 292 by 2007.[72]

Church officials tried to argue that the statute of limitations had run out on most claims, some going back almost 50 years. They maintained that the Diocese of Fairbanks was not responsible for other claims, specifically, those brought against the Jesuits, a religious order that is not subject to diocesan management.

The bishop of Northern Alaska, Donald J. Kettler, however, subsequently realized that this would not hold up in court. He announced that bankruptcy and reorganization were the "best way to bring all parties together and to provide for fair and equitable treatment of all who have been harmed."[73]

As a result, the diocese has mortgaged its conference center and the residence of the bishop and subordinate priests to pay sexual abuse claims. The federal bankruptcy court in 2009 also ruled that the diocese's insurance company was not liable for certain claims against pedophile priests in the 1970s as well. It has been reported that the diocese had been looking for loans and was even willing to sell its aircraft hangers to the Fairbanks airport.

In 2009, the Diocese of Wilmington, Delaware also declared bankruptcy, the result of 88 pending clerical abuse cases. In spite of the extension of the statute of limitations for such victims by the Delaware Child Victims Act of 2007, the court could not stop the Church's effort to pursue protection by Chapter 11 reorganization. At the time, its assets of about $100 million were offset by liabilities of almost $500 million.[74] This occurred just days after a $30 million claim brought by a victim of clerical sexual abuse was granted by the Wilmington court. The payout was the largest granted to one individual in all previous compensation cases in the United States. Legally significant was the fact that neither the diocese, nor a religious order, nor the parish, were completely responsible in the case. Instead, the parish was required to pay $3 million and the perpetrator $27 million.

One of the most recent bankruptcy cases occurred in the Archdiocese of Milwaukee. In January 2011, lawyers were trying to mediate 23 clerical sexual abuse lawsuits. This was after a bankruptcy court had ruled that the diocese's insurance companies were not bound to contribute to any financial settlement in clerical abuse cases during a specific five-year period of time. That time revolved partly around some of the molestations of 200 deaf boys by Father Lawrence Murphy.

The case became more than a financial suit; it became even more reprehensible with the allegations of a cover-up by hierarchical leaders who never aggressively pursued a canonical trial, a civil suit, or a criminal action against Murphy. The financial liability was beyond what the diocese could afford—a fact that hardly satisfied the victims of Murphy and other pedophile priests. In an official statement, the diocese claimed that it could not fairly compensate victims/survivors, carry out the essential ministries of the archdiocese, or meet the needs of its parishes.[75] Thus, Milwaukee became the eighth diocese to try to financially reorganize in order to move forward.

Just recently, in 2014, the Diocese of Helena, Montana also declared bankruptcy. In order to settle claims for about $15 million to over 350 victims of clerical sexual abuse, the diocese agreed to a financial settlement with survivors. It would be worked out and supervised by the US Bankruptcy Court in Montana. More than $2 million would also be set aside for other victims who might come forward in the future. The diocese also put mechanisms in place to protect children and apologized for the cover-up of priest predators in the past. It is anticipated that the church will still be able to carry out its social and religious ministry.

The Future

What is problematic in the bishops' responses to clerical sexual abuse are the unintended consequences of their attempts to rectify the situation. They rarely moved beyond words to substantive equitable actions to deal with the ramifications of their meager canonical attempts to redress the crisis.

Church reticence has warranted state action to redress the criminal aspects of clerical sexual abuse, to serve the compelling state interest to protect children from molestation, and even to challenge the traditional relationship between church and state in America. In all these cases, civil structures have been, and are continuing to be, used as the primary means with the power to resolve the organizational tension between church and state.

Questions of authority and enforcement have been at the basis of these legal strains, a sacred-secular unease that has been clearly visible during the last two decades, and which continues to be tested in a variety of civil, criminal, and canonical challenges today. The use of the subpoena, the elimination of confidentiality agreements, and the extension of statutes of limitations, have become the major criminal consequences of the Catholic clerical sexual abuse scandal. They have presented major ecclesiastical and civil challenges for the Church, which views the scandal through the lens of canonical authority. In essence, it means that the Church remains primarily concerned with priestly due process, internal governance, diocesan financial liabilities, and institutional accountability. On the other hand, civil authorities view the clerical abuse crisis as the justification for state investigations into current and past cases in order to ensure the enactment of legislation to protect children, to punish clerical predators, and to hold the Catholic Church responsible for the actions of its religious personnel.

The Church has also had to deal with financial problems that it was ill-prepared to handle. Using bankruptcy as a strategy for the equitable, limited distribution of funds for sexual abuse claims in financial mediations has also had church-state ramifications. Some Church leaders have feared, and have been unable to stop, courts from becoming involved in civil inquiries about the sources and use of Church funds from state to state.[76]

As a response, some bishops in California, specifically in San Diego as mentioned previously, attempted to split their diocese into individual parish corporations, with each pastor becoming his own corporation sole in order to limit the liability of the diocese. This strategy has been followed in a number of states with a variety of tactics. In Alaska for example, the bishop claimed that he did not own parishes or parish properties. As a result, he allowed the diocese of Fairbanks to set up the Catholic Trust of Northern Alaska in 2007 to protect the financial holdings of its parishes and to keep them immune from financial liability in clerical sexual abuses cases. Some opponents, however, have claimed that such legal maneuvering was simply an attempt to secretly shield Church monies really due to molestation victims.[77]

This concern about state intrusion into the finances of the Church has already materialized in Massachusetts, as also mentioned earlier. There the state legislature proposed a bill in 2006 to require the Catholic Church to give an accounting of its charitable finances to the attorney general, but it did not go forward.

Thus, there exists a potential church-state conflict regarding bankruptcy, due to state interference in deciding not only what Church assets are, but how they can or should be used—for the Church's religious mission or for its civil liability responsibilities to settle claims in clerical sexual abuse cases. At the same time, there is also the potential for the Church to use bankruptcy as a strategy to reorganize and hold on to as many of its valuable assets for the future while attempting to provide some sort of equitable settlement for clerical sexual abuse claims from the past and the present. In short, bankruptcy has become a significant legal response and a potential test of the power shift in the church-state relationship in the United States.

More broadly, the courts' inconsistent decisions show the uneven treatment of the Catholic Church before the law, and the future unexpected consequences that its adherents might have to anticipate should parish assets be sold without their approval. Such a lack of consistency means that the prevalence of further litigation by both the Church and the state in the future should be expected and that a ruling by the Supreme Court on the use of Church assets for financial claims may become necessary.

5
Pushback and Payback:
The Laity and the Lawyers

Introduction

Reporters and lawyers played the earliest roles in raising awareness about clerical sexual abuse. The press investigated and revealed heinous stories, helping to support civil authorities that prosecuted clerical molesters wherever they tried to hide.

Dedicated attorneys, as well, led the first legal actions against priest predators in Louisiana, Massachusetts, and other states. They came to the aid of survivors by helping them to attain redress for their victimization. It was their lawyers, who used aggressive and innovative tactics in civil suits, and criminal prosecutions who helped to assure justice for those caught in the most horrific scandal in Church history.

In the process of media and legal assertions against the Catholic hierarchy, the balance of power between church and state began to shift in the United States. Criminal actions of priests and the mismanagement of clerics by the hierarchy were brought to light by grand jury hearings. They resulted in the extensive use of subpoenas against Church leaders for clerical records and allowed the public depositions of bishops for the discovery of evidence. Civil suits challenged official Church financial settlements and confidentiality agreements. Bankruptcies became a fate hanging over the heads of diocese, providing a sense of fear that Church assets would be closely scrutinized and reorganized by the state.

The Catholic leadership has been a recalcitrant responder to the civil authorities. And, despite the bishops' efforts to create and implement a zero tolerance policy to protect children, time has shown that the bishops have continued to fall short of providing meaningful help to victims of clerical sexual abuse. Instead, many Church leaders are still placing obstacles in the way of financial redress, criminal prosecutions, and spiritual reconciliation. This is due to their continuing refusal to give up canonical power over what the bishops believe to be the Church's internal affairs and its traditional, ecclesiastical privileges.

Now almost a decade and a half after the Boston scandal in 2001, the battle for recognition, justice, and accountability among sexual abuse victims has, necessarily, intensified. This has occurred and become possible for two main reasons.

The first is due to the creation of a number of lay Catholic organizations that have taken an active, assertive, and often, adversarial role in the fight against the obstinate hierarchy. They have brought clerical sexual abuse victims and survivors together to counter the bishops' reluctance to punish priest predators. By mobilizing, engaging, pressuring, and even lobbying civil authorities, the Church laity is playing a critical role to unearth clandestine hierarchical practices and policies that excuse or cover up the illegal actions of priests. They are now fighting, along with civil authorities, for changes in civil law for the protection of children.

The second reason why the battle against the Church hierarchy has intensified is due to the efforts of aggressive lawyers. They are willing to pursue innovative legal strategies to hold Church leaders, including the pope, responsible for cover-ups, inaction, and benign rebuttals to the sexual abuse crisis. These attorneys have been able to take on the institutional Catholic Church, use the instrumentalities and processes of the American legal system, and help to bring justice to the victims of clerical sexual abuse. As a result, they have, consciously or unconsciously, helped to change Catholic Church-state relations, especially on matters of institutional, criminal, and financial liability.

Nonetheless, the hierarchy has continued, unsuccessfully, to pursue legal strategies that demand state recognition of its own traditional, canonical privileges and codes. It has done this even though it has consistently lost legal ground, public support, and lay confidence in its handling of clerical sexual abuse in the United States.

As a result of the work of lay organizations and the legal victories of many committed lawyers, civil authorities have found forceful allies in their attempts to prosecute pedophile priests and to protect children. The state has become more powerful in the church-state equation in both a legal and policy sense. It has garnered support for the punishment of clerical sexual abusers and judicial approval to end canonical and ecclesiastical privileges. It has gained new advocates for legislation designed to develop public policies to tighten statutes of limitations and punishments that deal with clerical sexual abuse. Consequently, the state has been able to more tightly control the formerly more tenuous relationship between church and state. Indeed, the state has emerged as the victor in the constitutional battles for hierarchical accountability, transparency, and justice in almost every case brought in state courts on major issues dealing with clerical sexual abuse.

Lay Responses: Survivors Network of those Abused by Priests (SNAP)

One of the first lay organizations established in response to clerical sexual abuse was the Survivors Network of those Abused by Priests (SNAP). The self-help group emerged in 1998, calling for the protection of victims and the prosecution of predator priests. It preceded the sexual abuse scandal in Boston, and was already in existence when the Geoghan, Shanley, and Porter stories broke after 2000.

SNAP was founded by Barbara Blaine. Twenty years earlier, as a student at St. Pius X Elementary School, she was molested by Father Chet Warren, the assistant pastor at her parish. The abuse continued though her senior year of high school until Blaine was finally able to confess the cleric's molestations to another priest while on a religious retreat. The priest told her that Jesus could forgive anything—a life-changing statement that gave her the courage and self esteem to tell herself "That's it. This isn't happening anymore."[1]

She went on to St. Louis University and earned a bachelor's degree, then to Washington University where she got a Master's in social work. But Blaine did not stop there. She went on to the Catholic Theological Seminary for a Master's Degree in Divinity and finally to DePaul

University School of Law, where she completed the full circle of her education. She also went through a lot of therapy.

In 1985, at the age of 29, Blaine told her family about the abuse she had suffered as a child and as a teenager. Her parents quickly brought suit against Warren's religious order, the Oblates of St. Francis DeSales, to assure the safety of other children. According to Blaine's family, the priest was sent for therapy, but stayed in ministry until he was finally defrocked in 1993.

Throughout a multiyear legal ordeal, the Blaine's felt that the Oblate leadership was "aloof;"[2] and cool. They were told that their daughter was Warren's only accuser, and that the religious order would closely monitor the priest. Dissatisfied, but persistent, the Blaine's finally received an $80,000 settlement, a financial payout tied to a confidentiality agreement. Warren was sent away for therapy, and the usual clerical sexual abuse story ended there—or did it?

Blaine was an educated woman and an empathetic advocate for the victims of clerical sexual abuse. This enabled her to begin her personal outreach to victims in 1988. She held meetings in the homeless shelter where she worked as a Chicago Catholic community worker. Word of her organization grew, according to newspaper accounts, by small ads and word of mouth. It "exploded," Blaine said after the revelations of the Boston scandals in 2001, at the time when the purpose of SNAP was "95%" about consoling victims.[3]

The mission statement of SNAP says it all: that it is an independent, confidential network of survivors and their supporters, all kinds of people who have suffered religious sexual abuse. As an organization, it is committed to protect the vulnerable, to heal the wounded, and to prevent priestly abuse in the future.

Thus, the purpose of SNAP has always been to expose predators and the people who shielded them. It has dedicated itself to build ways to protect children and to help individuals share their stories and confront truth. It also educates victims and communities about the effects of abuse.

To carry out this mission, SNAP needed to build a viable, caring, yet assertive organization. It has done this through the efforts of supportive leaders and activists committed to the recovery of victims and the punishment of molesters. It works for civil justice and criminal prosecutions, as well as changes in the law and civil procedures to assure justice and to prosecute predators. Just as importantly, it also demands accountability from Church authorities for enabling abuse and shielding predators.[4]

Through her persistent efforts over the years, Blaine has found that Father Warren's sexual deviance was known to his superiors in Rome. Frustrated by this information, and the lack of attention paid to it by the hierarchy, Blaine finally went public with certain aspects of her own story. She appeared on "The Oprah Winfrey Show," "Phil Donohue," and other television programs, hoping to raise awareness about clerical sexual abuse. Contacted by isolated victims after sharing the narrative of her abuse, Blaine also learned that there were other claims against Warren, a fact that had been hidden by his superiors over the years.

In 2002, Blaine was chosen as one of the Women of the Year by *Ms.* magazine for empowering survivors to tell their stories publicly. She worked for SNAP *pro bono* until 2004, when she started to finally receive a salary. Now she is married and continues her efforts on behalf of SNAP. Today, the organization claims to have over 12,000 members and more than 60 chapters in 56 countries

Since 1991, David Clohessy has worked with Blaine as the National Director of SNAP. A former community and union organizer, Clohessy was also a victim of clerical sexual abuse. He has revealed, too, that his brother, Father Kevin Clohessy, was accused of molestation while serving at a Catholic student center. Placed on leave, Kevin Clohessy was eventually sent for therapy to the St. John Vianney Renewal Center by his diocese, and then in May 2000 took an extended, voluntary leave of absence.

David Clohessy has publicly apologized for his brother. He has reportedly said, "I feel terribly sorry for anybody my brother victimized and for their families and for my family, especially my parents, and I hope that those people whom he hurt are able to come forward and get help."[5]

Blaine and Clohessy, then, have similar backgrounds: both were victims of clerical sexual abuse and both are committed advocates dedicated to help others who have suffered as they did. Clohessy has appeared on many television programs, too, and has received the Lifetime Achievement Advocacy Award by the Institute on Violence, Abuse, and Trauma for his compassion, wisdom, and work for victims.

From its inception, commentators have claimed that SNAP has been working under several assumptions. One is that the institutional Church is incapable of reforming itself because its decision-making structure is autocratic and privileged, and the other is that the organization, itself, is devoid of accountability.

As a result, SNAP has not worked within the Catholic establishment to redress clerical sexual abuse. Instead, it has taken on the character of an "outside agitator,"[6] playing a number of roles designed to protect survivors and prosecute clerical sexual abusers. In so doing, it has become an ally of civil authorities, rather than institutional reformers, seeking to change the power of a reluctant hierarchy when it comes to predator priests.

The first of the roles that SNAP plays is as a psychological shelter for victims of clerical sexual abuse. It provides psychic healing, maintaining the confidentiality of both victims and their stories recounted at meetings. It encourages such individuals to try to solve their own problems. Others are expected to listen. Silence is regarded as a time for reflection. Open discussion has also been viewed as part of healing.[7]

Second, SNAP has broadened its agenda since its inception, a fact that has resulted in legal challenges to Church authority. For example, in 2012, Clohessy, the organization's national director, was subpoenaed in a case involving four individuals who were members of SNAP and who were suing Reverend Michael Tierney and the Diocese of Kansas City-St. Joseph for clerical sexual abuse.

Although the statute of limitations had run out for the plaintiffs to legally make accusations, they claimed that they could now do so because they had recovered their repressed memories. In a role reversal, Church lawyers claimed that they needed to see 23 years of SNAP's confidential records and information relating to repressed memory about any priest in the diocese.

Clohessy was deposed and refused to give up any confidential information. He argued that "we think it's a horrific betrayal of trust and privacy."[8] In a series of appeals, Clohessy and SNAP ultimately took the case to the Supreme Court of Missouri in order to protect the identity, stories, and records of those who came to SNAP for shelter and healing.

The court sided with the organization's claims and rejected the arguments of the Church's lawyers. It ruled that the information they were seeking was neither discoverable nor remotely relevant—maintaining that the Church's attorneys were seeking an "incredibly broad spectrum of information."[9]

This example shows how SNAP has allied itself with civil authorities and consistently challenged the canonical positions of the Catholic Church. It has fought to protect victims and the confidentiality of their statements made at its meetings, as well as information provided by whistle-blowers. It protects the privacy that is expected by law enforcement officials and private communications with the press.[10] Some have claimed that the demand for confidential records was a way for the Church to silence SNAP,[11] but an official spokesperson for the USCCB categorically denied the allegation in a press release.

Third, SNAP acts as a go-between with those in positions of Church power and those sexual abuse victims who cannot speak out for themselves. This is a particularly relevant role as it pertains to the many legal and psychological disparities between alleged survivors and the Catholic leadership in the United States.

SNAP was reluctantly recognized as a legitimate organization by the American hierarchy and given credibility in 2002, when Clohessy was one of only four individuals invited to address the US Conference of Catholic bishops at its meeting in Dallas.

Working to craft their zero-tolerance policy to protect children, the bishops listened to lay calls for changes in their responses to clerical sexual abuse. For SNAP, the request to speak was, seemingly, a *quid pro quo,* that came only after the survivors' organization withdrew from participating in an earlier lawsuit against the USCCB and several dioceses.[12]

At the microphone, Clohessy called on the hierarchy to take four critical actions. These included making a radical change in their behavior, working for the prevention of clerical sexual abuse, lobbying to extend or eliminate statutes of limitations, and requiring all clergy members to be mandatory reporters of sexual abuse.

He was very clear, warning the bishops that words alone could not "miraculously transform a systemic problem that is deeply rooted in the power structure of the Church."[13] He challenged the laity to hold out for real change, because that was what their children deserved—and nothing less.

Fourth, SNAP serves in a political role, as well. It has acted to advocate for legislation to protect those sexually abused by priests. It also works as an activist for justice for those victims. It has done this by giving speeches, participating in demonstrations, giving press conferences, sending out mass mailings, holding annual meetings to raise public awareness, and educating others about how to survive clerical sexual abuse.[14]

In 2002, SNAP worked for the passage of a bill in California that extended the statute of limitations on child sexual abuse cases. It supported a similar, but failed, bill in 2006 in New York. It has continued to be reintroduced even to 2014, regardless of heavy Catholic opposition to it.

SNAP has also been challenging a number of bishops and their handling of sexual abuse cases in their diocese. These have included public statements about Archbishop Roger Mahoney in California, Bishop Robert Finn in Missouri, and many others. Indeed, there are so many cases that they simply cannot all be recounted here.

SNAP has also been politically active within the Catholic Church in a number of other ways to retaliate against those who have covered up clerical sexual abuse. In 2005, SNAP leaders traveled to Rome to protest the fact that Cardinal Law, the former head of the Boston Archdiocese during the Geoghan and Shanely cases, was celebrating a memorial mass for Pope John Paul II. In 2013, after Benedict XVI's retirement, SNAP members returned to Rome with a list of names of cardinals in a number of countries that they believed should not have been considered for the papacy. Specific cardinals were singled out because of their inadequate and ineffective policies of clerical sexual abuse.

Fifth, SNAP has been a defender of the vulnerable in the legal forum, participating in both civil and criminal lawsuits. It has filed *amicus* briefs, played a part in demanding large financial settlements, and provided damning publicity in the court of public opinion as well. It has given legal support to victims when the Church has delayed or attempted to evade culpability in many cases. It has even taken on religious orders such as the Franciscans in California,[15] where it gave support to victims in a case that ultimately resulted in a $28.5 million settlement for the accusers. The Franciscans subsequently opened their files in 2012 as well, leading to more information regarding clerical sexual abuse within their order from the past. The Diocese of Los Angeles, which was also involved in this particular lawsuit, subsequently published 12,000 pages of documents[16] as well.

The success in participating in such cases has led some scholars to claim that SNAP's major impact has been "to raise the costs of negligence and criminal behavior on the part of the church rather than to try to remake the organization."[17] But as a result of its involvement in the California case and others, SNAP has also brought about some church-state changes as well. This includes forcing the hierarchy and religious orders to become more transparent, and in turn, more accountable for their actions.

By 2011, SNAP moved from handling local cases and took a major legal leap forward. Joining with attorneys from the Center for Constitutional Rights (CCR) in New York, it became involved internationally by bringing a formal complaint against high-ranking officials at the Vatican for crimes against humanity.

These crimes included individual cases of molestations where letters and documents were exchanged between Vatican officials and members of the hierarchy. They also evidenced the Church leadership's lack of co-operation with civil law enforcement agencies and its refusal to hand over suspects for criminal prosecution in sexual abuse allegations.

In an 84-page document with over 20,000 pages of supporting materials[18] filed before the International Criminal Court in the Hague, SNAP and the CCR contended that the pope and certain members of his staff (i.e, the Vatican secretary of state and the head of the Congregation for the Defense of the Faith) were ultimately and directly responsible for the crimes of those below them. SNAP and the CCR estimated that this included anywhere between 6,000 and 20,000 members of the clergy, many of whom abused multiple child victims. They contended that the Vatican was "systematic" in its behavior, that it sheltered priests, obstructed, silenced, discredited and intimidated witnesses, and stone-walled prosecutors.[19]

The International Criminal Court, however, has declined to carry out a full investigation in the case, but has promised that it would do so if other evidence could be found to disprove its initial findings. In the meantime, Amnesty International also cited the Vatican, in 2011, for human rights violations by members of its clergy and the Holy See's failure to provide redress.[20]

Bouyed by its success, SNAP continues to fight to protect and extend the rights of victims of clerical sexual abuse while it also cooperates with civil authorities to prosecute offenders. Just recently, the organization joined with a number of legal groups in California to file an *amicus* brief in a case[21] to support victims of clerical sexual abuse who wanted to send letters to their alleged molesters in order to seek compensation for therapy and medical expenses. SNAP wanted the victims to gain the right to do this without the fear of being sued for extortion.

SNAP has also served as a launching pad for other organizations founded to help the survivors of clerical sexual abuse. One of these is SafeNet. Its co-founder, Paul Fericano, a former member of SNAP, recounts trying to channel his anger at being a victim of a predator priest at St. Anthony Seminary in Santa Barbara as a student. He said he tried to do this by handing out fliers, shouting down priests, lobbying for legislation, and even bringing a personal injury suit against the Franciscan Friars.

After a number of years in therapy, gaining the support of his family and friends, Fericano realized that speaking out was "essential" as was "listening to others." He claims that those two actions made it possible for him to "open a door to forgiveness," a portal that he described as "powerful" and "self-determined and deeply personal."[22]

SafeNet's co-founder was John McCord, an alumnus of St. Anthony's Seminary who was also abused by a priest on the faculty. After spending ten years in therapy, losing his wife and his job, McCord says that he is in the process of rebuilding trust and trying to help other survivors.

Other, small organizations continue to proliferate. One such example is "Road to Recovery." Founded by a former priest, Robert M. Hoatson, the northern New Jersey non-profit is also helped by a supporter/advocate, Father Kenneth Lash. Together, they try to help survivors by providing services and increasing public awareness about clerical sexual abuse. Their organization calls for change and works to get the support of the Church to provide healing for victims and their families.

Another newly formed lay group is "Catholic Whistleblowers." It is a network of current and former priests, nuns, and laypeople whose mission it is to support survivors of clerical sexual abuse. They provide moral and legal support while advocating for those who want to speak out about their ordeals. One of the founding members is Father Thomas Doyle, part of the triad with Mouton and Peterson in the prosecution of Father Gilbert Gauthe in Louisiana.

Just recently, a canon lawyer, Rev. James E. Connell, a member of Catholic Whistle-blowers, petitioned Pope Francis to take disciplinary action against Bishop Finn, mentioned earlier in this chapter. He was convicted of failing to report a priest in his diocese who was a pornographer and who is now serving a 50-year sentence in prison.

Many of these groups are small, and have been formed to deal with specific cases of sexual abuse in local areas. Their very presence, however, serves to show that survivors are everywhere, insist on being heard, and will be encouraged by lay groups to bring civil actions against the Church for redress of their grievances as well.

SNAP, which started out as a small but intense organization, has grown and been successful on a number of levels, particularly as it pushes to change the power relationship between church and state in America and global venues. However, it has not been without criticism or critics over the years. For example, when SNAP worked to extend the statute of limitations on child sexual abuse cases in California in 2002, some of its opponents questioned if its actions were a conflict of interest.

The bill to extend the statute of limitations was drafted by Laurence E. Drivon, a lawyer who represented 320 clergy sex abuse plaintiffs. The passage of a new bill would have allowed attorneys like him to file many more lawsuits in cases that had legally been considered beyond prosecution. It also would have been given him and others the opportunity to receive significant percentages of the settlements that resulted.

The problem? Drivon had also been a contributor to SNAP. This fact led members of the press and Church officials to question the propriety of the relationship between SNAP and the lawyers who would potentially earn huge salaries in Church settlements. Some reporters even asked if they were in a "symbiotic alliance."[23]

In 2004, SNAP did admit to accepting donations from some leading attorneys besides Drivon. These included major litigators against the Church such as Jeffrey Anderson, Michael S. Morey, and Joseph Klest. At the time, these lawyers together had handled more than 400 cases of clerical sexual abuse and had already won millions upon millions of dollars in settlements from dioceses in Minnesota, Illinois, and Kentucky.[24]

In 2012, Clohessy also admitted to publishing false information. During his deposition in the case of Tierney in Missouri, mentioned earlier in this chapter, Clohessy refused to provide confidential information in a case based on the repressed memory testimony of the priest's accuser. However, in the process of providing testimony, Clohessy also revealed that SNAP had knowingly issued a false press release. He admitted that SNAP was not, in fact, a rape crisis center, and that it did not have formal licensed counselors working for the organization. Instead, he continued to stress that SNAP publicized "lawsuits against priests,"[25] distancing himself from the psychological aspects of SNAP's mission.

Such behavior has only led to the inevitable question: does the end justify the means? SNAP has, in fact, been challenged by establishment, conservative Catholic lay organizations within its own Church.

The Catholic League for Religious and Civil Rights, located in New York, is just such an organization. Founded in 1973 by a priest, the late Father Virgil Blum, S. J., it is a Catholic advocacy group. It is currently led by William Donohue, a former teacher who holds a Ph.D. in sociology from New York University.

The author of a number of books and articles, Donohue is also the publisher of the Catholic League journal, *Catalyst*. He serves on the advisory boards of several of the most prestigious Catholic legal organizations and foundations, has received many teaching awards, and has appeared on many television and radio shows speaking on behalf of civil liberties and social issues. He is supported by leading members of the Catholic hierarchy and an influential board of directors. It is safe to say, then, that when Donohue talks, Catholic conservatives listen. When he challenges an organization such as SNAP, he has a certain amount of credibility.

Donohue has come out against SNAP on a number of occasions. In fact, he sees it as a "menace,"[26] saying that the organization "has decided to wage war on the Catholic Church."[27] Much of Donohue's opposition to SNAP comes from the investigations and discussions that it deals with at its annual conferences.

In 2014, SNAP will have held 25 yearly meetings with a recurring theme that Donohue characterizes as the "evil nature"[28] of the Catholic Church. He has attacked SNAP's relationship with Father Thomas Doyle, lawyers who are in business to simply sue the Church, and the fact that SNAP and its allies have "long pulled the wool over the eyes of many in the media."[29]

Other groups, such as the Knights of Columbus and Legatus, an organization founded by Tom Monaghan the original owner of Dominos's Pizza, are also staunch defenders of the Church. Along with the Catholic League, their assets alone could far surpass almost any financial challenge that SNAP might mount to destroy the monetary position of the Catholic Church in America.

What SNAP does have, however, is major visibility. This is a result of its enlarging agenda, especially in the international arena. It has served, and continues to play a critical role in providing a public and legal, lay response to clerical sexual abuse—in both the court of public opinion and in the judicial forum at home and abroad. It has shown that it can take on major players: the pope, the hierarchy, canon lawyers, and the die-hard, well-heeled members of the laity within the Church. By these actions, it has played a part in changing the American and international church-state dynamic. It has rallied thousands of people against the secrecy and reluctance of the Church to co-operate with civil authorities in the matter of clerical sexual abuse, thereby weakening the loyal religious and legal base of the hierarchy.

What SNAP reportedly lacks, however, is significant funding to participate in major legal actions against the Church. This could be another way for it to accomplish its original goals of helping the victims of clerical sexual abuse and of preventing priestly abuse in the future. To be more effective in these endeavors, SNAP will have to cooperate more exten-sively with legal authorities, form political coalitions, and create more meaningful relationships with other Catholic-activist organizations. As a result, SNAP could potentially penalize the Church and hurt it enough to bring about financial restitution for victims, real institutional reform, and hierarchical accountability in the future. Joining with other groups, then, SNAP could enlarge its original purpose and, either consciously or unconsciously, play a part in shifting more power to the state in the legal challenges associated with clerical sexual abuse.

SNAP must also guard against the possible loss of its own relevance. In light of the *ad hoc* proliferation of other organizations dedicated to the same goals as its own, it may be superseded by smaller, more intense, but short-lived groups who will solve problems in their parishes and locales and then disappear into the shadows. Their successes could pos-sibly lead to SNAP's demise.

Lay Response: Voice of the Faithful (VOTF)

Why would a hundred people get up early on a misty Fall Saturday morning to hear a theology professor lecture on "Eucharistic spiritual-ity"? Why did they want to learn about small faith communities and institutional Church reform? Why didn't they just turn over, go back to sleep, and get up later? That's what an outsider might ask, but the parking lot was full that day at the Lutheran Church. The Catholic attendees were wide awake and anxious to get started. They were there to participate in an education event sponsored by The Voice of the Faithful (VOTF).

Founded in Wellesley, Massachusetts in January of 2002, the organiza-tion's purpose was to respond to the revelations of clerical sexual abuse in the Boston area that were coming to light at the time. A group of about 30 concerned Catholic parishioners met in the basement of St. John the Evangelist Church, with the approval of their pastor, to pray on the prob-lem. But soon, they moved from contemplation to heated discussions, to outreach to survivors, and to the establishment of a focused faith based movement—all within about 90 days.

VOTF drew a growing number of Catholic and non-Catholic sup-porters to its meetings each week, garnering major media attention for its early attempts to pursue a limited, but critical agenda. It had a straightforward mission: to support the victims of clergy sexual abuse, to support priests of integrity, and to pursue structural change within the Church.

The burgeoning group hoped to accomplish these goals by being embedded within the official infrastructure of the Catholic Church, a position that it believed would give VOTF a type of insider status or role of "loyal opposition,"[30] and make it a true part of the post-Vatican II Church. It envisioned its organization to be a laity-empowered, social justice movement that would bring about institutional renewal and a new way of interacting with the world.

Without a decision-making role or any other kind of real power in the Church, the hierarchy believed that VOTF could only mount a limited, although potentially threatening, challenge to its power. Nevertheless, in a short time, it became apparent to everyone in the Boston Archdiocese that VOTF could build a consensus of concerned individuals who wanted to respond to clerical sexual abuse, and bring political pressure to bear to make changes in church-state relations in the State of Massachusetts.

Its very existence in a Church basement provided a physical place and a collective identity where the fledging group could meet. It created a forum for conversation and the possibility of collaboration with Church officials. More importantly, it established a means to mobilize a lay response to clerical sexual abuse.[31]

VOTF emerged as a full-blown organization by the end of 2002, and grew to a membership base of over 30,000 members across the United States and around the world. Today its website boasts of having chapters in every state with over 150 parish affiliations. It also reports that other similar groups exist in 21 nations now as well. Within a year, then, VOTF formed support groups, mobilized members, gained financial strength, and became politically active.

Underneath it all, the story of VOTF's responses to clerical sexual abuse revealed a deep sense of spiritual dissatisfaction with its Church leadership. Some say it was a result of frustration and discontent within the laity, feelings that moved it from reverence to reform. Others say it reflected the desire of Catholics to take back their Church and to become partners in institutional decision-making. In short, VOTF's members wanted to gain and ensure an authentic respect for the people in the pews. This was manifested by their demands for hierarchical accountability, transparency, renewal, and justice—the same expectations as those of the state.

VOTF was co-founded by Jim Muller and Jim Post, both intelligent and savvy organizers. Muller was a cardiologist and a faculty member at the Harvard Medical School for 25 years. A devoted Catholic, Muller attended Church elementary and secondary schools and was an alumnus of Notre Dame University. He graduated from the Johns Hopkins School of Medicine and was a specialist in coronary plaque ruptures that can lead to death. He was a committed social activist as well, having co-founded International Physicians for the Prevention of Nuclear War (PPNW). That organization won the Nobel Peace Prize in 1985. He received five honorary degrees from Catholic universities and was applauded by the Vatican. He is also currently the CEO of InfraReDx, Inc., a company that manufactures a medical device to identify plaque in patients undergoing cardiac procedures.

The co-founder of VOTF was Jim Post, a professor of management at Boston University. An authority on corporate governance, Post earned a PhD at the State University of New York in Buffalo and a JD from Villanova University. He is a well-known researcher and writer. His latest book[32] deals with corporate responsibility, and looks at ways to balance corporate self-interest with government regulation to meet the needs of consumers and employers. Post had worked at one time with the Rockefeller Foundation and the World Health Organization to institute a number of reforms that would create a code of conduct for marketing infant formula. It is easy to see how his business management skills translate to concerns about, and solutions for, ways to bring equilibrium to Church interests with the rights of the laity.

Both Muller and Post were the moving force behind VOTF in its earliest days. Muller recounts those times in his book, co-authored with Charles Kenney, *Keep the Faith, Change the Church.*[33] Muller was the one who pushed for consensus and creating a mission statement for the developing organization when there were so many disparate needs, concerns, agendas, and priorities—situations that eventually coalesced around the critical need to address clerical sexual abuse.

Simple but significant events sustained early interest in VOTF activities: a "healing Mass," "listening sessions," lectures by learned theologians, and plans to meet with Church leaders to discuss the tragedy and handling of clerical sexual abuse. When Cardinal Law, however, held a diocese-wide convocation on the problem, his attitude and actions did not satisfy VOTF attendees.

Muller contends that, in general, the cardinal was "aloof" and "unwilling to reach out to the laity,"[34] promising the people who came to the meeting that he would ponder what he had heard. Law's benign reaction led VOTF to respond in other ways to the sexual abuse crisis.

One member, David Zizik, attempted to start an association of parish councils to serve as a means of communication between laypeople and their archbishop. He challenged the appearance of a "culture of insularity and secrecy within the hierarchy,"[35] leading Law to order priests to refuse to cooperate with the VOTF leaders or any evolving association of parish councils. Law called such groups "superfluous and potentially divisive."[36] In essence, the cardinal maintained that equality for laypeople in the Church could only occur within the Church's traditional hierarchical structure. Translation: there is no equality of laypeople within the official Church organization. Subsequently, any groups seeking equality or inclusion were told to work with and under Law.

Those who disagreed were banned from holding meetings on Church property. James Post of the VOTF referred to these actions as "ludicrous"[37] but Law's punitive policies were followed in many other dioceses across the country. Early on, these included the Camden and Newark dioceses in New Jersey, Rockville Center, New York and Bridgeport, Connecticut.

Nevertheless, within a few months of its founding, VOTF was so strong that it was able to hold a meeting at the Hynes Convention Center in Boston to respond to clerical sexual abuse and the cover-up of such crimes by the hierarchy of the Church. VOTF opened its meeting by awarding a "Priest of Integrity Award" to Father Thomas Doyle, the priest who almost two decades before had tried to warn the Church hierarchy of the impending tragedy that was about to befall the Church as a result of clerical sexual abuse. To VOTF members, Doyle was a fitting hero and an inspiration to all.

As the meeting began to unfold, however, in September 2002, it became apparent that in the nine months since VOTF's inception, the concerns of the organization began to shift, intensify, and move away from its original focus. VOTF was becoming an umbrella organization to pull together a number of different religious and political agendas, a fact that could actually keep its organization viable and relevant, and a way to sustain media attention while increasing its resources.

The items discussed at the Hynes gathering now included panels, listening forums, and workshops about a broad range of issues. Some of these were about support for victims of clerical sexual abuse, the punishment of molesters, the responsibilities of bishops, the financial consequences of the abuse and the due process rights for the accused— challenges to canon law and stronger support for civil law—and by extension, challenges to the relationship between church and state.

But other matters also rose to the fore. These included the role of the laity in church governance, matters of sexual morality, the morale of priests, the place of women in the Church, the pathologies of clericalism, and concerns over the infallibility and Church teachings.[38]

Had VOTF opened the floodgates for religious reform and lost its focus on justice and transparency? Right after the convention, more conservative Catholic groups such as the Coalition of Catholics and Survivors questioned whether or not VOTF had focused sufficiently on sexual abuse.

Later, an anti-VOTF organization known as Faithful Voice, and its spokesperson, Carol McKinley, questioned the reform group's agenda. She called it "anti-Catholic" and made up of a "group of dissenters."[39] Media people such as Deal Hudson, the editor of *Crisis,* an influential Catholic magazine, even called VOTF "a wolf in sheep's clothing."[40]

Your Catholic Voice, an organization co-founded by Michael Galloway to present Catholic social teaching in the public forum as a basis for public policy decisions, claimed that VOTF was made up of "angry Catholics... who want to change the Church by their rules."[41] The spokesman for the group, Raymond Flynn, who was both the former mayor of Boston and a US ambassador to the Vatican, wondered if VOTF had moved from concerns about sexual abuse and structural reform to "almost radical doctrinal change."[42]

In spite of such criticism, Muller, VOTF's leader, remained optimistic in the face of lay and hierarchical challenges and believed that VOTF had been empowered after its convention. Because of its "positive world wide publicity,"[43] he and the energized VOTF leadership took on three immediate, concrete actions to advance its agenda. These were the 1) public evaluation of bishops, 2) the establishment of an independent fundraising effort for Church ministries, and 3) the solidarity with victim advocacy groups.

VOTF announced soon after its convention that it would begin to study the performance of the hierarchy based on individual bishops' compliance with "The Charter" and "The Essential Norms." The main VOTF affiliate in Boston anticipated that local chapters would do the assessments and then post them online. It was VOTF's way of doing what civil authorities were doing in court, only in a public, non-legal way.

At the same time, VOTF launched Voice of Compassion, a fundraising body that would accept donations from individuals who wanted diocesan transparency about how their monies were being used for charities, and other Church-related spending. Such information was not made public by the Boston Archdiocesan offices, but VOTF recognized financial power as a tool for change.

If Voice of Compassion were to be successful at its fundraising efforts, spokesmen said that they would have to establish new sites at other large urban dioceses. However, such efforts were totally opposed by the cardinal's spokesmen. Muller and his team were told that the "relationship between the archbishop and his church takes primacy over funding the programs and ministries of the archdiocese."[44] In short, raising money outside the aegis of the cardinal's office was understood to be a challenge to the power of the archdiocese's leader. Nevertheless, Voice of Compassion did raise money independently, offered it to the archbishop for the Church's charitable work, but was turned down. Voice of Compassion then offered its funds to Catholic Charities—which graciously accepted the donations.

VOTF also began to make contacts with other groups responding to clerical sexual abuse. These included a variety of associations such as SNAP, Survivors Alliance and Franciscan Exchange Network (SAFENET), and The Linkup to support their efforts for the healing of persons molested by clergy.

These early actions took on a life of their own. Slowly, VOTF affiliates began to seek ways to translate their original concerns over the abuse of children into "a more holistic reform"[45] that went beyond supporting the abused and priest of integrity, and changing the institutional structure of the Church. For example, when a number of women demonstrated on behalf of the "marginalized" female laity, VOTF embraced their challenges to hierarchical authority as a move toward a "constitutional process that will create a democratic body for the 1 billion Catholic laity of the world."[46] VOTF was quickly beginning to enlarge and change its original mission.

VOTF and the groups that it spawned demanded accountability, transparency, and a voice in Church decision-making, actions that were anathema to the traditional, autocratic, hierarchical infrastructure that has ruled the institutional Church for more than 2,000 years. Within this context, and five months after its inception, Cardinal Law agreed to allow a meeting between the leaders of VOTF and certain church officials[47] to discuss the clerical abuse scandal and how the hierarchy and laity could work together to improve the Church. Muller characterized the attitude of the cardinal's representatives as one of "arrogance," speaking to the VOTF leadership with a "hostile" and "accusatory" tone while working "back channels" against the organization.[48]

Finally, about six months later, in November of 2002, Law agreed to meet with the leadership of VOTF himself. Jim Post, the president at the time, summed up the two and a half hour conversation by saying that it was about one thing: authority. He said that the cardinal seemed unclear as to whether or not VOTF wanted to be an official church organization, or how the group would relate to the Church's leader. Law said that if it was about "shaping structural change," then it would be "troublesome."[49] Clearly, institutional reform could not only change the religious relationship between laity and hierarchy, but also the connections between church and state. The balance of power could surely shift in both equations if VOTF were allowed to pursue its growing mission.

Other discussions that were anticipated between VOTF and the cardinal, however, were not forthcoming. Law resigned one month later in December 2002, 11 months after the sexual abuse scandal broke in Boston. He had given a lengthy deposition before the grand jury and was also being pressured by VOTF.

From 2003 to 2006, VOTF revised its bylaws, increased its membership, and developed new ways of communicating with members across the United States and around the globe. It established a governing council, with a deliberative body of about 200 members that represented various VOTF affiliates across the United States. It became a national organization with a paid staff of more than 40 people and a large number of volunteers at its headquarters in Newton, Massachusetts. Sometime in the future, VOTF hopes to create an international council that will have representatives from around the world.

During its early growth, and while the Church maintained that its problems with regard to clerical sexual abuse were internal matters, VOTF responded with a different strategy: it would use technology to make clerical sexual abuse public—to share information and coordinate responses. It would show that the cases of clerical sexual abuse were not aberrations, but prove that the hierarchy knew what was going on for a long time.

Its tactics were simple: to build its organization through email, Internet innovations, and social media in order to establish collaborations with like-minded lay groups. The use of the Internet would be used to build a broad consensus for reform. In fact, some experts have claimed that the Internet, itself, has been another type of *affiliate* of VOTF.[50]

It allowed information to move beyond a locality and create a forum for individuals and small groups to participate in Church reform. The medium was cheap, instant, asynchronous, and capable of continually being modified. It was not only a forum to facilitate a one-on-one conversation, or a discussion between one person and many others, but it was also a platform for many people to interact with many other people for support. Although this new way of doing business demanded new behaviors[51] and responses from the Church, they never came.

In the meantime, VOTF grew stronger. It began lobbying and supported legislation to extend statutes of limitations for sexual abuse in Massachusetts and Pennsylvania.

By 2008, VOTF had expanded to the point that its leadership believed that it was necessary to refocus its original agenda. Having become a magnet for a series of lay groups that were dissatisfied with the Church, VOTF began to increase and divert its resources to examine, critique, and eventually call for both structural and *doctrinal* changes in the Church.

It began to recognize clerical sexual abuse as a symptom of more serious, seminal management problems within the hierarchy. These were understood to be inherent difficulties derived from an antiquated Church administration model: one that enabled and protected strict hierarchical secrecy and the culture of clericalism. In short, VOTF took on what it perceived to be a clerical sense of religious superiority—a pretentious, aloof attitude that pervaded and characterized its dealings with the laity.

As it shifted to bring about structural reform, then, VOTF's mission began to evolve more broadly into one that pursued doctrinal change, too. It included new and varied tactics to oppose the hierarchical, patriarchal structure of the Church, especially the demand for papal allegiance. VOTF rejected the attitude of clerics who were taught that they had undergone a change in their very human essence by becoming priests. These two facts, VOTF said, were the result of special isolated seminary education and training, the requirement for celibacy, the use of liturgical dress, and the special privileges afforded to priests with regard to compensation and lifestyle.[52]

In essence, VOTF maintained that "clericalism" was an "impediment"[53] to the healing and reform essential to the Catholic Church today. As a result, the organization intensified its efforts for doctrinal reform, hoping that its participation with other like-minded organizations would give greater weight to demands for a broader and deeper change in Church management.

Understanding this behavior as being intertwined with cover-ups, clerical superiority, and a lack of transparency, VOTF redirected its attention and began to move into new areas of discussion and analysis. These included taking up and questioning such doctrinal policies as priestly celibacy, the restriction on the ordination of women, and the clandestine, hierarchical control of Church monies.

It hoped to have a greater structural and doctrinal impact by participating in the formation of the American Catholic Conference (ACC), a burgeoning coalition of Church reform activists. The most radical of the groups in its organization was Call to Action, composed of several hundred small faith communities, for Church renewal and democratization.

The agenda of ACC is essentially doctrinal. It supports the ordination of women and an end to priestly celibacy. It calls for lay participation in the selection of bishops. ACC accepts active homosexual behavior and abortion. It recognizes that salvation is achieved by human accomplishment, and assures freedom of speech for all Catholic educators and theologians.[54]

VOTF has begun to ally itself now more openly with groups concerned with other seminal issues of Church reform, a fact that has put the organization in the middle of a power struggle between the Church leadership and a disaffected laity. The organization is no longer embedded within the Church. Rather it is outside, indeed, expelled from the official infrastructure. VOTF now acts independently, and without hierarchical collaboration or dialogue.

It has become increasingly obvious that VOTF is becoming more involved with matters that revolve around clericalism. For example, it responded negatively to the conclusions of the John Jay College report on the causes and the context of Catholic clerical sexual abuse that was published in 2003.[55] VOTF maintained that clericalism was basically at the root of priestly predatory behavior and that bishops were not complying with "The Charter to Protect Children and Young People" adopted by the NCCB in 2002, precisely due to the culture of clericalism.

In 2004, VOTF ran an ad in the *New York Times* that called for the sitting pope, John Paul II, to meet with clerical abuse survivors, to hold bishops responsible for transfers of pedophile priests, and to accept their resignations. It also wanted US bishops to disclose information about the transfers of abusive clergy. Their escalating public actions can be considered a "very public claim to a representative voice for the Church... [and] did garner attention."[56] By 2011, VOTF became more vocal, citing cover-ups in Philadelphia and Kansas City, and asking "Why anyone would trust the bishops' capacity and commitment to true accountability in light of their behavior since 2002... is beyond comprehension."[57]

In a letter to the USCCB, the VOTF called for a number of actions to return to the earlier promises of the American bishops to protect children. It wanted independent audits and open access to clerical records, totally independent diocesan review boards, victim assistance programs insulated from church officials and their law firms and insurance companies, support for an extension of statutes of limitations for crimes of clerical sexual abuse, listening sessions, and restrictions on NCCB participation by bishops who were stonewalling the actions required by "The Charter," and "The Essential Norms." Their actions continued to put further pressure on the Catholic hierarchy: pressure that was already being challenged in the courts and legislatures, and that had the long term effect of supporting unremitting legal actions by civil authorities.

By 2013, VOTF became more vocal, requesting that Pope Francis "act decisively"[58] on clerical abuse cases. Specifically, the organization called for Vatican action to hold three bishops accountable for failing to act on clerical sexual abuse: Archbishop John Myers of the Newark, New Jersey Archdiocese, retired Cardinal Roger Mahoney of the Los Angeles Archdiocese, and Bishop Robert Finn of Kansas City. To date, Archbishop Myers has not been removed from office, but has had a coadjutor named who will lead the diocese with him until he retires.

VOTF also sent requests for other long-term reforms to Rome in 2013 that it wanted the pope to consider.[59] Specifically it called for two actions that could have a bearing on canon law and in turn on US church-state relations. They were requests for disciplinary action for any bishop who covered up clergy sexual abuse, as well as accountability and transparency in Church financial matters.

Today, VOTF has several serious challenges. Organizationally, many members of the laity are simply leaving the Church rather than staying to try to reform it. The dwindling numbers of Catholic adherents, coupled with their increasing age, leaves VOTF in a state of creeping complacency. Establishing smaller groups might help to keep the organization relevant.[60]

Ideologically, VOTF also has problems, too. It cannot expect to have a decision-making voice within the Church infrastructure when its organization represents a challenge to the very foundations of the institution. VOTF's demands could bring about a weakened hierarchy, a fact that could portend a loss of Church influence and power within the civil state.

Politically, VOTF is also losing ground. It has tried to function as a special interest group advocating for the victims of clerical sexual abuse, but now it has pushed those interests to the back burner to advance its religious agenda for doctrinal reform. Thus, its involvement in the public arena has been severely compromised by its emphasis on religious reform rather than the compelling state interest to protect children. Such a change for institutional spiritual reform lessens its impact on the church-state dynamic: a pressure that could be used to effect great church-state cooperation on clerical sexual abuse.

Lay Responses to Clerical Sexual Abuse: bishop–accountability.org

The advent of technology has transformed the way that the Catholic hierarchy must deal with the laity. The people in the pews are most concerned with justice, reform, confidentiality, and accountability—while the bishops are still concerned with their own power to manage the clergy, enforce canon law, and lead the Church in its mission to teach, preach, and sanctify its adherents.

The hierarchy has done this for 2,000 years based on an autocratic leadership model shrouded in secrecy and justified by its own responsibility to protect the institution that is "the Church." This structure, however, has been shattered due to public access to the Internet and social media. Cyber advances, with their ability to go viral, have brought surprising internal, hierarchical practices to light—intricate, entrenched, fraternally-centered policies—former ways of acting that have been able to control civil access to ecclesiastical records and privileged policies.

The new technology has revealed the secret behavior and cover-ups of the hierarchy. It has been able to uncover and report this information to civil authorities and the general public through the effective use of web-based communications. The US hierarchy, however, has not been able to retool, respond, reform, and defend itself, as quickly as the laity has been able to report the Church's ineffectiveness to protect children, in spite of its zero tolerance policy.

The major technological organization that can be credited with creating an independent and objective openness within the secretive world of the bishops' authority is bishop-accountability.org. It was founded in 2003 by Terry McKiernan, who holds Master's degrees from the University of Wisconsin-Madison and the University of Bristol in England. The website is a nonprofit corporation that functions with a small staff. McKiernan is bishop-accountability's archivist. He curates all the information. Anne Barrett Doyle, who founded the Coalition of Catholics and Survivors in Boston, is the website's data analyst; she compares and assesses abuse statistics for bishop-accountability. The only other staff member is the website's treasurer, Ted O'Neill.

McKiernan has broadly defined the two missions of bishop-accountability. The first is to provide a full "account" of clerical sexual abuse from both individual and collective perspectives. To do this, his website has assembled and posts a "comprehensive archive"[61] of evidence. It claims that its archives contain over 45,000 documents just from records that were released as part of civil and criminal settlements.[62] They continue to grow daily.

Indeed, information has been gathered from a variety of sources: depositions, subpoenas, legal documents, financial settlements, newspaper reports, personal accounts, Vatican and diocesan directives/pronouncements, and Church records that have been required as part of legal remedies. SNAP now contends that bishop-accountability contains a total archive of over one million pages of information.

The second purpose of bishop-accountability.org is to hold bishops "accountable" for their improper handling of clerical sexual abuse. It is McKiernan's intent to encourage an informed public to demand indictments of bishops where possible and/or to bring about the removal of such bishops through requests to the pope to dismiss them. To provide information to the public, the website maintains a database of publicly accused priests, along with their pictures.

Bishop-accountability serves many different constituencies, and because it does, it has become the definitive source of information for the media, scholars, and lawyers seeking information related to clerical sexual abuse. It is, therefore, more than just a location for data. Some claim it is a technological step to truth. The use of its data is critical to those seeking to respond to clerical sexual abuse.

Just recently, bishop-accountability issued a report of its achievements in 2011. The statement gave insight into the kinds of things that the organization does besides collecting and providing information. First, it acts as an advocate for the release of diocesan information for its database of accused clerical abusers. It claims that its data "forced" Cardinal O'Malley of Boston to release the names of 159 accused priests, thus allowing its organization to link those names to a list of 276 former accused Boston priests and to a larger inventory of clerics released by 24 US bishops.[63]

This leads to its second purpose: to raise awareness about the scope of the problem of clerical sexual abuse. It compiles data, assesses it, and corrects claims of the bishops or others whose numbers or percentages are questionable. It posts links to documents, historical information, and reports. McKiernan is often invited to speak at major meetings of SNAP, VOTF, and other organizations. He is sought-after for media comments and commentary as well. Doyle works to get legislatures to extend statutes of limitations.

Third, bishop-accountability has moved into the international area, having provided the 20,000 pages of evidence in the case against the Vatican that was presented to the International Court at the Hague by SNAP. It has also begun to catalogue and provide information on the clerical sexual abuse cases that have been coming to light in Ireland.

Finally, bishop-accountability has also moved into the legal arena. In 2011, it acted as *amicus curiae*, along with SNAP, in a case of "ministerial privilege."[64] It joined with several other like-minded organizations to argue against a case that would have allowed religious organizations to make employment decisions regardless of civil laws, a policy which could have foreclosed discovery and litigation in cases brought by child sex abuse victims.

Opponents of bishop-accountability are rare, but do include some individuals who believe that the website has been unfair to accused priests. One group claims that "BishopAccountability.org profiles *countless* innocent priests on its site; so many, in fact, that the number of troubling examples could fill an entire book."[65] These accusations, however, have not been proven, nor do they undercut the important work of bishop-accountability. Its unique service to those seeking information to prosecute clerical sexual abusers and to bring about changes in the law, public policy, and Church administration remains unblemished.

Volunteer organizations, then, such as those profiled here, have opened the doors to assess the behaviors and policies of those who have, consciously or unconsciously, abetted the cover-up of clerical sexual abuse. They have done this by providing information, assuring greater hierarchical transparency, raising public awareness and entering into the legal forum. All of these actions have played a part in changing the church-state dynamic in the United States to one that is now victim-centered rather than one that is motivated by maintaining the balance of power between religious and civil power.

Legal Challenges to the Vatican and the Pope: The Tough Get Tougher

The church-state implications of Catholic clerical sexual abuse took on a more complex and ominous turn since a number of lawyers, such as Jeffrey Anderson, William McMurry, and others, decided to file suits against the government of the Vatican, referred to as the Holy See. These cases have challenged the Vatican state's sovereignty, the religious authority of the pope, his corporate responsibility and accountability, and the validity of canon law. The suits have tried to hold the pope himself, and other Church leaders, financially culpable for the clerical behavior of the Church's clergymen in sexual abuse allegations.

Indeed, the sexual abuse crisis has escalated and evolved into more aggressive, civil confrontations with the Holy See. This is a result of papal reticence to adjudicate such cases canonically, continuous Vatican confusion, and the clerical culture of confidentiality and superiority. As a result, these failures have added to growing church-state tensions, not just in the United States, but around the globe, posing a potentially increasing and more relevant challenge to the salvific social and political role of the Catholic Church in the secular world.

In the United States, especially, judicial claims have been made by sexual abuse victims demanding financial restitution from the Vatican as well as papal accountability for institutional inaction against accused abusive priests. After a decade of American clashes between canon and civil law,[66] two unique cases, *Doe v. Holy See*,[67] and *O'Bryan v. Holy See*,[68] worked their way through the US judicial system.

They challenged standard legal precedents, specifically a state's sovereign immunity, which under American law, allowed foreign states, such as the Vatican, to be exempt from certain types of civil suits. Now lawyers began to challenge whether or not such exclusions would apply to the crime of clerical sexual abuse, and whether or not they would apply to the Vatican.

Doe v. Holy See raised novel, but relevant, questions about the Vatican's financial liability in settling clerical molestation cases. It claimed that, as a state, the Vatican had legal and monetary obligations to victims of clerical sexual abuse since the institutional Church was the employer of pedophile priests.

O'Bryan v. Holy See brought suit for financial damages against the Holy See as well, but went further by petitioning the court for the right to depose leading Church personnel, including the pope, about the handling of clerical sexual abuse cases. Both cases reflected more assertive individual demands for greater civil and criminal accountability from the hierarchy and the governmental instrumentalities of the Holy See at the highest levels of the institutional Catholic Church.

A closer examination of the claims in *Doe v. Holy See* and *O'Bryan v. Holy See* raised a number of new church-state questions in the United States. At the national level, these included the secular, as well as the religious, responsibilities of Church leaders. Both cases challenged the Vatican's responsibility to manage its clerical personnel as well as its obligation to monitor the, often, negligent monitoring of alleged and *proven* perpetrators of sexual abuse. Indeed, these cases essentially asked if the obligations of a chief executive officer in a corporation were the same as, and applied to, both civil and ecclesiastical leaders in the same way.

More broadly, *Doe v. Holy See* and *O'Bryan v. Holy See* also challenged the nature of the immunity of the pope and the Vatican's diplomatic relations with the United States. They also raised legal problems about the financial liability of the Holy See in sexual abuse cases that occurred in the United States, a fact that continues to drive church-state tensions even to the present.

At the same time, such challenges also had the potential to lead to international monetary claims against the Vatican by victims from other countries. The possibility of global financial lawsuits has motivated the Holy See's lawyers in the United States to attack the legitimacy of American courts to adjudicate such claims against the Vatican. They also fuel the fear that financial clashes could compromise the moral integrity and political effectiveness of the papacy to bring the a moral dimension to the public policy debate.

These problems began to take shape in the early 2000s when the Sixth Circuit Court of Appeals, the Ninth Circuit Court of Appeals, and the US Supreme Court each handed down significant church-state rulings that resulted from cases dealing with Catholic clerical sexual abuse in the United States. Taken together, most of their decisions were narrow, but in some instances they overruled significant questions of authority and the immunity of the Vatican with regard to cases of clerical sexual abuse. In the process, however, the US courts also implicitly created tensions in American-Vatican relations as well.

Doe v. Holy See was a case brought before the courts in Oregon in 2002, a legal battle that lasted for a little more than a decade. Jeffrey Anderson, a lawyer from St. Paul who had previously sued thousands of Catholic priests, bishops and diocese over sexual abuse since 1983, brought the case. Among his most famous legal victories was his ability to obtain justice for the victims of Father James Porter in Boston in the 1990s.

By 2002, the newspapers and other media were continually reporting about his cases and his firm, Jeff Anderson and Associates. Its website clearly stated Anderson's view: that the firm doesn't just handle clients, but empowers survivors and reaches across time and the nation for justice.

As a lawyer, Anderson was motivated by this pragmatic philosophy. In newspaper articles, he was reported to have won around $60 million in settlements before taking on the case of *Doe v. Holy See*. But, it was his personal background that seemed to influence his approach to the case. Having become both an alcoholic and an atheist earlier in his life, Anderson rediscovered God while going though the recovery process in AA. He also had to deal with his adult daughter's revelation that she had been molested by a therapist as a child. The therapist had been a former Catholic priest.

Anderson admits to being driven, obsessed, and even manic about his work, but claims that his commitment to victims of clerical sexual abuse has nothing to do with Catholic theology or the Church. Instead, he says that it "has everything to do with what they're doing to kids."[69] In an interview with the *Huffington Post*, Andersen explained his evolution to a champion of the abused, then to a litigator against the Vatican, by saying that he "came to the stark realization that the problems were really endemic to the clerical culture, and all the problems we are having in the US led back to Rome…I realized nothing was going to fundamentally change until they did."[70] It is clear why Anderson would want to be involved in the case of *Doe v. Holy See*.

It arose from an individual allegation of clerical sexual abuse against a priest, Father Andrew Ronan. A member of the Order of the Friars Servants, Ronan was accused of molestation while serving at St. Albert's parish in the Archdiocese of Portland. Members of the parish were kept in the dark about the fact that Ronan had been accused of sexual abuse earlier and that he had been reassigned from Ireland to Chicago and, ultimately, to Portland.

The molestation accusations raised in *Doe v. Holy See* were similar to those in earlier cases, but these allegations were different because the suit was filed against the Vatican's governmental structure, the Holy See. It claimed that several sections of the Foreign Service Immunities Act (FSIA) could be used to challenge the Vatican and serve as the basis for the plaintiff's liability claims against the Holy See.

The case hinged on two legal principles within the FSIA: "vicarious liability" and "superior liability." Both held that sovereign states were responsible for the decisions of their instrumentalities and their domestic corporations abroad. Andersen argued that the Vatican should be held to the same standard. Part of these corporations and instrumentalities, he argued, essentially included the canonical decision of the archbishop of Portland, the incorporated "diocese" of Portland, the bishop of Chicago, and the Order of Friars Servants.

At the same time, lawyers for Doe argued that the principle of "superior liability" also applied in this case. It meant that states also had responsibility for the actions of their employees, as well as the obligation to warn individuals who came in contact with them if there were some kind of a problem. Andersen wanted the same principle to apply to the Vatican. He claimed that "superior liability" specifically applied to the reassignments of Ronan; parishioners should have been told about the former sexual allegations made against him and his "dangerous proclivities."[71]

The plaintiff in *Doe v. Holy See* brought suit against the Holy See, then, based on the "vicarious" and "superior" liability responsibilities established in FSIA. These arguments were countered by Church lawyers claiming an exemption defense. They argued that the Vatican, as both a sovereign and religious entity, was released from financial responsibility for the actions of its clergymen.

But Anderson and the other lawyers for Doe found two more points in FSIA to further their lawsuit based on vicarious and superior liability.

One was based on a "commercial activity exemption"[72] in FSIA. It makes a state responsible for an illegal act committed in the course of its commercial conduct or transactions abroad. And the second was an "injurious activity exemption."[73] This held a state responsible for the commission of an illegal act that occurred within the scope of a civil employee's job. Andersen argued that both applied to the Vatican regarding its spiritual work and those who carried it out globally.

The purpose of the Church's argument, of course, was to try to negate the liability implications of the suit. The financial settlements could be catastrophic. The lawyers for the Church, however, were thwarted when the district court accepted the argument of Doe's lawyers and ruled the Vatican responsible for the criminal actions of its priests.

After hearing the entire case, the district court made two critical rulings. First, it held that the commercial and tort exceptions in FSIA were unclear.[74] This left open the possibility of further litigation over whether or not an injurious act was committed within the scope of Ronan's employment. Second, in the absence of a federal precedent, the federal court turned to Oregon law and required Doe to prove that the sexual abuse by the prelate, Ronan, was committed within his duties as a priest. By ruling so broadly on this last point, the court allowed the case to go forward. No matter what its outcome, it was a ruling that implicitly upheld the plaintiff's right to challenge the financial liability, as well as the sovereign immunity exemption, of the Holy See in the matter of sexual abuse lawsuits.

At this point, the Vatican quickly appealed the case to a higher court, the Ninth Circuit Court of Appeals. The Church's lawyers argued two points. First, they claimed that the tort, or injurious, exceptions did not apply to the FSIA statute because the Holy See could not be sued for the day-to-day activities of each of its countless instrumentalities and personnel. The court ruled broadly in the Church's favor on this point. The justices of the Ninth Circuit concluded that the Holy See could not be sued for the daily work of the Archdiocese of Portland, the bishop of Chicago, or the Order of Friars Servants. And it went further: it ruled that Doe could not prove that any of them were inherently connected to the Vatican's governmental instrumentalities.

Second, the Church's lawyers argued that the Holy See was not responsible for "superior liability." On this point, the Ninth Circuit agreed with two lower court rulings. It held that Ronan was an employee of the Holy See who was acting within the scope of his employment under state law.[75] The court maintained that Ronan's pastoral duties were a "necessary precursor" and a "direct outgrowth" of conduct within the scope of his employment.[76] Consequently, Ronan's alleged molestation of Doe was considered to fall within the jurisdictional purview of the Holy See. The case was allowed to proceed.

Thus, by upholding Doe's liability claim, the Ninth Circuit also essentially *restricted* the Holy See's sovereign immunity in the United States. It limited the Vatican's liability exemptions by allowing suits to be brought in sexual abuse claims.

The Ninth Circuit also sent the case back to the district level for remand. That is, it wanted the lower court to reconsider whether or not FSIA preserves the right of sovereign immunity when discretionary acts,[77] or acts that are not part of a specific and mandatory policy, are carried out by employees. These would include acts such as molestation that could fall within the FSIA's tort exemption.

As soon as the decision to remand was handed down, the Church's lawyers recognized the foreign policy implications of the case and filed[78] for *certiorari,* or a motion requesting the views of the solicitor general of the United States. They even went further, and appealed to the US Supreme Court to grant the Church's petition against the removal of the Holy See's immunity in clerical sexual abuse cases.

Filing an *amicus* brief, the solicitor general agreed with the Church attorneys. He argued that *certiorari* should be granted: that the Court should vacate the judgment of the Ninth Circuit Court of Appeals, and send back the tort exception ruling for further consideration.

The government argued three points. First, it maintained that the Ninth Circuit erred in holding that Doe's claim fell within the FSIA's tort exception. Instead, the solicitor general maintained that injurious torts, such as sexual abuse, did not come within, or as a result of, the priest's (Ronan) scope of employment.[79]

Second, the government argued that the Ninth Circuit also erred by conflating the scope of employment inquiry with the question of superior liability in this case. It argued that to expand FSIA jurisdiction over claims against a foreign sovereign in this way should not apply without sufficient proof that the tort was within the scope of Ronan's employment.[80]

And third, the government contended that the Supreme Court should remand *Doe v. Holy See* for further consideration. It maintained that the question about whether or not the district court actually had jurisdiction over the vicarious liability claim under the FSIA's tort exception should be explored further.

Technically, then, the Obama administration sided with the Vatican on the matter of liability. However, in a surprising move, the Supreme Court did not accept all the arguments of the solicitor general. It declined to review the Vatican appeal to dismiss the lawsuit and returned part of the decision to the Ninth Circuit Court for remand. By its refusal to do this, the highest court in the United States also allowed the claim to limit the sovereign immunity of the Vatican, specifically in cases dealing with sexual molestation. At that point, it looked as though the lower court would rule in favor of Doe.

In 2012, however, the Ninth Circuit finally handed down a decision[81] that partially affirmed, reversed, and remanded claims of the original law suit. It held that Doe was not able to prove that the actions, obligations and liabilities of domestic corporations were attributable to the Holy See. It also held that the district court did not have jurisdiction over the Holy See for torts that might have been committed in the Archdiocese of Chicago, the Archdiocese of Portland, or by Ronan's order.

It did hold that there was no employer-employee relationship between Ronan and the Holy See. In fact, the Court even refused to accept the argument that the Vatican knew about his molestation of children for years before the priest was laicized. Under Oregon law, though, Ronan still could be considered an "employee" of the Vatican who acted within the scope of his employment. Therefore, the Holy See could financially be held liable for Ronan's actions under a discretionary exclusion. That holding left the door open for further litigation.

The court also ruled that there was no policy promulgated by the Holy See to cover up incidents of child abuse. It maintained that as a result of a lack of such evidence, it would not decide far-reaching questions on a nonexistent factual record.

Doe v. Holy See, and its potential impact on major legal, financial, and diplomatic implications for individuals seeking redress in sexual molestation cases against the Vatican State and its government instrumentalities, came to a close with a loss for its plaintiffs. The decision in the case failed to hold Church leaders or its government actors responsible for clerical sexual abuse. Soon after, Anderson responded that he was saddened by the decision and that he would appeal.

At the present, it is hard to know if individual suits against the Holy See, like the one in *Doe vs. Holy See*, will continue or will be successful, considering the legal requirements that have been set in this case to prove liability and complicity over sovereign immunity. Although the scales appear to be tilting toward the maintenance of international legal precedents involving the Vatican so far, there is no way of telling if other anticipated permissible claims against the Holy See will escalate. But, the possibility of major monetary pay-outs still exists, as does the spectre of the Church's limited ability to carry out its religious mission around the world.

Most importantly, however, is the fact that the results in this case maintained the sovereign immunity of Vatican leaders. The larger implication of *Doe v. Holy See* was that it erased possible challenges to the behaviors and actions of other sovereign leaders and members of their diplomatic services. The practice of recall and/or being declared a *persona non grata* for illegal acts might certainly have had to be reconsidered if Vatican sovereign immunity became a test case of exemptions in certain types of criminal behavior.

Nevertheless, other lawsuits, like those following the claims in *Doe v. Holy See*, had the distinct possibility of bringing the true implications of molestation and other crimes to the attention of those at the highest levels of the Catholic Church and other sovereign leaders after the case. In 2013, after a number of hearings and rehearing, the US District Court for the Ninth Circuit dismissed the final appeal in *Doe v. Holy See*. It was not the result of any settlement between the two parties to the legal challenge, but rather a decision made after the voluntary request of Anderson, the plaintiff's lawyer.

In a reaction to the end of the case, the Church's lawyer summed up the Holy See's view. He said the case was dropped because it was based on the erroneous fact that all priests are controlled by the Holy See. He emphasized for the record that the Church was not engaged in "commercial activity," that it was different from a large corporation, and that the pope was not simply its chief executive officer.[82] But, regardless of such a statement, it is possible to conclude that due to *Doe v. Holy See*, the Church also faced a critical challenge to its financial responsibility and managerial processes.

A second case, *O'Bryan v. Holy See*, also tested the legal and monetary responsibilities of those in the Vatican in 2004. Rather than argue for vicarious or superior liability as in the Doe case, this suit was based on the right of individuals to demand the deposition of high Vatican officials.

Three plaintiffs from Kentucky claimed that they were abused by members of the Catholic clergy. What made their case significant was the fact that an American district court allowed the plaintiffs to file their complaint against the Holy See, acting as a sovereign state, rather than simply against an accused priest,[83] or the legal corporation known as the "diocese,"[84] or its corporate head, "the bishop."

The context of the times, and the fact that other cases were emerging allowed the lawyer in the case to question what role the Vatican government (Holy See) played in allowing bishops to cover up sexual abuse. Even more importantly, the plaintiffs were also given permission to demand restitution from the Vatican if confidentiality was part of an official policy for a financial settlement.[85]

In response to this lawsuit, lawyers for the Holy See filed motions to dismiss the charges. They argued that as a sovereign state, the Vatican could not be sued in a district court based on exemptions, like the vicarious and superior exceptions in the FSIA.[86] So, they took the case to a higher court, the Sixth Circuit Court of Appeals.

At this point, however, O'Bryan and his fellow plaintiffs, took a different tack and requested that the Circuit Court give them the right to depose Benedict XVI, the sitting pope, and other high-ranking members of the Vatican hierarchy,[87] about matters of clerical sexual abuse. They contended that the officials' testimonies were critical to gathering information about their allegations against predator priests.

The plaintiffs from Kentucky argued that the pope, as the former head of the Vatican office known as the Congregation of the Doctrine of the Faith (CDF), which oversees sexual abuse matters, had the most extensive knowledge about molestation cases in the Vatican. They argued that in his position, he continued to maintain the system of complete secrecy about such issues, and that he best understood the policies and procedures of the Holy See during the duration of his leadership of the CDF and as pope. They also claimed that they had evidence of this, and that they possessed a number of documents that "directly implicate[d] Pope Benedict XVI's involvement in the Holy See's decision to cast a shroud of secrecy over clerical sexual abuse cases in the United States."[88]

O'Bryan's lawyers argued, then, that taking depositions from Vatican officials would illustrate the Holy See's extensive control over clergy in the United States. They believed they would be able to show the Vatican government's policy of mandated secrecy in known or suspected instances of child abuse, the lack of papal prosecution of accused clergy, and the Holy See's support of actions to protect the reputation of the church.

As a result of these arguments, the Circuit Court ruled that the plaintiffs could proceed with their case against the Vatican ecclesiastical authority.

Also, no longer constrained by the appeals process, the lower district court, in a stunning decision, approved the plaintiffs' earlier motion to depose Pope Benedict and other high-ranking Vatican officials. It claimed that the Pontiff "should be made to answer the most unfortunate question as to why children have been left vulnerable to avoid scandal."[89]

These decisions were unprecedented in American church-state relations. They raised questions about the scope of US subpoena powers, the definition of sovereign and diplomatic immunity, and the right of the state to require testimony from a head of state.

Lawyers for the plaintiffs in *O'Bryan v. Holy See* also sought copies of communications between the Vatican and all its US bishops related to sexual abuse issues. These included more than 3,300 cases going back as far as 90 years.[90]

In 2010, however, O'Bryan's lawyers dropped their civil lawsuit against the Holy See in American courts. They said it was for practical, rather than legal reasons. The attorneys claimed that to challenge the Vatican's sovereign immunity and to demand financial restitution would have required them to mount a major class action suit. It would have necessitated them getting thousands of victims to join in allegations against every US bishop and proving that each one acted as an agent of the Holy See. As a result, they were unable to prove the Vatican's financial liability for negligent American hierarchical supervision of abuser priests.

Thus, the case that sought to hold the Vatican financially culpable and responsible for the day-to-day management of all clergy was dropped. Although it failed to legally demand monetary restitution from the Holy See, the case was able to raise greater awareness about the internal workings and policies of the Catholic leadership in Rome. It shed light on ecclesiastical management and the pope's relationship to the hierarchy.

In a larger sense, *O'Bryan v. Holy See* raised significant church-state challenges as well. It provided a review of US policies regarding sovereign immunity, liabilities, and exemptions. These were critical to a deeper understanding of US diplomatic relations with states as independent and corporate actors in the international arena.

Later, another case also made demands for depositions from Vatican officials as well. It began in 2010 when the *New York Times* broke the story that the pope at the time, Benedict XVI, former head of the CDF and investigation of clerical sexual abuse, had not investigated allegations against a defrocked priest, Father Lawrence Murphy. These claims had been reported through ecclesiastical channels and advanced by

Archbishop Rembert Weakland of Milwaukee, the leader of the diocese at the time and his successor, the now-famous Cardinal Archbishop of New York, Timothy Dolan.

The accusers contended that Murphy had abused as many as 200 deaf children. They maintained that these molestations had occurred when the priest was chaplin at St. John's School for the Deaf in Milwaukee, but that no ecclesiastical action had been taken against him. The Vatican responded officially about the case by saying that the CDF "was not informed of the matter until some twenty years later."[91]

This case gained significant traction, however, when the Archdiocese of Milwaukee filed for bankruptcy in 2011. At that time, it revealed that it was expecting a huge number of lawsuits, possibly as many as 570 claims of clerical sexual abuse. Some dated as far back as 70 years, and a large number included allegations against Murphy. The plaintiffs who were seeking financial redress were being handled by Jeffery Anderson.

The Church claimed that it could not afford to pay the monetary claims of all the victims. The archdiocese contended that to do so would require it to use its financial resources as its donors had not intended. It argued that it had to carry on the essential ministries of the Church to meet the needs of its parishes, parishioners, and others who relied on Church services—as well as to use its monies to settle abuse claims. It could not afford to do both and remain solvent. Thus, it had to declare bankruptcy.

As part of its reorganization plan, the federal bankruptcy court required the Archdiocese of Milwaukee to provide the records and personnel files of 42 priests with credible claims of abuse. They also had to participate in the depositions of top church officials and to post the information on the Church's website.

Part of the correspondence that the archdiocese had to disclose revealed that the Holy See protected its abuser priests and did not report them to civil authorities. The Associated Press was able to obtain documents that showed that Benedict XVI had been recalcitrant, at best, about disciplining abusive priests.

In 2012, however, Anderson also quietly dropped this lawsuit against the Vatican. No specific reason was given. Some accused him of just seeking publicity in his earlier suit, but others said that his persistence and presence brought significant media attention to the sexual abuse perpetrated by Murphy.

In 2012, the case was made into a documentary in by Alex Gibney and entitled *Mea Maxima Culpa: Silence in the House of God*. Even though the

Murphy case never ended in a legal settlement against the Vatican, the media and the court of public opinion provided a significant forum to discuss the issues surrounding the case and the actions of other predator priests in the United States.

With these expanding and continuing state attempts to break through the walls of Vatican confidentiality, Church lawyers argued intensely that deposing Vatican officials is similar to compelling the testimony of the president of the United States and other high-ranking members of the US government. They also challenged the right of the US government to make civil and criminal demands on the leader of over one billion religious adherents.

Thus far, the pope, as a sovereign ruler is, in reality, still immune from American subpoenas and laws. To subject him to the jurisdiction of US federal or state courts is highly unlikely since reciprocal diplomatic courtesy has traditionally been the type of American political treatment afforded to foreign rulers. Indeed, the very act of serving a subpoena to the pope or even members of his inner ruling circle in the Vatican on US soil would be difficult, if not impossible, to perform, given the security that surrounds the hierarchical individuals.

The most significant result of these attempts, though, has been the indictment of the pope and the Church leadership in the media and the court of public opinion. This is often a more fatal arena for accusations and convictions within society. Such a blow, in the long term could seriously discredit the moral credibility, social justice work, and even the salfivic mission of the Church in the future.

Accusations and Responses of Pope Benedict and the Holy See

The escalation of suits against the highest levels of leadership in the Vatican also took on international proportions in March 2010, when the German press reported that the archbishop of Munich, the future Pope Benedict XVI, was made aware of a request from the Diocese of Essen to transfer a clerical sexual abuser to his diocese in Munich. This occurred in 1979 at a weekly meeting where the future pope approved the transfer, and was later reminded about the reassignment in a memo. The priest was returned to pastoral work within "days of beginning psychiatric treatment" and "later convicted of molesting boys in another parish."[92]

Reports of this incident and other stories in the German press generated a media indictment of Benedict XVI internationally, raising questions about his culpability and mishandling of sexual abuse cases prior to his election to the papacy in 2005.

Known as Joseph Cardinal Ratzinger before his accession to the papacy, Benedict XVI had been a Vatican insider since his appointment as head of the CDF in 1981 by his predecessor, Pope John Paul II. In that position, Ratzinger was tasked with examining and ruling on questions of religious orthodoxy for the entire Catholic Church. For example, he was empowered to inquire into the teachings of liberation theologians in Latin America, to silence them if necessary, and to condemn their theological positions—which he did.

The CDF also had authority over specific types of sexual abuse cases, a right that had been given to it since 1922 and reiterated in 1962. For the "two decades [Ratzinger] was in charge of that office," his opponents argued, "the future pope never asserted that authority, failing to act even as the cases undermined the church's credibility in the United States, Australia, Ireland and elsewhere."[93]

Benedict's supporters, on the other hand, argued that he was following standard canonical procedures during his tenure as Archbishop of Munich. According to the Vatican, what is misunderstood about the 1962 addendum to canon law on grave sins,[94] is that it only dealt with crimes against religious mandates, that is, *liturgical offenses,* rather than with broader violations of civil law.

For example, a section called "*Crimen Solicitationis*" in the 1962 addendum narrowly applied to crimes of solicitation that banned priests from trying to solicit sex during confession, an act that carried the penalty of excommunication. Such *canonical* crimes were to be reported in strict confidence to the CDF, but led to confusion among some canonists who interpreted the 1962 document to mean that church officials were also barred from contacting civil authorities with allegations of other charges of sex abuse against clerics in the church.[95]

Thus, as this convoluted misinformation came to light, widespread confusion among members of the hierarchy as to how to deal with cases of sexual abuse was also revealed. Some cases were reportedly sent to the CDF, and various other congregations or Church offices, as well as to the leadership at the Secretariat of State, the Court of Aposotolic Signatura, and the Pontifical Council for Legislative Tests.

This loose chain of command was further complicated by the misunderstood 1962 policy and the new Code of Canon Law that was issued in 1983. The latter set a five-year statute of limitations for canonical prosecution of accusations of clerical sexual abuse. Some bishops, nevertheless, allowed as much time as necessary to carry out a full canonical trial before dismissing a cleric from the priesthood. Coupled with criminal and civil laws in their respective countries and dioceses, many members of the hierarchy appeared to be confused, as well as conflicted, as to how to deal with predator priests—as criminals, or sinners, or both?

Thus, the Holy See in general and various popes specifically appear to have followed the standard operating canonical procedures as they understood them. As a result, they maintained and enforced what now appear to be inaccurate policies and clandestine practices. In the process, they also managed to essentially thwart the legal processes in the civil states where legal prosecutions were occurring, especially by making demands for the primacy of a confused code of canon law in a number of countries.

Reactions to these Church explanations of misunderstood canonical procedures and policies in US government inquiries have escalated in a number of other countries. For example, the summer of 2010 saw a "bold and provocative"[96] attack by Belgian authorities seeking information about Catholic clerical sexual abuse.

In the spring of 2010, the bishop of Bruges, Roger Vangheluwe, resigned after having admitted that he abused "a boy in my close entourage,"[97] a young man who turned out to be his own nephew. Reportedly, "hundreds of such claims"[98] against Belgian clerics quickly emerged after that admission, with the result that there was a general mistrust of an official, decade-old internal Church inquiry into sexual abuse. Leading to growing pressures on civil authorities, state officials pursued alleged hidden files and records related to molestations.

During a monthly meeting of the Belgian Bishops Conference, held at the official residence of the archbishop of Mechelen-Brussels, Belgian authorities entered the building and detained members of the Church hierarchy. The bishops were held for nine hours and questioned while authorities searched the premises. More than two truckloads of documents were seized, while at the same time, police confiscated computers at the Louvain office of the head of the Church committee investigating abuse. Government agents also seized materials from a ranking cardinal, and even drilled into the tombs of two deceased cardinals in the Brussels Cathedral, looking for possible hidden information.

In Belgium, the Church has no legal protections from such actions. Church property is usually owned by municipalities, priests are often paid by the government, and the church receives a tax exemption. But coupled with a formal accusation by the former president of the Church commission inquiring into sexual abuse that the church was hiding information, Belgian authorities felt justified in taking the actions they did. Indeed, these raids were clearly indicative of the fact that the Church would receive the same treatment as other organizations being investigated for alleged illegal activities.

Church reactions to the civil raids ranged from disbelief to resignation to outrage. The Belgian bishops issued an immediate statement opposing the seizures of the records of the Church commission of inquiry and the denial of victims' privacy rights in sexual abuse cases. Further, they addressed fears of potential breaches of confidentiality.[99] The head of the Church commission investigating sexual abuse said that he was "appalled" by the raid and felt that it reflected a growing "paranoia" within Belgium.[100] Four days later, he resigned.

The Vatican, in an official communiqué a day later, surprisingly acceded to the raid. The Holy See remarked, "It was not an agreeable experience, but everything was carried out correctly.[101] Then, in a complete turnabout 24 hours later, Cardinal Tarcisio Bertone, the Vatican secretary of state, called the detention of the bishops "serious and unbelievable."[102] Two days later, on a Sunday, Pope Benedict used his political and pastoral positions to make a serious statement, saying that the Belgian government's action was "surprising and deplorable," calling on civil authorities to respect both civil and canon law in their "reciprocal specificity and autonomy."[103]

As head of the Vatican, the pope stressed the need for Church autonomy to carry out its own investigations into clerical sexual abuse. As leader of the institutional Church, he expressed his solidarity with the Belgian clergy and hierarchy.

Tensions between the Vatican and the Belgian government continue to exist. The government is comparing the records it seized from the Church with those from the official inquiry commission. Its purpose is to evaluate whether or not there is a need for ecclesiastical secrecy and confidentiality to protect victims and their alleged molesters. Whatever the outcome, however, the relationship between church and state in

Belgium has been severely compromised, creating a situation in which Church credibility has been damaged. Indeed, the chief member of the Belgian hierarchy admitted that the persistent accusations of abuse show that "the reputation of church leaders was given a higher priority than that of abused children,"[104] leading lay Catholics to question Church authority.

In Ireland, a similar situation of mistrust exists. A series of inquiries into clerical sexual abuse began during the 1990s after a number of radio programs and media documentaries began to examine the predatory behavior of priests as well as nuns. They shocked the nation, and in response, the Irish Child Abuse Commission was officially established by the government in 2000. Subsequently, it carried out a nine-year investigation of clerical sexual abuse and issued a 2,600 page document,[105] popularly known as the Ryan Report. It revealed information that covered a period of more than 70 years, and produced data that officially recognized over 14,000 sexual abuse victims of priests and nuns.[106] Many of the abusers, prelates in a number of different religious orders, could not be identified, however, because of a right-to-privacy lawsuit that the Christian Brothers had won previously in the Irish courts during the hearings.

Nevertheless, the Ryan report exposed government and Church collusion in "perpetrating an abusive system"[107] of treatment toward children. It identified 18 orders of religious who were the perpetrators of such crimes, and it singled out the Irish Department of Education for its ineffective inspections and for allowing religious schools to essentially become workhouses.

The Irish government moved quickly to accept responsibility for what had gone unnoticed and/or unreported in most of its social service agencies and schools during the early part of the twentieth century. Apologizing for failing to intervene in sexual and other types of physical abuse cases, the Irish government officials at the time promised to reform Ireland's social services for children and filed motions against religious orders for criminal investigations.

The official Church, however, moved more slowly. Five years into the Ryan hearings, and without any real, official reforms put in place by the Irish hierarchy, another government investigation into sexual abuse allegations was carried out in the Diocese of Ferns. A report presented to the Irish Minister for Health and Children in 2006, recorded over 100 abuse accusations between 1996 and 2005 in that diocese,[108] and followed with a statement from the Bishop of Ferns citing his concerns, regrets, and prayers.

Pope Benedict expressed his "personal anguish and horror,"[109] as well, but he did not call for the criminal punishment of the alleged sexual abuse perpetrators. In fact, even after the publication of the second inquiry and the Irish government's issuance of the official Ryan Report in 2009, little was done in terms of clerical punishment. When four Irish bishops offered to resign their positions, and the heads of religious orders apologized, the Vatican accepted only one hierarchical resignation.[110] Instead, the pope called the Irish hierarchy to Rome, and after due consultation, issued a letter to the people of Ireland[111] in which he admitted that the victims of abuse had been betrayed, that their dignity was violated, and that no one had listened to them. "I openly express the shame and remorse that we all feel," he wrote to those who had been abused; to their abuser priests he said, "You betrayed the trust that was placed in you by innocent young people and their parents, and you must answer for it before Almighty God and before properly constituted tribunals."[112]

The pope, however, still did not accept the fact that Roman Catholic leaders should be disciplined by civil authorities for their negligence or their disregard for punishing those clerics who were involved in sexual abuse. Instead, when the pope apologized for their actions, he reiterated the Church's views that the contributing factors to clerical sexual abuse were "inadequate," "insufficient" and showed "misplaced concern for the reputation of the church...resulting in failure to apply existing canonical penalties" and safeguards.[113]

Even these statements could not justify papal inaction to recommend criminal prosecution for those responsible for sexual abuse. Nor could they excuse the lack of Vatican transparency and the need for a complete overhaul of the institutional Church infrastructure in Ireland. In 2009, another investigation occurred that looked into clerical sexual abuse in the Diocese of Dublin.

Eventually, as such inquiries increased, the pope did send a high-level Church delegation to Ireland to investigate the problem of clerical sexual abuse in a number of unnamed dioceses. The team promised that it would not interfere with civil officials or commissions in their investigations of clerical sexual abuse and a "widespread cover-up."[114]

One of the immediate church-state consequences of the government investigation in Ireland, however, was a dispute over the Church's compensation of victims of clerical sexual abuse. A number of leaders of the orders of priests and nuns met with members of the government in 2002, prior to the completion of the Ferns Report and the Ryan Report, and made a deal[115] with government representatives to settle financially with an uncertain number of victims. But as the list of the sexually abused continued to escalate, it became clear that the orders would end up paying only approximately 10% of the total cost of their settlements.

Indeed, some in the media reported that the government might have had to force the organizations of priests and nuns to make payments and ensure that compensation was given even to the point of "forcibly divesting them of properties."[116] Such a turn of financial events had the potential to pit the government against the Church, specifically as civil authorities demanded records of real estate holdings and insisted on other files that had previously been considered as ecclesiastically privileged. Further, disputes over settlements also had the potential to bring challenges by parishioners against the hierarchy about the ownership of Church buildings, schools, and other properties as well, thus bringing further state involvement into Church affairs.[117]

Questions have also arisen about the line between Vatican secrecy and the civil judicial process in Ireland. The press has reported that a 2001 clerical abuse directive issued by Benedict before he was pope, deepened confusion over the reporting processes established in the 1983 Code of Canon Law.

After becoming pope in 2005, Benedict's views appeared to have changed. Originally, as head of the CDF, Benedict directed bishops to send clerical abuse cases directly to his office, "even if a hint" of sexual abuse existed."[118] But as pope, he did nothing officially to move systematically beyond reporting and investigating such cases within the canonical infrastructure as well as the civil legal processes.

While these financial and political stories continue to unfold in the United States, Canada, Italy, Australia, Austria, Germany, and much of Western Europe, the political implications for the Catholic Church become more ominous. In order to deal with them, new clerical sexual abuse guidelines[119] were issued in July 2010 on Pope Benedict's watch. They were an attempt to clarify and, in some instances, revise canon law on the issue. They gave broader powers to Church authorities, specifically the CDF, when dealing with cases of molestation.

First, the substantive "Norms" that deal with *delicta graviora*,"[120] or grave crimes against the Church, were streamlined. In Article I, they make clear that the CDF is the only congregation to which cases against the sixth commandment are to be directed, and that it is the single office that can impose canonical sanctions. Second, the guidelines included new crimes, including predatory behavior against a minor below the age of eighteen, and perversions against "a person who habitually lacks the use of reason;" as well as the "acquisition, possession or distribution" of child pornography. Third, they also allowed allegations to be made as long as 20 years after an individual has reached his eighteenth birthday.[121] Conspicuous by its absence, however, was the lack of a canonical requirement to report predatory priestly behavior to civil authorities, thus leaving open the possibility of further church-state disputes over confidentiality, ecclesiastical records, clerical punishment, and financial liability.

The significance of these guideline changes, in the short term, reflected a more nuanced, *canonical,* Vatican explanation of existing sexual abuse policy, an attempt to clarify earlier confusion, and to provide some transparency. But what they appeared to do, in reality, was to equivocate on the criminal culpability of priests involved in sexual molestation and the authority of the state to deal with them.

Finally, in 2011, pushed by so many aggressive reactions to clerical sexual abuse by civil authorities around the world, the Vatican announced a new set of non-canonical guidelines to deal with the escalating problem. Designed by the CDF to assist bishops around the world in the development of a more systemized way of dealing with molestations, it called for spiritual and psychological assistance to the parents and families of victims, education and protection to provide safe environments for minors, and better development of priests and religious. Most importantly, however, from a church-state perspective, these guidelines also called for cooperation with civil authorities.

The CDF, for the first time, officially and clearly pointed out that the "Sexual abuse of minors is not just a canonical 'delict' but also a crime prosecuted by civil law. Although relations with civil authority will differ in various countries, nevertheless it is important to cooperate with such authority within their [bishops] responsibilities."[122] The CDF said in plain language that civil laws regarding the reporting of such crimes "should always be followed."[123]

The newly clarified, systematized guidelines provided a positive direction with which to deal with clerical sexual abuse. That said, however, the Vatican must still recognize the potential challenges to its financial liability in significant lawsuits against the Holy See from the United States and other countries. It must accept the possibility of a significant erosion of the sovereign immunity status of the Vatican in the future, and recognize possible further forceful state remedies to deal with escalating civil and criminal cases against the Holy See and the pope. In fact, some commentators argue that the denials of the Vatican under Benedict did "damage [to] Benedict's central goals of fortifying the church and fighting secularism in Europe."[124]

Indeed, it is possible to argue that increasing intrusions by civil authorities into Church affairs will necessarily reposition the relationship between church and state in reality, and ultimately erode the power of the Church in a variety of countries in the future. New international responses to clerical sexual abuse are an aggressive way to make the Vatican recognize, even if only canonically, that the compelling interest of the state to protect children from predators, both lay and clerical will prevail, regardless of what kind of ecclesiastical defenses or privileges the Church might claim, expect, or even demand.

An examination of the widening breach between canonical and civil responses to clerical sexual abuse shows that the days of the Catholic Church as a favored, "accommodated," or even tolerated interest within many countries is quickly coming to an end. This cataclysmic change, yet to be fully recognized or understood by the Holy See, portends the possible end of the Vatican's secret infrastructure, its management system, and its eroding social agenda. Indeed, the clerical sexual abuse tragedy also represents a potential end to the Vatican's ability to seize the moral high ground and have an impact on creating a more transcendent politics based on its social and charitable agenda and salvific mission

Closer to home, judicial challenges to canon law and the Vatican's administration of Church affairs by both lay organizations and aggressive lawyers also represent the increasing possibility of a split between the laity and the hierarchy in the United States. These phenomena necessarily raise inherently divisive choices, options that are exacerbated by the need for many members of the faithful to choose between obedience to the pope and the bishops versus the demands of their own individual consciences.

Can the new pope, Francis I, change this entire paradigm?

6
From Crisis to Power Shift and the Future

This book has examined the challenges, and ultimate power shift, in Catholic church-state relations in America, a result of clerical sexual abuse revelations over the last decade and a half. Traditionally, religion and government, as the two critical institutions in this country, have maintained a tenuous balance of power between the sacred and the secular. However, in the series of battles that ensued over priestly molestations and that have affected certain aspects of church-state relations, a different political rapport now exists: the state has tipped the scales and gained the upper hand in its relationship with the Catholic Church.

Now attorneys general, grand juries, judges, and lawyers have replaced the authority of Church officials. They have done this by legally obtaining civil control over the management of the clergy and certain institutional financial matters. Both of these areas have traditionally been held to be outside the purview of state control and treated, instead, as being within the Church's sphere of ecclesiastical authority.

Gaining greater secular control over religious power has been justified by civil authorities due to the fact that the state must deal with the heinous crimes perpetrated by priests on prepubescent children and teenagers. They claim that the state must do it because Church officials have not been able, or willing, to do it themselves. As a result, civil authorities have used the courts to gain the legal ability to investigate, monitor, sue, and prosecute members of the hierarchy, their "dioceses," and clerics. The right to do this, according to court precedent, has been justified by the compelling state interest of the government to protect children. Civil authorities recognize this as one of their primary responsibilities—to safeguard young people from the reprehensible acts of priests as well as the negligent and conscious hierarchical cover-ups of such predatory behavior carried out in the past and present.

The issue of clerical sexual abuse, then, has served as the battleground for a grand power struggle between both the leadership of the Catholic Church and US civil authorities. The bishops claim that they have the sole right to deal with matters within their ecclesiastical sphere of influence—particularly the treatment of its clergy and the administration of Church financial affairs. States argue that they have a compelling interest to protect children, a concern so critical that it overrides all Church authority in internal matters.

Both argue that their responsibilities and duties to those within their care require as much freedom as possible. The Church maintains the need for autonomy to assure its religious and social missions. The government claims the same right to meet its civil responsibilities.

Several seminal questions, then, arise within the context of this church-state conflict. What role should the US civil authorities play in handling the molestation crisis? How far should the state go in its attempts to provide justice for the victims of clerical sexual abuse? When do civil investigations move to the point of religious intrusion and even coercion? Under what circumstances, if any, does the Catholic Church have the right to invoke the First Amendment to protect its own ecclesiastical rights and privileges? Do Church officials have the unfettered privilege and duty to protect the due process rights of accused priests? Should the Church's legal system, canon law, have equal authority with civil law when dealing with clerical sexual abuse?

These questions are all critical to understanding how religious groups can, and must, function within established legal parameters designed to maintain the equilibrium between the rights and responsibilities of both church and state within a pluralistic society. At the same time, the answers to such problems, which have evolved in a series of court decisions and legislation, also reveal how the state has been able to maneuver though the delicate balance and counterbalance that legally enjoins, yet also entitles all members of various denominations as well as nonbelievers to exist peacefully within the United States.

What has occurred in the last 15 years, then, to change the traditional American Catholic church-state power relationship? Broadly speaking, civil authorities have, first, used their investigative powers to scrutinize the hierarchical management of clergy in clerical abuse cases. As a result, they have increased the use, and broadened the scope, of the state's subpoena powers in clerical sexual abuse investigations.

This began as far back as the Gauthe case in the 1980s, when the evidence collected and court proceedings were carried out under a seal of confidentiality. By 2001, however, the state became more involved and, within institutional Church thinking, even intrusive during the sexual abuse cases in Boston. In the Porter, Shanley, and Geoghan cases, the highest court in the State of Massachusetts set a precedent that allowed thousands of documents related to Church personnel matters to be made public for the first time.

Boston civil authorities also deposed high-ranking Church leaders publically for the first time as well. They were questioned and held responsible for the cover-ups of hundreds of molestations due their own ignorance, arrogance and decisions to reassign priests who had been shown to be sexual deviants. Church officials, from that point on, were required to turn over previously confidential personnel and medical records. This set a legal precedent that was eventually followed across the United States.

Beyond serving subpoenas for confidential, ecclesiastical records in clerical sexual abuse cases, an increasing number of states also enacted legislation to end the use of all confidential agreements between the Church and victims of clerical sexual abuse. Some states even required the publication of past secret settlements as well.

Other clerical sexual abuse cases, such as those in New Hampshire, resulted in state monitoring and oversight of church agencies that deal with children. And a number of states, such as Massachusetts, Delaware, California, New York, and New Jersey have attempted to extend the statutes of limitations to allow individuals who have been molested to come forward after the time had run out on their right to file such suits.

State investigative powers have also been augmented by other civil actions, specifically through litigation that has led to greater secular control over Church financial matters. This is the second way the state has limited Church autonomy in the United States. Civil authorities have necessarily done this since the judiciary has become involved in bankruptcy proceedings of Church dioceses. The courts have had to draw up and/or mediate financial reorganization plans, and make decisions about the use and disposition of assets that would have to be used to pay monetary settlements in clerical sexual abuse lawsuits.

This has raised questions about the corporate status and financial responsibilities of those dioceses going through the bankruptcy process. As a result, some state court decisions have challenged the financial administration of the Church, as well as how it should compensate victims of molestations. In Massachusetts, for example, the legislature attempted to give the attorney general increased oversight on the Church's use of charitable funds. The bill did not pass, but at issue was an attempt by the state to make the Boston Archdiocese accountable to the state in the way it dispersed its funds. The church-state implications were, and remain, significant according to religious authorities: the legality of governmental monitoring over the use of donated monies for charitable and other purposes.

These various legal challenges involving criminal prosecutions and civil lawsuits led to a growing constitutional battle between church and state over interpretations of the First Amendment. Church lawyers have invoked its "establishment clause" that part of the First Amendment that protects religious organizations from state interference in Church affairs.

This has been the basis for Catholic constitutional claims that civil authorities have intruded into internal religious matters in the prosecution of alleged clerical sexual abusers and the administration of Church financial transactions. Indeed, the Church's concern about the civil prosecution of priests for clerical sexual abuse, then, has been challenged on two fronts: first, its institutional claims for the legitimacy and superiority of its own canon law to deal with what the Church considers to be the management of its personnel, and second, the Church's right to constitutional protection of its internal affairs by the government. In short, these arguments have been the basis for Catholic legal demands for protection from civil intrusions into the handling of predatory priests.

While the Church has used the establishment clause of the First Amendment as its rationale for a number of its claims, so have civil authorities. In many cases, attorneys general and other civil legal experts have essentially argued that the state can become involved in the actions of a particular denomination (Catholic) for what the courts have defined as a "compelling state interest."

State authorities have justified their right to use this constitutional argument based on the precedent set by the Supreme Court in its 1963 ruling in *Sherbert v. Verner.*[1] In that case, the court ruled that the state could restrict religious practice, but only under "strict scrutiny," or specific guidelines. The limitations could only be imposed if they 1) served a compelling state interest, 2) were narrowly tailored to achieve a goal, and 3) used the least restrictive means possible.

Federal jurisprudence in this constitutional area had earlier allowed religious limitations to serve the compelling state interest to provide education,[2] to protect work conditions,[3] to assure national security, and now—with regard to clerical sexual abuse—to protect children. In short, the courts have ruled that the state may, in a number of circumstances, set limits on religious freedom without violating the establishment clause of the First Amendment.

Although this federal/state precedent was decided earlier, the constitutional responsibility and right in the matter of clerical sexual abuse has been fought with greater intensity as the escalating number of cases have come to light. The courts and a number of legislatures have worked to limit the Church's legal challenges and lobbying efforts, maintaining that such judicial and political actions were designed only to protect their own religious freedom and interests rather than those of sexually victimized children. Both the Catholic leadership and civil authorities continue to appeal to constitutional protections to enforce their own legal codes, administrative rights, prerogatives, and public duties.

Historically, the courts have taken the lead in trying to create a balanced church-state relationship by adjudicating cases where a public policy that is tangential to religious freedom or religious establishment has clashed. The courts have always attempted to maintain the notion of separation of church and state, but have often done this by walking a fine line between accommodating to the needs of religious groups, remaining neutral in religious-civil matters, or strictly avoiding any involvement, whatsoever, in a variety of cases.

In the numerous cases that have emerged since the trial of Father Gilbert Gauthe in 1984, then, certain parts of the First Amendment have been tested. The establishment clause and, in some situations, the freedom of religion clause in the First Amendment as well, have been used as a means to protect and challenge the ecclesiastical rights of the Catholic

Church, to provide justice for the victims of clerical sexual abuse, and to maintain the due process rights of accused priests.

In short, the clerical sexual abuse crisis has generated many legal battles within the states and a constitutional struggle on the federal level to maintain the tenuous relationship between church and state in America. These civil challenges reflect the actions of a conflicted Church hierarchy caught in a no-win situation. They mirror an autocratic cadre of bishops desperately trying to use both canon law *and* the Constitution to hold on to eroding ecclesiastical privileges. At the same time, they are still attempting to appear like team players who support a well-balanced church-state relationship. But the truth is simple: the Church has lost the battle.

At this time, however, it is not ready to face or really accept its defeat and all the ramifications that will come with it. The hierarchy still thinks that by using its own devices, specifically canon law, along with its prestige and wealth, its past glory and its former moral credibility, it can hold on to its religious power in the matter of clerical sexual abuse.

Too many questions persist to even consider such thinking. Can the hierarchy's strategies provide adequate justice for the victims of clerical sexual abuse, assure the protection of children in its care, and maintain it traditional religious and social missions?

Each case that has been heard in the courts has, in its own way, played a part in limiting the Church's power. But in attempts to deal with so many conflicting church-state issues and personal injuries, courts at different levels have sometimes also issued inconsistent decisions with mixed results across the United States. Thus, legal battles should be expected to continue; litigation will most likely go forward, and the clerical sexual abuse crisis will take a long time to reach some kind of resolution. What can be made of these conclusions?

The Supremacy of Civil Authority: The Continuing Tensions Between the Supremacy of Civil versus Canon Law

First, the decisions made by the civil and criminal courts in the United States have shown one basic fact: federal and state laws are superior to the canon, or Church law, in matters of clerical sexual abuse. They have clearly relegated canon law to a secondary position, showing that no religious organization can function above or outside the law of the land in criminal matters.

At the same time, court decisions have shown that Catholic hierarchical demands for ecclesiastical privilege and confidentiality are at an end. As a result, Catholic leaders must treat their religious personnel under the same legal guidelines set by state and federal authorities, rather than by mandates established in Rome, or themselves.

These two facts, the supremacy of civil law and the loss of ecclesiastical privileges, have changed the entire church-state dynamic in the United States. Justice and accountability are now meted out by civil authorities, rather than by religious leaders invoking canon law. The individual, rather than the religious institution, is the focus of civil law and its use. And as a result, the state will continue to prosecute those members of the clergy and hierarchy accused of clerical sexual abuse.

And how has the Catholic Church reacted to this change? It revised canon law in 1983 with later addendums, guidelines and clarifications. The USCCB adopted "The Charter" and "The Essential Norms." The hierarchy has also denied, obfuscated, and challenged thousands of clerical sexual abuse accusations and hundreds of convictions. It has fought legal/constitutional battles to maintain its authority. It has tried to limit financial settlements. In all of this, there has been an underlying ecclesiastical insistence on privileges. In all the state demands for specific documents, bankruptcy proceedings, and attempts to provide justice for victims, the Catholic Church has fought to protect its own institutional interests, its constitutional protections and its own reputation. As many victims have said: it has never deliberately or consciously placed the needs of victims over the good of the Church.

The Catholic church-state responses have been aggressive in federal courts: demanding constitutional protections, yet defensive in lower criminal and civil courts safeguarding its ecclesiastical rights. At both levels, however, the hierarchy's pragmatic, religious response to its adherents and the public sector has primarily been a canonical one. That is, Church lawyers have insisted on using its own legal code to justify its handling of clerical sexual abusers, to deal with the victims, to protect Church financial interests, and to continue its religious and social missions.

At the same time, the Church it has also used the tradition and past legitimacy of canon law as the strategy to challenge state and federal law in the United States. Where that has failed, it has turned to the First Amendment for government protection against secular involvement in its affairs and the guarantee for the right of religious freedom. It short, the Catholic Church has argued from both sides of the fence.

It was not until 2002, when the American bishops gathered for their biannual meeting in Dallas, however, that an official, legal, systematic, canonical attempt was made to redress the problem of clerical sexual abuse. Prior to that time, each bishop acted as his own judge and jury in such cases and dealt with molestation on an *ad hoc* basis. Sometimes he would make referrals to the Congregation for the Defense of the Faith (CDF) in Rome, but due to the complexity and time involved in adjudicating such cases, many bishops simply acted out of their own personal sense of justice or desire to protect the accused clergy members and the reputation of the Church. Thus, some prayers, some therapy, and many reassignments occurred—in secrecy—and were carried out without any real understanding, aftercare, or reports to civil authorities. No criminal prosecutions occurred as a result of their reporting of such incidents.

The Dallas meeting in 2002 showed that the US Catholic bishops were finally beginning to understand that in matters of clerical sexual abuse, the hierarchy could be held accountable to the state. Therefore, it also became apparent that Church leaders would have to adjust canon law to respond to this reality. Could they concede the right of the state to prosecute accused clergy, to subpoena their personnel records, to demand transparency, the possibly risk the reputation of the Church? Would the Vatican allow them to make such drastic changes in canon law, and as a consequence shift power in the Catholic church-state relationship?

Pragmatically, at the 2002 Dallas meeting, the American Catholic bishops realized that something had to be done to deal with the escalating problem of clerical sexual abuse. Their answer was to make concessions to civil law—adjusting canon law to the demands of civil law. The assembled bishops called for a "zero tolerance policy." They put an action plan in place to implement it. They established a national review board to oversee the zero tolerance policy and to create an office of child protection and safety. They set up offices to hear allegations of clerical sexual abuse. They ended the practice of confidentiality agreements. They set up diocesan review boards. They promised to provide safe environments for children. They supported improved seminary training.

Unfortunately, "The Charter" and "The Essential Norms" that emerged from the Dallas meeting were too little, too late and were originally passed without the approval of the Vatican. The Holy See refused to accept many of its recommendations. Canon law was still considered to be sacrosanct by officials in Rome. And certain bishops were simply unable or unwilling to accept such changes as well. A classic internal battle of wills within the hierarchy and with the Vatican ensued.

Even the head of the National Review Board, which was the watchdog body set up by the bishops up to monitor the recommendations of the Dallas meeting, agreed. Former Governor Frank Keating, who gave credibility to the review board, accused several bishops of acting "like the cosa nostra," or members of the Mafia—stonewalling his committee, hiding evidence and obstructing justice.[4] Keating subsequently resigned as the chairman of the Board.

His committee, however, continued on, working and commissioning the John Jay College of Criminal Justice to do a study entitled "The Nature and Scope of Sexual Abuse of Minors by Catholic Priests and Deacons in the United States, 1950–2002."[5] Released in February of 2004, the report attempted to ensure that sufficient steps were being taken by the hierarchy to protect minors from sexual abuse by clergy.

The report revealed some startling statistics as well: that 4,392 clergymen were accused of abusing 10,667 people between 1960 to 1984 (when the Gauthe case occurred in Louisiana) at a financial cost of $573 million dollars. It also showed that most of the victims were males between the ages of 11–14, that in 10% of the allegations, no action was taken against the priests, and that in 6% of the cases, the clerics were reprimanded and returned to ministry.[6] One can only assume that the rest were handled by the *ad hoc,* secret actions of individual bishops: treatments, therapy, retirements, transfers, and reassignments.

Thus, the complex and dated canon laws that existed before Dallas in 2002 reflected the hierarchical misunderstanding and lack of will on the part of bishops to deal with clerical sexual abuse in an effective way. But even more significant was the fact that many of the bishops continued to deal with clerical sexual abuse just as poorly after the passage of "The Charter" and "The Essential Norms" were drawn up in Dallas.

To this day, the bishops' implementation of guidelines to protect children remains inconsistent, incomplete, and without total acceptance of civil law at all levels of Church administration. At the same time, some bishops still refuse to accept the fact that canon law must defer to the laws of the state.

For example, in 2011, a second grand jury investigation of the Philadelphia Archdiocese found that Father Edward Avery and a number clerics accused of clerical sexual abuse had not been reported to civil authorities by their superiors, Monsignor Lynn and the deceased Cardinal Bevilaqua. That information came out a decade after the bishops had created "The Charter." Although no law had been in place to require Church officials to report clerical sexual abuse to civil authorities until 2005, Lynn had not adhered to the bishops' zero tolerance policy instituted in 2002. He was finally prosecuted and punished, sent to jail—and later released on the legal technicality that he had not violated state law. Nevertheless, Lynn, like other members of the religious leadership, simply had not adhered to the zero tolerance guidelines set down by his Church superiors a number of years earlier and had simply allowed Avery and others to continue in religious ministry.

In Missouri, Bishop Robert Finn of Kansas-St. Joseph has been convicted of failing to report a priest, Father Shawn Ratigan, for producing child pornography in 2013. Instead of informing civil authorities as he should have done under "The Charter" and civil law, the bishop simply confined Ratigan to a convent. However, civil authorities intervened and prosecuted the pornographer. Today Ratigan is in jail, and Finn is being monitored by the local prosecutor.

In Newark, New Jersey, Archbishop John J. Myers was accused of allowing a priest to continue working near young people after the priest had been convicted of groping a young boy but then released due to a judicial error. Myers, himself a canon lawyer, in a letter to his parishioners in 2013, admitted that church leadership had failed. He said that "the investigation uncovered certain operational vulnerabilities in our own systems. We found that the strong protocols presently in place were not always observed."[7]

He made this statement more than a decade after the Dallas zero-tolerance policy was enacted—it revealed ten years of either ignorance or non-compliance by an archbishop who was a canon lawyer himself. Myers is now being helped to run his archdiocese with a coadjutor bishop until he retires to his newly renovated, multi-million dollar residence.

In California, the release of Church documents filed in court as part of a $660 million dollar settlement for a 2007 clerical sexual abuse case revealed some startling information as well. The records in 2013 showed that Church leaders sent accused predator priests out of the state of California for psychological treatment so that they could circumvent the law that required them to report such cases to civil authorities.

In a press conference, the former head of the Los Angeles Archdiocese and one of the staunchest legal opponents of turning over clerical medical and personnel records to civil authorities, Roger Cardinal Mahoney, apologized to the many victims of clerical sexual abuse. Just as important, he also publicly admitted that while in a leadership position he was "naïve" and followed a policy of out of state therapeutic referrals,[8] thus bypassing "The Charter" guidelines as well as legal responsibility to report accused molesters to civil authorities.

Even as these kinds of revelations keep coming, some bishops still continue to oppose reasonable civil actions and laws to protect children. For example, in New York, religious leaders have continued to fight vigorously against legislation that would allow the suspension of the statute of limitations in clerical sexual abuse cases. With each day, such actions are accompanied by more information that trickles out as Church files are opened in the continuing allegations against priests, a requirement imposed by civil authorities for the compelling state interest to protect children and to adjudicate settlements in civil lawsuits.

In Wisconsin, just recently, thousands of pages of documents were opened in a sexual abuse case that also raised questions about the financial motives of Cardinal Timothy Dolan, who was the archbishop of Milwaukee during the allegations. It was revealed during bankruptcy hearings that Dolan asked the Vatican for permission to move nearly $57 million dollars of Church monies into a cemetery fund. He requested the right to do so in order to protect the trust from being invaded to pay off settlements in clerical sexual abuse cases. The cardinal vehemently denied press accusations that he was more concerned with the financial well-being of the Church than the justice due the sexual abuse victims. Ultimately, a state court held that such funds could not be used in a bankruptcy reorganization plan. However, situations like that continue to show the skepticism of the laity and the media and only help to cast doubt on the compassion and veracity of Church leaders across the United States. Now there's a new financial twist: Church funds are being protected by incorporating individual parishes in order to protect the larger financial assets throughout various American dioceses from liability claims.

In Chicago, in 2014, thousands of newly released documents have provided "a lurid history of abuses" and "halting responses from bishops"[9] with regard to clerical sexual abuse. Those records also show the civil prerogatives that Church officials were bold enough to ask for and to expect from public officials when dealing with the clergy—even when they were convicted pedophile priests.

Letters of the former archbishop, Cardinal Francis George, reveal that a priest, Father Norbert J. Maday, who had been jailed for sexual abuse, was allowed to pay his last respects to his deceased mother. To do so, civil officials permitted her body to be brought to the jail!

This was characterized as an "exceptional act of charity" by George[10] after former Governor Tommy Thompson of Wisconsin granted permission for this favor. No wonder Church authorities felt they could receive special treatment and ecclesiastical privileges by virtue of their religious positions.

What is the sad takeaway in all this new information and continuing revelations attached to clerical sexual abuse cases? That even after the USCCB adoption of "The Charter to Protect Children" in Dallas in 2002, all of the promises the bishops made to implement a zero-tolerance policy in clerical sexual abuse cases, and their assurances that they would comply with civil law to report such criminals, many members of the hierarchy continued to drag their feet in implementing those policies and obeying civil law. Too many Church leaders are still only giving those policies lip-service at best, and noncompliance at worst.

The reason for this belies an answer. Perhaps it is due to the continuing autocratic nature of the Church hierarchy. Bishops function like generals leading an army. They expect their orders to be followed without question. The chain of command flows from the pope on down, maintaining a structure that is essentially both undemocratic and dictatorial.

The clerical culture is also a problem. Superiority among many priests, due to their "special calling" and the religious nature of their work, still exists as well. Exemptions and privileges are considered as part of their elevated way of life. The treatment of the victims of clerical sexual abuse, therefore, is impersonal, detached, suspicious, and secondary to the role, reputation, and mission of the Church carried out through its esteemed personnel.

The laity has reacted with increasing opposition and anger to this type of clerical behavior. And it has established a variety of strategies to challenge and impact the continuing benign, ineffective, and unsatisfactory management practices of the hierarchy.

SNAP, VOTF, and a number of other organizations have taken on this task by supporting the victims of clerical sexual abuse, leading legal challenges in American courts, advocating for legislation for survivors, and pressuring state and Vatican officials to make needed changes for the redress of survivors' past injuries.

Some lay organizations are also demanding structural and doctrinal reform within the institutional Church itself. For example, SNAP brought suit against the Vatican at the International Criminal Court at The Hague and provided documentation for a significant number of cases of clerical sexual abuse. Although the Court indicated in 2013 that it would not open a full investigation, it said that it would reconsider that decision if new information or evidence emerged. It suggested that SNAP seek legal remedies with other human rights agencies. The organization did just that, submitting information to the UN committee investigating the Vatican's adherence to the Convention of the Right of the Child.

US lawyers have also reacted aggressively to the bishops and clerical sexual abusers. The church-state ramifications of a less than perfect acceptance and implementation of the zero tolerance policies of the bishops as well as the continuing legal abuses of hierarchical power and institutional cover-ups has resulted in a more intense and combative use of civil authority to assure the compelling state interest to protect children.

Their rationale is simple. The assertive lawyers maintain that if the Catholic Church will not report its clerical sexual abusers, if it will not cooperate with legal officials, if it will blatantly disobey civil law, then they will work with plaintiffs and the state for the right to impose stricter limitations on Church authority, and to demand financial restitution for such negligent management. They contend that it is the obligation of the State to prosecute all sexual predators, clerical or otherwise, and to punish those who protect them to the fullest extent of the law. Therefore, ecclesiastical privilege must be gone; accommodation must be gone; neutrality must be gone, and the notion of the separation of church and state must be reconsidered in light of the continued hierarchical reticence to punish clerical sexual abusers.

A Change in US Vatican Relations: Changes in Vatican Responses

A second church-state problem arising from the American clerical sexual abuse scandal has resulted in a spasm in United States-Vatican relations. This has come about due to legal challenges to the Holy See by

US attorneys and the Vatican's own inconsistent handling of the clerical sexual abuse crisis. This is a result of the way that two former popes, John Paul II and Benedict XVI, responded to the American clerical sexual abuse crisis.

Pope John Paul began his pontificate with an agenda to resuscitate Catholicism around the world. Committed to social justice and human rights, he traveled extensively to preach his religious message and instill the principles of the Church's social teachings wherever he went.

Part of his agenda was also to make needed changes within the institutional Church. In Latin America, for example, he challenged the clergy to be priests, rather than politicians. He put an end to the growing theological movement known as liberation theology, the notion that missionaries had a political role to play in helping the poor and marginalized.

Among his early reforms was the revision of the Code of Canon Law in 1983, a major institutional, legal change that could have streamlined and clarified the administration of the Church around the world. But the clerical sexual abuse crisis in the United States seemed to render the revised code almost irrelevant as the scandal broke and the updated canon law was still unable to provide clear rules and policies to deal with the priestly offenders.

At first, the official papal responses to the situation in America were theological, defensive, and confused. Stressing repentance and reconciliation for priest perpetrators, John Paul appeared to be only secondarily concerned with justice for their victims and clerical accountability to civil law. He seemed flummoxed by the entire scandal as it unfolded, seeing it essentially in terms of sin, within the purview of canon law, and thus a matter falling under his power and ecclesiastical privilege to adjudicate.

The pope did not effectively use the legal system he commissioned. It was at his disposal, but he did not move to enforce it with any real intensity. Instead, he simply made some statements during the 1990s to deal with clerical sexual abuse that reflected a pastoral attitude without criminal concerns. After the Boston cases in 2001, however, Pope John Paul wrote an Apostolic Letter systematizing the canonical procedures to be followed when allegations of clerical sexual abuse occurred. Entitled "The Norms of the Motu Proprio 'Sacramentorum Sanctitatis Tutela,'" it dealt with liturgical delicts, the solicitation of sex within the confessional, and the procedural norms to be implemented in canonical offenses against morality. These were clarified, and the CDF was granted total authority to deal with clerical discipline and to review all allegations of clerical sexual abuse and sins against the sixth commandment.

For the most part, however, the canonical procedures mandated by John Paul's 1983 revisions and 2001 systematization of canon law were bypassed by many members of the hierarchy. Each local diocese was responsible for the initial investigation of an allegation of sexual abuse; if there were some semblance of truth it was referred to the CDF. In turn, the CDF could authorize the local bishop to conduct a judicial trial within a Church tribunal. If guilty, a priest had the right of appeal to the CDF and its decision would be final. Priests who admitted their crimes could be required to live a life of prayer and penance and be restricted from public ministry. The most serious penalty would be dismissal from the clerical state. Some cases could also be directly referred to the pope, who could release a priest from his vows for the "good of the Church."[11] Up to this point, there was no pressure from Rome to follow civil law.

The person in charge of the CDF under Pope John Paul was Joseph Cardinal Ratzinger, the future Pope Benedict XVI. He seemed to understand the broader, pragmatic, criminal implications of the predatory behavior of the clergy. By 2005, just before he was elected pope, the *New York Times* reported that Benedict dealt with such matters every Friday morning and reviewed hundreds of clerical sexual abuse case files during his tenure in the CDF. He was the Vatican's most knowledgeable person regarding the matter when he assumed the papacy later on that year. He was the one person who knew the full scope of the clerical sexual abuse allegations. He had been privy to the worst of the worst. He had the power to prosecute and punish—or to look away. But he was only able to make marginal progress on his watch at the CFD.

The case of Father Marcial Maciel (Degollado) illustrates this point. Maciel, a Roman Catholic priest, had founded a religious order, the Legion of Christ and its lay arm, Regnum Christi, in Mexico in 1941. Through these two very conservative, but financially lucrative, organizations, Maciel set up schools, universities, and charitable agencies. During his lifetime, though, he was investigated for sexually abusing children and seminarians. In 1998, a formal case was brought against him, but it was quietly shelved by Ratzinger at the CDF. Some say this was on orders from his superior, Pope John Paul II. Clearly, the case showed conflicted attitudes between prosecution and compassion toward perpetrators of cleric sexual abuse at the very highest levels of Vatican authority. In

2006, however, Maciel was removed from active ministry by Benedict, who had become pope by that time. The aged priest, Maciel, was sent to spend his last days in prayer and penance. He was spared a canonical trial due to his advanced age. He died in 2008.

If John Paul was bewildered by the clerical sexual abuse crisis, Benedict was overwhelmed by the scandal as well as other problems within the Vatican. His plate was full: geopolitical problems in the Middle East compounded by his inability to reach out to Muslims; poor Vatican relations with atheistic countries such as Russia and China; difficulty in dealing with doctrinal problems such as abortion and gay marriage; financial questions arising from problems with the Vatican bank and internal struggles with the Vatican bureaucracy.

Early on in his pontificate, Benedict XVI reportedly recognized "how much filth there is in the Church,"[12] giving hope that such a realization would bring immediate change in the handling of clerical sexual abuse from the Vatican on down. But as far as Americans were concerned, they did not hear directly from the pope about the crisis in the United States until he addressed the United Nations in 2008. It was then, three years into his papacy, that he finally made several statements— words that seemed to show a change in the pontiff's attitude toward victims. He told reporters on the flight from Rome that he was "deeply ashamed"[13] of the scandal and that pedophiles would be excluded from sacred ministry.

The pope's words, perhaps too late, provided little compassion and no real sense of urgency. His later statements and those of the entire hierarchy were no more than what can be described as "episcobabble."[14] That is, a type of theological speech which essentially communicates little to nothing of substance. Today some refer to "episcobabble" as simply kicking the can down the road or using confusing religious notions to explain what goes on within the secret Church bureaucracy.

Just recently, the Associated Press was able to gather formerly confidential data showing how the CDF operated during Pope Benedict's papacy. His appointee, Cardinal William Levada, reportedly defrocked 384 priests after the clerical sexual scandal broke in Europe and other countries.[15] But to put the number in context, a member of the CDF claimed that it dealt with about 3,000 cases of diocesan and religious order priests merely between the years 2001 and 2010![16] This meant that the number of cases that resulted in dismissal from the clerical state was miniscule, at best.

In 2012, Levada and the CDF prepared yet another set of clear, systematized, and mandatory guidelines and procedures for every diocese in the world to follow in matters of clerical sexual abuse. Essentially, they fell into four categories. Legally, they called for each diocese to consider sexual abuse as a sin against the sixth commandment, to take into account the civil laws of every country, and to consider anyone under the age of 18 a minor. In terms of rights, they called for respect for the accuser and for the Church to offer spiritual and psychological assistance to victims. Accused clerics were to be afforded due process rights. Canonically, all investigations of allegations were to be held in privacy. Structurally, bishops would still retain authority over their review boards.

However, the new guidelines seemed to grudgingly recognize the authority of civil law. They said that bishops must "make allowance" for the specific civil legislation of each particular country with regard to the molestation of minors. Finally, the guidelines stated that "the return of a cleric to public ministry is excluded if such ministry is a danger for minors or a cause of scandal for the community."[17] Some canonical progress seemed to be at hand.

The generation of another new framework for handling clerical sexual abuse situations, however, was not enough to satisfy Benedict's critics. The way that he handled the matter in the past has been considered one of the reasons for his resignation in 2013, an action that had not occurred since the fifteenth century.[18] Benedict's decision to retire was officially said to be due to the infirmities of his advanced age. His departure was characterized by the press as an exit that left the Vatican in a state of discord: reeling from scandals and filled with intrigue as well as internal struggles.

Benedict's responses to the pedophilia crisis must be viewed in the context of all these situations and other assertive actions by civil authorities in many countries beyond the United States. Taken together, state reactions to clerical sexual abuse around the globe escalated on his watch, and as they grew they created larger, peripheral damages to international Catholic church-state relations.

First among these were legal challenges to the authority of the Holy See from American legal experts. They accosted the state-sovereignty of the Vatican and demanded accountability from the pope and his subordinates. Several cases such as *Doe v. Holy See* and *O'Bryan v. Holy See*, discussed previously, created some tension with the Vatican on matters of corporate financial responsibility and diplomatic immunity. They challenged the administration, agenda, transparency, and accountability of Church authorities and gave impetus to legal challenges from other states in their dealings with the Vatican as well.

Leaked cables obtained by Wikileaks showed that as early as 2002, the secretary of state under Pope John Paul registered his "displeasure"[19] at several lawsuits served against the Vatican. The cables revealed that the Church's attitude was that it was one thing to sue bishops, "but another thing entirely to sue the Holy See."[20]

Putting its credibility on the line, the Obama administration tried to support the Vatican's claims for sovereign immunity in several later suits, but essentially was unable to persuade the Supreme Court that the Holy See had absolutely no responsibility for the actions of its clergy world-wide. The court allowed the lower courts to continue to reconsider sexual abuse liability challenges. After more legal wrangling, a lower court dismissed charges against the immunity of the pope, and lawyers agreed to drop their cases as well. The various legal challenges and decisions reflected both a political difference and a legal division in the relationship between the United States and the Vatican, a challenge based on the diplomatic, financial immunity of its leadership.

At this point then, America and the Vatican continue to carry out positive diplomatic relations, a pragmatic diplomatic and political necessity, since the Church claims membership from almost 25% of the American population. A delicate diplomatic balance, therefore, joins the similarly delicate church-state balance at home, one that could affect a critical electoral constituency for individuals seeking and serving in public office in the future.

A New Papal Direction

The question everyone is asking now is whether or not the new pope can reverse the course of the previously ineffective Catholic leadership and its inadequate, convoluted Church policies on clerical sexual abuse matters. Will Francis I be able to restore trust in the clergy and the credibility of the hierarchy? Can he embody the Church's needed institutional remorse and apologize to the victims of sexual abuse in sincere, pragmatic ways for the clergy's sins and crimes? In short, will he be able to provide the pastoral leadership to help sexually molested victims to heal and their abusers to be punished? Will he be able to resuscitate the ailing legitimacy of canon law? Will he be able to make a difference in American-Vatican relations? Will he be able to implement the Church's social policies based on transcendent values? It is difficult to say, as the new pope tries to deal with such problems as well as the hobbled agenda left behind by his successor.

Currently, there is a change in tone, if not doctrine, on the part of the new pontiff. Chosen as "The Man of the Year" by *Time* at the end of 2013, Francis I holds out the hope of a renewed, compassionate, and accountable Church.

The former cardinal and archbishop of Buenos Aires, Jorge Mario Bergoglio is the first Latin American pope. He was born in Argentina after his parents emigrated there from Italy. He entered the Jesuit seminary in 1966, and in only a few years became the leader of the Jesuit order of priests in Argentina. He became a university rector and a bishop in 1992. From that point on, he quickly rose up the ecclesiastical ranks, serving as a member of a number of Vatican congregations, or official government departments. His theological emphasis has always revolved around the principle of compassion—for both the poor and the marginalized in society.

On becoming pope, Francis continued to stress social and economic inequality, evangelizing about issues that deal with the family, marriage, and the end of life. He has also attempted to rein in and control various congregations, or departments within the Holy See, actions that reflect a change in a number of internal priorities of his predecessors.

As far as the matter of clerical sexual abuse, the new pope has characterized the protection of children as a major concern of the Vatican. In early December 2013, in an address to the bishops of the Netherlands, he gave the hierarchy assurances that he would pray and continue to express compassion to the victims of sexual abuse and their families.

Three months later, in March of 2014, Francis formally announced the establishment of a special papal commission to deal with the ongoing clerical sexual abuse problem. Appointing Sean Cardinal O'Malley of Boston to lead it, the Pope made sure that the commission included many different kinds of people who could provide a systematic implementation for change— including laypeople and a sexual abuse victim.

Their participation represents a seismic shift in the way that the Vatican has done business in the last two thousand years. For the first time, the laity might have significant input into policymaking on critical institutional moral matters. It could potentially turn the institutional structure of the Church upside down. Instead of imposing doctrines and policies from the top, a new bottom-up model would necessarily change the way the hierarchy and Church members would communicate, make policies, and implement consensus decisions. Such a turnabout could begin to create a new sense of community, democratize the Church infrastructure, and in turn change the type of relationship that it would have with states.

For his part, Cardinal O'Malley has promised to be open and to bring about change. He has assured the public that he will work with the commission to "propose inititatives to encourage local responsibility around the world and the mutual sharing of 'best practices' for the protection of all minors, including programs for training, education, formation and responses to abuse."[21]

The pope has begun to show his sincere commitment to the victims of priestly predatory behavior and has also taken personal responsibility for the harm done to children. He has promised to deal with the "moral damage"[22] done to them and to impose sanctions on their abusers. To back this up, has also met with a number of victims.

Pope Francis has also taken a more assertive role in punishing ranking members of the hierarchy for sexual abuse. Under his direction, the Vatican has given support to those seeking justice for the predatory actions of Jozef Wesolowski, a former archbishop from Poland and nuncio to the Dominican Republic. He was defrocked in 2014 by the Congregation for the Doctine of the Faith for sexual abuse and will also be prosecuted in a Vatican criminal court since he holds citizenship in the sovereign city state.

These changes under Francis I seem to have substance, and they have also been matched by an official Vatican presentation about children's rights before the United Nations in January 2014. However, that report left the Church open to major criticism. A spokesman for the Holy See discussed issues such as clerical sexual abuse before the Committee on the Convention of the Rights of the Child and the Optional Protocols, to which the Vatican is a signatory. The outcome of this exchange between Vatican officials and UN committee members proceeded with questions about how far the new pope appears to be willing to go to regain the Church's moral credibility.

Monsignor Silvano Tomasi highlighted the Vatican's policies and procedures designed to help eliminate abuse as well as the Holy See's collaboration with civil authorities. He stressed its commitment to listen to victims and to provide physical, emotional and spiritual services to young people and their families. As examples, the spokesman cited changes in the laws of the Vatican State regarding child rights, its promotion and participation in UN attempts to deal with such problems, and its work to "develop effective measures within their jurisdiction and in conformity with canonical legislation"[23] to deal with the protection of children. Further, he stressed the fact that many local churches have developed guidelines to deal promptly with abuse in accordance with national laws. These were positive changes put forward in the right direction by the Vatican.

The Vatican, however, refused to provide the UN panel with information about specific clerical sexual cases, the total number of such allegations, or its alleged lack of transparency in dealing with such matters. Tomasi also made the point that "priests are not functionaries of the Vatican,"[24] but citizens of their own states, and therefore, under the jurisdiction of their own countries, rather than the Holy See. Attempting to distance the Vatican from culpability, both financial and legal, he said that the Vatican would welcome any suggestions that the committee might have to assist it in ensuring "efficient implementation" of Vatican reforms.[25]

The United Nations Committee responded with criticisms that the Vatican did not expect. In its observations of the Vatican's report on behalf of working for the rights of children, it called on the Holy See to act in greater compliance with the UN and to create a mechanism to accomplish this. In fact, the committee even went so far as to raise the damaging fact that the Holy See has taken both ineffective measures and "adopted polices and practices which have essentially led to the continuation of the [sexual] abuse by and the impunity of the [clerical] perpetrators."[26]

In short, the diplomats were very undiplomatic as they criticized the Vatican. They faulted the Holy See for the transfers of clerical sexual abusers, the secrecy involved in such movements, and the fact that such priests were treated as sinners rather than criminals.[27]

Clearly, the reputation of the papacy and Church leadership is under scrutiny from many sides: national governments such as those in Ireland, Belgium, Australia, and other states; international organizations such as the United Nations and the International Criminal Court at The Hague; and from aggrieved individuals seeking financial redress from the sovereign state of the Vatican and its leadership. But just recently, Pope

Francis, in response to criticism from the United Nations, defended the Church and its actions to deal with clerical sexual abuse. He has said that "The Catholic Church is perhaps the only public institution to have acted with transparency and responsibility. No one else has done more. Yet the Church is the only one to have been attacked."[28] These remarks have been met with criticism and disappointment, indeed, even with fear: that the Church will continue to defend its institution at all costs— even by this new pope.

Regardless, the court of public opinion has pronounced its own damning verdict—in the media and in the cyber world. There is no more time or space for the Vatican and its leadership to defend its indefensible positions on clerical sexual abuse.

So the new pope must begin to develop and implement major reforms, ones that are deep, both structurally and culturally. First, from an institutional perspective, he must move beyond the ineffective crisis management of his predecessors. He needs to establish and implement carefully considered reforms that will move the Vatican from autocracy to democracy, from secrecy to transparency, and from irresponsible behavior to accountability. These changes must be so profound that they will affect Church management and its leadership at all levels and in all countries.

For example, the institutional Catholic Church in America, led by the USCCB and the superiors of religious orders, must participate with the Vatican in the development of management changes. They must start to function as more modern, corporate, transparent, administrative *teams* within the United States' pluralistic political and societal structure.

In the past, Church leaders have failed in their own varied attempts at crisis management[29] by acting in *ad hoc*, inconsistent ways. Members of the hierarchy have refused to admit the extent of clerical sexual abuse, to accept responsibility for such crimes, or even to recognize the victims of clerical sexual abuse in many cases. They did little to nothing to establish corrective actions until 2002 in Dallas, and even then, many religious officials were recalcitrant about putting reformed canonical policies into practice.

Such behavior is evidence of a hostile hierarchical environment, due in part to the condescending and often, patronizing, Catholic clerical culture. This is the other change that the pope must make. He must alter and replace that culture with a positive, sincere, and caring attitudinal response to others, especially toward those who claim to be victims of priestly sexual abuse. He must turn around 2,000 years of ingrained religious superiority.

In his own way, he has begun to do this. Pope Francis is leading by his personal example—moving from the papal apartments to a smaller home, driving his own car, showing public love and compassion to the sick, the poor, and the marginalized. Now he must guide and influence the hierarchy and clergy to accept this unpretentious way of life. He must encourage them to embrace priestly humility rather than clerical superiority, to raise human compassion for children and others, and to give more attention to such concerns over the protection of the reputation of the institutional Church. But he cannot do this if he makes statements that do not reflect his own behavior.

People must be treated with human dignity, as individuals who are more important than impersonal organizations. The pope must bring about a behavioral change in the hierarchical and clerical mind-set; in so doing, he might be able to reconcile authentic attitudinal reform with the skepticism of many unbelieving civil authorities and the members of the general public who doubt their willingness to fully engage and embrace the needs of victims and the demands of civil law.

This change can only come slowly, and it will take more than revisions to canon law to make it work. It will be more difficult to bring about, even though it is as critically important as structural change.

The struggles and need to reform the structure and culture within the Church has created a situation where the Catholic Church is no longer able to act as an equal in the American church-state equation. It can no longer make arguments demanding that canon law supersede civil law or even be equal to it. It can no longer hide behind the First Amendment. It has brought legal, strict scrutiny on itself. It has lost its legal credibility, a position that has exploded its canonical secrecy and institutional power by civil inquiries into the most confidential clerical records of the Church.

The revelations of confidentiality agreements and cover-ups have shown the moral and legal culpability of a religious organization gone amuck, so concerned with its own position, reputation, and privilege that it has stopped at nothing to protect its own existence. In the process, the loss of legal credibility in both civil lawsuits and criminal prosecutions has led to a loss of something even bigger: the loss of the Catholic Church's moral legitimacy in the public arena. It is this loss that will stymie the social mission of the Church. It will compromise the ability of the Catholic Church to advocate for transcendent values and to use any kind of moral credibility to inject them to the public policy debate. It will silence the Church in its role of trying to be the voice of the voiceless and the spiritual champion of social justice and human rights. In the eyes of many, the Catholic Church has lost its right to speak for the poor, the vulnerable, and the marginalized. Its social, political, and moral influence is eroding quickly and will soon be totally lost without strong leadership, reformed policies, a change in attitude, and many prayers for a renewed, compassionate, accountable Church in the world.

Notes

1 Early Warnings and Denials: Father Gauthe

1. See, for example: Father Thomas Doyle, O. P. and Stephen C. Rubino, "Catholic Clergy Sexual Abuse Meets the Civil Law," *Fordham Urban Law Journal* 31, no. 2 (2003): Article 6. Accessed at http://ir.lawnet.fordham.edu/ulj.

2. For example, see his encyclicals titled *Sapientiae Christianae* (Promulgated 10 January 1890), *Immortale Dei* (Promulgated 1 November 1885), *Longinque Oceani* (Promulgated 1 January 1885), *Inscrutibili Dei Consilio* (Promulgated 21 April 1878), and *Testem Benevolentiae* (Promulgated 22 January 1899). All accessed at http://www.vatican.va.

3. Pope Leo XIII, "*Longinque Oceani*, Section 8," 6 January 1895, http://www.vatican.va/holy_father/leo_xiii/encyclicals /documents/hf_l-xiiI_enc_06011895_longinqua_en.html.

4. Pope Leo XIII, "*Immortale Dei*, Section 33," 1 November 1885, http://www.vatican.va/holy_father/leo_xiii/encyclicals /documents/hf_l-xiii_enc_01111885_immortale-dei_en.html.

5. Pope Leo XIII, "*Sapientiae Christianae*, Sections 22 and 24," 10 January 1890, http://www.vatican.va/holy_father/leo_xiii /encyclicals/documents/hf_l-xiii_enc_10011890_sapientiae -christianae_en.html.

6. See Jo Renee Formicola, "Catholic Moral Demands in American Politics: A New Paradigm," *Journal of Church and State* 51, no. 1 (Winter 2009): 4–23. See, for example, the religious challenges and responses by Al Smith, John F. Kennedy, John Kerry, and Rudolph Giuliani in their quests for the presidency.

7. See his main articles on the subject: "Freedom of Religion I: The Ethical Problem," *Theological Studies,* 6 (June 1945): 229–286; "Contemporary Orientations of Catholic Thought on Church and State," *Theological Studies* 10 (June 1949): 177–234;

"Governmental Repression of Heresy," *Proceedings of the Third Annual Convention of the Catholic Theological Society of America* (Chicago: Catholic Theological Society of America, 1948) pp. 26–98; "The Problem of State Religion," *Theological Studies* 12 (June 1951) pp, 155–178; and "Leo XIII on Church and State: The General Structure of the Controversy," *Theological Studies* XIV (March 1953): 1–30; "Leo XIII: Separation of Church and State," *Theological Studies* 14 (March 1953): 145–214. Murray was subsequently censured for these ideas and not allowed to write on the subject of church-state relations. For a more complete explanation, see Jo Renee Formicola, "American Catholic Political Theology," *Journal of Church and State* 29, no. 3 (Autumn 1987): 457–474.

8. The General Council (known as Vatican II) lasted from 1962–1965. Its purpose was to bring about Church renewal. For a compendium of documents that were promulgated at the meeting, see Walter M. Abbott, gen. ed., *The Documents of Vatican II* (New York: Herder and Herder, 1966).

9. *Lumen Gentium,* in Abbott, *Documents of Vatican II*, Section 41, p. 241.

10. Ibid., Section 76, pp. 287–288 in Abbott, *Documents of Vatican II*.

11. *Dignitatius Humane,* Section 2, pp. 678–679 in Abbott, *Documents of Vatican II.*

12. See, for example, earlier works that continued to be influential regarding American Catholic thought on Church State relations by Father John A. Ryan, Moorehouse F. X. Millar, SJ. and Father Francis J. Boland. See especially, John A. Ryan and F. X. Millar, *The State and the Church* (New York: Macmillan, 1922) and John A. Ryan and Francis A. Boland, *Catholic Principles of Politics* (New York: Macmillan, 1940).

13. Pope Leo XIII, *Immortale Dei.*

14. Jason Berry, *Lead Us Not into Temptation* (Urbana: University of Illinois Press, 2000), http://www.bishop-accountability.org/news/1986_01_30_Berry_Anatomy Of.htm.

15. David Kohn, "The Church on Trial, Part 1: Rage in Louisana," CBS News Report, 11 June 2002, http://cbsnews.com/stories/2002/06/11/6011/main511845 .html.

16. Ibid.

17. Ibid.

18. Berry, *Lead Us Not into Temptation*, p. 7.

19. Ibid., p. 11.

20. Jason Berry, "Anatomy of a Cover Up: The Diocese of Lafayette and Its Moral Responsibility for the Pedophilia Scandal," *The Times of Acadiana,* 30 January 1986, http://www.bishop-accountability.org/news/1986_01_30_Berry_Anatomy Of.htm.

21. One family, the Campbell's, disagreed with this strategy and in the end, wanted to return the settlement money they received in order to have their son testify in a subsequent action against Gauthe.

22. Berry, *Lead Us Not into Temptation*, p. 23.

23. Rev. Dr. Thomas Kane, "House of Affirmation, International Theraputic Center for Clergy and Religious: Give Me Your Hand," September 1973, p. 3, http://www.bishop-accountability.org/treatment/HoA/1973_09_Kane_House_of_Affirmation.pdf.

24. Rev. Dr. Thomas Kane, "The House of Affirmation," in *Brothers Newsletter* 17, no. 2 (1976): 19, http://www.bishop-accountability.org/treatment/HoA/1976_Kane_House_of_Affirmation.pdf.

25. Investigative Staff of *The Boston Globe*, *Betrayal: The Crisis in the Catholic Church* (New York: Little, Brown and Company, 2002), p. 172.

26. Ibid., p. 175.

27. Berry, *Lead Us Not into Temptation*, p. 6, his description.

28. Kohn, "The Church on Trial."

29. Berry, *Lead Us Not into Temptation*, 51.

30. Ibid., p. 10.

31. Eamonn O'Neil, "What the Catholic bishop Knew," *The Guardian*, 2 April 2010, New York, http://www.theguardian.com/world/2010/apr/02/catholic-bishop-william-levada.

32. Berry, *Lead Us Not into Temptation*, p. 37.

33. Kane, House of Affirmation, "House of Affirmation, International Theraputic Center," p. 3.

34. Ibid.

35. Berry, *Lead Us Not into Temptation*, p 39.

36. The cases had a number of hearings. See *Gastal v. Hannan*, No. 84-CC-1833 Supreme Court of Louisiana. 459 So. 2d 526; 1984. 7 December 1984. *Gastal v. Hannan*, No. 84-OC-2070. Supreme Court of Louisiana. 462. So. 2d 201; 1984. 20 December 1984. *Gastal v. Hannan*, No. 85-CD=0102, Supreme Court of Louisiana. 463 so. 2d. 593, 1985. 27 February 1985. *Gastal v. Hannan*, No. 85-CD-0512. Supreme Court of Louisiana. 466 So. 2d. 450; 1985. 12 April 1985. *Gastal v. Hannan*, No. 85-CD-1213. Supreme Court of Louisiana. 472 So. 2d 923; 1985. 28 June 28 1985.

37. Berry, *Lead Us Not into Temptation*, p. 57.

38. This diplomatic shift reflected a changed attitude in church-state thinking in the United States, especially at the Vatican. Both Ronald Reagan and Pope John Paul II had similar concerns: the power of the atheistic Communist regime in Eastern Europe to stifle freedom, both political and religious. Some saw this as a possible reason for a diplomatic symbiosis between the United States and the Holy See. For a fuller and more historical explanation, see Jo Renee Formicola, "US Vatican-Relations: Toward a Post-Cold War Convergence?" *Journal of Church and State* 38 (Autumn 1996): 799–816.

39. See, for example, Carl Bernstein, "The Holy Alliance," *Time* 139 (24 February 1992): 28–35; Alex Alexiev, "The Kremlin and the Vatican," *Orbis* 27 (Fall 1983): 554–565.

40. Berry, *Lead Us Not into Temptation*, p. 56.
41. Father Thomas Doyle, O. P., "A Short History of *The Manual*," Weirdload.com, http://www.weirdload.com/pd-manual.html.
42. Ibid., p. 1.
43. In 2001, the organization changed its name from the National Conference of Catholic Bishops (NCCB) to the United States Conference of Catholic Bishops (USCCB). The United States Conference of Catholics Bishops (USCCB) was the original name of the bishops' *administrative* organization housed in Washington, DC.
44. O'Neill, "What the Catholic Bishop Knew," p. 3.
45. Doyle, "A Short History of *The Manual*," p. 5.
46. Ibid., p. 6.
47. Ibid., p. 7.
48. Carl M. Cannon, "Priests Who Molest," San Jose Mercury News, 31 December 1987, p. 3. Accessed at bishop-accountability.org.
49. Berry, *Lead Us Not into Temptation*, p. 155.
50. Kohn, "The Church on Trial."
51. Ibid.
52. Ibid.
53. Ibid.
54. O'Neill, "What the Catholic Bishop Knew," p. 2.
55. Paulson, "Lessons Unlearned," p. 2.
56. The Investigative Staff of *The Boston Globe, Betrayal*, p. 39.
57. Laurie Goodstein, "Audit Finds Sex Abuse Was Topic Decades Ago," *The New York Times*, 19 June 2013, p. A14.
58. The National Review Board for the Protection of Children and Young People, *A Report of the Crisis in the Catholic Church in the United States* (Washington, DC: The United States Conference of Catholic bishops, 2004), p. 46, http://www.bishop-accountability.org.
59. Bishops' Ad Hoc Committee on Sexual Abuse, "Restoring Trust: A Pastoral Response to Sexual Abuse, Volume I," Binder of Materials Presented to the NCCB at its Annual Meeting in Washington, DC, November 1994. "Restoring Trust: A Pastoral Response to Sexual Abuse Volume II," November 1995; and "Restoring Trust: A Pastoral Response to Sexual Abuse Volume III," 1996. All accessed at http://www.bishop-accountability.org/reports/1994-11-RestoringTrust/.
60. Eric Rich and Elizabeth Hamilton, "Doctors: Church Used Us," *Hartford Courant*, 24 March 2002, http://www.bishop-accountability.org/news9/2002-03-24.
61. Ibid.
62. Bishops' Ad Hoc Committee on Sexual Abuse, "Restoring Trust,... Volume I," p. 23.

2   Revelations and Scandals: Boston and Beyond

1. Thomas Farragher, "Behind Walls, Trouble Built to a Brutal End," *The Boston Globe*, 2 December 2003, http://www.boston.com/news/local/massachusetts/articles/2003/12/02/behind_walls_trouble_built_to_a_brutal_end/?page=full.

2. Ibid.

3. The scene is available on YouTube. Youtube.com, "Joseph Druce #1," http://www.youtube.com/watch?v=IjkHXDtoXAo.JosephDruce#1YouTube. Upload 12 June 2007.

4. Daniel J. Wakin and Katie Zezima, "Abusive Ex-Priest, John Geoghan, Is Killed in Prison," *The New York Times*, 24 August 2003, http://www.snapnetwork.og/news/massachusetts/boston/geoghan_murder.

5. CNN Staff, "Prosecutor: Inmate Considered Geoghan 'A Prize.'" CNN, 26 August 2003, http://cnn.com/2003/US/08/25/geoghan/index.html.

6. Farragher, "Behind Walls."

7. John Geoghan, "Letter of Father John Geoghan to Bishop Daily," 4 April 1980, http://www.bishop-accountability.org/ma-boston/archives/PatternAndPractice/0303-Geoghan-II-06705–06706.pdf.

8. Ibid.

9. Dr. Robert W. Mullins, "Letter of Dr. Robert W. Mullins to Reverend Oates," 20 October 1984, http://www.bishop-accountability.org.

10. Dr. John Brennan, "Letter of Dr. John Brennan to Reverend Banks," 14 December 1984, http://www.bishop-accountability.org.

11. For chronology, see: Globe Staff, "Geoghan's Troubled History," *The Boston Globe*, 7 January 2002, www.boston.com/globe/spotlight/abuse/stories/010702_history.htm.

12. Dr. Robert Swords, "Letter of Dr. Robert Swords to Reverend Robert Banks," 13 Decemter 1989, http://www.bishop-accountability.org.

13. David Arnold and Michael Rezendes, "Law Deposition Ends, for Now," *The Boston Globe*, 14 May 2002, p. B1.

14. Walter V. Robinson, "Shining the Globe's Spotlight on the Catholic Church," *Neiman Foundation for Journalism at Harvard: Neiman Reports*, Spring 2003, http://www.nieman.harvard.edu/reports/article/101186/Shining-the-Globe.

15. Matt Carroll, Kevin Cullen, Thomas Farragher, Steven Kurkjan, Michael Paulson, Sara Pfeiffer, Michael Rezendez, and Walter V. Robinson, among others.

16. The investigative staff of *The Boston Globe*. *Betrayal: The Crisis in the Catholic Church* (New York: Little, Brown and Company, 2002), p. vii.

17. Robinson, "Shining the Globe's Spotlight," p. 5.

18. See the following cases: WestlawNext, *Leary v. Geogha*n, 26 November 2001; WestlawNext, *Globe Newspaper Co. Inc. v. Clerk of Suffolk County Superior Court*,

4 February 2002; WestlawNext, *Globe Newspaper Co. Inc. v. Clerk of Middlesex County Superior Court*, 5 March 2002.

19. Robinson, "Shining the Globe's Spotlight," p. 1.

20. United States District Court District of Massachusetts, "Local Rules of the United States District Court for the District of Massachusetts. Rule 83.2B 'Special Orders for the Protection of the Accused or the Litigants in Widely Publicized or Sensational Criminal or Civil Cases,'" 1 September 1990, p. 84, http://www.mad.uscourts.gov/general/pdf/lc/localrulescombined .pdf.

21. Andrea Kuperman, "Case Law on Entering Protective Orders, Entering Sealing Orders," July 2010, p. 1, http://www.uscourts/.gov/uscourts/rulesand policies.

22. Between 3–12 April 1989, Geoghan was at St. Luke Institute. His evaluation led to this diagnosis. See: Globe Staff, "Geoghan's Troubled History," *The Boston Globe*, 7 January 2002, http://www.bishop-accountability.org.

23. Associated Press. "Files Show Archdiocese Paid $21 Million in Abuse Cases," *The New York Times*, 13 August 2003, p. 20.

24. Michael Rezendes and the *Globe* Spotlight team, "Church Allowed Abuse by Priests for Years," *The Boston Globe*, 6 January 2002, http://www.boston.com /globe/spotlight/abuse/stories/010602_geoghan.htm.

25. Founded in 1978, the NAMBLA website claims it was "inspired by the success of a campaign based in Boston's gay community to defend against a local witchhunt." It's goal is "to end the extreme oppression of men and boys in mutually consensual relations" and itsmembership is open to everyone "sympathetic" to man/boy love and personal freedom. See http://www.nambla .org/welcome.html

26. Globe Spotlight Team, "Excerpts from Judge Sweeney's Ruling," *The Boston Globe*, 26 November 2002, p. A14.

27. Ibid.

28. Westchester County April "E" 2002 grand jury, *Report of the April "E" 2002 Westchester Country Grand Jury Concerning Complaints of Sexual Abuse and Misconduct against Minors by Members of the Clergy.* 19 June 2002, http://www.bishop-accountability .org/resource/resourcefiles/report/WestchesterGrandJuryReport.pdf.

29. Ibid., p. 15.

30. Hamilton County Prosecutors. "Settlement Agreement between the archdiocese of Cincinnati and the Hamilton Country Prosecuting Attorney," Signed by Michael K. Allan and Archbishop Daniel E, Pilarczyk, 20 November 2003, http://www.bishop-accountability.org.

31. See Archbishop Daniel E. Pilarczyk, "Statement by Archbishop Daniel Pilarczyk," *Catholic Telegraph*, 20 November 2003, http:///www.bishop-accountability/org /resources.

32. Walter V. Robinson and Michael Rezendes, "Geoghan Victims Agree to $10M Settlement," *The Boston Globe*, 19 September 2002, http://www.bishop -accounability/org/ma-bos/settlements.

33. Stephen Kurkjian and Walter V. Robinson, "Archdiocese Abandons Deal in Geoghan Case, Committee Rebuff Law, Cites Serious Fiscal Threat," *The Boston Globe*, 4 May 2002, http://www.bishop-accountability.org/ma-bos/setttlements.

34. Robinson and Rezendes, "Geoghan Victims Agree to $10M Settlement."

35. Office of the Attorney General, Commonwealth of Massachusetts, "The Sexual Abuse of Children in the Roman Catholic Archdiocese of Boston," 23 July 2003, p. 16, http://www.bishop-accountability.org/downloads/archexecsumm.pdf.

36. Ibid., p. 25.

37. Ibid., p. 27.

38. Ibid., p. 28.

39. Ibid., p. 30.

40. Ibid., p. 31.

41. Associated Press. "Judge Rebuffs Church's Motion to Halt Law's Testimony Today," *The New York Times*, 22 January 2003, p. A 12.

42. Office of the Attorney General, Commonwealth of Massachusetts. p. 73. Accessed at www.ago.state.ma.us

43. See, for example: Massachusetts General Laws: Chapter 265, Section 13 (Indecent Assault and Battery on a Child Under 14); Section 22A (Rape of a Child; Use of Force); Section 23 (Rape and Abuse of Child); Section 24B (Assault of Child; Intent to Commit Rape). See also Massachusetts General Laws: Chapter 119; Section 21 (Mandated Reporters Defined); Chapter 119, Section 51A (Mandated Reporting Explained). See also Massachusetts General Laws: Chapter 277, Section 63 (State of Limitations for Criminal Cases). This now allows a period of 27 years from reporting or from a victim turning 16. Massachusetts General Laws, Chapter 260, Section 4C (State of Limitations for Civil Cases). This now allows a victim to bring suit three years from the act or three years from when the victim "discovered or reasonably should have discovered that an emotional or psychological injury or condition was cased by said act." Information accessed at http://www.lawlib.state.ma.us /subject/about/childsexabuse.html.

44. Michael Paulson, "Citing Deficit, Archdiocese Eyes Substantial Budget Cuts," *The Boston Globe*, 24 March 2005, http://www.boston.globe.

45. Michael Paulson. "Leaving 'Little Rome' for Braintree," *The Boston Globe*, 26 June 2008, p. Al.

46. Abby Goodnough, "Archdiocese of Boston Lists Priests Tied to Abuse," *The New York Times*, 28 August 2011, p. A12

47. Pam Belluck and Frank Bruni, "A Yearlong Crisis," *The New York Times*, 14 October 2002, p. A1.

48. Office of the Attorney General of the Commonwealth of Massachusetts, "The Sexual Abuse of Children," pp. 32–33.
49. Daniel J. Wakin, "Brooklyn Bishop Ending Tenure amid Storm over Scandal," *The New York Times*, 2 August 2003, http://www.bishop-accountability.org/news 2003_07_12/2003_08_02_Wakin_BrooklynBishop.htm.
50. Ibid., p. 43.
51. Sam Dillon, "In New Hampshire, Abuse Cases Undermine a Catholic Bishop," *The New York Times*, 18 18 October 2002, p. 51, http://www.snapnetwork.org /news/otherstates/NH_NYTimes_on_McCormick.htm.
52. Ibid.
53. Peter W. Heed, N. William Delker, James D. Rosenberg, *Report on the Investigation of the Diocese of Manchester* (No. 02–8-1154), p. 1. Overview of the Investigation, Office of the Attorney General, 3 March 2003. http://www .bishop-accountability.org/reports/2003_03_03_NHAG.
54. Ibid., p. 2.
55. *Lemon v. Kurtzman* 403 U. S. 602 (1971). The test established in the case was based on three questions: (1) Does the government advance a secular or legislative purpose? (2) Does its primary effect neither support nor inhibit religion? and (3) Does the government's action create an entangling alliance between Church and State?
56. Dave Wedge, "John Geoghan Killer Joe Druce Posted to Marry," *Boston Herald*, 6 October 2012, http://www.freerepublic.com/focus/f-chat/2601937/posts.
57. John R. Ellement and Jonathon Saltzman. "Defrocked Priest Shanley Is a Victim of 'Injustice,' His Attorney Says," *The Boston Globe*, 15 January 2010, http://www.boston.com/news/local/breaking_news/2010/01/sjc_rules _in_sh.html.
58. Pam Belluck, "A Prominent Accuser in Boston Abuse Scandal Is Found Dead," *The New York Times*, 24 February 2008, p. A18.

3   Challenge and Complexity: Canon Law and Civil Law

1. *Acts of the Apostles*, 8:3.
2. Ibid., 9:12.
3. 1 Timothy 3.
4. Titus 1.
5. 1 Timothy 3.
6. 1 Corinthians 2:7.
7. Ibid.
8. See Peter Kirby, "The Didache. The Lord's Teaching through the Twelve Apostles to the Nations." Chapter 2 translated by Bishop John Robertson and

Sir James Donaldson. 16 April 2009. http://www.earlychirstianwritings.com/text/didache-roberts.html.

9. Father Thomas Doyle, O. P. and Stephen C. Rubino, Esq., "Catholic Clergy Sexual Abuse Meets the Civil Law," *Fordham Urban Law Journal* 31, no. 2 (2003): 32, Article 6, http://ir.lawnet.fordham.edu/ulj.

10. Fr. Brendan Daly, "Sexual Abuse and Canon Law," *Compass* 43 (Spring 2009): 34.

11. Ibid.

12. Doyle and Rubino, "Catholic Clergy Sexual Abuse," p. 15.

13. Edward Peters, trans., *The 1917 Pio-Benedictine Code of Canon Law* (San Francisco: Ignatius Press, 2001).

14. Nicholas P. Cafardi, *Before Dallas: The US Bishops' Response to Clergy Sexual Abuse of Children.* (Mahwah, NJ: Paulist Press, 2008). See Chapter 4 and his specific references from Adam J. Maida, "The Selection, Training and Removal of Diocesan Clergy," *Catholic Lawyer* 33 (1990): p. 60, and John G. Proctor, "Clerical Misconduct: Canonical and Practical Consequences," *CSLA Proceedings* 49 (1987): p. 237.

15. These were instructions from the Supreme Sacred Congregation of the Holy Office and approved by Pope John Paul II on 16 March 1962. The orders were addressed to all of the members of the Church leadership with a caveat that said that they were "to be kept carefully in the secret archive of the Curia for internal use," that they were not for public discussion, and that they were not to be "published or augmented with commentaries." Accessed at http://www.vatican.va/resources/resources-crimen-sollicitationis-1962.

16. Ibid., specifically see Sections l, 2, 3, and 4 for the actual procedures that must be followed.

17. *The Code of Canon Law* (1983), Book VI, Part II, Canon 1395, para. 2, http://www.vatican.va/archives/ENG1104/-56.HTM.

18. Ibid.

19. Ibid., 1718, para. 1.

20. Ibid., 1341.

21. See Ibid., 1324, Section 1, paras. 1, 2, and 3.

22. Cafardi, *Before Dallas.* See specifically Chapter 3 for a fuller explanation.

23. Rembert W. Weakland, *A Pilgrim in a Pilgrim Church* (Grand Rapids, MI: Eerdmans, 2009), p. 268.

24. Ibid., pp. 269–270.

25. Ibid., p. 170.

26. Cafardi, *Before Dallas*, p. 63.

27. These became revisions to canon law in 2001 and were promulgated by Pope John Paul in his Apostolic Letter to the Congregation for the Doctrine of the Faith, *The Norms of the Motu Proprio' Sacramentorum Sanctitatis Tutela'* (2001), http://www.vatican.va/resources/resource.into-storica-en-html.

28. Matthew 16: 18–19.

29. Tad Szulc, *Pope John Paul II: The Biography* (New York: Pocket Books, 1995), p. 262.

30. Ibid., p. 379.

31. Jo Renee Formicola, *John Paul II: Prophetic Politician* (Washington, DC: Georgetown University Press, 2000). See specifically Chapters 2 and 5.

32. Reuters, "Society Shares Blame for Scandals, Vatican Says: Catholic Church: Permissiveness is 'real culprit' in Abuse of Children," *Los Angeles Times*, 26 June 1993, p. B5.

33. Ibid.

34. Ibid.

35. William D. Montalbano, "Pontiff Assails US Church, Sex Abuse by Priests," *Los Angeles Times*, 15 August 1993, p. A1.

36. Pope John Paul II, *Ecclesia in Oceana*, December 1998, Chapter IV, para. 39, http://www.vatican.va.

37. Congregation for the Doctrine of the Faith, *The Norms*.

38. Melinda Henneberger, "Vatican to Hold Secret Trials of Priests in Pedophilia Cases," *The New York Times*, 9 January 2002, p. A8.

39. Ron Howell, "Vatican Focuses on Gay Priests," *Newsday* (Queens edition), 21 March 2002, p. A6.

40. Melinda Henneberger, "Scandal Left to US Catholics," *The New York Times*, 14 April 2002, p. A9.

41. John Paul II, *Ad Tuendam Fidem, by Which Certain Norms Are Inserted into the Code of Canon Law and into the Code of Canons of the Eastern Churches*, promulgated 18 May 1998, http://www.vatican.va/holy_father/john_paul_ii /motu_proprio/documents.

42. Ibid.

43. The National Review Board for the Protection of Children and Young People. *A Report on the Crisis in the Catholic Church in the United States* (Washington, DC: The United States Conference of Catholic Bishops, 2004), p. 43, http:// www.bishop-accountability.org.

44. See Richard Boudreaux and Larry B. Stammer, "US Catholics and Vatican Face a Cultural Chasm in Coping with Sex Scandal," *Los Angeles Times*, 23 April 2002, p. A1, http://www.articles.latimes.com/2002/apr/23.

45. Ibid.

46. Henneberger, "Scandal Left to US Catholics," p. A9.

47. Vatican, "Final Communique" of the Meeting between the cardinals of the United States and the pope," 24 April 2002, http://www.vatican.va/roman _curia/cardina...rdinal_20020424_final-communique_en.html.

48. "Pope's Speech to American Cardinals on Church Crisis," *The New York Times*, 24 April 2002, p. A22.

49. Ibid.

50. Ibid.

51. Patricia Rice, "Gregory Hails Pope's Response to US Scandal: 'He Gets It,'" *St. Louis Post-Dispatch*, 28 April 2002, p. B1.

52. Ibid.

53. Anne E. Kornblut, "Crisis in the Church, Vatican Visit; President Weighs in on Church Scandal," *The Boston Globe*, 29 May 2002, p. A14.

4 Too Little, Too Late: The Hierarchy Responds

1. The Quinnipiac Polling Institute, "Sex Abuse Priests and The Bishops Who Hid Them Should Go, American Catholics Tell Quinnipiac University Poll; Catholics 3–1 Want Equal Say in Dealing with Issue," Quinnipiac University, 12 June 2002, http://www.quinnipiac.edu/institutes-and-centers/polling-institute /national/release-detail?ReleaseID=476.

2. John Bookser Feister, "US Bishops Prepare for Key Meeting," AmericanCatholic.org, 12 June 2002, http://www.americancatholic.org/news /clergysexabuse/USCCB-Dallas_Wednesday.asp.

3. Ibid.

4. Gary Wills, "Bishops at Bay," *The New York Review of Books*, 15 August 2002, p. 7, http://www.nybooks.com/articles/archives/2002/aug/15/the-bishops-at -bay.

5. Ibid., p. 5.

6. Ibid.

7. Ibid., 7.

8. Wilton D. Gregory, "Comments of Bishop Wilton D. Gregory to the Religion Newswriters Association," Archdiocese of Milwaukee, 5 September 2003, http://www.archmil.org/ArchMil/Resources/bishopgregoryaddress.pdf.

9. Congregation for the Doctrine of the Faith, *The Code of Canon Law, 1983*, Canons 290–293, 1717 and 1719, http://www.vatican.va/archives/ENG1104/-56.HTM.

10. Thomas F. Reilly, "The Sexual Abuse of Children in the Roman Catholic Archdiocese of Boston: Executive Summary and Scope of Investigation," Office of the Attorney General Commonwealth of Massachusetts, 23 July 2003, p. 1 and 1–1 in Appendix 1, http://www.bishop-accountability.org /downloads/archdiocese.pdf.

11. *Stogner v. California*, 539 US 607 (2003).

12. The Court of Appeal of the State of California, Second Appellate District Division Three re: Los Angeles County Superior Court, No. BH0011928 (B177852) and Los Angeles Country Superior Court No. BH0011928 (B180696).

13. Decision of the Court of Appeals of the State of California in Archdiocese of Los Angeles v. Superior Court of Los Angeles County (and Doe 1 and 2 v Superior Court of Los Angeles County [BH001928]), p. 4, http://www .lawlink.com/research/caselevel3/82533.

14. Archdiocese of Los Angeles., *Report to the People of God: Clergy Sexual Abuse, Archdiocese of Los Angeles (1930–2003)*, 17 February 2004, pp. 7, 11. http://www.la-archdiocese.org/org/protecting/reports/Documents/2004 -0217_ADLA_CSA_Report.

15. Westchester County April "E" 2002 Grand Jury, *Report of the April "E" 2002 Westchester Country Grand Jury Concerning Complaints of Sexual Abuse and Misconduct against Minors by Members of the Clergy*, Issued 19 June 2002, www.Bishop-accountability.org/resources/resourcefiles/report/Westchester GrandJuryReport.pdf. p. 29–30.

16. Suffolk County Supreme Court Special Grand Jury. *Grand Jury Report CPL $190.85(1)(C)*, 6 May 2002. Issued 17 January 2003, http://www.bishop -accountability.org/reports/2003_02_10_SuffolkGrandJury/Suffolk_Full _Report.pdf.

17. Ibid., pp. 106, 142, 144.

18. Canon law says that the statute expires after a victim turns 28 or ten years after turning 18.

19. Laurie Goodstein, "Catholic Orders Might Keep Abusive Priests," *The New York Times,* 22 July 2002, p. A9.

20. Sam Dillon, "Catholic Religious Orders Let Abusive Priests Stay," *The New York Times,* 10 August 2002, p. A8.

21. Giovanni Battista Re, Letter of Cardinal Giovanni Battista Re to Bishop Wilton Gregory, 14 October 2002, http://www.bishop-accountability.org/resources /resource-files/churchdocs/Gregory.htm.

22. Bishop David J. Malloy, *The Charter for the Protection of Children and Young People, USCCB,* 16 June 2011, Footnote to Article 2. First Draft. http://www.usccb .org/issues-and-action/child-and-youth-protection/upload/Charter-for-the -Protection-of-Children-and-Young-People-revised-2011.pdf.

23. Ibid.

24. Ibid.

25. USCCB, *Charter for the Protection of Children and Young People.* Final, Revised Edition (Washington, DC: 2002). Footnote to Article 2. http://www.usccb .org/issues-and-action/child-and-youth-protection/upload/Charter-for-the -Protection-of-Children-and-Young-People-revised-2011.pdf.

26. Ibid.

27. Ibid.

28. Hamilton County Prosecutors, "Settlement Agreement between the Archdiocese of Cincinnati and the Hamilton County Prosecuting Attorney," signed 20 November 2003, p. 2, http://www.bishop-accountability.org/resources /resource-files/courtdocs/2003–11–20-Pilarczyk-Agreement.pdf.

29. Ibid., p. 3.

30. Ibid., p. 6. For the archbishop's reaction see: Daniel E. Pilarczyk, "Statement by Archbishop Daniel E. Pilarczyk," *Catholic Telegraph*, 20 November 2003, http://

www.bishop-accountability.org/resources/resource-files/timeline/2003–11
–20-Pilarczyk-Statement.htm.

31. Joseph A. Reaves, "Romley, O'Brien Clash Over Substance of Deal; Bishop
Denies He's Admitting Cover-Up," *Arizona Republic*, 3 June 2003, http://
www.bishop-accountability.org/news2003_01_06/2003_06_03_Reaves
_RomleyOBrien.htm.

32. "Text of Agreement between the State of Arizona ex.rel. Richard M
Romley, Maricopa Country Attorney; Thomas J. O'Brien, Bishop of the
Roman Catholic Diocese of Phoenix and the Roman Catholic Diocese of
Phoenix," a corporation sole ("the diocese"), 3 May 2003, http://www.bishop
-accountability.org/az-phoenix/phoenix-agreement-resignation.htm.

33. *Arizona Republic* Staff, "Text of Bishop O'Brien's News Conference," *Arizona
Republic*, 2 June 2003, http://www.bishop-accountability.org/az-phoenix/phoenix
-agreement-resignation.htm.

34. Ibid.

35. David O'Reilly and Nancy Phillips, "Grand Jury Harshly Criticizes
Archdiocese for Hiding Clergy Sexual Abuse," *Philadelphia Inquirer*, 21
September 2005, p. l.

36. Lynne Abraham, District Attorney of Philadelphia. *Report of the Grand Jury*. In
the Court of Common Pleas First Judicial District of Pennsylvania Criminal
Trial Division. *In Re: County Investigating Grand Jury*. Misc. No. 03-00-239.
Introduction. Section IV, 59–76. 17 September 2003, http://www.bishop
-accountability.org

37. R. Seth Williams, District Attorney of Philadelphia. *Report of the Grand Jury*.
Grand Jury Hearing XXIII in the Court of Common Pleas Hearing XXIII
of the First Judicial District of Pennsylvania. Misc. No. 0009901–2008,
p. 34.

38. Ibid., p. 23.

39. Ibid., p. 29.

40. Ibid., pp. 43–44.

41. Associated Press, "Pennsylvania: Ex-Priest Recants Guilt in Abuse Case," *The
New York Times*, 18 January 2013, p. A17.

42. Sam Hemingway, "Vermont Roman Catholic Diocese, Priest Abuse
$17.65 Million Settlement," *Burlington Free Press*, 14 May 2012, http://www
.burlingtonfreepress.com/article/20100514/news.

43. Laurie Goodstein, "Defying Civil and Canon Laws, Church Failed to Stop a
Priest," *The New York Times*, 8 September 2012, p. A1. Bishop Finn was found
guilty on one misdemeanor charge and sentenced to two years of court-
supervised probation.

44. Sam Hemingway, "Diocese Settles 11 Priest Sex Abuse Cases in Burlington,
Federal Court," 9 January 2013, http://www.burlingtonfreepress.com/article
/2013109/news.

45. Associated Press, "Cardinal to be Questioned about Role in Abuse Cases," *The New York Times*, 17 February 2012, p. 23.

46. *Economist* Staff, "Briefing: The Catholic Church in America," *The Economist*, 18 August 2012, p. 19.

47. John Jay College of Criminal Justice. In February 2005, a second *Report on the Implementation of "The Charter" for the Protection of Children and Young People Issued by the Office of Child and Youth Protection of the USCCB* reported that 1,092 new accusations of abuse were made. See http://www.nccbuscc.org/ocyp/dioceseo405–039.html.

48. Associated Press, "Catholic Church's Costs Pass $1 Billion in Abuse Cases," *The New York Times*, 12 June 2005, p. A33.

49. See report of the US Conference of Catholic Bishops issued on 30 March 2006, which reported that $467 million had been paid out in settlements during the year. Accessed at http://www.catholic.org/national. These include financial settlements such as an $85 million payout by the Archdiocese of Boston, another settlement for 88 claims for $75,000 each, and a third group of about 70 other victims waiting to make further accusations. In Orange Country, California, the archdiocese was required to pay out $104.7 million to settle claims against its priests for sexual abuse, the largest ever. In Louisville, the archdiocese agreed to a settlement of $25.7 million to resolve 243 civil suits, an agreement that has depleted more than half of the diocese's cash assets. In Covington, Kentucky, the diocese settled for $120 million. Smaller payouts have included a $6.3 million settlement by the Christian Brothers, a $5 million payout in New Jersey, $3.4 million in Miami, and numerous private settlements to individuals to end embarrassing litigation in an ever-increasing number of dioceses across the United States. These individual reports are available in the media, but an aggregate of this information is available currently through the website of the US Catholic Bishops at http://www.usccb.org.

50. No official amounts are available from the Catholic Church presently. This figure is from Cathy Lynn Grossman, "Clergy Sex Abuse Settlements Top $2.5 Billion Nationwide," *USA Today*, 13 March 2013. The number continues to escalate with each subsequent settlement. Accessed at: http://www.usatoday.com/story/news/nation/2013/03/13/sex-abuse-settlement-cardinal-roger-mahony/1984217/.

51. *Economist* Staff, "Briefing," p. 20.

52. Colin Fogarty, "Bankruptcy Bills 'Staggering' for Portland Archdiocese," Oregon OPB Online, 25 October 2005.

53. Priests who belong to "orders," such as Jesuits, Dominicans, etc., are under the authority of abbots or the heads of their orders, rather than bishops or archbishops. Bishops can remove parish priests from religious service, but only the Vatican, with the approval of the pope, can laicize or defrock a priest.

54. In Washington State, for example, this includes all churches, schools, cemeteries, and parcels of land.

55. Mark E. Chopko, "Shaping the Church: Overcoming the Twin Challenges of Secularization and Scandal," 53 *Catholic University Law Review* 125 (Fall 2003): p. 151.

56. Ibid. Chopko argues from *New Hampshire v. Presbyterian Church* 998 P.2d, 592, 598.(USA.).

57. United State Bankruptcy Court, D. Oregon. *In Re Roman Catholic Archbishop of Portland in Or., 335 B. R. 842 (Bankr. D. Or. 2005)* Bankruptcy Case No. 04–37154, Adversary No., 04-3292. https://www.courtlistener.com/orb/8QCL /in-re-roman-catholic-archbishop-of-portland-in-or/

58. Ibid. p. 21 at 9–11; 15–17; and p. 24 at 5–7.

59. To add to the complexity of this situation, all archdioceses and/or dioceses are not incorporated. For example, Boston is, but Philadelphia is not incorporated hence, the Philadelphia grand jury's recommendation to hold unincorporated entities (as associations) liable as incorporated ones.

60. United States Bankruptcy Court, D. Oregon, p. 29 at 14.

61. Ibid. p. 31 at 19. In 2005, the state Bankruptcy Court ruled that a test group of nine Catholic churches and one school could be sold to pay sexual abuse claims. However, a reorganization plan was mediated that made the point moot. It protected parish properties and provided acceptable settlements for the plaintiffs in 2007.

62. United States Bankruptcy Court, D. Oregon, p. 32 at 6. The court specifically said individuals did not "have a constitutional right to worship in any particular building."

63. Ibid., p 34 at 12. In response, the Archdiocese of Portland appealed to the US Bankruptcy Court for protection of a $36 million trust fund, claiming that it should not be forced to liquidate those monies to pay for sexual abuse claims. The court held for the Church in the matter.

64. Up to $39.7 million was paid through Church loans and assets. Another $51.75 million was paid by Church insurance. About $17 million in attorneys' fees will have to be absorbed by the archdiocese. See: Ashbel S. Green and Aimee Green, "Parishioners Welcome Settlement," *The Oregonian*, 20 December 2006, http://www.BishopAccountability.org.

65. Nicholas K. Geranios, "Lawyer for Victims of Abuse Seeks to Include Parish Property," *The Associated Press*, 12 April 2005.

66. United States Bankruptcy Court, Summary Judgment of Judge Patricia Williams, filed 25 August 2005, NO. 04–08822-PCW11, Chapter 11.

67. United States District Court for the Eastern District of Washington, Committee of Tort Litigants, et. al. vs. Catholic Diocese of Spokane, et.al., No. 05-CV-274-JLQ, Bkty. Ct. No. 04–08822-PCW11.

68. For a breakdown of how the claims will be paid and allocated, see: John Stucke and Virginia de Leon, "Diocese Files Settlement," *The Spokesman-Review*, 5 January 2007, http://www.spokesmanreview.com.

69. Arthur H. Rotstein, "Tuscon Diocese Bankruptcy Effectively over a Year Later," *Associated Press*, as carried in the *Seattle Post-Intelligencer*, 18 September 2005, http://www.bishop-accountability.org.

70. Thomas Geyer, "Davenport Diocese Files for Bankruptcy," *Quad-City Times*, 12 October 2006, http://www.qctimes.com/news/local/davenport-diocese -files-for-bankruptcy/article_fdbe9ddd-8bc7–58ea-8da6-cdbb4c9561a0.html.

71. Mark Sauer, "San Diego Catholic Diocese Files for Bankruptcy," *The San Diego Union-Tribune*, 28 February 2007. http://www.signonsandiego.com/news /metro/20070228–9999–7n28diocese.html.

72. Associated Press, "Claims of Abuse by Priests Double," 9 January 2007, http:// www.adn.com/news/alaska.

73. Bishop Donald J. Kettler. Press Release: "Fairbanks Diocese Seeks A Consensual Plan for Reorganization," 13 February 2008, http://www.bishop -accountability.org/news.

74. Ian Urbina, "Delaware Diocese Files for Bankruptcy in Wake of Abuse Suits," *The New York Times*, 20 December 2010, p. A10.

75. Statement of The Archdiocese of Milwaukee. "Love One Another," 4 January 2011. Available at http://www.archmil.org/reorg.htm.

76. Chopko, "Shaping the Church," p. 17.

77. Mary Beth Smetzer, "Court Ruling Leaves Fairbanks Diocese without Insurance in Abuse Cases," *News Miner*, 3 October 2009, http://www.bishop -accountability.org/news2009.

5   Pushback and Payback: The Laity and the Lawyers

1. Bill Frogameni, "Toledo Native Barbara Blaine Crusades against Sexual Abuse in the Catholic Church," *Toledo City Paper*, 29 April 2004, http://www .bishop-accountability.org/news2004_01_06/2004_04_frog.

2. Ibid.

3. Ibid.

4. Jerimee Richir, "SNAP Mission Statement," 2012, http://www.snapnetwork .org/mission_statement.

5. Patricia Rice, "Priest Accused of Abuse Was Given Parish Job," *Post-Dispatch*, 8 April 2002, http://www.bishop-accountability.org/news3/2002_04_08_Rice _PriestAccused.

6. Peter McDonough, *The Catholic Labyrinth: Power, Apathy and a Passion for Reform in the American Church* (New York: Oxford University Press, 2013, p. 149.

7. Richir, "SNAP Mission Statement."

8. David Clohessy, "A50A471 Deposition in Case # 1016CV29995," 2 January 2012, p. 42, http://www.themediareport.com/wp-content/uploads/2012/03/CLOHESSY-DEPOSITION-010212.pdf.

9. *David Clohessy v. The Honorable Ann J. Mesle*, "Writ of Prohibition," 19 July 2012, https://d3n8a8pro7vhmx.cloudfront.net/snap/pages/1114/attachments/original/1343231724/Petition_for_Writ_July_19_2012.pdf?1343231724.

10. Clohessy, "A50A471 Deposition," p. 42.

11. Laurie Goodstein, "Catholic Church Puts legal Pressure on Survivors' Network," *The New York Times*, 13 March 2012, http://www.nytimes.com/2012/03/13/us/catholic-church-pressures-victims.
The author attributes this statement to Marci Hamilton, a law professor at Yeshiva University, who is an advocate for clergy sex abuse victims.

12. United States Conference of Catholic Bishops, Office of Media Relations. "Conference President Invites Continued Dialogue with 'SNAP,'" 10 June 2002, http://old.usccb.org/comm/archives/2002/02-109.shtml.

13. David Clohessy, "Impact Statement," given to the USCCB Meeting in Dallas, Texas, 13 June 2002, http://www.bishop-accountability.org/resources/resource-files/timeline/2002-06-13-Clohessy-ImpactStatement.htm.

14. Michael D'Antonio, *Mortal Sins: Sex, Crime, and the Era of Catholic Scandal* (New York: St. Martin's Press, 2013).

15. In 1993, sexual abuse allegations were leveled against a number of Franciscan Friars at St. Anthony's Seminary in Santa Barbara, California, from 1964 to 1987. A board of inquiry was set up to investigate the matter and confirmed 34 allegations. Finally in 2006, after pressure from SNAP and some of its members who were also victims in this predatory situation, a number of cases were brought against Rev. Mario Cimmarrusti, OFM, former prefect of discipline at St. Anthony Seminary. The Franciscans settled with 25 local plaintiffs against Cimmarrusti and others for $28.5 million.

16. Ashley Powers, "Secret Files Detail Clergy Abuse," *Los Angles Times*, 24 May 2012, http://www.latimes.com/20112/may/24/local.

17. McDonough, *The Catholic Labyrinth*, p. 150.

18. Barbara Blaine, "Why the Pope Must Fact Justice at The Hague," *The Guardian*, 17 September 2011, http://www.theguardian.com/commentisfree/ciefarmerica/2011/sep/17/pope--clergy-sex-abuse-hague.

19. Ibid.

20. Amnesty International, *Annual Report*, 2011, http://www.amnesty.org/en/annual-report2011.

21. *Malin v. Singer* (2013) to repudiate *Gerbosi v. Gaims* (2011) 193 Cal. Appr. 4th 435, http://www.casp.net/uncategorized/five-amici-briefs-filed-to-challenge-gerbosi.

22. Paul Fericano, "Bridge of Understanding," *Santa Barbara Independent*, 12 August 2004, http://mysafenet.org/?q=node/47.

23. Daniel Lyons, "Paid to Picket," *Forbes*, 15 September 2003, http://www.forbes.com/forbes/2003/0915/054.html.

24. Ibid.

25. Michelle Bauman, "SNAP Director Admits to Publishing False Information," *Catholic News Agency*, 6 March 2012. Accessed at http://ww.catholicnewsagency.com/news/snap-director-admits-to-publishing

26. Laurie Goodstein. "Catholic Church Puts Legal Pressure on Survivors' Network," *The New York Times,* 12 March 2012, http://www.nytimes.com/2012/03/13/us/catholic-church-pressures-victims.

27. Catholic League for Religious and Civil Rights, "About Us," n.d., http://www.catholicleague.org.

28. Ibid.

29. Ibid.

30. McDonough, *The Catholic Labyrinth*, p. 171.

31. Tricia Colleen Bruce, *Faithful Revolution: How Voice of the Faithful is Changing the Church.* (New York: Oxford University Press, 2011).

32. See: A. B. Carroll, K. J. Lipartito, J. E. Post, P. H. Werhane, and K. E. Goodpaster, *Corporate Responsibility: The American Experience* (Cambridge: Cambridge University Press, 2012).

33. James E. Muller and Charles Kenney, *Keep the Faith, Change the Church* (New York: St. Martin's Press, 2011).

34. Ibid., p. 50.

35. Michael Paulson, "Law Seeks to Curb Organizing by Laity," *The Boston Globe*, 27 April 2002, p. A1.

36. Ibid.

37. Michael Paulson, "Bishop Bans Group from meetings at Parish," *The Boston Globe*, 1 October 2002, p. A1.

38. James Carroll, "Let Church Reform Begin," *The Boston Globe*, 16 September 2002, p. A15.

39. Paulson, "Bishop Bans Group," p. A1.

40. Deal Hudson, "When Wolves Dress Like Sheep: Close Look at Voice of the Faithful," *Crisis Magazine*, 8 August 2002, http://www.staycatholic.com.

41. Greg Byrnes, "Some Attending Voice of the Faithful Meetings Find They Have No Voice," 2003, http://www.staycatholic.com/no_voice_at_voice_of_the_faithful.htm.

42. Ibid.

43. Muller and Kenney, *Keep the Faith* p. 175

44. Ibid., p. 115.

45. Bruce, *Faithful Revolution*, p. 62.

46. Michael Paulson, "Catholic Group to Rate bishops," *The Boston Globe*, 20 September 2002, p. A1.

47. These included Bishop Walter Edyvean, the vicar for administration, and Father Mark O'Connell, the canon lawyer for the Boston Archdiocese.

48. Muller and Kenney, *Keep the Faith*, pp. 5–6.

49. Michael Paulson, "In His First Meeting with Voice of the Faithful, Law Seeks Answers," *The Boston Globe,* 27 November 2002, p. B1.

50. Clay Shirky, *Here Comes Everybody* (New York: Penguin Books, 2008), p.148.

51. Ibid.

52. Voice of the Faithful, "Clerical Culture among Roman Catholic Diocesan Clergy," No Date, http://www.votf.org/clericalism.pdf.

53. Voice of the Faithful, "Clericalism: Reality and Concerns," No Date, http://votf.org/page/clericalism-reality-and-concerns/18094.

54. Stephanie Block, "Is It the Voice of the Faithful?" CatholicCulture.org, No Date, http://www.catholicculture.org/culture/lobaray/view.cfm?recnum-7303.

55. VOTF was concerned that the report did not address clericalism by name, that it lacked an analysis of the priestly culture, and that without a modification of it, clericalism would do "harm to victims and their families, to the members of faith communities, and to clergy." See: Voice of the Faithful, "Conclusion about the John Jay College Report: 'The Causes and Context of Sexual Abuse of Minors by Catholic Priests in the US 1950–2010,'" 11 October 2011, p. 9, http://www.votf.org/Govt_reports/VOTF_Conclusions_Report.pdf.

56. Bruce, *Faithful Revolution*, p. 138.

57. Voice of the Faithful, "Conclusion about," p. 10.

58. Voice of the Faithful. Press Release. "Voice of the Faithful Urges Pope Francis to 'Act Decisively' Regarding Bishops, Clergy Sexual Abuse and His Message to Vatican Congregation." 6 June 2013. http://votf.org/featured/18098.

59. Voice of the Faithful. "The Six Most Important Reforms VOTF Would Like to Discuss with His Advisors in October," 24 September 2013, http://voicefaithful.wordpress.com/2013/09/24/the-six-most-important-reforms-voice-of-the-faithful-would-like-pope-francis-to-discuss-with-his-advisors-in-october/.

60. Muller and Kenney, pp. 279–80.

61. Bishop-Accountability.org, "Who We Are," June 2003, http://www.bishop-accountability.org/Who_We_Are.

62. Bishop-Accountability.org, "Introduction to the Archives," n.d., http://www.bishopsaccountability.org/Introduction_to_the-Archives.

63. Bishop-Accountability.org, "Some Things You Helped Us Achieve in 2011," n.d., http://www.bishopaccountability.org/2011.

64. *Hosanna-Tabor Evangelical Lutheran Church and School v. Equal Employment Opportunity Commission*, No. 10–553, 9 August 2011, http://www.Americanbar.org.

65. TheMediaReport.com, "Bishop-Accountability.org Exposed: The Self Professed Chroniclers of Abuse Smearing Innocent Priests," 4 April 2013.

The article refers to the case of Father Roger N. Jacques, who underwent a four-year investigation for clerical sexual abuse and was exonerated. His name, however, was not removed from the list of those "publicly accused" on the website. Accessed at http://www.themediareport.com/2013/04/or/bishop -accountability-org.

66. For a fuller discussion of the clash between civil and canon law in America, see: Jo Renee Formicola, "The Vatican, the American bishops, and the church-state Ramifications of Clerical Sexual Abuse," *Journal of Church and State* 46 (Summer 2004): 479–502.

67. *Doe v. Holy See*, US Court of Appeals for the Ninth Circuit, No. 06–35563 and 06–35587.

68. *O'Bryan v. Holy See*, US Court of Appeals for the Sixth Circuit. No. 07–5078, 07–5163, argued 24 November 2008 (490 F. Supp. 2nd 826, 832).

69. Monica Davey, "A Frenzied Pace for the Lawyer behind Suits against the Vatican," *The New York Times*, 28 April 2010, p. A14.

70. Patrick Condon, "Jeff Anderson: One Man's Crusade against the Catholic Church," *The Huffington Post*, 29 March 2010, http://www.huffingtonpost. com/2010/03/29/efff-anderson-one-mans-cr_n_516658.html.

71. United States Court of Appeals for the Ninth Circuit, No. 06–35587 D.C. No. C.V-02–004-MWM, p. 2549.

72. FSIA does not define "commercial." For a fuller discussion, see: Edan Burkett, "Victory for Clergy Sexual Abuse Victims: The Ninth Circuit Strips the Holy See of Foreign Sovereign Immunity in *Doe v.Holy See*," *BYU Law Review* 2010, no. 1 (January 2010): 35–39.

73. FSIA does not define "employment." See Burkett, "Victory for Clergy," for a longer discussion.

74. 28 US C. 1605 (a)(5)(A) (2006).

75. The first case was *Fearing v. Bucher*, 977, P.2d 1163 (Or.1999). It spelled out three requirements by the court to determine whether or not actions are carried out within the course and scope of employment: "1) the acts must have occurred substantially within the time and space limits authorized by the employment; 2) the employee must have been motivated, at least partially, by a purpose to serve the employer; and 3) the act must have been of a kind which the employee was hired to perform." *Fearing v. Bucher* 1168. The second case was *Minnis v. Oregon Mut. Ins. Co.* 48 P.3d 137 (Or. 2002) that applies the state of Oregon's three requirement test to intentional torts as well See: Ninth Circuit holding in *Doe v. Holy See*, p. 2573.

76. *Fearing*, 1168.

77. The Ninth Circuit also refused to consider a cross-appeal on the commercial activity exception, claiming that it did not have jurisdiction in the matter.

78. Petitioner's Reply Brief, In the Supreme Court of the United States, 27 October 2009, No. 09–1.

79. Subsequently, however, the Oregon Supreme Court held that "sexual assault was not within the scope of [the priests] employment in *Schmidt v. Archdiocese of Portland,* 180P.ed 160, 177 (Or.Ct. App. 2008)." This case was cited later in the *amicus* brief of the solicitor general when it was heard by the Supreme Court of the United States.

80. *Holy See v. John V. Doe,* "Brief for the United States as *Amicus Curiae,*" No. 09–1, May 2010, p. 9.

81. United States Court of Appeals for the Ninth Circuit. *Doe v. Holy See,* Appeal No. 06–35563 Affirmed in part, Reversed in part and Remanded. Cross Appeal No. 06–35587 Dismissed. D.C. No. CV-02–00430-MWM, Opinion, pp. 2543–2579.

82. Vatican Radio Staff, "Holy See's lawyer: Dismissed Lawsuit in US 'Never Should Have Been Filed,'" Vatican Radio, 7 August 2013, http://en.radiovaticana.va/storico/2013/08/07/holy_sees_lawyer_dismissed_lawsuit_in_us_never_should_have_been/en1-717667.

83. In a significant number of lawsuits, clerics, bishops, and even US cardinals have been deposed and thousands of pages of documents have been subpoenaed for grand jury investigations, but none of these have reached as high as the Vatican. For further information about the use and abuse of subpoenas in sexual abuse cases, see Jo Renee Formicola, "The Further Legal Consequence of Catholic Clerical Sexual Abuse," *Journal of Church and State* 49 (Summer 2007): 445–466.

84. A "diocese" is an ecclesiastical term used to designate a specific geographical territory. Often a diocese is incorporated so that the Church may carry out financial or other civil business with the state. The bishop, or religious head of a diocese, therefore, is also head of the legal corporation and embodies the corporation as the "corporation sole." Some dioceses are incorporated, making is easier to bring lawsuits in civil courts against the dioceses or the bishop, but other dioceses are not, thus creating more complex civil actions.

85. Plaintiffs argued that the Holy See "circulated a document containing a set of procedural norms for dealing with the solicitation of sex in confession, clergy sex with minors, homosexual relations, and bestiality." See *O'Bryan v. Holy See,* US Court of Appeals, 07–5078/5163, 24 November 2008. pp. 2–3. Dubbed the "1963 policy" by the media, this document was made public in July 2003 with the claim that the Holy See refused to require US bishops to report childhood sexual abuse to civil authorities. The Vatican, however, maintains that the media was referring to a 1962 update of its 1922 Code of Canon Law titled *"Crimen Sollicitationis"* that only included the crime of soliciting sex with a confessor. It was covered by a strict code of confidentiality meant to protect all persons concerned. "It was not intended to represent the entirety of the policy of the Catholic Church regarding sexual improprieties on the part of the clergy. Rather, its sole purpose was to establish a procedure that

responded to the singularly delicate situation." See: *The Norms of the Motu Proprio "Sacramentorum Sanctitatis Tutela"* (2001) issued by Pope Benedict XVI on 21 May 2010. Accessed at http://www.vatican.va/resources/resources .introd-storica.en.html.

86. Historically, the United States has granted foreign sovereigns immunity from American lawsuits, but in 1952 the State Department restricted immunity only to their public acts. In 1976, Congress passed the FSIA to incorporate that principle into law, but subsequent cases identified two exceptions when sovereigns could be sued: in matters of illegal commercial activity, or when tortious (injurious) acts had been committed by their employees in the scope of their employment.

87. These included Tarcisio Cardinal Bertone, the Vatican secretary of state, William Cardinal Levada, prefect of the Congregation for the Doctrine of the Faith, and Archbishop Pietro Sambi, the Vatican's *nuncio* (i.e., ambassador) to the United States.

88. *O'Bryan v. Holy See*, US District Court. Western District of Kentucky at Louisville, Civil Action No. 3:04CV-338-H. p. 2.

89. Ibid.

90. Ibid.

91. Zenit.org Staff, "Vatican Statement on the 'Murphy Case,'" Zenit.org, 25 March 2010, http://www.zenit.org/en/articles/vatican-statement-on-the-murphy-case.

92. Nicholas Kulish and Katrin Bennhold, "Pope Was Told Pedophile Priest Would Get Post," *The New York Times*, 26 March 2010, p. A10.

93. Laurie Goodstein and David M. Halbfinger, "Amid Sexual Abuse Scandal, an Office that Failed to Act," *The New York Times*, 2 July 10, p. A1.

94. Pope Benedict XVI, *Norms of the Motu Proprio*.

95. Dan Gilgoff, "Vatican to Pursue New Legal Strategy in U. S Lawyer Says," CNN, 17 May 2010, http://www.cnn.com/2010/CRIME/05/7/vatican.abuse /index.html.

96. Rachel Donadio, "Vatican Protests after Belgian Police Drill into Tombs in Sex Abuse Inquiry," *New York Times*, 26 June 2010, p. A4

97. Elisabetta Povoledo, "Bishop, 73, in Belgium Steps Down Over Abuse," *The New York Times*, 24 April 2010, p. A4.

98. Stephen Castel and Nicholas Kulish "Belgian Police Raid Offices of Church in Abuse Case," *The New York Times*, 25 June 2010, p. A6.

99. Ibid.

100. Ibid.

101. Official Communiqué of the Vatican. "Vatican, Belgian bishops on Raids of Church Offices: It was Not an Agreeable Experience," 25 June 2010, http:// www.zenit.org/en/articles/vatican-belgian-bishops-on-raids-of-church -offices.

102. Rachel Donadio, "Raid on Church in Belgium Was 'Deplorable,' Pope Says," *The New York Times*, 28 June 2010, p. A4.
103. Pope Benedict XVI, "Benedict XVI's Solidarity with Bishops of Belgium," 27 June 2010, http://www.press.catholica.va/news.
104. Povoledo, "Bishop, 73."
105. Its report was issued on 20 May 2009. It is available on www .childabusecommission.com/rpt/pdfs/.
106. Shawn Pogatchnik, "Irish Say Religious Groups in Abuse Case Hide Wealth," *The Philadelphia Inquirer*, 28 May 2009, p. B13.
107. Sarah Lyall, "Blaming Church, Ireland Detail Scourge of Abuse," *The New York Times,* 21 May 2009, p. A1.
108. "Pope Expresses Personal Anguish and Horror over Priestly Sex Abuse," 27 October 2006, Statement of Pope Benedict, 2006 accessed at http://www .ewtn.com/vnews/getstory.asp?number=7271.
109. Ibid.
110. It finally accepted the resignation of Bishop James Moriarity of Kildare and Leighlin in April 2010. The Vatican did not accept the resignations of auxiliary bishops Eaomon Walsh and Bishop Ramond Field. They were assigned "revised responsibilities within the diocese," according to the Associated Press. See the Associated Press, "Ireland: Vatican Rejects Resignations," *The New York Times*, 12 August 2010, p. A14.
111. Pope Benedict XVI, "Text of the Pastoral Letter of the Holy Father Pope Benedict XVI to the Catholics of Ireland," 19 March 2010, www .vatican.va/holy_father/Benedict xvi/letters/2010/documents/hf_ben-xvi _let_20100319_church-ireland_en.html112.
112. Ibid., Sections 6 and 7.
113. Ibid., Section 4.
114. Associated Press, "Ireland: Vatican Sending Team to Check Effectiveness of Its Response to Abuse," *The New York Times*, 13 November 2010, p. A7.
115. Lyall, "Blaming Church."
116. Ibid., Father Thomas Doyle, O. P., canon lawyer and chief critic of the Church leadership on clerical sexual abuse as quoted in article.
117. For a further discussion of such real estate disputes and bankruptcies in the United States, see: Formicola, "The Further Consequences," pp. 445–465. For example, the members of St. Stanislaus Kostak Church in St. Louis have been in a dispute with the Archdiocese of St. Louis over $8 million in assets. Fearing that the archdiocese might use them to settle sexual abuse settlements, the parish has withheld sending funds to the bishop. The parish has been told by the Supreme Tribunal of the Apostolic Signatura that the actions of St. Stanislaus's lay board and its parish priest constitute a "schism," with the automatic penalty of excommunication. For a fuller explanation, see:

Malcom Gay, "Renegade Priest Leads a Split St. Louis Parish," *The New York Times,* 14 August 2010, p. A10.

118. Melinda Henneberger, "Vatican to Hold Secret Trials of Priests in Pedophilia Cases," *The New York Times,* 9 January 2002, p. A8.

119. Pope Benedict XVI, *Norms of the Moto Proprio.* Quotes taken from the official document accessed at http://www.Vatican.va. These new norms were based on the mandates of the 1918 Code of Canon Law that recognized a number of canonical crimes, or "delicts," to be handled by the CDF, and addendums from 1922 and 1962 Code that explained administrative procedures and further definitional refinements. From that time to 1983, the Vatican claims that there were different canonical approaches to clerical sexual abuse. These included therapy as well as spiritual reconciliation In 1983, when new Code of Canon Law was established by John Paul II, the sexual abuse of a minor below the age of 16 years was to be punished even to the point of exclusion from the clerical state if the case so warranted. In 1994, the American bishops were able to amend the law and raised the age of a minor to 18 in the United States; the same age change was applied to Ireland in 1996. In 2001, canon law was again amended to allow allegations made by an individual ten years after his/her eighteenth birthday.

120. Vatican.va. Text of the "Substantive Norms on *delicta graviora*" promulgated 21 May 2010, www.vatican.va/resources/resources_norme_en.html.

121. See Articles, 1, 6, and 7 of the "Substantive Norms."

122. Congregation of the Doctrine of the Faith, "Circular Letter to Assist Episcopal Conferences in Developing Guidelines for Dealing with Cases of Sexual Abuses of Minors Perpetrated by Clerics," 3 May 2011, http://www.vatican.va /roman_curia/congregations/cfaith/documents/rc_con.

123. Ibid.

124. Rachel Donadio, "Pope Offers Apology, but No Punishment, for Clergy's Abuse," *The New York Times,* 21 March, 2010, p. A6.

6   From Crisis to Power Shift and the Future

1. *Sherbert v. Verner,* 374 US 398 (1963).
2. *Wisconsin v. Yoder,* 406 US 205 (1972).
3. *Employment Division v. Smith,* 494 US 872 (1990).
4. Laurie Goodstein, "Chief of Panel on Priest Abuse Will Step Down," *The New York Times,* 16 June 2003, p. A1.
5. John Jay College of Criminal Justice, *The Nature and Scope of Sexual Abuse of Minors by Catholic Priests and Deacons in the US 1950–2002,* 25 February 2004, http://www.usccb.org/issues-and-action/child-and-youth-protection

/upload/The-Nature-and-Scope-of-Sexual-Abuse-of-Minors-by-Catholic
-Priests-and-Deacons-in-the-United-States-1950–2002.pdf.

6. Ibid.

7. Marc Santora and Laurie Goodstein, "Newark Monsignor Loses Job for Failing
to Stop Priest's Work with Children," *The New York Times*, 26 May 2013, p. 16.

8. Ian Lovett, "Los Angeles Cardinal Hid Abuse, Files Show," *The New York Times*,
22 January 2013, p. 16.

9. Steven Yaccino and Michael Paulson, "In Files, a History of Sexual Abuse by
Priests in Chicago Archdiocese," *The New York Times,* 22 January 2014, p. A1.

10. Ibid.

11. See: Congregation for the Doctrine of the Faith, "Guide to Understanding
Basic CDF Procedures Concerning Sexual Abuse Allegations," 2010, http://
www.vatican.va/resources/resources_guid-CDF-procedures_en.html.

12. Pope Benedict XVI, "How Much Filth There Is in the Church," Good Friday
Services, April 2005, http://www.conchiglia.us/uk/us-pap/uk_sporcizia_nella
_Chiesa.html.

13. John Holusha and Ian Fisher, "Pope Begins US Visit; Says He Is
Ashamed of Sex Scandal," *The New York Times,* 16 April 2008, http://
www.nytimes.com/2008/04/16/us/nationalspecial2/15cnd-pope.html?
pagewanted=all&_r=0.

14. This term was brought to my attention by David R. Edwards, a colleague
at Seton Hall University, who provided these definitions and a variety of
resources to further explore the notion. One suggestion is: http://www
.firstthings.com/onthesquare/2006/11/hylden-schoris-agenda.

15. Laurie Goodstein, "384 Priests Defrocked Over Abuse in 2 Years," *The New
York Times,* 18 January 2014, p. A8.

16. Gregory Erlandson and Matthew Bunson, *Pope Benedict XVI and the Sexual
Abuse Crisis: Working for Reform and Renewal* (Huntington, IN: Our Sunday
Visitor, 2010), p. 30. The authors recount an interview in an article published in
an Italian Catholic newspaper, *L'Avvenire.* They do not give a date, but ascribe
these statistics to Monsignor Scicluna, a Vatican official with the CDF.

17. Congregation for the Doctrine of the Faith, "Circular Letter to Assist
Episcopal Conferences in Developing Guidelines for Dealing with Cases
of Sexual Abuses of Minors Perpetrated by Clerica," 3 May 2011, Signed
by William Cardinal Levada, Prefect, http://www.vatica.va/roman_curia
/congregations/cfaith/document.

18. The last resignation occurred in 1415 by Pope Gregory XII who gave up his
position to end the Western Schism or the "Babylonian Captivity," a time
when there were two (and at one point, three) popes ruling the Church,
one in Rome and one in Avignon. The matter was settled by the Council of
Constance and the election of Pope Martin V.

19. Rachel Donadio, "Leaked Cables Show Vatican Tensions and Diplomacy with US," *The New York Times*, 12 December 2011, http://www.nytimes .com/2010/12/11/world/europe11vatican.html.

20. Ibid.

21. Josephine McKenna, "Cardinal Sean O'Malley on sexual abuse crisis: 'There is so much denial,'" Religion News Service, 3 May 2014. http://www.religionnews .com/2014/05/03/cardinal-sean-omalley-sexual-abuse-crisis-much-denial/

22. Elisabetta Povoledo "Pope Takes Responsibility in Priests' Abuse Scandal," *The New York Times*, 12 April 2014, A 11.

23. Msgr. Silvano Tomasi, "Presentation by H. E. Msgr. Silvano Tomasi of the Periodic Report of the Holy See to the Committee on the Convention of the Rights of the Child and the Optional Protocols," 16 January 2014, http://www .vatican.va/roman_curia/secretariet_state/2014/documents.

24. Ibid.

25. Lizzy Davies, "UN Panel Grills Catholic Hierarchy on Handling of Child Sex Abuse by Priests," *The Guardian*, 16 January 2014, http://www.theguardian .com/world/2014/jan/16/un-criticises-vatican-coverups-child-sex-abuse -catholic-priests.

26. United Nations Committee on the Rights of the Child. "Concluding Observations on the Second Periodic Report of the Holy See," 25 February 2014. p. 9, http://tbinternet.ohchr.org/Treaties/CRC/Shared Documents /VAT/CRC_C_VAT_CO_2.

27. Ibid.

28. Jim Yardley, "Pope Moves to Delfate Breathless Portrayals of Stardom," *The New York Times*, 6 March 2014, p. A 7.

29. For an excellent discussion, see: Tom Barth, "Crisis Management in the Catholic Church: Lessons for Public Administrators," *Public Administration Review* 70, no. 5 (September–October 2010): 780–791.

Bibliography

Abbott, Walter M., gen. ed. *The Documents of Vatican II*. New York: Herder and Herder, 1966.

Abraham, Lynn. *Report of the Grand Jury*. In the Court of Common Pleas. First Judicial District of Pennsylvania. Criminal Trial Division. Misc. No. 03–00–239. 17 September 2003. http:// www.bishop-accountability.org.

Albach, Susan Hogan. "USCCB Committee Bishops Accused of Abuse Cover-Up." *Dallas Morning News*, 19 January 2004.

Alexiev, Alex. "The Kremlin and the Vatican." *Orbis* 27 (Fall 1983): pp. 554–565.

Allen, John, Jr. "Plantiffs Drop Lawsuit against Vatican." *National Catholic Reporter*, 10 August 2010. http://ncronline.org/news /accountability/plaintiffs-drop-lawsuit-against-vatican.

Amnesty International. *Annual Report*, 2011. http://www.amnesty .org/en/annual-report/2011.

Anderson, Jeff. "Press Release: Statement of Jeff Anderson re: John V. Doe v. Holy See." Jeff Anderson & Associates PA. 20 August 2012. http://www.andersonadvocates.com/Posts/News-or-Event /1154/Press-Release-Judge-dismisses-historic-child-sexual-abuse -case-involving-Vatican%E2%80%99s-role-in-clergy-abuse -cover-up.aspx

Anderson, Jeff, and Associates PA. "Attorneys: Jeff Anderson, Trial Attorney." http://www.andersonadvocates.com/Attorney Profiles.aspx.

Archdiocese of Los Angeles. *Report to the People of God: Clergy Sexual Abuse, Archdiocese of Los Angeles (1930–2003)*. 17 February 2004. http://www.la-archdiocese.org/org/protecting/reports /Documents/2004-0217_ADLA_CSA_Report.pdf

Archdiocese of Milwaukee. "Love One anoter," 4 January 2001. www.archmil.org/reorg/Listecki-Loa.htm

Archdiocese of Milwaukee. "Questions and Answers." *The Archdiocese of Milwaukee*, 16 October 2012. http://www.archmil.org/offices/sexual-abuse-prevention/restricted -priests/QA.htm.

Archdiocese of Milwaukee. "Questions and Answers: Information and Answers about Clergy Sexual Abuse in the Archdiocese of Milwaukee and its Chapter 11 Bankruptcy Proceeding." *The Archdiocese of Milwaukee*, March 2012.

Arizona Republic Staff. "Text of Bishop O'Brien's News Conference." *Arizona Republic*, 2 June 2003. http://www.bishop-accountability.org/az-phoenix/phoenix -agreement-resignation.htm.

Arnold, David, and Michael Rezendes. "Law Deposition Ends, for Now." *The Boston Globe*, 14 May 2002, p. B1.

Associated Press. "Boston: Court Upholds Former Priest's Conviction." *The New York Times*, 16 January 2010, p. A12.

Associated Press. "Cardinal to be Questioned about Role in Abuse Cases." *The New York Times*, 17 February 2012, p. A23.

Associated Press. "Catholic Church's Costs Pass $1 Billion in Abuse Cases." *The New York Times*, 12 June 2005, p. A33.

Associated Press. "Claims of Abuse by Priests Double," 9 January 2007. http://www .adn.com/news/alaska

Associated Press, "Files Show Archdiocese Paid 21 Million in Abuse Cases." *The New York Times*, 13 August 2003, p. A20.

Associated Press. "Ireland: Vatican Rejects Resignations." *The New York Times*, 12 August 2010, p. A14.

Associated Press, "Judge Rebuffs Church's Motion to Halt Law's Testimony Today." *The New York Times*, 22 January 2003, p. A12.

Associated Press. "Los Angeles Archdiocese Releases More Files on Sexual Abuse. *The New York Times*, 1 August 2013, p. A13.

Associated Press. "Missouri: Priest Gets 50 Years in Child Pornography Case." *The New York Times*, 13 September 2013, p. A17.

Associated Press. "Pennsylvania: Ex-Priest Recants Guilt in Abuse Case." *The New York Times*, 18 January 2013, p. A17.

Attorney General of Hamilton County. "Settlement Agreement between the Archdiocese of Cincinnati and the Hamilton County Prosecuting Attorney." Bishop-Accountability.org. 20 November 2003. http://www.bishop-accountability .org/resources/resource-files/courtdocs/2003–11–20-Pilarczyk-Agreement.pdf.

Banerjee, Neela. "Boston Archdiocese Halves Offers in Open Abuse Cases." *The New York Times*, 31 December 2005, p. A10.

Banerjee, Neela. "Boston Archdiocese Opens Books, Including Abuse Details." *The New York Times*, 20 April 2006, p. A16.

Banerjee, Neela. "Boston Church Panel Will Allow Archdiocese to Weigh Bankruptcy." *The New York Times*, 5 December 2002, p. A1.

Banerjee, Neela. "Boston Church Papers Released: A Pattern of Negligence is Cited." *The New York Times*, 4 December 2002, p. A1.

Banerjee, Neela. "Boston Study Traces Patterns of Sexual Abuse by Priests." *The New York Times*, 27 February 2004, p. A22.

Banerjee, Neela. "Cardinal Law Said His Policy Shielded Priests." *The New York Times*, 14 August 2002, p. A1.

Barth, Tom. "Crisis Management in the Catholic Church: Lessons for Public Administrators." *Public Administration Review* 70, no. 5 (September–October 2012): pp. 780–790.

Battista Re, Cardinal Giovanni. Letter of Cardinal Giovanni Battista Re to Bishop Wilton Gregory. 14 October 2002. http://www.bishop-accountability.org/resources /resource-files/churchdocs/Gregory.htm.

Bauman, Michelle. "SNAP Director Admits to Publishing False Information." *Catholic News Agency*, 6 March 2012. http://www.catholicnewsagency.com /news/snap-director-admits-to-publishing-false-information/.

Belluck, Pam. "Boston Archdiocese Opens Books, Including Abuse Details." *The New York Times*, 20 April 2006, p. A16.

Belluck, Pam. "Boston Church Panel Will Allow Archdiocese to Weigh Bankruptcy." *The New York Times*, 5 December 2002, p. A1.

Belluck, Pam. "Boston Church Papers Released: A Pattern of Negligence is Cited." *The New York Times*, 4 December 2002, p. A1.

Belluck, Pam. "Boston Study Traces Pattern of Sexual Abuse by Priests." *The New York Times*, 27 February 2004, p. A22.

Belluck, Pam. "Cardinal Law Said His Policy Shielded Priests." *The New York Times*, 14 August 2002, p. A1.

Belluck, Pam. "Judge Denies Church's Bid to Seal Records on Priests." *The New York Times*, 26 November 2002, p. A18.

Belluck, Pam. "A Prominent Accuser in Boston Abuse Scandal Is Found Dead." *The New York Times*, 24 February 2008, p. A18.

Belluck, Pam, and Frank Bruni. "A Yearlong Crisis." *The New York Times*, 14 October 2002, p. A1.

Belluck, Pam, and Adam Liptak. "For Boston Archdiocese, Bankruptcy Would Have Drawback." *The New York Times*, 3 December 2002, p. A26.

Bernstein, Carl. "The Holy Alliance." *Time* 139 (24 February 1992): pp. 28–35.

Berry, Jason. "Anatomy of a Cover-Up: The Diocese of Lafayette and Its Moral Responsibility for the Pedophilia Scandal." *The Times of Acadiana*, 30 January 1986. http://www.bishop-accountability.org/news/1986_01_30_Berry_AnatomyOf.htm.

Berry, Jason. *Lead Us Not into Temptation*. Urbana: University of Illinois Press, 2000. http://www.bishop-accountability.org/news/1986_01_30_Berry_AnatomyOf.htm.

Berry, Jason. "The Tragedy of Gilbert Gauthe: Part I." *The Times of Acadiana*, 23 May 1985. http://www.bishop-accountability.org/news/1985_05_23_Berry_The Tragedy.htm.

Berry, Jason. "The Tragedy of Gilbert Gauthe: Part II." *The Times of Acadiana*, 30 May 1985. http://www.bishopaccountabiliy.org/news/1985_05_30_Berry_TheTragedy ofGilbertGauthe.

Berry, Jason, and Gerald Renner. *Vows of Silence: The Abuse of Power in the Papacy of John Paul II.* London: Free Press, 2004.

BishopAccountability.org. "Geoghan Documents." 1954–2002. http://www.bishop-accountability.org/docs/boston/geoghan/doc_list.htm.

Bishop-Accountability.org. "Introduction to the Archives." No Date. http://bishopaccountability.org/Introduction_to_the_Archives/.

Bishop Accountability.org. "Some Things You Helped Us Achieve in 2011." No Date. http://www.bishopaccountability.org/2011/.

BishopAccountability.org. "Who We Are." June 2003. http://www.bishop-accountability.org/Who_We_Are.

Bishops' Ad Hoc Committee on Sexual Abuse. "Restoring Trust: A Pastoral Response to Sexual Abuse Volume I." Binder of Materials Presented to the NCCB at its Annual Meeting in Washington, DC, November 1994. http://www.bishopaccountability.org/reports/1994_11_NCCB_Restoring_Trust/rt94_01_policies.

Bishops' Ad Hoc Committee on Sexual Abuse. "Restoring Trust: A Pastoral Response to Sexual Abuse Volume II." November 1995. http://www.bishopaccountability.org/reports/1994_11_NCCB_Restoring_Trust/rt94_01_policies.

Bishops' Ad Hoc Committee on Sexual Abuse. "Restoring Trust: A Pastoral Response to Sexual Abuse Volume III." 1996. http://www.bishopaccountability.org/reports/1994_11_NCCB_Restoring_Trust/rt94_01_policies.

Bishop Donald J. Kettler. Press Release: "Fairbanks Diocese Seeks A Consensual Plan for Reorganization," 13 February 2008, http://www.bishop-accountability.org/news

Blaine, Barbara. "Why the Pope Must Fact Justice at the Hague." *The Guardian*, 17 September 2011. http://www.theguardian.com/commentisfree/cifamerica/2011/sep/17/pope-clergy-sex-abuse-hague.

Block, Stephanie. "Is It the Voice of the Faithful?" CatholicCulture.org, No Date. http://www.catholicculture.org/culture/library/view.cfm?recnum=7303.

Boorstein, Michelle. "U. S. Courts Allow Sex Abuse Cases against Vatican to Be Proved in Rare Legal Move." *The Washington Post*, 27 March 2010, p. A5.

Boudreaux, Richard, and Larry B. Stammer. "U. S. Catholics and Vatican Face a Cultural Chasm in Coping with Sex Scandal." *Los Angeles Times*, 23 April 2002. http://www.articles.latimes.com/2002/apr/23.

Brennan, Dr. John. "Letter of Dr. John Brennan to Reverend Banks," 14 December 1984. http://www.bishop-accountability.org

Bruce, Tricia Colleen. *Faithful Revolution: How Voice of the Faithful Is Changing the Church.* New York: Oxford University Press, 2011.

Burge, Kathleen. "Judge's Ruling Frees Documents in Geoghan Case." *The Boston Globe*, 30 November 2001. http://bishopaccountability.org/news5/2001_11_30_Burge_Judges_Ruling.htm.

Burkett, Edan. "Victory for Clergy Sexual Abuse Victims: The Ninth Circuit Strips the Holy See of Foreign Sovereign Immunity in *Doe v Holy See*." *BYU Law Review* 2010, no. 1 (January 2010): 35–39.

Butterfield, Fox. "Boston Archdiocese, Hunting Financially, Warns of Layoffs." *The New York Times*, 18 June 2003, p. A22.

Butterfield, Fox. "Church in Boston Offers 55 million or Abuse Claims." *The New York Times*, 9 August 2003, p. Al.

Butterfield, Fox. "Deal Reflects Archbishop and His Franciscan Roots." *The New York Times*, 11 September 2003, p. A10.

Butterfield, Fox. "Leader in Boston Is Praised by Priests and Lay Catholics Alike." *The New York Times*, 14 December 2002, p. A21.

Butterfield, Fox. "789 Children Abused by Priests Since 1940, Massachusetts Says." *The New York Times*, 24 July 2003, p. A1.

Byrne, Matt. "Advocacy Groups Seek Hearing on Abuse Scandal." *The Boston Globe*, 14 March 2010.

Byrnes, Greg. "Some Attending Voice of the Faithful Meetings Find They Have No Voice." 2003. http://www.staycatholic.com/no_voice_at_voice_of_the_faithful.htm.

Cafardi, Nicholas P. *Before Dallas: The U. S. Bishops' Response to Clergy Sexual Abuse of Children.* Mahwah, NJ: Paulist Press, 2008.

Cannon, Carl M. "Louisiana Case Brought Pedophilic Priests into the Open." *San Jose Mercury News*, 31 December 1987. http://www.bishopaccountability.org/news/1987_12_31_Cannon_LouisianaCase.htm.

Carroll, A. B., K. J. Lipartito, J. E. Post, P. J. Werhane, and K. E. Goodpaster. *Corporate Responsibility: The American Experience.* Cambridge: Cambridge University Press, 2012.

Carroll, James. "Let Church Reform Begin." *The Boston Globe*, 16 September 2002, p. A15.

Castel, Stephen, and Nicholas Kulish. "Belgian Police Raid Offices of Church in Abuse Case." *The New York Times*, 25 June 2010, p. A6.

Catholic Bishop of Northern Alaska. Press Release of Bishop Donald J. Kettler. 13 February 2008. http://www.bishop-accountability.org/ak_fairbanks/2008_02_13_Hannon_Press_Release.pdf

Catholic League for Religious and Civil Rights. "About Us." http://www.catholicleague.org/about-us/. n.d.

Catholic News Agency. "Pope Benedict Expresses Personal Anguish and Horror Over Priestly Sex Abuse." 27 October 2006. http://www.ewtn.com/vnews/getstory.asp?number=72712.

Catholic Whistleblowers. "Who We Are." http://www.catholicwhistleblowers.org.n.d.

Chopko, Mark E. "Shaping the Church: Overcoming the Twin Challenges of Secularization and Scandal." *Catholic University Law Review* 53, no. 1. (Fall 2003): 125–159.

Chua-Eoan, Howard, and Elizabeth Dias. "The People's Pope." *Time* 182, no. 26 (23 December 2013): 46–75.

Clohessy, David. "A50A471 Deposition in Case # 1016CV29995." 2 January 2012. http://www.themediareport.com/wp-content/uploads/2012/03/CLOHESSY-DEPOSITION-010212.pdf.

Clohessy, David. "Impact Statement." Given to the USCCB Meeting in Dallas, Texas. 13 June 2002. http://www.bishop-accountability.org/resources/resource -files/timeline/2002–06–13-Clohessy-ImpactStatement.htm.

CNN Staff. "Prosecutor: Inmate Considered Geoghan 'a Prize.'" CNN, 26 August 2003. http://www.cnn.com/2003/US/08/25/geoghan/index.html.

Colbert, Chuck. "Clerical Sexual Abuse Scandal Widens in Boston Archdiocese." *National Catholic Reporter*, 8 February 2002. http://www.snapnetwork.org/news /massachusetts/boston/BOS_scandal_widens.html.

Committee on Rules of Practice and Procedure. "Case Law on Entering Protective Orders, Entering Sealing Orders, and Modifying Protective Orders." July 2010. http://www.uscourts.gov/uscourts/RulesAndPolicies/rules/Caselaw_Study_of _Discovery_Protective_Orders.pdf.

Condon, Patrick. "Jeff Anderson: One Man's Crusade against the Catholic Church." *The Huffington Post*, 29 March 2010. http://www.huffingtonpost.com /jeff-anderson-one-mans-cr_n_516658.html.

Congregation for the Doctrine of the Faith. "Circular Letter to Assist Episcopal Conferences in Developing Guidelines for Dealing with Cases of Sexual Abuses of Minors Perpetrated by Clerics." 3 May 2011. http://www.vatican.va/roman _curia/congregations/cfaith/documents/rc_con_cfaith_doc_20110503_abuso -minori_en.html.

Congregation for the Doctrine of the Faith. "Guide to Understanding Basic CDF Procedures Concerning Sexual Abuse Allegations." 2010. http://www.vatican .va/resources/resources/guide-CDF-procedures.en.html.

Congregation for the Doctrine of the Faith. *The Code of Canon Law.* 1983. http:// www.vatican.va/archives/ENG1104/-56.HTM.

Congregation for the Doctrine of the Faith. "The Norms of the Motu Proprio 'Sacramentorum Sanctitatis Tutela.'" 2001. http://www.vatican.va/resources /resources_introd-storica-en.html.

Court of Appeal of the State of California. Second Appellate District Division Three re: Los Angeles County Superior Court, No. BH0011928 (B177852) and Los Angeles Country Superior Court No. BH0011928 (B180696).

Daly, Fr. "Sexual Abuse and Canon Law." *Compass* 43 (Spring 2009): 33–40.

D'Antonio, Michael. *Mortal Sins: Sex, Crime, and the Era of Catholic Scandal.* New York: St. Martin's Press, 2013.

Davey, Monica. "A Frenzied Pace for the Lawyer Behind Suits against the Vatican." *The New York Times*, 28 April 2010, p. A14.

David Clohessy v. The Honorable Ann J. Mesle. "Writ of Prohibition." 19 July 2012. https://d3n8a8pro7vhmx.cloudfront.net/snap/pages/1114/attachments /original/1343231724/Petition_for_Writ_July_19_2012.pdf?1343231724.

Davies, Lizzy. "UN Panel Grills Catholic Hierarchy on Handling of Child Sexual Abuses by Priests." *The Guardian*, 16 January 2014. http://www.theguardian .com/world/2014/jan/16/un-criticises-vatican-coverups-child-sex-abuse -catholic-priests.

Davies, Lizzy. "Vatican Refuses to Give UN Panel Full Details of Clerica Sex Abuse Cases." *The Guardian*, 4 December 2013. http://www.theguardian.com /world/2013/dec/04/vatican-refuses-un-panel-details-clerical-sex-abuse-cases.

Dillon, Sam. "Bishops Take No Action on Calls for Audit." *The New York Times*, 14 November 2002, p. A30.

Dillon, Sam. "Catholic Religious Orders Let Abusive Priests Stay." *The New York Times*, 10 August 2002, p. A8.

Dillon, Sam. "In New Hampshire, Abuse Cases Undermine a Catholic Bishop." *The New York Times*, 18 October 2002. http://www.snapnetwork.org/news /otherstates/NH_NYTimes_on_McCormick.htm.

Dillon, Sam. "Means Found to Prosecute Decades-Old Abuse Cases." *The New York Times*, 28 August 2002, p. A16.

Doe v. Holy See. U. S. Court of Appeals for the Ninth Circuit. No. 06–35563 and 06–35587.

Donadio, Rachel. "A Constant Drumbeat Hastened the Pope's Exist." *The New York Times*, 13 February 2013, p. A14.

Donadio, Rachel. "As Pope Departs, Discord Remains at Vatican." *The New York Times*, 1 March 2013, p. A1.

Donadio, Rachel. "Leaked Cables Show Vatican Tensions and Diplomacy with U. S." *The New York Times*. 12 December 2011. http://www.nytimes.com/2010/12/11 /world/europe/11Vatican.html.

Donadio, Rachel. "Reports Suggest Internal Struggles." *The New York Times*, 24 February 2013, p. A6.

Donadio, Rachel. "Pope Offers Apology, but No Punishment, for Clergy's Abuse." *The New York Times,* 21 March, 2010, p. A6.

Rachel Donadio, "Raid on Church in Belgium Was 'Deplorable,' Pope Says," *The New York Times*, 28 June 2010, p. A4.

Donadio, Rachel. "Vatican Protests after Belgian Police Drill into Tombs in Sex Abuse Inquiry." *New York Times*, 26 June 2010, p. A4.Donohoe, William. "SNAP EXPOSED: Unmasking the Survivors Network of those Abused by Priests." *Catholic League Special Report*, 22 August 2011. http://www.catholicleague.org /snap-exposed-unmasking-the-survivors-network-of-those-abused-by -priests/.

Doyle, Thomas O. P., "The Archives and the Secret Archives Required by Canon Law." 6 April 2002. http://www.theharrowing.com/secretarch.html.

Doyle, Thomas O. P. "A Short History of *The Manual*." 12 October 2010. http:// www.awrsipe.com/Doyle/pdf_files/Manual-History%20%2010-12-2010.pdf.

Doyle, Thomas O. P., F. Ray Mouton, and Father Michael Peterson. "The Problem of Sexual Molestation by Roman Catholic Clergy: Meeting the Problem in a Comprehensive and Responsible Manner." 1985. http://www.bishop -accountability.org.

Doyle, Thomas O. P., and Stephen C. Rubino, Esq. "Catholic Clergy Sexual Abuse Meets the Civil Law." *Fordham Urban Law Journal* 31, no. 2 (2003): 1–42, Article 6.

http://bishop-accountability.org/news5/2004_01_01_Doyle_CatholicClergy .pdf.

Doyle, Thomas O. P., Richard Sipe, and Patrick J. Wall. *Sex, Priests, and Secret Codes: The Catholic Church's 2,000 Year Paper Trail of Sexual Abuse.* Lanham, MD: Taylor Trade, 2006.

Economist Staff. "Briefing: The Catholic Church in America." *The Economist,* 18 August 2012, p. 19.

Ellement, John R., and Jonathan Saltzman. "Defrocked Priest Shanley Is a Victim of 'Injustice,' His Attorney Says." *The Boston Globe,* 15 January 2010. http://www .boston.com/news/local/breaking_news/2010/01/sjc_rules_in_sh.html.

Employment Division v. Smith. 494 U. S. 872 (1990).

Erlandson Gregory, and Matthew Bunson. *Pope Benedict XVI and the Sexual Abuse Crisis: Working for Reform and Renewal.* Huntington, IN: Our Sunday Visitor, 2010.

Euart, Sr. Sharon. "Canon Law and Clergy Sexual Abuse Crisis: An Overview of the U. S. Experience." 25 May 2010. http://www.dioslc.org/images/tribunal /USCCB%20CANON%20LAW%20SEMINAR%202010%20EUART.doc.

Faris, Stephan. "Could the Vatican Go to Court for Human-Rights Abuses?" *Time,* 20 September 2011. http://content.time.com/time/world/article/0,8599,2093771,00 .html.

Farragher, Thomas. "Behind Walls, Trouble Built to a Brutal End." *The Boston Globe,* 2 December 2003. http://www.boston.com/news/local/massachusetts /articles/2003/12/02/behind_walls_trouble_built_to_a_brutal_end/?page=full.

Farragher, Thomas. "Patterns of Abuse Found Nationwide." *The Boston Globe,* 14 December 2002. http://www.boston.com/globe/spotlight/abuse/stories3/121402 _impact.html.

Farragher, Thomas. "Settlement Doesn't Heal Victims' Hearts." *The Boston Globe,* 20 September 2002. http://www.boston.com/globe/spotlight/abuse/stories3/092002 _victims.html.

Fearing v. Bucher. 977. P.2d 1163 (Or.1999).

Feister, John Bookser. "U.S. Bishops Prepare for Key Meeting." 12 June 2002. http:// www.americancatholic.org/news/clergysexabuse/USCCB-Dallas_Wednesday .asp.

Fericano, Paul. "Bridge of Understanding." *Santa Barbara Independent,* 12 August 2004. http://www.mysafenet.org/?q=node/47.

Fogarty, Colin. "Bankruptcy Bills 'Staggering'" for Portland Archdiocese." Oregon OPB Online, 25 October 2005.

Formicola, Jo Renee. "American Catholic Political Theology." *Journal of Church and State* 29 (Autumn 1987): 457–474.

Formicola, Jo Renee. "Catholic Clerical Sexual Abuse: Effects on Vatican Sovereignty and Papal Power." *Journal of Church and State* 53, no. 4 (Autumn 2011): 523–544.

Formicola, Jo Renee. "Catholic Moral Demands in American Politics: A New Paradigm," *Journal of Church and State* 51, no. 1 (Winter 2009): 4–23.

Formicola, Jo Renee. "*Everson* Revisited: 'This is Not…Just a Little Case over Bus Fares.'" *Polity* 28, no. 1 (Fall 1995): 49–66.

Formicola, Jo Renee. "The Further Legal Consequences of Catholic Clerical Sexual Abuse." *Journal of Church and State* 49 (Summer 2007): 445–466.

Formicola, Jo Renee. *John Paul II: Prophetic Politician*. Washington, DC: Georgetown University Press, 2000.

Formicola, Jo Renee. "The Vatican, the American Bishops, and the Church-State Ramifications of Clerical Sexual Abuse." *Journal of Church and State* 46 (Summer 2004): 479–502.

Formicola, Jo Renee. "U. S. Vatican-Relations: Toward a Post-Cold War Convergence?" *Journal of Church and State* 38 (Autumn 1996): 799–816.

Frawley-O'Dea, Mary Gail. *Perversion of Power*. Nashville, TN: Vanderbilt University Press, 2007.

Frogameni, Bill. "Toledo Native Barbara Blaine Crusades against Sexual Abuse in the Catholic Church." *Toledo City Paper*, 29 April 2004. http://www.bishop accountability.org/news2004_01_06/2004_04_29_Frogameni_ToledoNative .html.

Gastal v. Hannan. No. 84-CC-1833. Supreme Court of Louisiana. 459 So. 2d 526; 1984. 7 December 1984.

Gastal v. Hannan. No. 84-OC-2070, Supreme Court of Louisiana. 462 So. 2d 201; 1984. 20 December 1984.

Gastal v. Hannan. No. 85-CD-0102, Supreme Court of Louisiana. 463 So. 2d 593, 1985. 27 February 1985.

Gastal v. Hannan. No. 85-CD-0512. Supreme Court of Louisiana. 466 So. 2d 450; 1985. 12 April 1985.

Gastal v. Hannan. No. 85-CD-1213. Supreme Court of Louisiana. 472 So. 2d 923; 1985. 28 June 1985.

Gay, Malcom. "Renegade Priest Leads a Split St. Louis Parish." *The New York Times*, 14 August 2010, p. A10.

Geoghan, John. "Letter of Father John Geoghan to Bishop Daily." 4 April 1980. http:// www.bishop-accountability.org/ma-boston/archives/PatternAndPractice/0303 -Geoghan-II-06705-06706.pdf.

Geranios, Nicholas K. "Lawyer for Victims of Abuse Seeks to Include Parish Property." *The Associated Press*, 12 April 2005.

Geyer, Thomas. "Davenport Diocese Files for Bankruptcy." *Quad-City Times*, 12 October 2006. http://www.qctimes.com/news/local/davenport-diocese-files-for -bankruptcy/article_fdbe9ddd-8bc7-58ea-8da6-cdbb4c9561a0.html.

Globe Newspaper Co. Inc. v. Clerk of Middlesex County. No. CIV.A.2001–5302.C, Superior Court of Massachusetts, 5 March 2002.

Globe Newspaper Co., Inc. v. Clerk of Suffolk County. No.01–558*F, Supreme Court of Massachusetts, 4 February 2002.

Globe Staff. "Geoghan's Troubled History." *The Boston Globe.* 7 January 2002. www .boston.com/globe/spotlight/abuse/stories/010702_history.htm.

Globe Staff. "The Council Members Expressed Grave Concern." *The Boston Globe*, 4 May 2002. http://www.boston.com/globe/spotlight/abuse/print2/050402_text .html.

Gilgoff, Dan. "One Lawyer Behind Many allegations of Catholic Church Abuse." CNN U.S, 20 April 2010. http://www.cnn.com/2010/US/04/26/church.abuse .victims.lawyer/.

Gilgoff, Dan. "Vatican to Pursue New Legal Strategy in U. S Lawyer Says." CNN. 17 May 2010. http://www.cnn.com/2010/CRIME/05/17/vatican.abuse/.

Globe Spotlight Team. "Church Allowed Abuse by Priest for Years." *The Boston Globe*, 6 January 2002. http://www.boston.com/globe/spotlight/abuse/stories /010602_geoghan.html.

Globe Spotlight Team. "Excerpts from Judge Sweeney's Ruling." *The Boston Globe*, 26 November 2002, p. A14.

Globe Spotlight Team. "Geoghan Preferred Preying on Poorer Children." *The Boston Globe*, January 7, 2002. http://www.bishopaccountability.org/news/2002 _01_07_Pfeiffer_GeoghanPreferred.html.

Goodnough, Abby. "Archdiocese of Boston Lists Priests Tied to Abuse." *The New York Times*, 28 August 2011, p. A12.

Goodstein, Laurie. "Abuse Victims Ask Court to Prosecute the Vatican." *The New York Times*, 14 September 2011, p. A15.

Goodstein, Laurie. "Audit Finds Sex Abuse Was Topic Decades Ago." *The New York Times*, 19 June 2013, p. A14.

Goodstein, Laurie. "Bishops Won't Focus on Abuse Policies." *The New York Times*, 15 June 2011, p. A10.

Goodstein, Laurie. "Catholic Church Puts Legal Pressure on Surivors' Network." *The New York Times*, 12 March 2012. http://www.nytimes.com/2012/03/13 /us/catholic-church-pressures-victims-network-with-subpoenas.html? pagewanted=all&_r=0.

Goodstein, Laurie "Catholic Orders Might Keep Abusive Priests." *The New York Times*, 22 July 2002, p. A9.

Goodstein, Laurie. "Chief of Panel on Priest Abuse Will Step Down." *The New York Times*, 16 June 2003, p. A1.

Goodstein, Laurie. "Church Using Priest' Cases to Pressure Victims' Network." *The New York Times*, 13 March 2012, p. A1.

Goodstein, Laurie. "Church Whistle-Blowers Join Forces on Abuse." *The New York Times*, 21 May 2013, sec. A, p. 12.

Goodstein, Laurie. "Defying Civil and Canon Laws, Church Failed to Stop a Priest." *The New York Times*, 8 September 2012, p. A1.

Goodstein, Laurie. "Files Show Dolan Sought to Protect Church Assets." *The New York Times*, 2 July 2013, sec. A, p. 10.

Goodstein, Laurie. "New Sexual Abuse Files Cast Shadow on Legacy of Los Angeles Cardinal." *The New York Times*, 23 January 2013, sec. A, p. 11.

Goodstein, Laurie. "Order Dismisses a Priest Trying to Ordain Women." *The New York Times*, 9 August 2011, p. A14.

Goodstein, Laurie. "384 Priests Defrocked Over Abuse in 2 Years," *The New York Times,* 18 January 2014, p. A8.

Goodstein, Laurie. "Wisconsin: Church Will Release Files on Abuse." *The New York Times*, 4 April 2013, sec. A, p. 15.

Goodstein, Laurie, and Erik Eckholm. "Church Battles Efforts to Ease Sex Abuse Suits." *The New York Times*, 14 June 2012, p. A1.

Goodstein, Laurie, and David M. Halbfinger. "Amid Sexual Abuse Scandal, an Office that Failed to Act." *The New York Times*, 2 July 10, p. A1.

Gregory, Bishop Wilton D. "Comments of Bishop Wilton D. Gregory to the Religion Newswriters Association." Archdiocese of Milwaukee. 5 September 2003. http://www.archmil.org/ArchMil/Resources/bishopgregoryaddress.pdf.

Gregory, Bishop Wilton D. "Reflection on the U.S. Bishop's Efforts to Combat Sexual Abuse of Children." Archdiocese of Milwaukee, September 2003. http://www.archmil.org/ArchMil/Resources/bishopgregoryaddress.pdf.

Green, Ashbel S., and Aimee Green. "Parishioners Welcome Settlement." *The Oregonian*, 20 December 2006. http://www.bishopaccountability.org/news2006/11_12/2006_12_20_Green_ParishionersWelcome.htm.

Griffith, Thomas B. "The Tension Within the Religion Clause of the First Amendment." *BYU Law Review* 2011, no. 3 (2011): 597–604.

Grossman, Cathy Lynn. "Clergy Sex Abuse Settlements Top $2.5 Billion Nationwide." *USA Today*, 13 March 2013. http://www.usatoday.com/story/news/nation/2013/03/13/sex-abuse-settlement-cardinal-roger-mahony/1984217/.

Hamilton County Prosecutors. "Settlement Agreement between the Archdiocese of Cincinnati and the Hamilton County Prosecuting Attorney." Signed 20 November 2003, p. 2. http://www.bishop-accountability.org/resources/resource-files/courtdocs/2003–11–20-Pilarczyk-Agreement.pdf.

Hamilton, Marci. "The Case for Abolishing Child Abuse Statutes of Limitations, and for Victims' Forgoing Settlement in Favor of a Jury Trial." 17 July 2003. http://www.bishop-accountability.org/ma-bos/settlements.

Heed, Peter W., N. William Delker, and James D. Rosenberg. *Report on the Investigation of the Diocese of Manchester* (No. 02–8-1154). Office of the Attorney General, 3 March 2003. http://www.bishop-accountability.org/reports/2003_03_03_NHAG.

Hemingway, Sam. "Diocese Settles 11 Priest Sex Abuse Cases in Burlington, Federal Court." 9 January 2013. http://www.bishopaccountability.org/news2013/01_02/2013_01_10_Hemingway_DioceseSettles.html.

Hemingway, Sam. "Vermont Roman Catholic Diocese, Priest Abuse $17.65 Million Settlement." *Burlington Free Press,* 14 May 2012. http://www.burlingtonfreepress .com/article/20100514/NEWS02/100513034/Vermont-Roman-Catholic-diocese -priest-abuse-victims-reach-17–65-million-settlement.

Henneberger, Melinda. "Scandal Left to U.S Catholics." *The New York Times,* 14 April 2002, p. A9.

Hennenberger, Melinda. "Vatican to Hold Secret Trials of Priests in Pedophilia Cases." *The New York Times,* 9 January 2002, p. A8.

Herzog, Karen. "What the Church Documents Reveal." *Journal Sentinel,* 20 July 2013. https://rapevictimsofthecatholicchurch.wordpress.com/category/manchester -diocese-of-the-roman-catholic-church/.

Hoatson, Robert M., and Rev. Kenneth Lasch. 2013. "Home." http://www.road-to -recovery.org.

Holusha, John, and Ian Fisher. "Pope Begins U. S. Visit; Says He Is Ashamed of Sex Scandal." *The New York Times,* 16 April 2008. http://www.nytimes .com/2008/04/16/us/nationalspecial2/15cnd-pope.html?pagewanted=all&_r=0.

Holy See v. John v. Doe. "Brief for the United States as *Amicus Curiae* before the Supreme Court." No. 09-l. May 2010.

Holy See v. John v. Doe. "Petitioner's Reply Brief." 27 October 2009. http://www .bishop-accountability.com.

Holy See Press Office. "Briefing on the Meeting of the Council of Cardinals." 5 December 2013. http://www.vatica.va/resourses/resources_briefing-consiglio -cardinali_2014.

Hosanna-Tabor Evangelical Lutheran Church and School v. Equal Employment Opportunity Commission, et al. "On Writ of Certiorari to the United States Court of Appeals for the Sixth Circuit: Brief of BishopAccountability.org, The Cardozo Advocates for Kids, Child Protection Project, The Foundation to Abolish Child Sex Abuse, Jewish Board of Advocates for Children, Inc., Kidsafe Foundation, The National Black Church Initiative, The National Center for Victims of Crime, Survivors for Justice, And the Survivors Network of Those Abused by Priests as Amici Curiae in Support of Respondents." Supreme Court of the United States, August 2011., http://www.Americanbar.org.

Howell, Ron. "Vatican Focuses on Gay Priests." *Newsday* (Queens edition), 21 March 2002, p. A6.

Hudson, Deal. "When Wolves Dress Like Sheep: Close Look at Voice of the Faithful." *Crisis Magazine,* 8 August 2002. http://www.staycatholic.com.

Hylden. Jordan. "Schori's Agenda." First Things. 2006. http://www.firstthings.com /web-exclusives/2006/11/hylden-schoris-agenda.

Investigative Staff of *The Boston Globe. Betrayal: The Crisis in the Catholic Church.* New York: Little, Brown and Company, 2008.

Jaccino, Steven, and Michael Paulson. "In Files, a History of Sexual Abuse by Priests in Chicago Archdiocese." *The New York Times,* 22 January 2014, p. A10.

John Jay College of Criminal Justice. *The Nature and Scope of Sexual Abuse of Minors by Catholic Priests and Deacons in the U. S. 1950–2002.* 25 February 2004. http://www.usccb.org/issues-and-action/child-and-youth-protection/upload /The-Nature-and-Scope-of-Sexual-Abuse-of-Minors-by-Catholic-Priests-and -Deacons-in-the-United-States-1950–2002.pdf.

John Jay College Research Team. *The Causes and Context of Sexual Abuse of Minors by Catholic Priests in the U. S. 1950–2010.* USCCB, May 2011. http://www.bishop -accountability.org.

John Paul II. *Ad Tuendam Fidem, by Which Certain Norms Are Inserted into the Code of Canon Law and into the Code of Canons of the Eastern Churches.* 18 May 1998. http://www.vatican.va/holy_father/john_paul_ii/motu_proprio/documents /hf_jp-ii_motu-proprio_30061998_ad-tuendam-fidem_en.html.

John V. Doe v. Holy See. Nos. 06–33563 & 06–33587: Appeal from the United States District Court for the District of Oregon. United States Court of Appeals For The Ninth Circuit, 3 March 2009.

Johnson, Annysa. "8,000 Instances of Abuse Alleged in Archdiocese Bankruptcy Hearing." *Milwaukee Wisconsin Journal Sentinel,* 9 February 2012. http://www .jsonline.com/news/religion/achdiocese-bankrusptcy-judge-allows.

Johnson, M. L. "Clergy Sex Abuse Victims to See Milwaukee Archdiocese Files." *Associated Press,* 24 June 2013. http://rapevictimsofthecatholicchurch.wordpress .com/2013/06/24/clergy-sex-abuse-victims-to-see-milwaukee-archdiocese -files/.

Kamal, Sameea. "Knights of Columbus Insurance Program Passes $90 Billion Mark." *The Courant,* 11 July 2013. http://articles.courant.com/2013–07–11/business /hc-knights-of-columbus-insurance-20130711_1_knights-insurance-companies -families.

Kane, Rev. Dr. Thomas, "The House of Affirmation." *Brothers Newsletter* 17, no. 4 (1976): 18–27. http://www.bishopaccountability.org/treatment/HoA/1976_Kane _House_of_Affirmation.pdf.

Kane, Rev. Dr. Thomas. "House of Affirmation, International Therapeutic Center for Clergy and Religious: Give Me Your Hand." September 1973. http://www .bishopaccountability.org/treatment/HoA/1973/09/KaneHouseofAffirmation.pdf.

Kettler, Bishop Donald J. "Fairbanks Diocese Seeks a Consensual Plan for Reorganization." Press Release. 13 February 2008. http://www.bishop-account ability.org/news

Kirby, Peter. "The Didache: The Lord's Teaching through the Twelve Apostles to the Nations." 24 June 2014. http://www.earlychristianwritings.com/text /didache-roberts.html.

Kirkjian, Stpehen, and Walter V. Robinson. "Archdiocese Abandons Deal in Geoghan Case, Committee Rebuff Law, Cites Serious Fiscal Threat." *The Boston Globe,* 4 May 2002. http://www.bishopaccountability.org/mabos/settlements /SettlementBostonGeoghan.html.

Knights of Columbus. "Knights of Columbus—Safe, Secure." Kofcknights.org, 2012. http://www.kofcknights.org/Photos/KofC%20Financial%20Strength%20 2012%286%29.pdf.

Kohn, David. "The Church on Trial, Part 1: Rage in Louisana." CBS News Report. 11 June 2002. http://www.cbsnews.com/stories/2002/06/11/60II/main511845 .shtml.

Kornblut, Anne E. "Crisis in the Church, Vatican Visit; President Weigh in on Church Scandal." *The Boston Globe*, 29 May 2002, p. A14.

Kulish, Nicholas, and Katrin Bennhold. "Pope Was Told Pedophile Priest Would Get Post." *The New York Times*, 26 March 2010, p. A10.

Kuperman, Andrea. "Case Law on Entering Protective Orders, Entering Sealing Orders." July 2010, p. 1. http://www.uscourts/.gov/uscourts/rulesandpolicies.

Lavoie, Denise. "88 People Agree to Settlement in Boston Clergy Abuse Cases." *USA Today*, 10 March 2006, p. 3a.

Leary v. Geoghan. Nos. SUCV199900371, SUCV199901109, Superior Court of Massachusetts, 26 November 2001.

Lemon v. Kurtzman. 403 U.S. 602 (1971).

Liptak, Adam. "Scandal's in the Church: The Impact; Cardinal's Resignation Won't Stop Lawsuits, but Alters Atmosphere," 14 December 2002. http://www.nytimes .com/2002/12/14/us/scandals-church-impact-cardinal-s-resignation

Lovett, Ian. "Los Angeles Cardinal Hid Abuse, Files Show." *The New York Times*, 22 January 2013, sec. A, p. 16.

Lyall, Sarah. "Blaming Church, Ireland Detail Scourge of Abuse." *The New York Times*, 21 May 2009, p. A1.

Lyons, Daniel. "Paid to Picket." *Forbes*, 15 September 2003. http://www.forbes.com /forbes/2003/0915/054.html.

Lytton, Timothy D. "Clergy Sexual Abuse Litigation: The Policymaking Role of Tort Law." *Connecticut Law Review* 39, no. 3 (February 2007): 809–895.

Lytton, Timothy D. "Using Tort Litigation to Enhance Regulatory Policy Making: Evaluating Climate Change Litigation in Light of Lessons from Gun-Industry and Clergy Sexual Abuse Lawsuits." *Texas Law Review* 86, no. 7 (2008): 1837–1876.

Malin v. Singer (2013) to repudiate *Gerbosi v. Gaims* (2011) 193 Cal. Appr. 4th 435. http://www.casp.net/uncategorized/five-amici-briefs-filed-to-challenge -gerbosi.

Malloy, Bishop David J. *The Charter for the Protection of Children and Young People.* USCCB. Revised.16 June 2011. http://www.usccb.org/issues-and-action/child-and -youth-protection/upload/Charter-for-the-Protection-of-Children-and -Young-People-revised-2011.pdf.

Marchocki, Kathryn. "Alleged Abuse Victim Meets with Church Task Force." *Manchester Union Leader*, 2 November 2002. http://www.bishop-accountability .org/NH-Manchester/JBMcCormack-2002–11.html.

Marchocki, Kathryn. "Court, NH Can Oversee Audit of Diocese." *The Union Leader*, 23 March 2005. http://www.bishopaccountability.org/news2005_01_06 /2005_03_23_Marchocki_CourtNH.html.

Marchocki, Kathryn. "Priest Leaves Jaffrey after Admitting Affair." *Nashua Telegraph*, 3 November 2002. http://www.bishop-accountability.org/news/2002_11_03_AP _PriestLeaves.html.

Mashberg, Tom. "Geoghan Victims Get $10M; Judge Oddly Praises All Parties." *Boston Herald*, 20 September 2002. http://www.bishopaccountability.org/mabos /settlements/SettlementBostonGeoghan.html.

Mascagni, Evan. "Five Amici Briefs Filed to Challenge Gergosi and Support the Broad Construction of Anti-SLAPP Law." 26 March 2013. http://www.casp.net /uncategorized/five-amici-briefs-filed-to-challenge.

Massachusetts Laws about Child Sexual Abuse. Massachusetts General Law, Chapter 265, Sections 13B (Indecent Assault and Battery on Child Under 14); Section 22A (Rape of a Child; Use of Force); Section 23 (Rape and Abuse of Child); Section 24 B (Assault of Child; Intent to Commit Rape). See also Massachusetts General Law Chapter 119, Section 21 (Mandated Reporters Defined); Section 51 A (Mandated Reporting Explained); Massachusetts General Law Chapter 277, Section 63 (Statute of Limitations for Criminal Cases); Massachusetts General Law, Chapter 260, Section 4C (State of Limitations for civil Cases). 5 November 2013. http://www.lawlib.state.ma.us/subject/about /childsexabuse.html.

McCord, John. "When Litigation Ends." *Survivors Alliance and Franciscan Exchange Network*, 12 December 2003. http://www.mysafenet.org/?q=node/36.

McDonough, Peter. *The Catholic Labyrinth: Power, Apathy and a Passion for Reform in the American Church*. New York: Oxford University Press, 2013.

McKenna, Josephine. "Cardinal Sean O'Malley on sexual abuse crisis: 'There is so much denial,'" Religion News Service, 3 May 2014. http://www.religionnews .com/2014/05/03/cardinal-sean-omalley-sexual-abuse-crisis-much-denial/

McKiernan, Terence. "Governments Must Step into Priest Sex Abuse Cases." CNN, 19 March 2010. Accessed at: http://www.cnn.com/2010/OPINION/03/19 /mckiernan.catholic.sex.abuse/.

McNamara, Eileen. "Reclaiming Their Church." *The Boston Globe*, 14 April 2002. http://www.boston.com/globe/spotlight/abuse/stories/041402_mcnamara.htm.

McVeigh, Karen. "Pope Accused of Crimes against Humanity by Victims of Sex Abuse." *The Guardian*. 13 September 2011. http://www.theguardian.com /world/2011/sep/13/prop-crime-humanity.

Meichtry, Stacy, and John L. Allen Jr. "Vatican: 'Its Forgiveness.' Victims: 'It's More Pain.'" *National Catholic Reporter*, 11 April 2005. http://www.national catholicreporter.org/update/conclave/pt041105d.htm.

Montalbano, William D. "Pontiff Assails U. S. Church, Sex Abuse by Priests." *Los Angeles Times*, 15 August 1993, p. A1.

Mueller, Mark. "Archbishop Denounced for Support of Priest." *Star-Ledger*, 30 April 2013, p. A1.

Mueller, Mark. "Papers Reveal Another Priest Accused of Sex Abuse." *Star-Ledger*, 2 August 2013, p.A 14.

Muller, James E., and Charles Kenney. *Keep the Faith, Change the Church.* New York: St. Martin's Press, 2004.

Mullins, Dr. Robert w. "Letter of Dr. Robert W. Mullins to Reverend Oates." 20 October 1984. www.bishop-accountability.org

Murray, John Courtney, S. J. "Contemporary Orientations of Catholic Thought on Church and State." *Theological Studies* 10 (June 1949): 177–234.

Murray, John Courtney, S. J. "Freedom of Religion I: The Ethical Problem." *Theological Studies* 6 (June 1945): 229–286.

Murray, John Courtney, S. J. "Governmental Repression of Heresy." *Proceedings of the Third Annual Convention of the Catholic Theological Society of America.* Chicago: Catholic Theological Society of America, 1948, pp. 26–98.

Murray, John Courtney S. J. "Leo XIII on Church and State: The General Structure of the Controversy." *Theological Studies* 14 (March 1953): 1–30.

Murray, John Courtney, S. J. *We Hold These Truths: Reflections on the American Proposition.* New York: Sheed and Ward, 1960.

NAMBLA. North American Man/Boy Association. "Who We Are," http://www.nambla.org/welcome.html

National Review Board. "A Ten Year Progress Report." 13 June 2012. http://www.usccb.org/issues-and-action/child-and-youth-protection/upload/10-Year-Progress-Report-Summary.pdf

New Hampshire Judicial Branch. "Decision of Superior Court of Judge Carol A. Conboy. No 2–8-1154." 22 March 2005. http://www.courts.state.nh.us/superoders/grandjury/pdf.

New Hampshire v. Presbyterian Church 998 P.2d, 592, 598 (USA).

New York Times Staff. "Files Show Archdiocese Paid $21 Million in Abuse Cases." *The New York Times*, 13 August 2003, p. A20.

Office of the Attorney General, Commonwealth of Massachusetts. "The Sexual Abuse of Children in the Roman Catholic Archdiocese of Boston." 23 July 2003. http://www.bishop-accountability.org/downloads/archexecsumm.pdf.

Official Communiqué of the Vatican. "Vatican, Belgian Bishops on Raids of Church Offices: It Was Not an Agreeable Experience." 25 June 2010. http://www.zenit.org/en/articles/vatican-belgian-bishops-on-raids-of-church-offices.

O'Bryan v. Holy See. Civil Action No. 3:04CV-388-H before the U. S. District Court Western District of Kentucky at Louisville. Filed 4 January 2010.

O'Bryan v. Holy See. US Court of Appeals for the Sixth Circuit. No. 07–5078, 07–5163. Argued 24 November 2008 (490 F. Supp. 2nd 826, 832).

O'Neill, Eamonn. "What the Catholic Bishop Knew." *The Guardian*, 2 April 2010. New York. http://www.theguardian.com/world/2010/apr/02/catholic-bishop -william-levada.

O'Reilly, David, and Nancy Phillips. "Grand Jury Harshly Criticizes Archdiocese for Hiding Clergy Sexual Abuse." *Philadelphia Inquirer*, 21 September 2005, p. l.

Paulson, Michael. "Bishop Bans Group from Meetings at Parish." *The Boston Globe*, 1 October 2002, p. A1.

Paulson, Michael. "Catholic Group to Rate Bishops." *The Boston Globe*, 20 September 2002, p. A1.

Paulson, Michael. "Church Struggle Pain La. Region Stung by Abuse in "80s." *The Boston Globe*, 12 June 2002. http://www.boston.com/globe/spotlight/abuse /stories2/061202_louisiana.html.

Paulson, Michael. "Citing Deficit, Archdiocese Eyes Substantial Budget Cuts." *The Boston Globe*, 24 March 2005. p. 1. http://www.boston.globe.

Paulson, Michael. "In His First Meeting with Voice of Faithful, Law Seeks Answers." *The Boston Globe*, 27 November 2002, p. B1.

Paulson, Michael. "Law Seeks to Curb Organizing by Laity." *The Boston Globe*, 27 April 2002, p. A1.

Paulson, Michael. "Leaving 'Little Rome' for Braintree." *The Boston Globe*, 26 June 2008, p. A1.

Paulson, Michael. "Lessons Unlearned." *The Boston Globe*, 12 June 2002. http:// www.boston.com/globe/spotlight/abuse/stories2/061202_louisiana.htm.

Perry, Kimball. "Archdiocese Found Guilty of Criminal Charges." *Cincinnati Post*, 21 November 2003, p. A1.

Peters, Edward, trans. *The 1917 Pio-Benedictine Code of Canon Law*. San Francisco: Ignatius Press, 2001.

Petitioner's Reply Brief. In the Supreme Court of the United States, 27 October 2009, No. 09–1.

Pilarczyk, Archbishop Daniel E. "Statement by Archbishop Daniel E. Pilarczyk." *Catholic Telegraph*, 20 November 2003. http://www.bishop-accountability.org /resources/resource-files/timeline/2003–11–20-Pilarczyk-Statement.html.

Pogatchnik, Shawn. "Irish Say Religious Groups in Abuse Case Hide Wealth." *The Philadelphia Inquirer*, 28 May 2009, p. B13.

Pope Benedict XVI. "Benedict XVI's Solidarity with Bishops of Belgium." 27 June 2010. http://www.press.catholica.va/news.

Pope Benedict XVI. *The Norms of the Motu Proprio "Sacramentorum Sanctitatis Tutela"*. 2001. http://www.vatican.va/resources/resources_introd-storica_en.html.

Pope Benedict XVI. "How Much Filth There Is in Church." Good Friday Services, April 2005. http://www.conchiglia.us/uk/uk/_pap/uk_sporcizia_nella_Chiesa.htm.

Pope Benedict XVI. "Text of the Pastoral Letter of the Holy Father Pope Benedict XVI to the Catholics of Ireland." 19 March 2010. http://www

.vatican.va/holy_father/benedict_xvi/letters/2010/documents/hf_ben-xvi_let
_20100319_church-ireland_en.html112.

"Pope Expresses Personal Anguish and Horror over Priestly Sex Abuse," 27 October 2006, Statement of Pope Benedict, 2006 accessed at. http://www.ewtn .com/vnews/getstory.asp?number=72712.

Pope Francis I. "Address of Pope Francis to Bishops of the Episcopal Conference of the Netherlands on Their 'Ad Limina' Visit." 2 December 2013. http:// www.news.va/en/news/to-the-bishops-of-the-episcopal-conference-of-the -Netherlands.

Pope John Paul II. *Ecclesia in Oceana.* December 1998. http://www.vatican.va.

Pope John Paul II. *"On the Manner of Proceeding in Causes of Solicitation,"* (*Crimen Sollicitudionis*). Supreme Sacred Congregation of the Holy Office, 16 March 1962. http://www.vatican.va/resources/resources_crimen-sollicitationis-1962 _en.html.

Pope John Paul II. "*The Norms of the Motu Proprio "Sacramentorum Sanctitatis Tutela"* http://www.bishop-accountability.org/resources/resource-files/churchdocs /SacramentorumAndNormaeEnglish.htm. 30 April 2001.

Pope Leo XIII. *Immortale Dei.* 1 November 1885. http://www.vatican.va/holy_father /leo_xiii/encyclicals/documents/hf_lxiii_enc_01111885_immortale-dei_en.html.

Pope Leo XIII. *Inscrutabili Dei Consilio.* 21 April 1878. http://www.vatican.va/holy _father/leo_xiii/encyclicals/documents/hf_l-xiii_enc_21041878_inscrutabili -dei-consilio_en.html.

Pope Leo XIII. *Longinque Oceani.* 1 January 1885. http://www.vatican.va/holy_father /leo_xiii/encyclicals/documents/hf_l-xiii_enc_06011895_longinqua_en.html.

Pope Leo XIII. *Sapientiae Christianae.* 10 January 1890. http://www.vatican.va /holy_father/leoxiii/encyclicals/documents/hf_l-xiii_enc_10011890 _sapientiae-christianae_en.html.

Pope Leo XIII. *Testem Benevolentiae.* 22 January 1899. http://www.Vatican.va.

"Pope's Speech to American Cardinals on Church Crisis," *The New York Times,* 24 April 2002, p. A 22.

Post, James E. "Voice of the Faithful—A Decade of Catholic Activism." *Voice of the Faithful,* No Date. http://www.votf.org/2012Conference/VOTFADecadeof CatholicActivism.pdf.

Povoledo, Elisabetta. "Bishop, 73, in Belgium Steps Down Over Abuse." *The New York Times,* 24 April 2010, p. A4.

Povoledo, Elisabetta. "Catholic Leaders Meet to Discuss Abuse Prevention." *The New York Times,* 7 February 2012, p. A11.

Povoledo, Elisabetta, "Clear Rules Eyed on Church Sex Abuse,: *The New York Times,* 6 May 2014, p. A8.

Powers, Ashley. "Secret Files Detail Clergy Abuse." *Los Angeles Times,* 24 May 2012. http://articles.latimes.com/2012/may/24/local/la-me-0523-franciscan -abuse-20120524.

The Quinnipiac Polling Institute. "Sex Abuse Priests and Bishops Who Hid Them Should Go, American Catholics Tell Quinnipiac University Poll; Catholics 3–1 Want Equal Say in Dealing with Issue." Quinnipiac University. 12 June 2002. http://www.quinnipiac.edu/institutes-and-centers/polling-institute /national/release-detail?ReleaseID=476.

Reaves, Joseph A. "Romley, O'Brien Clash Over Substance of Deal; Bishop Denies He's Admitting Cover-Up." *Arizona Republic*, 3 June 2003. http://www .bishopaccountability.org/news2003_01_06/2003_06_03_Reaves_RomleyO Brien.htm.

Reaves, Joseph A. "Unsung Judges Lead Way in Priest Investigations." *The Arizona Republic*, 23 February 2003. http://www.snapnetwork.org/legal_courts/stories /unsung_judges_leadway.html.

Reilly, Thomas F. "The Sexual Abuse of Children in the Roman Catholic Archdiocese of Boston: Executive Summary and Scope of Investigation." Office of the Attorney General Commonwealth of Massachusetts. 23 July 2003. http:// www.bishop-accountability.org/downloads/*arIchexecsumm*.pdf.

Religion and Ethics Newsweekly, 9 July 2004. Episode No. 745.

Rendezes, Michael. "Judge Accepts Geoghan Settlement." *The Boston Globe*, 20 September 2002. http://www.boston.com/globe/spotlight/abuse/stories3/092002 _settlement.html.

Reuters. "Society Shares Blame for Scandals, Vatican Says: Catholic Church: Permissiveness is 'real culprit' in Abuse of Children." *Los Angeles Times*, 26 June 1993, p. B5.

Rice, Patricia. "Gregory Hails Pope's Response to U.S. Scandal: "He Gets It." *St. Louis Post-Dispatch*, 28 April 2002, p. B1.

Rice, Patricia. "Priest Accused of Abuse Was Given Parish Job." *Post-Dispatch*, 8 April 2002. http://www.altarboys.tripod.com/archives/Priest_Accusex .html.

Rich, Eric, and Elizabeth Hamilton. "Doctors: Church Used Us." *Hartford Courant*, 24 March 2002. http://www.bishopaccountability.org/news9/2002_03_24_Rich _DoctorsChurch.htm.

Richir, Jerimee. "SNAP Mission Statement." 2012. http://www.snapnetwork.org /mission_statement.

Rivera, Ray. "Prosecutor Seeks to Force Rabbis to Report on Abuse." *The New York Times*, 23 May 2012. http://www.nytimes.com/2012/05/24/nyregion/brooklyn -prosecutor-seeks-bill-requiring-rabbis-to-report-claims-of-abuse.html.

Robinson, Walter V. "Shining the Globe's Spotlight on the Catholic Church." *Neiman Foundation for Journalism at Harvard: Neiman Reports*. Spring 2003. http://www.nieman.harvard.edu/reports/article/101186/Shining-the-Globe.

Robinson, Walter V., and Michael Rezendes. "Geoghan Victims Agree to "10M Settlement." *The Boston Globe*, 19 September 2002. http://www.bishop-accountability .org/ma-bos/settlements.

Rotstein, Arthur H. "Tuscon Diocese Bankruptcy Effectively over a Year Later." *Associated Press,* as carried in *the Seattle Post-Intelligencer,* 18 September 2005. http://www.bishopaccountability.org/news2005_07_12/2005_09_18_Rotstein _TucsonDiocese.htm.

Ryan, John A., and Francis A. Boland. *Catholic Principles of Politics.* New York: Macmillan, 1940.

Ryan, John A., and F. X. Millar. *The State and the Church.* New York: Macmillan, 1922.

Santora, Marc, and Laurie Goodstein. "Newark Monsignor Loses Job for Failing to Stop Priest's Work with Children." *The New York Times,* 26 May 2013, p. 16.

Sauer, Mark. "San Diego Catholic Diocese Files for Bankruptcy." *The San Diego Union-Tribune,* 28 February 2007. http://www.signonsandiego.com/news/metro /20070228–9999–7n28diocese.html.

Sennott, Charles, *Globe* Staff, and Jason Horowitz, "Seminarians follow the bishops' debate." *The Boston Globe,* 20 April 2002, p. A24.

Sherbert v. Verner. 374 U. S. 398 (1963).

Shirky, Clay. *Here Comes Everybody.* New York: Penguin Books, 2008.

Shultzberger, A. G., and Laurie Goodstein. "Bishop Indicted; Charge is Failing to Report Abuse." *The New York Times,* 15 October 2011, p. A1.

Slovick, Sam. "Sacred Monsters: Terence McKiernan." 12 July 2013. http://www .MissionandState.org.

Smetzer, Mary Beth. "Court Ruling Leaves Fairbanks Diocese without Insurance in Abuse Cases." *News Miner,* 3 October 2009. http://www.bishopaccountability .org/news2009/09_10/2009_10_03_Smetzer_CourtRuling.htm.

Spadaro, Antonino, SJ "A Big Heart Open to God." 30 September 2013. http://www .americamagazaine.or/pope-interview.

State v. Gastal. 731 So. 2d 273 (1998).

Stogner v. California. 539 U. S. 607 (2003).

Stucke, John, and Virginia de Leon. "Diocese Files Settlement." *The Spokesman-Review,* 5 January 2007. http://www.spokesman.com/stories/2007/jan/05/diocese -files-settlement/.

Suffolk County Supreme Court Special Grand Jury. *Grand Jury Report CPL §190.85(1) (C),* 6 May 2002. Issued 17 January 2003. http://www.bishopaccountability.org /reports/2003_02_10_SuffolkGrandJury/Suffolk_Full_Report.pdf.

Supreme Sacred Congregation of the Holy Office. "Instruction on the Manner of Proceeding in Causes Involving the Crime of Solicitation." 1962. http://www .vatican.va/resources/resources_cimen-sollicitationis-1962_en.html.

Survivors Network of Those Abused by Priests. "MissionStatement." Snapnetwork. org, n.d. http://www.snapnetwork.org/mission_statement.

Swords, Dr. Robert. "Letter of Dr. Robert Swords to Reverend Robert Banks." 13 December 1989. www.bishop-accountability.org.

Szulc, Tad. *Pope John Paul II: The Biography.* New York: Pocket Books, 1995.

"Text of Agreement between the State of Arizona ex.rel. Richard M Romley, Maricopa Country Attorney; Thomas J. O'Brien, Bishop of the Roman

Catholic Diocese of Phoenix and the Roman Catholic Diocese of Phoenix," a corporation sole ("the diocese"), 3 May 2003, http://www.bishop-accountability .org/az-phoenix/phoenix-agreement-resignation.htm.

TheMediaReport.Com. "Att'y Jeff Anderson Quietly Drops Vatican Lawsuit, Publicity Stunt Exposed." 1 March 2012. http://www.themediareport.com/2012 /03/01/atty-jeff-anderson-quietly-drops-vatican-lawsuit/.

TheMediaReport.Com. "BishopAccountbility.org Exposed: The Self Professed Chroniclers of Abuse Smearing Innocent Priests." 4 April 2013. http://www .themediareport.com/2013/04/04/bishop-accountability-org-anti-catholic/.

The National Review Board for the Protection of Children and Young People. *A Report on the Crisis in the Catholic Church in the United States*. Washington, DC: The United States Conference of Catholic Bishops, 2004. http://www.bishop -accountability.org.

Times Wires. "Connecticut Priest Accused of Abuse commits Suicide," *St. Petersburg Times*, 17 May 2002. p. 5A.

Tomasi, Msgr. Silvano. "Presentation by H. E. Msgr. Silvano Tomasi of the Periodic Report of the Holy See to the Committee on the Convention of the Rights of the Child and the Optional Protocols." 16 January 2014. http://www.vatican.va /roman_curia/secretariat_state/2014/documents/rc-seg-st-20140116_tomasi -child-rights_en.html.

United Nations Committee on the Rights of the Child "Concluding Observations on the Second Periodic Report of the Holy See." 25 February 2014. http://tbinternet .ohchr.org/Treaties/CRC/Shared Documents/VAT/CRC_C_VAT_CO_2_.

United States Bankruptcy Court, Summary Judgment of Judge Patricia Williams. Filed NO. 04–08822-PCW11, Chapter 11. 25 August 2005.

United States Bankruptcy Court., D. Oregon. *In Re Roman Catholic Archbishop of Portland in Oregon as Successors*, a Corporation Sole, DBA the Archdiocese of Portland in Oregon, Debtor. No. 04–37154-elp11, 338 B. R. 414. 17 January 2006. https://www.courtlistener.com/orb/8QCL/in-re-roman-catholic-archbishop -of-portland-in-or/.

United States Conference of Catholic Bishops, Office of Media Relations. "Conference President Invites Continued Dialogue with 'SNAP.'" 10 June 2002. http://old.usccb.org/comm/archives/2002/02–109.shtml.

United States Conference of Catholic Bishops, Office of Media Relations. "Effort to Combat Clergy Sexual Abuse against Minors: A Chronology." www.archmil .org/Archmil/resources/timeline.pdf June 2002.

United States Conference of Catholic Bishops. "The Charter to Protect Children and Young People." http://www.bishop-accountability.org/resources/resourcefiles /Churchdocs/Dallas. June 2002.

United States Conference of Catholic Bishops. "The Essential Norms for Diocesan/ Eparchical Policies Dealing With Allegation of Sexual Abuse of Minors by Priests of Deacons." 2002. http://www.bishop-accountbility.org/resources /resourcesfiles/Churchdocs/finalnorms.html.

United States Conference of Catholic Bishops. "The Nature and Scope of Sexual Abuse of Minors by Catholic Priests and Deacons in the U. S. 1950–2002." February 2004. http://www.usccb.org/issues-and-action/child-and-youth -protection/upload/The-Nature-and-Scope-of-Sexual-Abuse-of-Minors-by -Catholic-Priests-and-Deacons-in-the-United-States-1950–2002.pdf.

United States Conference of Catholic Bishops. *Report of the National Review Board*. 29 July 2003. http://www.bishopaccountability.org/news2003_07_12/2003_07_29 _Chicago_ReportOf.htm.

United States Court of Appeals for the Ninth Circuit. No. 06–35587 D.C. No. C.V-02–004-MWM, p. 2549.

United States District Court: District of Massachusetts. "Local Rules of the United states District Court for the District of Massachusetts Rule 83.2B 'Special Orders for the Protection of the Accused or the Litigants in Widely Publicized or Sensational Criminal or Civil Cases.'" 1 September 1990. http://www.mad .uscourts.gov/general/pdf/lc/localrulescombined.pdf.

United States District Court for the Eastern District of Washington. *Committee of Tort Litigants, et. al. vs. Catholic Diocese of Spokane, et.al.* No. 05-CV-274-JLQ, Bkty. Ct. No. 04–08822-PCW11.

Urbina, Ian. "Delaware Diocese Files for Bankruptcy in Wake of Abuse Suits." *The New York Times*, 20 December 2010, p. A10.

Vatican. "Final Communique" of the Meeting between the Cardinals of the United States and the Pope." 24 April 2002. http://www.vatican.va/roman_curia /cardina...rdinal_20020424_final-communique_en.html.

Vatican Radio Staff. "Holy See's Lawyer: Dismissed Lawsuit in US 'Never Should Have Been Filed.'" Vatican Radio, 7 August 2013. http://en.radiovaticana.va /storico/2013/08/07/holy_sees_lawyer_dismissed_lawsuit_in_us_never_should _have_been/en1-717667.

Vitello, Paul. "Bishop Avidly Opposes Bill Extending Times to File Child-Abuse Suits." *The New York Times*, 5 June 2009, p. A18.

Vitello, Paul. "Religious Leaders Fight Bill to Open Abuse Cases." *The New York Times*, 12 March 2009, p. A1.

Voice of the Faithful. "Clerical Culture among Roman Catholic Diocesan Clergy." No Date. http://www.votf.org/clericalism.pdf.

Voice of the Faithful. "Clericalism: Reality and Concerns." No Date. http://votf .org/page/clericalism-reality-and-concerns/18094.

Voice of the Faithful. "Conclusions about the John Jay College Report: 'The Causes and Context of Sexual Abuse of Minors by Catholic Priests in the U. S. 1950–2010.'" 11 October 2011. http://www.votf.org/Govt_reports/VOTF _Conclusions_Report.pdf.

Voice of the Faithful. "The Six Most Important Reforms VOTF Would Like to Discuss with His Advisors in October." 24 September 2013. http://voicefaithful .wordpress.com/2013/09/24/the-six-most-important-reforms-voice-of-the -faithful-would-like-pope-francis-to-discuss-with-his-advisors-in-october/.

Voice of the Faithful. "Voice of the Faithful Urges Pope Francis to 'act decisively' regarding Bishops, clergy sexual abuse and his message to Vatican Congregation," 6 June 2013. http://votf.org/featured 18098.

Wakin, Daniel J. "Brooklyn Bishop Ending Tenure amid Storm over Scandal." *The New York Times*, 2 August 2003. http://www.nytimes.com/2003/08/02/nyregion /brooklyn-bishop-ending-tenure-amid-storm-over-scandal.html.

Wakin, Daniel J., and Katie Zezima. "Abusive Ex-Priest, John Geoghan, Is Killed in Prison." *The New York Times*, 24 August 2003. http://www.snapnetwork.org /news/massachusetts/boston/geoghan_murder.htm.

Walsh, Andrew. "Bishops in the Dock." *Religion in the News* 14, no. 1 (Spring 2012): pp. 6–9.

Walsh, Andrew. "No Peace for the Church." *Religion in the News* 6, no. 3 (Winter 2006): pp. 17–19.

Weakland, Rembert W., OSB. *A Pilgrim in a Pilgrim Church*. Grand Rapids, MI: Eerdmans, 2009.

Wedge, Dave, "John Geoghan Killer Joe Druce Poised to Marry." *Boston Herald*, 6 October 2010. http://www.freerepublic.com/focus/f-chat/2601937/posts.

Westchester County April "E" 2002 Grand Jury. *Report of the April "E" 2002 Westchester Country Grand Jury Concerning Complaints of Sexual Abuse and Misconduct against Minors by Members of the Clergy.* 19 June 2002. http://www.bishopaccountability .org/resources/resourcefiles/reports/WestchesterGrandJuryReport.pdf.

Williams, R. Seth. District Attorney of Philadelphia. *Report of the Grand Jury.* Grand Jury Hearing XXIII in the Court of Common Pleas of the First Judicial District of Pennsylvania. Misc. No. 0009901–2008.

Wills, Gary. "Bishops at Bay." *The New York Review of Books*, 15 August 2002. http:// www.nybooks.com/articles/archives/2002/aug/15/the-bishops-at-bay.

Wisconsin v. Yoder. 406 U. S. 205 (1972).

Yaccino, Steven, and Michael Paulson. "In files, a History of Sexual abuse by Priests in Chicago Archdiocese." *The New York Times*, 22 January 2014, p. A1.

Yardley, Jim. "Pope Moves to Deflate Breathless Portrayals of Stardom." *The New York Times*, 6 March 2014, p. A7.

Youtube.com. "Joseph Druce #1." 12 June 2007. http://www.youtube.com /watch?v=IjkHXDtoXAo.JosephDruce#1YouTube.

Zenit.org Staff. "Vatican Statement on the 'Murphy Case.'" Zenit.org, 25 March 2010. http://www.zenit.org/en/articles/vatican-statement-on-the-murphy-case.

Zezima, Katie. "Archdiocese Is Hamstrung in Reform, Report Says." *The New York Times*, 8 April 2006, p. A11.

Zezima, Katie. "Boston Archdiocese to Sell Land to Raise $100 Million." *The New York Times*, 11 April 2004, p. A21.

Index

Ad Tenendam Fidem (John
  Paul), 105
Aga, Mohamet Ali, 101
Alaska, 142–3, 145
American Catholic Conference
  (ACC), 167
American Catholics
  Church integral in lives
    of, 15
  political loyalties of, 13
  in US economic and social
    structures, 14
Amnesty International, 5, 155
Anderson, Jeffrey, 72
  in *Doe v. Holy See,* 172, 174–6,
    178
  in Murphy cases, 182
  SNAP and, 157
archbishops
  incorporation by, 231n59
  legal liability of, 139
Avery, Edward, 134–5, 201–2

"Babylonian Captivity," 241n18
bankruptcies, 138–46, 148, 196
  of Milwaukee Archdiocese,
    182
  of St. Louis Archdiocese,
    239–40n117
Belgium, 185–7
Bencomo, Raul, 20–1

Benedict XVI (pope; Joseph
  Ratzinger), 4–5
  accusations against, 183–91
  change in US-Vatican
    relations under, 207–10
  Congregation for the
    Defense of the Faith
    under, 104, 126, 207
  McCarrick named cardinal
    by, 115
  meets with American
    bishops, 107
  new sexual abuse guidelines
    issued under, 189,
    240n119
  in *O'Bryan v. Holy See,* 180, 181
Berry, Jason, 6, 17
Bertone, Tarcisio (cardinal),
  186, 238n87
Bevilacqua, Anthony
  (cardinal), 132, 133, 135,
  136, 202
bishop-accountability.org,
  169–72
bishops, 10, 16
  acting on behalf of dioceses,
    54, 237n83
  authority of, 194
  "Charter for the Protection
    of Children and Young
    People" by, 116–18, 125

bishops—*Continued*
  Code of Canon Law on powers of, 89
  on Code of Canon Law on sexual
      abuse cases, 96–7
  consequences of Gauthe case for, 41–3
  Dallas meeting of (2002), 111–14, 116
  John Paul II and, 102, 103, 105–8
  National Conference of Catholic
      Bishops organization of, 34–6,
      220*n*43
  sexual abuse allegations to be
      investigated and tried by, 92–6
  Vatican II on authority of, 98
  Vatican versus, 125–30
Blaine, Barbara, 149–51
Blum, Virgil, 157
The Book of Gommorah (Peter
    Damien), 85
Borden, Shirl, 72–3
Boston, Archdiocese of
  after sexual abuse scandals, 67–70
  attempts to seal records of, 52
  Boston Globe suit against, 55–6
  costs of settlements by, 230*n*49
  depositions of leaders of, 59–60
  Geoghan and other civil suits
      against, 57–8
  Reilly's investigation of and report
      on, 62–6
  sexual abuse settlements by, 53–4, 105
  under Law's leadership, 61–2
  Voice of the Faithful in, 159–65
Boston (Massachusetts), 3, 195
  attorney general's investigation and
      report in, 62–6, 120
Boston College, 67
Boston Globe, 5–6
  Boston Archdiocese sued by, 55–6
  on Geoghan case, 50–5, 105
Brennan, James, 134, 136
Brennan, John, 49
Brooklyn, Diocese of (New York), 69

Bullaria, 84
Bush, George W., 108, 115
Byzantium (Constantinople; Istanbul), 81

California, 120–3, 202–3
  costs of settlements in, 230*n*49
  incorporation in, 145
  legislation in, 153
  SNAP in, 155–7
Call to Action (organization), 167
Campbell family, 218*n*21
canon law, 2
  challenged in Gauthe case, 26
  "Charter" and "Essential Norms" in
      conflict with, 126–8
  Congregation of the Doctrine of the
      Faith authority to enforce, 184
  in early Church history, 77–82
  "Essential Norms for Diocesan/
      Eparchial Policies Dealing
      with Allegations of Sexual
      Abuses..." on, 118–19
  establishment of, 84
  history and evolution of, 75–7
  judicial challenges to, 191
  on punishment for sexual abuse, 85–6
  on sexual abusers, 91–2
  supremacy of civil law over, 198–205
  supremacy over civil law of, 52
  in twentieth-century world, 87–91
  as used by popes, 4–5
  Vatican on supremacy of, 201
Capuchins (religious order), 40
cardinals, 60
Castro, Fidel, 115
Catholic Charities, 67, 137–8, 164
Catholic Church. *See* Roman Catholic
    Church
Catholic League for Religious and
    Civil Rights, 157–8
Catholic Whistleblowers
    (organization), 156

Catholicism, 12

CDF. *See* Congregation of the Doctrine of the Faith

celibacy, for clergy, 83, 86
  American Catholic Conference on, 167
  Code of Canon Law on, 90
  not linked to pedophilia, 108
  VOTF on, 166

Center for Constitutional Rights (CCR), 154–5

Chaput, Charles (archbishop), 133–4

Charlemagne (emperor, Holy Roman Empire), 83

"The Charter for the Protection of Children and Young People," 116–19, 125–30, 199
  ineffectiveness of, 136, 200–1
  VOTF on compliance with, 163–4, 167, 168

Chicago (Illinois), 203–4

children
  Boston Archdiocese policies on, 63
  "Charter for the Protection of Children and Young People" on, 116–18, 125–9
  legislation protecting, 66
  at risk in Boston, 64
  state interest in protection of, 197
  Vatican on rights of, 212–13
  see also victims

China, 117, 127

Chopko, Mark, 36, 139

Christian Brothers (order), 187, 230n49

Christianity
  beginning of, 78–9
  Constantine's conversion to, 80

Christians
  earliest, 78–9
  Nicene Creed for, 81
  in Roman Empire under Constantine, 80

Church hierarchy, 16–17
  bishop–accountability.org and, 169–72
  "Charter" and "Essential Norms" on, 125–6
  Council of Trent defines, 86
  depositions of, 59–60
  development in Roman Empire of, 80
  legal strategy of, 148–9
  loss of political power of, 198
  pope at top of, 97
  power relationships between clergy, laity, and, 11
  traditional view of, 12–13
  VOTF challenge to, 166–9

church-state issues
  in bankruptcies, 140–1, 146
  in California case, 121–3
  change in relations between Vatican and US, 205–10
  concordats between Church and civil states, 11
  courts on, 197
  current balance of power in, 193–5
  in depositions of Church leadership, 59–60
  in diplomatic recognition of Vatican, 31–2
  erosion of Church power in, 191, 215
  financial aspects of, 138
  in Gauthe case, 26–7, 30, 38–9
  in Geoghan case, 52, 56
  Lemon v. Kurtzman on, 72, 224n55
  Murray on, 13, 217–18n7
  in Reilly's investigation of Boston Archdiocese, 63
  sovereign immunity of Vatican as, 181

Cimmarrusti, Mario, 233n15

Cincinnati, Diocese of, 130–1

Cincinnati (Ohio), 57

civil law
    canon law supremacy over, 52, 84, 88
    Congregation of the Doctrine of the
        Faith on, 190, 209
    "Essential Norms for Diocesan/
        Eparchial Policies Dealing
        with Allegations of Sexual
        Abuses..." on, 118–19
    Justinian Code as, 82–3
    popes immune to, 183
    supremacy over canon law of, 198–205
civil states
    Belgium, 186
    current balance of power between
        Church and, 193–5
    Germany, 183–4
    Ireland, 187–9
    Leo XIII on relationship between
        Church and, 11–12
    Vatican II documents on, 13–14
civil suits, 147–8
    bankruptcies resulting from, 138–44
    against Boston Archdiocese, 53–4,
        56–8
    depositions in, 59–60
    against dioceses, 133
    Doe v. Holy See case against Vatican,
        172–9
    financial consequences of, 137,
        230n49
    against Gauthe, 21, 24–31, 35, 37
    John Paul II on, 102
    O'Bryan v. Holy See, 179–81
    against SNAP, 152–3
clergy
    celibacy for, 83, 86
    clerical culture of, 204, 214–15
    see also Church hierarchy; priests
clerical culture, 204, 214–15
clericalism, 167, 235n55
Clinton, Bill, 115
Clohessy, David, 151–3, 157

Clohessy, Kevin, 151
Coalition of Catholics and Survivors,
    163, 170
Code of Canon Law, 88–90, 184
    American bishops on, 96–7
    changes of 2001 to, 225n27
    changes under John Paul II to, 206
    civil law and, 91
    Crimen Sollicitationis in, 237–8n85
    on sexual abusers, 92–5, 240n119
College of Cardinals, 60
commercial activity exemption
    (in FISA), 176
Conference of Major Superiors of
    Men, 128–9
confidentiality
    in Blaine's case, 150
    in Boston cases, 54–6, 58
    "Charter for the Protection of
        Children and Young People"
        on, 117, 118
    in civil cases, 148
    of court records, 52
    Crimen Sollicitationis on, 237–8n85
    elimination of, 145
    legislation ending, 195
    in *O'Bryan v. Holy See,* 180
    of priest-penitent communications,
        122
    of privileged communications, 59
    in Rockville Center case, 124
    in settlement agreements, 21, 91, 123
    of SNAP records, 152–3
    of Vatican communications, 63, 183
    in Westchester County case, 57, 123
Congregation of the Doctrine of the
    Faith (CDF), 125
    bishops referrals to, 200
    canon law appeals to, 93
    on clerical sexual abuse, 189–90
    given total authority under John
        Paul II, 206–7

in *O'Bryan v. Holy See,* 180
under Levada, 41, 208–9
under Ratzinger (Benedict XVI),
    104, 108, 126, 181–2, 184
Wesolowski defrocked by, 212
Connell, James E., 156
Constance, Council of, 241*n*18
Constantine (emperor, Roman
    Empire), 80–1
Constantinople (Byzantium;
    Istanbul), 81
Constitution (US)
    First Amendment to, 196–200
    Leo XIII on, 11–12
Convention of the Rights of the Child,
    205, 212
Cooke, Terence (cardinal), 115
*Corpus Juris Canonici (Decretum
    Gratiani),* 84
Cote, Roland, 70
Council of Trent (1545–1563), 86
Covington (Kentucky), 230*n*49
Crimen Sollicitationis, 90, 184, 237–8*n*85
criminal cases, 147
    against dioceses, 133
    against Gauthe, 21, 24–31, 37
    against Geoghan, 51, 57
    in Los Angeles, 136
    in Philadelphia, 133–6
    against Porter, 51
    against Shanley, 56
    Vatican on, 101–2
Cuba, 127
Cushing, Richard (cardinal), 50

Daily, Thomas (bishop), 49, 62, 69
Dallas (Texas)
    bishops, meeting in (2002), 111–14,
        200
    "Charter" and "Essential Norms"
        passed at bishops' meeting in,
        116, 118–19, 125–8

D'Antonio, Michael, 6
Davenport (Iowa), 120, 142
decretals (spiritual rulings), 82
*Decretum Gratiani (Corpus Juris
    Canonici),* 84
depositions, 59–60
    of Vatican officials, 180, 183, 237*n*83
*The Didache: The Teachings of the Twelve
    Apostles,* 79
Dignitatas Humane (Vatican II
    document), 14
dioceses
    bankruptcies of, 138–46
    bishops acting on behalf of, 54
    definition of, 237*n*83
    incorporation by, 231*n*59
    sexual abuse allegations to be
        investigated and tried by,
        92–6
    see also bishops
Doe v. Holy See (US, 2013), 172–9
Dolan, Timothy (cardinal), 182, 203
Donohue, William, 157–8
Doran, Thomas (bishop), 114
Doyle, Anne Barrett, 170, 171
Doyle,Thomas, 3, 7
    at Chicago NCCB meeting, 35, 102
    on financial consequences of
        scandal, 137
    as founder of Catholic
        Whistleblowers, 156
    Gauthe case and, 32–4, 36–7, 39–40
    guidelines proposed by, 96, 116
    honored by VOTF, 162
    SNAP and, 158
Drivon, Laurence E., 157
Druce, Joseph, 46–8, 72–3
Dublin, Diocese of (Ireland), 188

Eagan, Edward (cardinal), 43
Eastern Catholic Church (Eastern
    Orthodox Church), 81–2

Edwards, David R., 241*n*14
Edyvean, Walter (bishop), 235*n*47
Effinger, Bill, 94–5
Endal, George, 143
Englehardt, Charles, 134, 136
ephebophilia, 1
episcobabble, 208
"The Essential Norms for Diocesan/
    Eparchial Policies Dealing
    with Allegations of Sexual
    Abuses of Minors by Priests
    or Deacons," 116, 118–19,
    125–6, 130, 199
  ineffectiveness of, 136, 200–1
  VOTF on compliance with, 163–4,
    168
Evans, Richard, 45
Evers, Charles, 61

Fairbanks (Alaska), 142–3
Faithful Voice (organization), 163
Fearing v. Bucher (Oregon, 1999),
    236*n*75
federal courts
  on balance between Church and
    state, 197
  bankruptcies under, 140–1
  Church positions in, 199
  Doe v. Holy See in, 172–9
  O'Bryan v. Holy See in, 179–81
  see also Supreme Court
Fericano, Paul, 155–6
Ferns, Diocese of (Ireland), 187–8
Field, Ramond (bishop), 239*n*110
Finn, Robert W. (bishop), 136, 154, 156,
    168, 202
First Amendment, 196–200
  Sherbert v. Verner on, 197
First Latern Council (1123), 83
Flynn, Raymond, 163
Foreign Service Immunities Act
    (FSIA), 175–7, 180, 238*n*86

Francis I (pope; Jorge Mario
    Bergoglio), 5, 68, 97
  Catholic Whistleblowers's petition
    of, 156
  sexual abuse policies of, 210–12,
    214–15
  VOTF on, 168
Franciscans (order), 154, 233*n*15
  SAFENET organization of survivors
    of, 155–6, 164
Franklin, William (bishop), 142
freedom of religion
  California case on, 121–3
  Sherbert v. Verner on, 197
  Vatican II on, 14
Frey, Gerard (bishop), 18–21, 23, 26,
    29–31, 33, 41

Gale, Robert, 70
Galileo, 104
Galloway, Michael, 163
Gastal, Scott, 24–6, 29–31, 34, 37, 38
Gauthe, Gilbert, 2–3, 9, 17–18, 195
  after prison, 38
  civil and criminal charges against,
    20–1, 24–37
  consequences of case of, 38–44
  first allegations against, 18–19
  guilty plea by, 37
  life of, 23–4
  settlement in case of, 21
  suspended, 19–20
Geoghan, John, 3, 73
  Boston Globe coverage of, 6, 51–5
  civil suits against, 56–8, 105
  criminal case against, 57, 65, 66
  murder of, 48
  in treatment, 49–50
George, Francis (cardinal), 204
Germany, 183–4
Gibney, Alex, 182
Globe. See Boston Globe

Gonzalez, Alberto, 115
grand juries, 120
Gratian, 84
Gregory, Wilton (bishop), 106, 108
    at Dallas bishops' meeting, 112, 114,
        118
Gregory XII (pope), 241*n*18

Hannan, Philip (archbishop), 26, 33, 34
Helena (Montana), 144
Henry (Louisiana), 17
Herbert, Paul, 19–22
Hoatson, Robert M., 156
Holy Roman Empire, 83
Holy See. *See* popes; Vatican
homosexuality, 85, 105
House of Affirmation, 21–2, 64
    Gauthe treated in, 20, 21, 28–9
Hoye, Daniel (bishop), 36
Hudson, Deal, 163
Hughes, James, 51

Ignatius of Antioch (saint), 80
injurious activity exemption
    (in FSIA), 176
Institute of Living, 42
    dispute between Eagan and, 43
    Gauthe in, 29
    Geoghan in, 49–50
Institutes of Consecrated Life
    (ICL), 128
International Criminal Court
    (the Hague), 155, 171, 205
International Physicians for the
    Prevention of Nuclear War
    (PPNW), 161
Internet
    bishop–accountability.org on,
        169–72
    information sources on, 5
    used by VOTF, 166
Ireland, 187–9, 239*n*110

Irish Child Abuse Commission, 187
Irish immigrants, 15

Jacques, Roger N., 235–6*n*65
Jesuits, 143
Jesus Christ, 78, 98
John XXIII (pope), 13, 98
John Jay College of Criminal Justice
    report, 167, 201
John Paul I (pope), 100
John Paul II (pope; Karol Wojtyla), 4,
        31, 115, 219*n*38
    Benedict XVI appointed head of
        CDF by, 184
    change in US-Vatican relations
        under, 206–8
    on "Charter" and "Essential Norms,"
        126, 127
    on clerical sexual abuse crisis, 101–8
    Code of Canon Law revised
        under, 89, 90, 225*n*15,
        225*n*27, 240*n*119
    Law and, 61, 69, 154
    life of, 98–101
    Shanley defrocked by, 56
    VOTF on, 168
Justinian (emperor, Roman
    Empire), 82
Justinian Code, 82–3

Kane, Thomas, 21, 22, 28, 64
Kansas City-St. Joseph, Diocese of, 136,
        152, 202
katoliki (early Christians), 80
Keating, Frank, 118, 201
Kennedy, John Fitzgerald, 14
Kenney, Charles, 161
Kettler, Donald J. (bishop), 143
Klest, Joseph, 157
Knights of Columbus (organization),
        158
Krol, John (archbishop), 35, 132

Laghi, Pio (archbishop), 31, 32
laity
  bishop-accountability.org, 169–72
  organizations of, 148
  power relationships between clergy,
    Church hierarchy, and, 11
  Survivors Network of those Abused
    by Priests, 149–59
  Voice of the Faithful, 159–69
Larroque, Henri Alexandre, 18–20,
  26–8, 30, 31, 33, 41
Lash, Kenneth, 156
Lateran, Council of the (1215), 83
Lateran, Treaty of the (1929), 97
Law, Bernard (cardinal), 32
  after sexual abuse scandals, 67
  apology of, 65
  Boston Archdiocese under
    leadership of, 61–2
  at Chicago NCCB meeting, 35
  civil suit settlement agreed to by,
    57–8
  depositions of, 59–60, 65
  Geoghan under, 50–3
  life of, 60–1
  meets with John Paul II, 107
  Reilly's report on, 64
  retirement of, 68–9
  on Shanley case, 56
  SNAP protest against, 154
  VOTF and, 161–2, 165
lawyers (attorneys), 147, 157
lay investiture, 83, 117
Legatus (organization), 158
Legion of Christ (Mexican order), 6,
  207
legislation
  in California, 121, 156–7
  ending confidentiality, 195
  in Massachusetts, 66, 223n43
  in New York State, 123
  in Pennsylvania, 133

recommended by grand juries, 120
  SNAP on, 153
  VOTF on, 166
Lemon v. Kurtzman (US, 1971), 72, 224n55
Leno, Jay, 67
Leo III (pope), 83
Leo XIII (pope), 11–12
Levada, William (cardinal), 34–5, 41,
  208–9, 238n87
liberation theologians, 184, 206
The Linkup, 164
Los Angeles, Archdiocese of, 120–3,
  136, 154, 203
Los Angeles County, 102–3
Louisville (Kentucky), 230n49
Lumen Gentium (Vatican II document),
  13–14
Lundowski, Joseph, 143
Lynn, William, 134–6, 202

Maciel, Marcial (Degollado), 6, 207–8
Maday, Norbert J., 204
Maderios, Humberto (cardinal), 50, 62
Mahan, Paul, 70
Mahoney, Roger (cardinal), 136, 154,
  168, 203
Manchester (New Hampshire),
  Diocese of, 70–2, 130
The Manual (Doyle, Mouton, and
  Peterson), 34–6, 41, 42
marriage
  among early priests, 79, 81
  banned for priesthood, 83–4
Martin V (pope), 241n18
mass media. *See* media
Massachusetts, 195
  legislation in, 66, 145, 223n43
  see also Boston; Boston Archdiocese
McCarrick, Theodore (cardinal), 114–16
McCord, John, 156
McCormack, John (bishop), 62, 69–71
McKiernan, Terry, 170, 171

McKinley, Carol, 163

McMurry, William, 172

McSorley, Patrick, 73

Mea Maxima Culpa: Silence in the House of God (film, Gibney), 182

media, 6, 147

  on Benedict XVI, 183–4

  at Dallas meeting of bishops, 111–13

Mejia, Jorge (archbishop), 103

Miami (Florida), 230*n*49

Milwaukee, Archdiocese of, 143–4, 182, 203

ministerial privilege, 171

Minnis v. Oregon Mut. Ins. Co. (Oregon, 2002), 236*n*75

Monaghan, Tom, 158

Morey, Michael S., 157

Moriarity, James (bishop), 239*n*110

Mother Teresa, 115

Mouton, F. Ray, 3

  at Chicago NCCB meeting, 35, 102

  on financial consequences of scandal, 137

  in Gauthe case, 27–9, 31–4, 36, 37

  guidelines proposed by, 96, 116

  leaves Church, 39

Muller, Jim, 161–5

Mullins, Robert, 49

Murphy, Lawrence, 144, 181–3

Murray, John Courtney, 13, 14, 217–18*n*7

Myers, John J. (archbishop), 114, 168, 202

National Conference of Catholic Bishops (NCCB), 39, 220*n*43

  consequences of Gauthe case for, 41–4

  founding of, 98

  John Paul II and, 102, 104

  secret Chicago meeting of, 34–6

  on sexual abuse cases, 106

  see also United States Conference of Catholic Bishops

National Review Board of the Catholic Laity, 137, 201

Navarro-Valls, Joaquin, 105

New Hampshire, 71–2, 130

New Jersey, 230*n*49

New Life Center, 42–3

New York (state), 203

  Suffolk County in, 123–4

  Westchester County in, 57, 123

New York Times, 5, 6, 105

  on Benedict XVI, 181–2, 207

  VOTF advertisement in, 168

Nicea, Church Council at (325), 81

Nicene Creed, 81

Nigeria, 107

Norms of the Moto Proprio (Benedict XVI), 240*n*119

The Norms of the Moto Proprio "Sacramentorum Sancititatis Tutela" (John Paul II), 104

North American Man Boy Love Association (NAMBLA), 55, 222*n*25

Obama administration, 178, 210

Oblates of St. Francis DeSales (order), 150

O'Brien, Thomas (bishop), 131

O'Bryan v. Holy See (US, 2008), 172–3, 179–81

O'Connell, Mark, 235*n*47

O'Connor, John (cardinal), 32

Office for Youth and Child Protection, 118

O'Malley, Sean (cardinal), 67–8, 171

  special papal commission on sexual abuse headed by, 211, 212

O'Neill, Ted, 170

Orange Country (California), 230*n*49

Order of Friars Servants, 175

Our Lady of Peace Hospital, 42

papacy. *See* popes; Vatican
Papal States, 86
parishes
    councils of, in Boston, 162
    incorporation of, 142, 145, 202
pastors, 16
Paul (saint; Saul), 77–9
Paul VI (pope), 22, 100
pedophiles
    in prison, 45–8
    recidivism among, 64
pedophilia
    canon law on, 85
    Code of Canon Law on, 89, 90
    definition of, 1
    not linked to celibacy, 108
Peter (saint), 98
Peter Damien (saint), 85
Peterson, Michael, 3
    at Chicago NCCB meeting, 35, 36, 102
    death of, 41
    on financial consequences of
        scandal, 137
    Gauthe case and, 28, 31–4, 37–8
    guidelines proposed by, 96, 116
Pharisees, 78
Philadelphia (Pennsylvania), 132–6, 201–2
Phoenix (Arizona), 131
Pilarczyk, Daniel E. (archbishop), 57,
        96, 113
Pius IX (pope), 86
Pius X (pope), 88
Poland, 99–101
Polcino, Anna, 21
popes (papacy; Holy See)
    immune to US laws, 183
    legal challenges to, 172–83
    political power seized by, 83
    resignations of, 209, 241n18
    as Vatican ruler, 97–8
    as Vicar of Christ on Earth, 86
    see also *individual popes*

Porter, James, 51, 174
Portland, Archdiocese of (Oregon),
        231n63, 231n64
    bankruptcy of, 139–41
    in *Doe v. Holy See,* 175, 176
Post, James (Jim), 161, 162, 165
press. *See* media
priests, 16–17
    celibacy for, 83
    clericalism of, 167, 235n55
    Code of Canon Law on pedophilia
        by, 89
    Council of Trent on moral lives of, 86
    earliest, marriage among, 79, 81
    in earliest Church, 79
    "Essential Norms for Diocesan/
        Eparchial Policies Dealing with
        Allegations of Sexual Abuses..."
        on, 116, 118–19, 125–8
    marital sex banned for, 82
    marriage banned for, 83–4
    reassignments for, 10, 50, 53, 55–6,
        69, 112, 134
    in religious orders, 230n53

Quinn, A. J. (bishop), 33, 35, 36

Ratigan, Shawn, 136, 202
Ratzinger, Joseph (cardinal).
        See Benedict XVI
Reagan, Ronald, 31, 219n38
Reagan Administration, 31, 100
Regina Cleri (residence for retired
        priests), 53
Regnum Christi (organization), 207
Reilly, Thomas F., 59, 62–7, 69
religious orders, 128, 230n53
    in Ireland, 187–8
Renner, Gerald, 6
respondent superior (legal principle), 25
Restoring Trust (NCCB), 42–4
Rice, Condoleeza, 115

Rigali, Justin (cardinal), 135
Road to Recovery (organization), 156
Robichaux, Pete, 19, 28, 38
Robichaux, Roy, 19
Robinson, Walter V., 50
Rockville Center, Diocese of, 123–4
Roman Catholic Church
    canon law established for, 84
    canon law used by, 76
    consequences of Gauthe case for, 41
    current balance of power between
        government and, 193–5
    Eastern Catholic Church and, 81–2
    financial consequences of clerical
        sexual abuse for, 137–46
    groups urging reform of, 167
    historic relationships between civil
        states and, 11–12
    loss of credibility for, 66
    political power assumed by, 82
Roman Empire, 80–1
Rome (Italy), 82
Romley, Richard M., 131
Ronan, Andrew, 175–8
Rosenkranz, George, 70
Russia, 127
Ryan Report (Ireland), 187–8

SAFENET (organization).
        See Survivors Alliance and
        Franciscan Exchange Network
Sagrera, Craig, 18, 28, 31, 38
Sagrera, Wayne, 18–19
Sambi, Pietro (archbishop), 238n87
San Diego (California), 142, 145
Schwartz, Harold, 43
separation of Church and state.
        See church-state issues
Servants of the Paraclete (order), 42, 43
settlements
    by Boston Archdiocese, 53–4, 56
    in Cincinnati, 131

confidentiality in, 123
costs of, 137, 230n49
by Franciscans, 233n15
in Gauthe case, 21
in Geoghan case, 58, 105
in Ireland, 189
in McSorley case, 73
in Portland (Oregon), 141
in San Diego, 142
in Vermont, 136
in Westchester County, 57
won by Anderson, 174
sexual abuse and crimes
    American bishops on, 95–7
    canon law on, 85–6
    "Charter for the Protection of
        Children and Young People"
        on, 116–18
    Code of Canon Law on, 90, 92–5
    confusion in American Church over
        handling of, 90–1
    varied definitions of, 22
    Vatican on definition of, 129
Shanley, Paul, 3, 55–8, 65, 66, 73
Sherbert v. Verner (US, 1963), 197
Shero, Bernard, 134, 136
Simon, J. Minos, 25–6, 29–30, 37–9
Siricius (pope), 82
skinners (child molesters in prison),
        45–6
Solidarity (union, Poland), 101
Southdown (treatment facility), 42,
        43, 49
sovereign immunity, 173
    of Vatican, 176–9, 181, 191, 210
Spellman, Francis (cardinal), 13
Spokane, Diocese of (Washington), 141–2
St. John Vianney Hospital, 42, 43, 135, 151
St. Louis, Archdiocese of, 239–40n117
St. Luke Institute, 42, 43
    founded by Peterson, 28, 31, 33
    Geoghan in, 49

St. Michael's Community, 42

Stansbury, Nathan, 20, 24–6, 28, 30, 37

statutes of limitation
  in California, 121
  in Code of Canon Law, 90, 94, 96, 156–7, 184
  legislation on, 195
  in Massachusetts, 66
  Supreme Court on, 121
  Vatican on, 128
  VOTF on, 166

Stephen (biblical), 78

Suffolk County (New York), 123–4

superior liability, 175–6

Supreme Court (US)
  on clerical sexual abuse, 174
  on *Doe v. Holy See,* 178
  on *Lemon v Kurtzman,* 72, 224*n*55
  on *Sherbert v. Verner,* 197
  on sovereign immunity of Vatican, 210
  on statutes of limitation, 121

survivors. *See* victims

Survivors Alliance and Franciscan Exchange Network (SAFENET), 155–6, 164

Survivors Network of those Abused by Priests (SNAP), 4, 149–59, 204–5
  bishop-accountability.org and, 170, 171
  Doyle honored by, 40
  VOTF and, 164

Sweeny, Constance, 55, 56, 65

Third Latern Council (1179), 86

Thompson, Tommy, 204

Tierney, Michael, 152, 157

Timothy (biblical), 78

Titus (biblical), 78, 79

Tomasi, Silvano, 212–13

treatment facilities, 42–3

Trent, Council of (1545), 83

Tuscon (Arizona), 142

United Nations, 5, 208
  in conflicts with Vatican over rights of children, 212–13

United States
  change in relations with Vatican, 205–10
  current balance of power between Church and state in, 193–5
  in *Doe v. Holy See,* 177–8
  John Paul II on sexual abuse caused by culture of, 102, 103
  legal actions against Vatican taken in, 172–4
  threats to Church authority in, 117
  Vatican recognized by, 31–2, 100

United States Catholic Conference (USCC), 220*n*43
  on sexual abuse cases, 106

United States Conference of Catholic Bishops (USCCB), 220*n*43
  on costs of settlements, 230*n*49
  Dallas meeting of, 111–14, 116, 200
  founding of, 98
  management changes in US Church and, 214
  McCormack appointed to sexual abuse committee by, 72
  Office for Youth and Child Protection in, 118
  represented on Vatican commission, 126
  SNAP recognized by, 153
  VOTF letter to, 168
  Washington meeting of, 67
  website of, 5

Vangheluwe, Roger (bishop), 185

Vatican (Holy See), 4
  accusations against Benedict, 183–91

American bishops and, 96–7, 125–30
on Belgian raid, 186
change in relations with US, 205–10
Code of Canon Law modified by, 90, 225n15
in conflicts with UN over rights of children, 212–13
Doe v. Holy See case against, 172–9
on Gauthe case, 33–4
O'Bryan v. Holy See against, 179–81
official responses to American clerical sexual abuse crisis by, 101–9
papacy distinguished from, 97–8
SNAP complaint against, 154–5, 205
special papal commission on sexual abuse established in, 211
US diplomatic recognition for, 31–2, 100
website of, 5
Vatican II (General Council), 13–14, 60, 98, 218n8
Ventura County (California), 120–1
Vermont, 136
vicarious liability, 175–6
vicars, 119, 120
victims
accepting Church authority, 10
bishops' *Restoring Trust* documents on, 42
Boston Globe request for, 52
canon law not applied to, 91
"Charter for the Protection of Children and Young People" on, 116–18

confidentiality in Church settlements with, 54–5, 57
at Dallas bishops' meeting, 113
Francis I on, 211, 212
in Ireland, 188
John Paul II on, 103
legislation on, 223n43
statutes of limitation for, 121
Survivors Network of those Abused by Priests, 149–59
Voice of the Faithful, 159–69
Voice of Compassion (organization), 164
Voice of the Faithful (VOTF; organization), 4, 159–69, 204–5

Walensa, Lech, 100
Walsh, Eamon (bishop), 239n110
Warren, Chet, 149–51
Weakland, Rembert G. (archbishop), 6, 94–5, 182
Wesolowski, Jozef (archbishop), 212
Westchester County (New York), 57, 123
Williams, Seth, 133
Wilmington (Delaware), 143
Wisconsin, 203
Wojtyla, Karol. *See* John Paul II
women
ACC on, 167
VOTF on, 164

Your Catholic Voice (organization), 163

Zizik, David, 162

Printed and bound by CPI Group (UK) Ltd, Croydon, CR0 4YY